Rupert D. V. Glasgow

The Minimal Self

Rupert D. V. Glasgow

The Minimal Self

Würzburg
University Press

Dissertation, Julius-Maximilians-Universität Würzburg
Graduiertenschule für Geisteswisenschaften, 2017
Gutachter: Prof. Dr. Roland Borgards, Prof. Dr. Martin Heisenberg, Prof. Dr. Karl Mertens

Impressum

Julius-Maximilians-Universität Würzburg
Würzburg University Press
Universitätsbibliothek Würzburg
Am Hubland
D-97074 Würzburg
www.wup.uni-wuerzburg.de

©2017 Würzburg University Press
Print on Demand

Coverdesign & Layout: Christina Nath

ISBN: 978-3-95826-52-8 (print)
ISBN: 978-3-95286-53-5 (online)
URN: urn:nbn:de:bvb:20-opus-145252

Except otherwise noted, this document – excluding the cover – is licensed under the Creative Commons Attribution-ShareAlike 3.0 DE License (CC BY-SA 3.0 DE):
http://creativecommons.org/licenses/by-sa/3.0/de/

The cover page is licensed under the Creative Commons Attribution-NonCommercial-NoDerivatives 3.0 DE License (CC BY-NC-ND 3.0 DE):
http://creativecommons.org/licenses/by-nc-nd/3.0/de/

Acknowledgements

First I should like to thank Roland Borgards both for supporting my application to be a PhD student at the Graduate School of the Humanities, Würzburg University, and for providing me with expert guidance throughout the thesis project. I should also like to thank Martin Heisenberg and Karl Mertens for being such discerning and thoughtful members of the thesis committee. The discussions we had not only helped me shape and refine my argument, but were stimulating and thoroughly enjoyable in their own right.

Special thanks go to Bertram Gerber of the Leibniz Institute of Neurobiology in Magdeburg. Bertram not only encouraged me to pursue this line of thought in the first place, but raised countless biological questions in our many discussions, undertook meticulous readings of the text, and gave invaluable advice on structure and presentation. I am especially grateful for the unstinting generosity of his moral support and friendship.

My gratitude also goes to the organizers and participants in the courses and talks I have given in recent years on the 'The Phylogeny of the Self', who have spurred me on with their perspicacity and enthusiasm. In particular, I thank (in alphabetical order) Mirjam Appel, Achim Engelhorn, Alex Gómez Marín, Apollonia Heisenberg, Manos Paissios, Alois Palmetshofer and Ayse Yarali. Many thanks go to Christina Nath for making such a fine job of the layout and illustrations, and I further owe a great debt of gratitude to Bertram Gerber, Roland Borgards, Martin Heisenberg, Manos Paissios and Ayse Yarali for making the illustrations possible. My friends in Zaragoza and elsewhere have given me wonderful support as ever: special mention goes to Carmen Canales and to Winni Schindler and Sarah Lothian for sharing ideas and intuitions with me, as well as to Barbara Glasgow in Berkhamsted and Faith Glasgow and Tony Doubleday in Stoke Newington.

RDVG
Zaragoza, Spain

The Minimal Self between Cultural Animal Studies and the New Ethology

Foreword by Roland Borgards

In the last 20 years a new way of thinking about animals has emerged in the natural sciences as well as in the Humanities. For the Humanities, this development is associated with philosophers such as Giorgio Agamben or Cary Wolfe, it is articulated by ethnologists such as Philippe Descola or Eduardo Viveiros de Castro, and it is greatly influenced by Jacques Derrida's deconstruction, Bruno Latour's new materialism and Donna Haraway's science studies. What all these different thinkers have in common is that they don't take the notion of the animal for granted. For them, there is no such thing as 'The Animal'. There are – in a decisive plural – only different animals, and different gazes at these different animals, and different circumstances for different gazes at different animals. Most of all: for them there is no insuperable line holding apart humans and animals, but only a multitude of crossings, entanglements and differentiations. Arguing within this framework, research on human-animal relations is on the point of being institutionalised in the Humanities under the name of *Cultural Animal Studies*, as was the case with gender studies in the 1980s and postcolonial studies in the 1990s.

For the natural sciences a complementary development may be sketched, as in the last 20 years ethology has found a new starting point in comparing the abilities of non-human animals with those of humans. Until the 1990s the burden of proof lay with those who considered animals to be endowed with human-like abilities: if you were bold enough to think that animals other than humans have a theory of mind or some kind of culture, that there is morality or personality in animals, that they can love and lie, and that they know they will die, then it was up to you to prove it. Well, proof has been given, evidence has been found, thanks to ethologists such as Marc Bekoff, Andrew Withen,

Frans de Waal, William McGrew, Volker Sommer, Kurt Kotrschal, John Bradshaw or Martin Heisenberg. Today, the burden of proof thus seems to lie with those who deny that there are animals with human-like abilities. No longer is it the gap between humans and animals that is taken for granted, but their common ground as a starting point for further differentiations. It is this research attitude that I want to call the *New Ethology*.

The primary object of both Cultural Animal Studies and the New Ethology was the ape. The issue was clear: if you could prove for just one animal that its closeness to us is more important than its distance from us, you had won the case against the entire ideology of human exceptionality. If there exists a cultured chimpanzee, culture is no longer exclusively human. And if there exist cultured apes, a novel displaying the cultural abilities of a chimpanzee – a novel such as Franz Kafka's *Bericht für eine Akademie* – is no longer mere fiction.

Since their beginnings both Cultural Animal Studies and the New Ethology have broadened their focus to include cats, birds, fish, even flies. This tendency towards 'lower' animals of lesser complexity grounds the current debate: how far can we go?

With his book on *The Minimal Self* Rupert Glasgow gives an answer to this question by turning it round 180 degrees. Not how far can we go? But how early can we begin? That a human being is a self seems to be self-evident. That a chimpanzee is a self seems – though new – to be common sense. That a bird, let's say a crow, is a self seems not unfounded. A fish? Some think so. A fly? Probably. But Glasgow doesn't ask if something is still a self, but if something is already a self. He doesn't start with man, therefore, approaching the frontiers of selfhood from above, but with self-organizing whirlpools, approaching them from below. With this bottom-up method Glasgow provides us with fundamental research into key notions for both Cultural Animal Studies and the New Ethology.

Ultimately, Glasgow's study thus addresses a double readership: on the one hand, readers from the Humanities interested in the question of animals; on the other hand, readers from the natural sciences interested in the epistemological foundations of the life sciences. And as a side effect it proves that there are common grounds, common questions and common interests for the 'two cultures' of research: if Glasgow shows that the *minimal self* gives rise to the distinction between life and non-life, he demonstrates in the very same gesture that the *minimal self* calls for the unification of the natural sciences and the Humanities.

Preface

The present work attempts to analyse the notion of a 'minimal self', focusing on the transition from entities that are not quite 'selves' to things that are, such as unicellular and multicellular organisms. It is conceived as part of a larger project, with broader ramifications. In an attempt not to exhaust the reader's patience and good will, however, the idea is to divide this project into more manageable chunks. Accordingly, *The Minimal Self* will be followed by a separate study of how minimal selfhood provides a foundation for the possibility of rudimentary consciousness. Further studies are planned.

Contents

I.
Introduction: Intrinsic Reflexivity

The Concept of a 'Self'. 17
Forms of Intrinsic Reflexivity (1): Self-Maintenance. 27
    Self-Organization. 27
    Self-Production 32
    Self-Adaptation and Self-Transformation 36
Forms of Intrinsic Reflexivity (2): Self-Reproduction. 38
Forms of Intrinsic Reflexivity (3): Self-Containment 46
Self and Self-Interest: Self as an End in Itself 51
Self, Sameness and Unity 57
Self and Flow **63**
    Self-Assembly. 63
    Self and Stasis. 66

II.
Flux, Fire and Auto-Mobiles

Fluid Flow. 75
Combustion 84
    Wild Fires, Tamed Fires 84
    Auto-Mobiles and the Containment of Combustion. 89

III.
Selfish Genes and DNA

Selfishness.. 101
The Selfishness of Genes 105
Self-Like Macromolecules.. 110
Cosmopolitan Genes... 116
Selfish DNA 121
Mobile DNA 127
    LTR Retrotransposons..128
    Non-LTR Retrotransposons 130
    DNA Transposons 131
    Mobile Bacterial Retroelements 133
The Containment of Alien Selfishness............................ 135

IV.
Viruses and other Selves-Within-Selves

Coat-Wearing Genes 147
    Preliminary Considerations 147
    Collective Viral Selfhood...................................152
The Streamlined Selves of Small Viruses and Viroids 156
You Are What You Wear 163
Selfhood Recruited or Hijacked 168
Other Intracellular Selves 173
    Rickettsia and Mitochondria...............................173
    Buchnera and '*Candidatus* Tremblaya Princeps'............182
Postscript: Minimum Genomes, Minimum Selves 187

V.
The Urself, LUCA and the Origins of Life

Urself and Überself 193
Soups, Genes and Catalysts..................................... 201
    Warm Ponds and Hot Soups....................................201
    Genetic and Metabolic Approaches............................203
Microdroplets and Membranes 208
Hemi-Cells and Semi-Selves..................................... 212

Mineral Surfaces 212
Inside-Out Cells 215
Inorganic Microcompartments 216
Escape to Selfhood 218

VI.
Cellf and Self-Containment

Introduction: (More or Less) Containing One's Self 223
Forms of Container 229
    Membranes, Walls and Tests 229
    Epithelium, Epidermis 235
Functional Unity as Self-Containment 239
    Organisms as Self-Containing Entities 239
    The Strange Case of the Social Amoebae: *Dictyostelium Discoideum* 244
    Genetic Individuals 247
    Chimeras and Symbionts 250
    Farming, Love and Other Shared Selfhood 255
Immune Containment: Distinguishing Self from Non-Self 259
    Immunity and Selfhood: A Complex Relationship 259
    Immunity and Selfhood: A Necessary Relationship? 265
Managing the Interface of Self and Non-Self 270
    Respiration 270
    Osmoregulation 274
    Thermoregulation 277
Extending One's Self 279
    Houses and Other Shells 279
    Tools as Extensions of Self 284
Transcending One's Self 287

Glossary 291
List of Figures 303
Endnotes 305
Bibliography 369

I.

Introduction:
Intrinsic Reflexivity

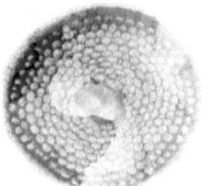

The Concept of a 'Self'

The aim of this work is to examine the minimum conditions that must be met to be able to ascribe a 'self' to an entity. The term 'self' is rarely given a satisfactory definition: it is often used in a rather vague sense to mean 'what you really are', or it is conflated with 'mind'. It is frequently claimed that no such thing exists, or that selfhood is another of the illusions to which the philosophically naive are prone. I argue, however, that if properly defined the concept of 'selfhood' is supremely useful and avoids many of the metaphysical connotations of the term 'mind', in particular the mental-physical dichotomy that tends to divorce minds from their specific material embodiment. The objective in this Introduction is to define the concept 'self' in terms of what I shall call 'intrinsic reflexivity'. Three underlying categories of such intrinsic reflexivity are distinguished: self-maintenance, self-reproduction and self-containment. When the 'self' is analysed within such a framework, the claim that no such thing exists can be seen to be unjustified.

A self defined in such terms is not a uniquely human phenomenon, although the human self certainly *is* unique. The narrative or autobiographical selfhood specific to humans – our ability to use concepts to define ourselves and tell ourselves and others a story about ourselves – is regarded by most as a 'pinnacle' of selfhood and has been studied with great depth and insight by many thinkers. The breathtakingly complex human self, however, is built upon and thus presupposes the more ancestral forms of selfhood that are the subject here. The aim is to analyse the logical preconditions for the transition from a world, or a universe, bereft of selfhood to one in which selves are present.

In analysing how selfhood has emerged, it is essential to examine the fuzzy borderlines between entities to which selfhood can be ascribed and those which fail to fulfil the criteria. This will allow us to establish a level of 'minimal selfhood', a mode of being that is shared by all selves in their capacity as selves. Unicellular organisms will provide a paradigm of such minimal selfhood, in that they display all three forms of intrinsic reflexivity that are here considered necessary and sufficient for full minimal selfhood.[1] Multicellular organisms such as animals can also be characterized in terms of the intrinsically reflexive processes of self-maintenance, self-reproduction and self-containment, so they too embody full minimal selfhood. Such minimal selfhood provides the foundation for the more complex manifestations of selfhood that have evolved in animals such as birds and mammals.

Understood in such terms, full minimal selfhood may be seen to coincide with life itself, and an analysis of minimal selfhood would accordingly be tantamount to an analysis of the nature of life.[2] While this is certainly a large part of the truth, it should be stressed that the focus here is *primarily* on selfhood, for which I attempt to provide a definition, and only *secondarily* on life, which I at no point seek to define (instead citing the definitions of others and relying on presumably shared intuitions of 'life as we know it'). The possible existence in some remote (or not so remote) corner of the universe of life-forms that are *radically* different from what we know opens an unsavoury can of epistemological worms owing to the problem of circularity. The question is how we could ever recognize a radically different life-form *as a living entity* unless we already knew what we were looking for, which in practice means looking for some of the properties that characterize earthly life-forms.[3]

Before coming to the full minimal selfhood of unicellular (and multicellular) organisms, however, the focus will be on the self-like[4] nature of non-living but life-like phenomena such as forest fires and whirlpools and the status of 'selfish' genes and DNA, as well as *viroids*, viruses and intracellular *endosymbionts*, where it is a matter of controversy whether they are described as 'living' or otherwise. The task will thus be to ascertain what is entailed by attributing selfhood to a paramecium, an amoeba or a dinoflagellate, and why we may be more reluctant to ascribe it to a gene or a virus, however *selfishly* they may seem to behave.

It is often said that selves are a figment of the imagination. In his book *The Metaphysics of Mind*, the philosopher Anthony Kenny claims that 'the self of the philosophers' is a mythical entity.[5] In fact, Kenny is here referring to the concept of the 'self' as understood not only by certain philosophers, but also by various philosophically challenged poets, dramatists and presumably psychologists. He continues, this time wisely putting his 'self' in inverted commas:

> *'the self' is a piece of philosopher's nonsense consisting in a misunderstanding of the reflexive pronoun. To ask what kind of substance my self is is like asking what the characteristic of ownness is which my own property has in addition to being mine. When, outside philosophy, I talk about myself, I am simply talking about the human being, Anthony Kenny; and my self is nothing other than myself. It is a philosophical muddle to allow the space which differentiates 'my self' from 'myself' to generate the illusion of a mysterious metaphysical entity distinct from, but obscurely linked to, the human being who is talking to you.*

Healthy though it is to have one's philosophical muddles periodically unmuddled, the following analysis of selfhood will not be following Kenny's route in summarily dismissing it as an illusion generated by grammatical delinquency. At the same time, it will avoid any talk of 'substance' (whatever that is), its aim being to define 'self' in a way that is empirically testable rather than mythical or metaphysical.

For a start, we need to go a little further with our grammatical analysis. English is not the only language in which we humans refer to ourselves or to our selves. The Germans do so too, perhaps not surprisingly given that our languages are siblings, and our philosophical cultures so closely intertwined. However, when the Germans reflexively refer to 'myself' or 'himself', they use *mich* or *sich*, whereas when their philosophers reify the reflexive into Kenny's 'mythical entity', they usually refer to *das Selbst*. Clearly something slightly different is going on. Admittedly, German philosophers have not been inclined to use the substantive *Selbst* as much as English-speaking philosophers have used 'self', resorting instead to an armoury of alternatives such as *das Ich* (the I) or *das Subjekt* (the subject) or attaching *Selbst* as a prefix to a mode of cognition to produce self-consciousness or self-perception or self-experience. The early Heidegger was among the most prolific in referring to *das Selbst* in a philosophical context, and we shall encounter some of his insights below.[6]

The reason for this discrepancy is that the everyday word 'self' from which the philosophical noun is derived has two or even three distinct uses. It can function as part of a reflexive pronoun (as in 'I wash myself') but also as part of an emphatic pronoun (as in 'I did it myself').[7] As in English, these two uses coincide in approximately 45 percent of the world's languages, including Arabic *(nafs)*, Mandarin *(zijĭ)*, Persian *(xod-)* and Turkish *(kendi-)*. However, this double usage is not present in German, where the emphatic *selbst* is clearly distinguished from the reflexive *sich*, in Russian *(sam* versus *sebja)*, or in French or Spanish *(même or mismo versus se)*.[8] Given that German philosophers such as Heidegger have tended, if at all, to use the *emphatic* 'self' for reification into 'the' self, it is all the more remarkable to find the following example of the *reflexive* 'self' being utilised for the same purpose by the 14th-century German mystic Henry Suso (Heinrich Seuse) in his *Book of Truth*: 'You must know that every person has a fivefold self *(fúnfley Sich)*. The first self he has in common with the stone, and this is being; the second he has in common with the plant, and this is growth; the third with the animals, and this is sensation; the fourth, which all human beings share, is general human nature ...; the fifth, which belongs to him alone, is his personality, in respect of both nobility and chance.'[9] Unsurprisingly, this use of *sich* as a noun *(das Sich)* sounds stranger to modern-day German ears than *das Selbst* does.[10]

Common to both the emphatic and reflexive uses of the word 'self' is an association with sameness or identity. This is particularly manifest in languages such as German, French or Spanish, where the emphatic terms for 'self'– *selbst, même* or *mismo* – are clearly associated with the identity function (cf. *derselbe* etc. in German). When it is said that 'the president himself opened the meeting', the emphatic 'self' evokes alternative referents (it could have been the president's wife or the vice-president who opened the meeting), but only in order to negate them and effectively *re*-iterate the identity of the agent.[11] In the case of the reflexive 'self' (as in 'I wash myself'), the point is that both the subject of the sentence and the subsequent personal pronoun refer to the *same* entity. However, there is duality in this unity; that very same entity is both subject and object,[12] donor and recipient, active and passive. Such duality or double-functionality is essential to reflexivity, and, as will become clear below, it is this interplay of duality and unity that takes the concept of the 'self' beyond the realm of mere tautology or empty self-identity.

None of the above would necessarily appease a common-sense philosopher such as Kenny objecting to the misuse of a humble pronoun – whether reflexive, emphatic or both – as a metaphysical-sounding noun. So where does this tendency come from? Kenny is perhaps thinking of a strain of British empirical philosophy that goes back to John Locke and David Hume, who strove to find 'himself' or his self by introspection but merely stumbled upon the particular perception he happened to have at the time.[13] In *Sources of the Self: The Making of the Modern Identity*, Charles Taylor suggests that the creation of the substantive 'self', preceded with a definite or indefinite article, is a reflection of our modern

The Concept of a 'Self'

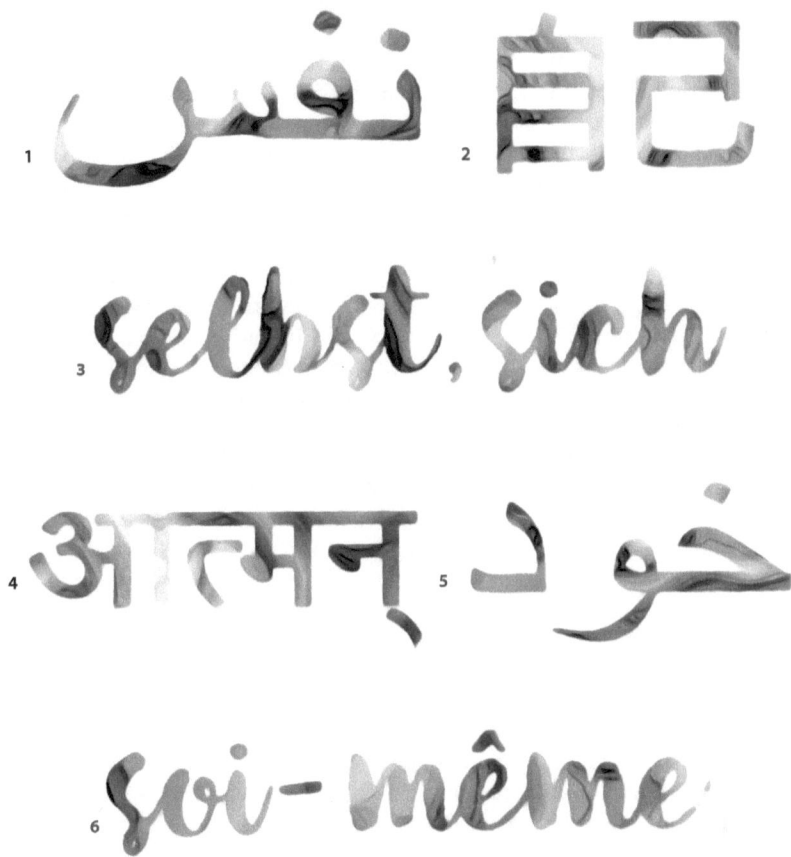

1 Arabic – nafs   **2** Mandarin – zìjǐ   **3** German – selbst, sich
4 Sanskrit – atman   **5** Persian – xod   **6** French – soi-même

Figure 1: Self across cultures and scripts

sense of agency.¹⁴ Yet 'modernity' is not usually considered to stretch back as far as the 14th century, when Suso was writing of the 'fivefold self'. The concept seems to have transcended cultural boundaries in provoking a more general urge to indulge in grammatical gymnastics. Even further in the past, Aristotle's *Nicomachean Ethics* famously defined a friend as 'another self' (*allos autos*) and as a 'different self' (*heteros autos*).¹⁵ Admittedly, this is thought to have sounded odd to contemporaries and subsequent interpreters. There does not appear to be any other example in Classical Greek of the pronoun *autos* being used as a noun in this way, and commentators such as Cicero and Aquinas noted the stylistic strangeness of the phrase.

Unlike Greek, however, ancient Indian philosophy had a marked tendency to substantivize the 'self'. The Hindu notion of *atman* (meaning the real or true Self) has been traced back to the ancient Sanskrit of the *Rig Veda* at least three millennia ago, where it is thought to have originated either in the word for 'breath' or in the reflexive pronoun *tman*.¹⁶ The early Suttas of Buddhism frequently use the word *atta* (the Pali equivalent of *atman* in Sanskrit) to refer to a changing, empirical self (though not a metaphysical Self), and the Pali language seems to have had a special affinity for reifying 'self' into *the* self.¹⁷ In Arabic too, a link between the reflexive 'self' and breath (a metonym for life itself) comes to light in the word *nafs*: the *Qu'ran* uses *nafs* both as a reflexive and an emphatic pronoun and as a noun denoting the lower or bodily self: the great struggle, for Islam, is the struggle against *nafs*. The word is clearly cognate with the ancient Arabic word for 'breath' *(nafas)* and with *nephesh* in Hebrew. As in Sanskrit, reflexive selfhood seems inextricably tied up with breath and by extension with life itself. Given such interdependence, the question of which came first – reflexivity or life – is perhaps unanswerable.¹⁸

If so many thinkers from so many cultures, using so many languages, have fallen prey to the same habit of turning a harmless reflexive or emphatic pronoun into a noun denoting the living being that one is, it seems parochial to spurn it as the muddle-headedness of a particular philosophical tradition. Something interesting is going on with the languages, or the concepts, in question. What is the nature of this relationship between reflexive/emphatic selfhood and life? Why have they recurrently been linked in so many diverse contexts?

We can here draw a distinction that helps shed light on this relationship. This distinction is between intrinsic reflexivity, where the reflexive activity or relation is constitutive of the entity in question, and extrinsic reflexivity, where it is not.¹⁹ When we say 'I shave myself' or 'I wash myself',²⁰ the reflexive activity is extrinsic in the sense of being contingent in relation to whatever it is that is the dual subject-object of the sentence (i.e. in relation to whatever it is that 'I' am): I can shave or wash (myself) or not, but I will still *be*, which amounts to saying that

I will still be *myself*. In such cases, the common-sense philosopher is certainly right to insist that we do not mean 'I shave my self' or 'I wash my self'. I am unlikely to regard my 'self' – whatever it may be – as the sort of entity that grows stubbly or gets covered in grime.

When we say 'I create myself' or 'I produce myself', by contrast, the reflexive activity is intrinsic to the entity in question. The idea is that I myself, *as a self*, am just the sort of thing that is engaged in and constituted by intrinsically reflexive processes such as self-production or self-creation (in ways that will become apparent below), and if I cease to engage in these intrinsically reflexive activities (e.g. if I cease to produce myself), I shall cease to be. In this respect, there is no reason for the typographical gap in 'I produce my self' to raise our hackles. Self-production and self-creation seem to pertain to what we are as living beings, and ultimately as *selves*, in a way that self-depilation and auto-grooming do not. However, any such distinction is far from absolute. It might be countered that it is indeed essential to me to wash and to shave (myself); this may be considered a vital part of my identity and thus of what I am.[21] The distinction between intrinsic and extrinsic reflexivity is thus to be taken as gradual or non-absolute, its value heuristic.[22]

Figure 2: Me, myself and a typographical gap

The crucial point is that processes or activities embodying intrinsic reflexivity – processes or activities such as self-organisation or self-production or self-creation – reflect the two underlying features of selfhood: reflexivity and sameness. If I create myself, reflexivity is manifest in the duality of subject and object, cause and effect, creator and created. At the same time, sameness or unity is manifest in the continuity of the process; it is logically guaranteed by the use of the first-person for both constituents of the duality. There is a logical and causal link between the self that creates itself and the self that is created by this process of self-creation. In this sense, a self is an entity that exists in a relation of intrinsic reflexivity to itself. Implicit in any such notion of selfhood are the ideas of process and time. A self is an ongoing participant in a dynamic, intrinsically reflexive process such as self-organization, self-production or self-creation.

It might be objected that to understand 'selfhood' in terms of reflexivity is to ground biology in grammar. Such an objection might run that what is common to selves defined in this way – as a category that not only includes phenomena characterized as living or as possessed of a 'mind' but incorporates a whole range of non-biological self-organizing systems – is nothing more than a grammatical feature of the verbs used to describe the processes of which they consist. Surely this is the emptiest of formalisms? Well, perhaps it is. But it is a rather special category of formalism. To the extent that intrinsically reflexive processes are constitutive of a type of entity that in some sense *forms* itself or forms its *self* (whatever that 'self' might be), it might be termed *self-formalism*. The act of self-formation marries formalism with a (reflexive) process.[23] Moreover, as will become clearer below when a distinction is drawn between self-organization and self-assembly,[24] the grounding of selfhood in intrinsic reflexivity results in a conception of selfhood that is dependent upon ongoing energetic flow and the dictates of thermodynamics. Far from being a purely formal construct, therefore, an intrinsically reflexive self is a necessarily *thermodynamic self*.

It might also be objected that such an approach suggests that the human self can be 'reduced' to a process of (for example) mere self-organization, disregarding everything that makes human selfhood so lofty and sublime and so *different* from a muddy whirlpool or a lowly grub (not that 'lowly grubs' can be explained away by self-organization either). Yet there is an abundance of ways in which intrinsic reflexivity can manifest itself. Far from being reductionistic, such a definition of selfhood is appropriately circular: while telling us that a self is an entity constituted by an intrinsically reflexive relationship to itself, or that produces itself out of a pre-existing self to form a post-existing self, it tells us nothing about what the self that is constituted in this way actually *is* (whether it be a controlled flow of energy, a unit of genetic material, an organism, a living individual, a human being, a community of individuals, a biosphere or even a universe). One of the tasks of the following pages is to consider the range of manifestations of intrinsic reflexivity – the variety of forms of selfhood – of which the human self is just one, albeit one that is of characteristic interest to us.

A further distinction should be drawn at this point. This is the distinction between intrinsic reflexivity (as in 'I *produce* myself' or 'I *create* myself') and tautological self-identity (as in 'I *am* myself'): it is a distinction between a concept of selfhood that is dynamic and requires a process in time, and one that is static, i.e. prone to be undermined by the passage of time. The latter, static notion of 'selfhood' is surprisingly widespread, based as it is on the emphatic use of 'self' (I am myself, for no-one else can be me; my 'self' is what only I am) to the exclusion of the reflexive use. It gives rise to the common use of 'self', often deployed in expressions such as 'real self' or 'true self' or 'inner self', to denote 'what I *really* am' or some sort of unchanging private essence. And this, in turn, gives philosophers and psychologists the pleasure of arguing that there is no such thing as the self. This sounds radical, deep and satisfyingly Nietzschean (the self is dead, dutifully following in God's footsteps), and it attracts its adherents by suggesting that they do not really exist, at least not in the way they thought they did. In fact, what it really claims is that there is no inner, true, essential 'core' 'within' me, and if I thought there was, then I misunderstood what I really am.

Such views come to light, for example, in Bruce Hood's *The Self Illusion* (2012), which operates with a notion of the self as 'something at the core of someone's existence' or 'the essence of who someone is'.[25] This true, unitary 'self' is also taken to imply 'sovereignty', i.e. a capacity for independent decision-making.[26] Any evidence that a self is subject to outside influences such as group pressure or stereotyping is understood as undermining genuine selfhood: 'if it is a self that flinches and bends with tiny changes in circumstances', suggests Hood, 'then it might as well be non-existent'.[27] Thomas Metzinger's *The Ego Tunnel: The Science of the Mind and the Myth of the Self* (2009) explicitly seeks to convince the reader that 'there is no such thing as a self'. Contrary to popular opinion, he writes, 'nobody has ever *been* or *had* a self'.[28] Everything that has previously been understood in terms of selfhood can in fact be explained away as a 'phenomenally transparent self-model' – by which he means a model or representation of the organism that is not experienced as a model or whose representational nature is hidden from us. A biological organism is not a self, he continues,[29] for the self is 'merely a form of representational content – namely, the content of a transparent self-model activated in the organism's brain', this content comprising our bodily sensations, emotions and perceptions. The 'self' does not properly *exist*, Metzinger seems to be saying, because it is just a representation and not the 'reality'. Our delusive sense of self arises precisely because we are constitutionally unable to realize that it is just a representation – or perhaps rather a *mis*representation – in the brain.[30]

In their rigorous and sensible *Philosophical Foundations of Neuroscience* (2003), M. R. Bennett and P. M. S. Hacker likewise follow the line of argument embarked upon by Anthony Kenny, focusing on the specifically English typographical gap opened up from 'myself' to 'my self' and dismissing the noun 'self' *merely* as an aberration and an innovation produced by a conjunction of slipshod philosophy and wilful grammatical vandalism.[31] Their point, in fact, is to call into question the notion of a persistent inner entity to which only 'I' have introspective access. As such, their attack is thoroughly justified as an attack on 'mind' – an entity that is generally considered to be private, inner and enduring. However, I will argue that such a persistent private core is not what a self is.

The tautological or static use of 'self' will not feature in the following pages. The 'self' that is the focus of the following study is not specifically 'real' or 'inner'; its unity may well be problematic, and its 'persistence' – so far as it extends – is not at all similar to that of an unchanging and timeless essence. The self in question is intrinsically reflexive and bound up with the dynamic nature of non-equilibrium systems. The following three subchapters will analyse selfhood in terms of a variety of forms of intrinsic reflexivity, highlighting the three underlying categories to which these various forms belong, namely the categories of self-maintenance, self-reproduction and self-containment.

Forms of Intrinsic Reflexivity (1): Self-Maintenance

Self-Organization

It has long been understood that the essence of life is a tendency to perpetuate itself. This reflexivity is manifest in the *Acaranga Sutra*, the oldest extant text of the Jains of ancient India, which dates from the 4th century BCE: 'All beings are fond of life', it is said; 'they like pleasure and hate pain, shun destruction and like to live, they long to live'.[32] In Western thought the idea has found expression in the term *conatus* (Latin for 'striving' or 'effort'), developed by thinkers such as Thomas Hobbes and Baruch Spinoza[33] and generally taken to refer to the fundamental striving of a (living) being to continue to exist; Arthur Schopenhauer developed the concept of the will to life (*der Wille zum Leben*); while more recently Hans Jonas has focused on what he designates 'concern' or 'self-concern'.[34] The underlying idea is that the primordial 'concern' of any living organism is keep on living, to maintain its structure and form in the face of the constant threat of disorder or death. To this extent, a living being is an entity with 'interests', its fundamental interest being to stay alive, whether in itself or possibly through its offspring.[35]

Clearly, any such definition of life in terms of a tendency or a striving to stay alive tells us no more about what life actually *is* than the notion of self-creation betrays what the 'self' is that is creating and being created.[36] Yet this in itself highlights a feature common to selfhood and life: whatever they are, they both tend or strive to perpetuate themselves *as* whatever they are. The striving of the living organism – with its metabolic processes and activities – can thus be understood in terms of self-causation; at any one moment, a living organism is giving rise to the organism it will be in the next moment. The concept of an organism as a system of causally interdependent functional components (its organs) highlights such self-causation, graphically illustrated by the way an organism will cease to perpetuate itself as an organism if any one of its constituent organs (say, its liver) fails to function. It is thus possible not only to specify the function of each component in terms of its role *within* the organism (e.g. detoxifying the system), but also to describe it in more general terms as being to help maintain the self-maintaining self: on this level, all the components have the same function. To this extent, the functioning whole not only *entails* the functioning of all its components, but is likewise *entailed* by their proper functioning. There is thus a sense in which – via the mediation of its component parts – the organism as a whole is both the cause and the effect of itself. Self-causation of this order may also come to light in *action* and *behaviour* insofar as an organism is conceived as being the *cause* of what it does: when a lion chases after a gazelle or an amoeba after a tasty paramecium, at least part of the causal explanation lies within the predator (its 'inner' state).

For philosophers, though not for biologists, the circularity of self-causation – i.e. of a self that causes self that causes self – has been a perennial headache. Spinoza's notion of such a *causa sui* or self-cause was ridiculed by Schopenhauer as evoking the tale of Baron von Münchhausen pulling himself and his trusty steed out of a quagmire by his own hair.[37] As we all know (it is assumed), nothing can be its own cause. Disconcertingly (it might be countered), nothing can *indeed* be its own cause: 'nothing' is a sort of *causa sui* precisely to the extent that nothing comes from nothing. As a result, 'nothing' has delighted rhetoricians and paradoxists down the ages for its ability to give rise to itself. But this will do not (comes the sober reply): 'nothing' is not a 'thing' but a purely verbal construction.[38] Self-causation is generally repudiated by rational thought as a trick associated with omnipotent deity, punning metaphysical mumbo-jumbo or tall tales told by unrepentant story-tellers.

In fact, the notion of self-causation or self-generation is only empty if taken in an atemporal sense. The concept of 'time' provides a way out from the impasse: in practice, a self always generates itself *out of* a pre-existing self and *into* a post-existing self. Philosophers, but not biologists, have tended to fret about the riddle of which came first, the chicken or the egg.[39] The theory of evolution can be understood to relieve biologists of such worries, postulating a regressive lineage of selves emerging from earlier selves emerging from still earlier selves back to the dawn of selfhood.

Of course, this does raise the question of the *ur*-self: what gave rise to the first self (if such a concept even makes sense)? We shall postpone addressing this question more fully until Chapter 5. But at least part of the answer is that all living selfhood depends upon and thus presupposes a flux of energy. The self-causation that is characteristic of living beings is not a feat of magic, like a rabbit hoisting itself into existence from a conjurer's top hat. The 'self' does not produce itself from nowhere, out of nothing, but uses an energy flux to produce itself *from itself*. A minimum condition, therefore, is a universe with an energy gradient, and the resulting flow of energy. Such a universe makes possible, for a start, the phenomenon known as self-organization.

The concept of self-organization goes back to the 18th-century German philosopher Immanuel Kant, who describes a natural organism – as opposed to a manmade artefact – as something that is both an 'organized and a self-organizing being'.[40] More recently, however, the term has been adopted by Ilya Prigogine and Isabelle Stengers to describe the seemingly 'spontaneous' emergence of order in systems comprising turbulent fluids or certain chemical reactions when the system in question is driven far from thermodynamic equilibrium by an influx of energy.[41] Prigogine has coined the term 'dissipative structures' for such systems, by which he means a structure able to maintain itself through a process of dynamic interaction with its environment, an inflow and outflow of energy and matter. The phenomenon has even been described as a law to the effect that 'the flow of energy from a source to a sink through an intermediate system orders that system', where 'ordering' is taken to imply increased 'complexity'.[42]

Such systems include eddies and whirlpools, hurricanes and the convection cells that are produced when oil is gently heated in a pan, but they also include chemical systems such as flames and the much-discussed Belouzov-Zhabotinsky (BZ) reaction, a mixture of reacting chemicals that – when kept far from equilibrium by the addition of a constant supply of the appropriate chemical ingredients – soon starts to oscillate between two colours with metronomic regularity.[43] The mechanisms underlying this 'chemical clock' have been summarized as an 11-step sequence of chemical reactions one of which produces a chemical that in turn influences its own manufacture, and this element of feedback (in this case the ability of a chemical species to catalyse its own production) is perhaps one of the keys to self-organization. What it amounts to is a form of reflexivity in which self – i.e. the system or a part or a product of that system – is 'fed back' into itself, thus acquiring a dual nature as cause and effect. Reflexivity of this sort appears to be essential to the emergence of order. The result is a temporal or spatial pattern of coherent or structured events in which local components sustain the global order while the global structures constrain the behaviour of the individual components: a circular causality in which the whole determines the parts and the parts determine the whole.

Prigogine himself discerned in his dissipative systems something akin to a 'pre-biological adaptation mechanism' in that the eddy, the chemical clock or the convection roll may well modify its structures in response to a change in the control parameters.[44] Others have refused to run any such risk of animism or anthropomorphism.[45] Either way, the self-organizing processes of flowing water and flame have served as timeless metaphors for life and the living, and self-organization in its various forms is pervasive in biology. Self-organizing 'laws of form' or 'morphogenetic fields' rooted in systems dynamics are thought to constrain and shape both the development of individual organisms and the evolution of whole lineages,[46] while clock-like chemical autocatalytic processes share the self-organizing structure and rhythmic regularity essential to the biological clocks of our circadian rhythms.

The use of computational or mathematical models of self-organization to understand how biological systems work has been criticised by some. It has been argued that the principles of self-organization, far from revealing the 'secrets of life', show us 'what living things have in common with the rest of the universe'.[47] Yet this is not quite fair. Self-organization is not something that life has in common with all non-life (there is neither life nor self-organization in thermodynamic equilibrium); it is something life has in common with forms of non-life that are nonetheless *life-like*. Self-organization characterizes both life and the life-like, and as such it provides ideal ground for analysing the difference and drawing a boundary between the living and the merely life-like.

The relationship between self-organization and life also depends on our conception of life. If life is conceived not in terms of individual organisms but the biosphere on which every living organism is logically dependent, then an understanding in terms of self-organization makes more patent sense. Robert Shapiro and Gerald Feinberg thus famously define the biosphere – which they regard as the fundamental unit of life – as a 'highly ordered system of matter and energy characterized by complex cycles that maintain or gradually increase the order of the system through an exchange of energy with its environment'.[48] They pinpoint three conditions to be met if life is to arise: there must be a flow of free energy; a system of matter able to interact with the energy and use it to become ordered; and enough time to build up the necessary complexity.[49] In these terms, the self-organizing self is the global whole, whose sustained structures – evolving and increasing in complexity – are powered by a stream of solar or possibly geochemical energy; this planetary self maintains and progressively transforms itself using the flow of low-entropy light energy, in turn radiating away higher-entropy energy in the form of heat. The emergence and evolution of life is to be grasped primarily as a result of thermodynamic drive. The process of evolution by natural selection is itself sometimes considered an aspect or dimension of such self-organization, reproductive 'fitness' being a matter of energetic 'efficiency'.[50] Alternatively, another reflexive term, 'self-adaptation', might be judged to be preferable to 'self-organization' in underscoring that the self-perpetuation of this biospherical 'self' involves it constantly adjusting itself to its non-self, i.e. to the ever-changing environmental framework in which it finds itself and on which it depends.

Such claims are not uncontroversial. The motivation behind the definition proposed by Shapiro and Feinberg was in part to free our understanding of 'life' from a vision associated exclusively with terrestrial biology (a 'carbaquist' approach to life), allowing them to entertain the possibility of life-forms based not on water and carbon-based compounds, but on liquid ammonia, hydrocarbons or silicates (at the appropriate temperatures). But in taking this path they have sacrificed a lot of the properties considered essential in fuller and more rounded definitions of life, properties such as reproduction and heredity. Moreover, the idea of an ongoing 'complexification' of the biosphere has undeniable teleological undertones. An originally self-organizing self ends up as a self-complexifying self, leaving one wondering where this directionality comes from and how necessary it is: does the self really 'have' to become more complex?[51] Is complexity in any sense 'better' than simplicity (can we speak of 'progress')? Does a whirlpool or a chemical clock 'strive' to become more complex too? Deeper claims about complexity are worryingly unfalsifiable. What seems to be a long-term trend can always – in the bigger picture – prove to be a transitory fluctuation. Perhaps we are currently perched on the brink of a big drop in complexity. Perhaps, given enough complexity, we are *always* perched on the brink of a big drop in complexity.

Irrespective of the complexity of the self-organizing biosphere of which we form a part, most self-organizing systems – such as whirlpools, hurricanes and flames – tend not to be regarded as living entities, at least literally. By the same token, it may seem counter-intuitive to designate them 'selves'. In Chapter 2 we shall look at why, for all their metaphorical suggestiveness, they fail to meet the necessary criteria. Yet given our definition of selfhood in terms of intrinsic reflexivity, what are we to make of these non-living selves? Three closely related options present themselves. A first option is simply to accept that this is where our definition takes us, like it or not: a self, in a broad sense, need not necessarily be alive; it may just be *life-like*. A second option is to put such 'selves' in scare quotes, though this lays us open to charges of conceptual cowardice (an honest thinker should call a spade a spade, not a 'spade'). A third option is to dilute our 'selves' with a prefix such as proto, pseudo or quasi. This may be taken to imply some sort of progression or scale of selfhood, perhaps with human selfhood as the unquestioned peak. In fact, the deeper implication is simply that there are various criteria of selfhood, or various categories of intrinsic reflexivity. In the many cases of less-than-full selfhood only some – but not all – of these criteria are met.[52] These three options can co-exist, more or less coherently, and they are the options favoured in the present argument.

One further option available to those who have qualms about 'reducing' selfhood to anything as lowly as a merely self-organizing system is to deny point-blank that self-organizing selves really are selves, 'selves' or even proto-selves. It might be claimed, for example, that the term 'self-organization' is a misnomer; the system in question does not really exhibit intrinsic reflexivity, for it is not organizing *itself*. In the present context, however, this would be inconsistent insofar as there is no obvious reason for *not* counting self-organization as a form of intrinsic reflexivity as defined above. In *Mind in Life*, Evan Thompson implies that self-organizing systems are not yet individuals 'in a sense that begins to be worthy of the term self'.[53] Here it seems to be a matter of value, in that the attribution of selfhood is something of which an entity is deemed 'worthy' or not, but it is not clear where this value has come from. What remains true is that the notion of a self-organizing system does not provide an adequate characterization of the type of living selves that we are. There are other forms of intrinsic reflexivity that will help provide us with a fuller concept of selfhood.

Self-Production

Biologists have tended to highlight two sets of definitions of life and living organisms. Both exhibit intrinsic reflexivity.

The first may start with certain properties associated with individual organisms in the here-and-now. Life is 'that which is squishy,' suggests Gerald Joyce as a popular definition,[54] but too many non-living things are squishy for this to be of much help. Alternatively, living organisms may intuitively be identified as things that can eat other things, or that grow, move or respond to stimuli (although this raises the question of which of these things they do, and when). Underlying and grounding these more contingent features, however, is a universal property: metabolism. The matter and energy that make up an organism are not a permanent part of its structure, but are being constantly imported from the environment (in the form of light, water, oxygen or food), utilized to perform the work of maintaining the structure of the organism, and eventually returned to the environment as heat and waste.[55] A metabolic system is consequently a self-maintaining system. Many biologists have been wary of this metabolism-based definition because it fails to distinguish clearly between biological systems and the proto-metabolisms of flames or hurricanes[56]; greater specificity is felt to be required to differentiate living systems from 'merely' self-organizing ones.

The second approach – often adopted by those heedful of the inadequacies of the first – is to follow John Maynard Smith and Eörs Szathmáry in describing as living 'any population of entities possessing those properties that are needed if the population is to evolve by natural selection'. In other words, living beings are specified as having the properties of multiplication, variation and heredity, or as descending from such entities (as in the case of sterile hybrids, such as mules).[57] This entails that living entities are self-reproducing – or perhaps self-replicating[58] – entities. As with the self-maintenance of metabolism, intrinsic reflexivity resides in the production of self by self. In this case, however, the self-relationship spans the evolution of a lineage rather than the development of an individual organism; it is phylogenetic rather than ontogenetic. Whether such heredity involves informational macromolecules such as RNA or DNA or a form of gene-less or compositional information embodied in the persisting structures of the entity need not be specified at this point.

A common tendency has been to combine these two approaches to life. One of the best-known formulations is Joyce's 'working' definition of life as 'a self-sustained chemical system capable of undergoing darwinian evolution'.[59] Others, by contrast, have laid emphasis on one approach or the other. A relevant analysis of self-maintenance in this context was expounded by Martin Heidegger in his lectures on *The Fundamental Concepts of Metaphysics* from the 1929/30 winter term at the University of Freiburg. Without phrasing it in terms of intrinsic reflexivity, Heidegger explicitly links his notion of selfhood to the reflexive activity of an organism, referring to the self-production, self-guidance and self-renewal of an organism as features that distinguish it from a manmade machine.[60] Elsewhere he subsumes all these terms under the more general notion of *Selbsterhaltung* or self-maintenance.[61] The activity by which an organism maintains itself – i.e. guides itself, produces itself and renews itself – manifests what he terms the 'character of selfhood'.

Yet Heidegger is quick to defuse the potentially subversive implications of what he is saying, adding that the 'selfhood' shown by animals – by analogy with the human self – has tended to lead to overhasty talk of an 'animal soul', a temptation that he feels should be resisted.[62] Recognizing that selfhood is liable to be associated with subjectivity, consciousness and even personality (attributes he unquestioningly denies to animals), he is thus forced to restrict 'selfhood' to humans and find a different set of terms to refer to whatever it is that animals have.[63] Admittedly, he does subsequently refer to the 'specific selfhood [*Selbstsein*] of animals' as 'self in a wholly formal sense',[64] but by this stage it is too late: animals have clearly been refused the real thing. Given that we have so far come nowhere near ascertaining what 'subjectivity', 'consciousness' or 'personality' actually are (and why, if at all, they should be denied to animals), we would be unwise to follow Heidegger in his dogmatism. Having established – albeit by formal criteria – that all organisms are selves, there is no reason to backtrack by excluding from selfhood all organisms except the particular species of organism that happens to include Heidegger.

Another, related term implying intrinsic reflexivity that has come to prominence in recent years is *autopoiesis* or self-production, which has been developed by Humberto Maturana and Francisco Varela and others. The paradigmatic autopoietic system is the single cell (the foundation and core of all life on Earth), comprising as it does a bounded network of chemical transformations that continually regenerates the components and the boundary required to maintain that very network of chemical transformations. The fundamental contrast is with an *allopoietic* system such as a factory assembly line, where the product (say, a car or a cooker) is different from the system that produces it.[65] The class of autopoietic systems (self-producing bounded networks of molecules) is in fact part of a broader class of *autonomous* systems, where the boundary in question need not necessarily be material and which may thus extend to include other entities such as multicellular organisms, microbial communities or insect colonies.[66] Yet the principle of intrinsic reflexivity is equally present in both cases, embodied in the prefix *auto* as opposed to the *allo* (other) of assembly-line production.[67] Both autopoietic and autonomous systems are systems that produce themselves from themselves, and that regulate the process by which self gives rise to self. The precise nature of the boundary separating self from non-self is a question central to any analysis of selfhood and forms the particular focus of Chapter 6.

Maturana and Varela themselves resort at times to rather misleading imagery: 'the most striking feature of an autopoietic system', they write, 'is that it pulls itself up by its own bootstraps and becomes distinct from its environment through its own dynamics'.[68] Such bootstrapping is disconcertingly reminiscent of the 'nothing' that comes from 'nothing', evoking an acrobatic exercise worthy of Münchhausen and suggesting that an autopoietic system can hoist itself into existence on its own. It cannot. Further confusion has been caused by an emphasis on what they have called the 'organizational' or 'operational' closure of such systems, which has been misunderstood as implying material or energetic closure in relation to the environment (whereas what is meant is the circular or recursive relationship among the component processes that make up the system).[69] The concept of autopoiesis has consequently been accused of failing to take account of the thermodynamic requirements of any such living system. As Kepa Ruiz-Mirazo and Álvaro Moreno have put it, the self-productive logic of an autopoietic system should not be conceived as operating in isolation from the environment that provides the thermodynamic framework or from the associated energetic-material constraints.[70] Amongst other things, it must be 'nourished' by an inflow of energy or matter. The critique eloquently voiced by these two authors thus leads to their own notion of 'basic autonomy', defined as 'the capacity of a system to *manage* the flow of matter and energy through it so that it can, at the same time, regulate, modify and control: (i) internal self-constructive processes; and (ii) processes of exchange with the environment. Thus, the system must be able to generate and regenerate all the constraints – including part of its boundary conditions – that define it as such, together with its own particular way of interacting with the environment'.[71]

The underlying point is that any system of metabolic self-maintenance or self-production involves the preservation of organization within far-from-equilibrium conditions, and in order to achieve this – i.e. to resist the tendency towards disorder and disorganization – the system must be thermodynamically open. Metabolism thus implies a thermodynamic factor from the outset; the relational or self-constructive dimension of the autopoietic or autonomous system cannot be disentangled from the interactive dimension, i.e. its dynamic relationship to the environment in which it is embedded.

So how is a biologically self-maintaining entity to be distinguished from a 'merely' self-organizing entity? How do we get from the dissipative structures of physico-chemical self-organization described by Prigogine and Stengers to autopoietic systems such as bacteria or amoebae? As we shall see in Chapter 2, various factors play a role. First, as the name implies, dissipative systems fail to 'contain' or 'control' the energy that passes through them. Instead of being made to do 'work', there is a greater tendency for the energy to be lost as 'heat' to the surrounding environment, exemplified by the combustive proto-metabolism of a forest fire in comparison with the controlled combustion of an animal's metabolism. By contrast with dissipation, work requires the imposition of some sort of control or constraint on the system's energetic processes. Though the Second Law of Thermodynamics dictates that whenever energy does work, some fraction of that energy will be lost to random molecular motion as heat (whence the implacable net increase in disorder), autonomous living systems show a capacity for using and reusing their energy to maintain their own structural organization before expelling it in the form of relatively high-entropy waste. There is a deep link between such control and the concept of self-containment.

A second point, related to the first, is that such systems – characterized in particular by an ability to maintain their organization in the face of external perturbations, i.e. by incipient homeostasis – are chemical as opposed to merely physical systems.[72] The requisite chemical energy transfer is based on a universal energetic currency, the molecule *ATP*, which fosters the efficient transmission of energy between the system's constituent processes by coupling spontaneously occurring exergonic processes to endergonic processes, i.e. the 'uphill' or non-spontaneous processes required for aspects of self-construction such as *polymer* synthesis.[73] This makes it possible for building work to be done. Within an overall category of self-maintenance, one might thus differentiate between 'merely' *energetic* self-maintenance on the one hand, which refers to self-perpetuating energy flow patterns and incorporates phenomena such as self-organizing fluid flow and the self-propagation characteristic of flames and fires, and *structural* self-production on the other hand, which involves the ongoing manufacture of relatively stable structures such as proteins and other complex biomolecules. It is the degree and form of structural self-containment that determines whether a particular self-maintaining self is best regarded as a case of self-organization or self-propagation or as a self-producing system. This may determine how far we are inclined to regard it as a 'living' being.

Self-Adaptation and Self-Transformation

The idea of a self-maintaining or self-producing system may nonetheless seem too passive or inward to do justice to what goes on in even the simplest living organisms. Consider Schrödinger's oft-quoted reference to an organism's 'astonishing gift of concentrating a "stream of order" on itself and thus escaping the decay into atomic chaos – of "drinking orderliness" from a suitable environment'.[74] The principle of 'self-nourishment' or 'self-nutrition' (*trophe di' hautou*) was recognized by Aristotle as a defining characteristic of the living soul.[75] In modern terms, this can be taken to suggest not merely passive self-maintenance, but an active manipulation of the environment in order to concentrate the energy flow that it will use to sustain itself. A meaningful contrast might thus be drawn between an entity that just 'happens' to benefit from the flow of a 'stream of order' upon itself (and that persists only for as long as this low-entropy energy flow is readily available) and an entity that is able to modify itself or the environment – to fine-tune the relationship between self and non-self – in such a way that the energy flow is available and its effects last for longer than would have otherwise been the case.

This contrast between 'passive' and 'active' self-maintenance is very much a matter of degree. The homeostatic self-regulation[76] by which an organism maintains a constant internal medium in the face of the vicissitudes of the external world may be outwardly passive, but it nevertheless involves a process of self-adaptation that might be described as a form of *internalized* self-movement. More patently active self-adaptation occurs when an organism *moves itself* – engages in locomotion – within the environment around it. When *Escherichia coli* bacterial cells swim towards amino acids such as aspartate, they are *actively striving* to steer a 'stream of order' upon themselves; agency and motility are the attributes that enable them to make this leap. When they swim away from toxic metals, they are likewise seeking conditions conducive to their continuing self-organization. Self-maintenance is not just a matter of passively perpetuating oneself, in other words, but may involve forms of *self-adaptation* that vary in the degree of activity they imply. The category of 'self-adaptation' thus refers to the capacity of an organism to modify the relationship between self and non-self – i.e. attune itself to its surroundings – in such a way as to sustain its continuing existence as the self that it is. One specific mode of self-adaptation, the active self-adaptation of directed self-movement, will be the focus of recurrent attention throughout this analysis of minimal selfhood. A forthcoming study will look at how certain forms of self-movement generate the need and provide the foundation for the possibility of consciousness.

This moment-to-moment self-adaptation – the flexibility of an entity that can move itself and manipulate non-self – is in turn founded on forms of longer-term adaptability such as the evolutionary attunement fixed in the 'genetic' memory of a lineage; it may further incorporate the cognitive plasticity (the 'neural' memory) of an individual organism learning through experience about how best to deal with its environment. In such cases one might even speak of self-transformation rather than self-adaptation, the former suggesting a relatively permanent or enduring modification as opposed to the reversible response to circumstantial changes implied by the latter. Yet the deeper point is the same: an adaptive or self-transforming self is a self that maintains itself by modifying itself.[77] It might seem that the category of self-adaptive or self-transformative activity is best subsumed *within* the more general category of self-maintenance in that the former is grounded upon the latter and not vice versa: a self can only adapt or transform itself as *part* of an underlying process of self-maintenance. Yet this is not the whole truth: a self-maintaining self that fails to adapt itself to circumstances will soon cease to be a self.[78] There is a sense, therefore, in which the two categories of self-maintenance and self-adaptation are mutually dependent, or two sides of the same coin. To the extent that self-maintenance is a dynamic process and involves a dynamic relationship to non-self, *some* self-change must be present from the start. This notion of self-modification or self-transformation is inextricably bound up with paradox in that the 'essence' of a self may be not only to maintain itself but also to change itself, indeed to maintain itself *by* changing itself.

Forms of Intrinsic Reflexivity (2): Self-Reproduction

Proponents of an autopoietic approach to living systems have tended, not surprisingly, to see self-production as a more fundamental feature of life than multiplication and evolution. Their argument is based on the apparent logical priority of self-production over self-reproduction. As Maturana and Varela express it, 'reproduction cannot be a part of the organization of living beings because to reproduce something, that something must *first* constitute a unity and have an organization that defines it'. A living being, they say, 'must be capable of existing without reproducing itself. It is enough to think of a mule to realize that this must be so'.[79] Nor are most sexually reproducing selves strictly capable of *self*-reproduction, for two are required; in these cases self is dependent upon an 'other'. Hermaphroditic forms of reproduction – appropriately designated 'selfing' and commonly found in gastropods, fish and certain plants – may enable certain organisms to get round such restrictions on reproductive autonomy, but here too self-reproduction is logically dependent on the prior existence of a self-*producing* self.

On this view, autopoiesis is logically presupposed by reproduction, but not vice versa. Once we have a self-maintaining and self-producing system, this may or may not reproduce, mutate and evolve. In practice, this will depend on its inner conditions and its external circumstances. In extreme conditions, so-called adversity/stress-selected organisms face a trade-off between self-preservation and self-reproduction. For terrestrial animals to survive the low temperatures of the Antarctic, for example, they must produce special sugars such as trehalose and antifreeze proteins, diverting valuable metabolic resources away from other functions such as growth or reproduction. Accordingly, such organisms tend to have long life cycles, low growth rates and low rates of reproduction.[80]

In microbial communities found in nutrient-poor sediments deposited thousands or even millions of years ago, the cells also seem to operate at or near the lower limit for the metabolism of life, appearing dead but absorbing food when it is available; they might be described, with understatement, as 'slow selves'. In such energy-poor circumstances, reproduction is not a viable option because dividing in two would create new rivals for nutrients that are already scarce. It makes more sense for the cells to use what energy they can garner to repair cellular damage.[81] In extreme conditions such as these, self-maintenance certainly seems to come before self-reproduction.

The autopoietic perspective has thus been portrayed as focusing on the 'here and now'. As Thompson puts it, the claim is that 'for an individual entity, here and now, to be characterized as a living system, it must realize the autopoietic organization (...). In other words, no system that deserves, here and now, to be called living can fail to be autopoietic'.[82] By contrast, the other main approach to life, which focuses on reproduction and evolution and finds its best-known expression in Joyce's 'self-sustained chemical system capable of undergoing darwinian evolution',[83] has implications that go beyond the self-maintaining self here and now. One such implication is that life can only be a collective phenomenon. As made clear by the definition of Maynard Smith and Szathmáry, life is something attributed to a *population* of entities; the individual life cannot be separated from its synchronic and diachronic context, i.e. from the community of other living beings with which it is competing and cooperating and from the historical lineage of self-maintaining, self-reproducing, evolving entities that have given rise to it. Yet this raises a clutch of puzzling questions about the precise nature of the self-reproducing self in question.

Every cell's dream, according to François Jacob, is to become two cells. Given half a chance, *E. coli* bacteria proliferate wildly, doubling their number in as little as 20 minutes.[84] But who or what is the self that is living its dream so prodigally? In the case of self-maintenance, it seems clear that the self that is produced is the same as the self *from which* it is produced. The self-producing self has 'interests' (its own persistence in time), and it 'acts' in these interests. But reproduction seems different: is the self that reproduces itself really the same as the self that is reproduced? Is self-reproduction merely a radical case of self-transformation? Can we speak of 'interests' here? Whose interests? Does the cell really 'want' to become two, or to multiply? For whose sake? In terms of selfishness, the reproduction of an organism cannot be said to occur *for the sake of* the organism itself; rather, it occurs for the sake of the lineage, or the species, or some other level of selfhood. In many cases, reproduction is essentially linked to the apparent demise of the reproducing self. Take the case of an amoeba that reproduces itself by fission: which of the two offspring does the mother amoeba become? Both?

Or perhaps neither? Can one entity be 'the same as' or 'identical to' two subsequent entities? It may be felt that the question simply has no answer.[85] The puzzle seems even more intractable in the case of fusion, as when gametes fuse to form a *zygote* in sexual reproduction. Again, the principle of numerical identity is undermined, this time with 'two' becoming 'one' instead of 'one' becoming 'two'. The difference between self-production and self-reproduction can thus be pinpointed as the breach of numerical identity that is entailed either by fission or fusion. Although identity is infringed by self-reproduction, however, continuity – defined in terms of causality or temporal contiguity – remains unscathed. Offspring are a continuation of their progenitors.

Indeed, there is a sense in which all the cells in my body form part of a venerable and unbroken lineage going back not only to an original zygote formed from the union of two gametes a few decades ago, but to the first ever individual or collective *ur*-self, i.e. to a primordial RNA-based protocell or a community of such protocells perhaps 3.5 billion years ago. As such, they are distant siblings of every other prokaryotic and eukaryotic cell ever in existence. Perhaps the indeterminacy of the self-dividing (and uniting) cellular self across the generations hints at the primacy of the species self or the global self, a constantly self-organizing and self-renewing biosphere. In these terms, the indeterminate identity of the cellular self over time is made irrelevant by the unity of the whole at a higher level.

Or perhaps these conceptual difficulties suggest that (self)-reproduction is not a genuine case of intrinsic reflexivity in the sense we are looking for, and as such not truly pertinent to the nature of selfhood. Perhaps reproduction is more akin to *allo*-production than *auto*-production. Whereas self produces self in the course of the normal life cycle, there is a discontinuity – a jump in selfhood – whenever a new life cycle begins, whether the life in question be that of a single cell such as an amoeba or a multicellular organism such as an animal. Yet this too is only half the story. In fact, the unanswerability of the question is reflected in the notion that the newborn self is both a continuation *and* a new start. Our natural tendency as biological 'individuals' – where our individuality is defined and demarcated by the beginning and ending of our life cycle in time, our birth and our death – seems to be to give priority to the individual over the sequential or collective viewpoint. Few of us would regard ourselves as *nothing but* a strict continuation of our parents, or our offspring *simply* as a perpetuation of ourselves. The stress on biological individuality may be compounded by a culturally specific craving for uniqueness, by the ideological individualism that encourages wealthy modern-day humans to fly the parental nest and develop a self 'of their own'. At a deeper level, while our unconscious genetic memory goes back through the generations, our brain-based narrative memory, which provides the foundation for the autobiographical selfhood that *matters* to us so much, is perforce restricted to the life-span[86] of the individual living in the here and now. It is perhaps our very nature as individuals – our selfhood defined in terms of what we can consciously recall[87] – that predisposes us to privilege the individual over the trans-individual perspective. The fact that I have no conscious memory of my previous 'incarnations' as my human forefathers, not to mention my primate, mammalian, vertebrate, *metazoan* or unicellular ancestors, inclines me to separate my selfhood from theirs; I tend, for example, to think of myself as a different self from the worm-like proto-chordate that I/we used to be.

The bigger picture, however, is that I should gratefully appreciate the genetic memory that I have inherited from my ancestry, including the 37 percent of my genes that have counterparts in bacteria and are the bequest of the common ancestor we share from over two billion years ago.[88] It may be natural and healthy to restrict selfhood to the extant biological individual ('me'), but it runs the risk of a certain sort of solipsism.

If we stress the autopoietic, 'here-and-now' dimension of life, reproduction is secondary and may require nothing more than a simple process of cellular growth followed by division. In such a scenario, inheritance need not be associated with a genetic record such as DNA but could pass through a structural inheritance system based on persisting features of the cytoskeleton or membrane. Understood thus, the very constitution of the cell is what is bequeathed from one generation to the next; it is the self-maintaining configuration of the self that is passed from progenitor to progeny, from self to self. Yet there are limitations to such a conception of heredity that dispenses with specialized informational macromolecules. The problem is that the higher the complexity of such systems, the more fragile or brittle they become, and without some form of reliable genetic inheritance system, there is no way to fix or record any organizational novelties that may arise. As Ruiz-Mirazo and Moreno suggest, 'in order to start a process of open-ended evolution, autonomous systems have to incorporate genetic machinery, where informational records are partly decoupled from all the muddle of metabolic reactions'. The apparent limitations of a purely structural inheritance system 'can only be overcome with the invention of a new kind of organization, based on the development of hereditary mechanisms which are metabolically "off line"'.[89]

Ruiz-Mirazo and colleagues (2004) have thus traced what amounts to an evolution of intrinsic reflexivity, progressing from self-organization via self-maintaining chemical autocatalysis and basic autonomy to 'hereditary autonomy' based on self-replicating macromolecules capable of open-ended evolution.[90] Others have placed the self-replication of these informational macromolecules at the very root of life. When the first hypotheses explaining the origins of life through natural processes were proposed in the first half of the 20th century, the U.S. geneticist H. J. Muller suggested that the first living organisms were primitive genes, and the camps were divided into 'nucleocentric' and 'cytoplasmist' schools of thought, depending on whether they put genetic material or metabolism first.[91] In the second half of the century the gene-centred viewpoint propounded by Richard Dawkins and others continued to be influential; the fundamental units of life were seen not as cells or as organisms, but as genes or replicators which competed with each other by producing 'vehicles' through which they interacted with the environment with varying degrees of success.[92] Such replicators preceded cells both logically and chronologically. Life was an expression of self-replicating information.

On this view, the intrinsic reflexivity that is relevant would not be the logically ambiguous self-reproduction of cells, but the self-replication of informational macromolecules made of DNA. This too raises the question of what 'self' is being replicated in the process. Chapters 3 and 4 will look in greater detail at the possible ascription of selfishness and selfhood to units of genetic material, both in cellular chromosomes and in the form of viruses. For the present let a few preliminary logical considerations suffice. First, there is a certain asymmetry between the logic of cellular reproduction and that of DNA replication. Whereas the former implies the seamless continuity of (say) cellular growth followed by fission, the latter involves the manufacture of 'replicas' using a template.[93] Like cellular reproduction, DNA replication violates the principle of numerical identity in that the relationship of prior self to subsequent self is no longer one-to-one, and it remains unclear whether the resulting macromolecules are best characterized in terms of qualitative identity[94] or mere continuity. The use of a template for the replication of a DNA molecule sounds suspiciously like a form of *allo*-replication: the template and the replica may be highly similar or exactly alike (as identical, perhaps, as a 'mirror image'), but the newly produced strand – indeed ultimately both of the strands in the two resulting double-stranded molecules – has been assembled by means of processes that are external to itself. To the extent that *all* DNA molecules are in the end just replicas, one may be left asking oneself where the 'original' self is to be found.[95]

But this is surely over-pedantic. In practice, the product of replication is likely to be identical to, or continuous with, its progenitor in every respect that could possibly *matter*. What counts is that it should embody the same information, for it is through its informational identity that it exerts an effect on its environment. At the same time, individual molecules are so remote from our ordinary perception that there may be a tendency to consider them statistically rather than as individual entities anyway. This ambiguity is present in Dawkins's own work, where a replicator is described in one passage as 'potentially the ancestor of an indefinitely long line of descendant replicators' and in the next paragraph as 'potentially immortal'.[96] The idea is clearly that the self-replicating macromolecule in some sense 'lives on' in its structurally identical descendants, which are a continuation of itself. Yet this has some strange logical implications, one of the most striking being that the successful replicator is the ancestor *of itself* (albeit its subsequent self); it is its own ancestor.[97] In view of the statistical nature of the identity of atoms and small molecules, this is perhaps less likely to worry us than it would if we were talking about humans. Yet there are gradations in size and perceptibility. The chromosomes of the human genome each contain billions of atoms, and are clearly much more 'identifiable' than a mere hydrogen molecule. Given the wonders of modern microscopy, two such macromolecules can hardly be said to be indiscernible. This is all the more relevant since the crux of the genocentric viewpoint is in fact that the self-replicating macromolecules are *supposed* not to be fully identical, for they are (collectively) *supposed* to evolve. No two replicates are exactly alike; mis-replication is essential. In the case of sexual reproduction, moreover, genetic recombination opens up new dimensions of evolvability. Seen in this light, what matters is not informational identity, but informational *continuity* – the continuity of a self-adapting or self-transforming lineage of information-bearing molecules.

A further complication in focusing on DNA as a self-replicating entity is that DNA is not in itself strictly self-replicating. While it is true that the specific sequence of bases in a DNA molecule serves as the template for the construction of a new chain complementary to itself, an enzyme called *DNA polymerase* is always required for the replication of any DNA sequence. To be sure, it is the DNA itself that encodes the DNA polymerase that is needed for its replication, but the whole process is dependent on the controlled conditions of a cellular environment to allow for the *translation* of the encoded information into the requisite sequence of amino acids, properly folded to form each enzyme.[98] In itself DNA does not show the *reflexivity* required of life and selfhood. It is perfect for the storage of information; one gram of DNA is thought to be enough to hold about two petabytes of data, the equivalent of three million CDs.[99] If kept cold, dry and dark, the DNA does not require constant maintenance and appears to be highly accurate. Yet this is not the point. DNA may be a highly efficient medium of information storage, but information storage relies on immobility and stasis; in general there is no flow, no process, no life and no self.

A clue to the connection between DNA and selfhood, however, is provided by RNA, the macromolecule that is commonly thought to have preceded DNA in the early evolution of life. A major difference between DNA and RNA is that RNA molecules are not merely linear sequences of symbols like barcodes, but are endowed with a dimensionality that makes them behave more like proteins.[100] The sequence of nucleotide bases not only encodes information, but also specifies how the molecules fold in solution, for RNA molecules – as a consequence of *base pairing* between different parts of the molecular chain – are able to loop back on themselves to form complicated two and three-dimensional topographies. The molecules thus adopt distinctive shapes determined by the sequence of their nucleotides.

The result is that RNA is characterized by the duality or double-functionality that lends itself to intrinsic reflexivity: on the one hand it embodies information in the sequence of its nucleotides, while on the other hand it embodies biological function, specified by its distinctive folded structure. It is this dual nature as both 'data' and 'program' that bestows upon it the capacity to interact with itself, in so doing creating order. According to Wolfgang Banzhaf and colleagues (1999), RNA is a macromolecule that not only serves 'as a storage device for biological information (like DNA, only less stable), but that also shows some biological activity (like proteins, only weaker)'. What this means is that RNA has the property of 'being able to serve (at times) as operator and (at other times) as operand. The only "trick" nature uses to achieve that is to fold strings of ribo-nucleotides, the linear sequence of which can be interpreted as information, into a two- and sometimes three-dimensional form that can act on other RNA strings and sometimes even on itself'.[101] As Francis Crick first realized, this implies that RNA not only serves as a template but is also capable of behaving as an enzyme and possibly thus catalyzing its own self-replication. This self-feeding circularity depends on the duality of RNA as information and program, where the function of the program is to maintain itself (both as information and program) in the face of entropy.

Subsequent evolution, it is widely thought, divided the one-polymer world of RNA (the so-called RNA world) into the two-polymer world of DNA and proteins. The reflexivity that had previously been encapsulated in RNA molecules still existed, but no longer inherent within a single type of macromolecule; it was now embodied within the duality of DNA molecules, which provided more reliable information storage, and proteins, which make better catalysts: a sort of self-division of labour.[102] The upshot is that although DNA may be incapable of directly catalysing its own replication, it at least *encodes the instructions* for catalysing its own replication – as well as for providing the right conditions for this in an appropriate cellular microenvironment. If not directly self-replicating, it can perhaps be said to be *indirectly* self-replicating. While this lack of metabolic self-sufficiency may exclude DNA from the realm of full selfhood in its own right, it suggests that it is the self-reproducing cell – the cellular microenvironment within which self-replicating DNA may operate – that represents a more relevant unit of selfhood.

Having thus pinpointed self-maintenance in its various forms (including self-organization, self-production and self-adaptation) and self-reproduction (including self-replication) as two fundamental and perhaps inextricable aspects of the intrinsic reflexivity of living selfhood, this notion of an enclosed microenvironment brings us to a third fundamental aspect that requires attention.

Forms of Intrinsic Reflexivity (3): Self-Containment

A self is an entity that not only maintains itself and adapts itself to its surroundings, and not only reproduces itself; it is an entity that *contains itself*. This concept of self-containment suggests two ideas. The first idea is that the entity in question is held within a boundary that is intrinsic to that entity, just as every individual cell is enclosed within a *lipid* membrane produced by the cell itself. The second idea is that the entity is self-contained in the more usual sense of 'self-sufficient' or autonomous. In both cases, this self-containment is differentially 'porous' or 'permeable'. However self-contained it may be, any self is always dependent on the environment that sustains it with a flow of energy and matter. The boundary must thus allow nutrients in and waste out, but at the same time keep the internal environment strictly separate from the external environment.

The term is ambiguous in other senses. A boundary or limit represents the point at which self coincides with non-self, to this extent infringing the law of identity. The boundary thus has a 'double identity' as something that both links and separates self and non-self.[103] As we shall see in Chapter 6, moreover, living organisms tend to be *pervaded* by their boundaries, which are anything but restricted to 'outer' limits. The human gut, for example, is topologically part of the outside world (we are doughnuts in this sense, the hole in the middle running from mouth to anus), so while we may think of our skin as the main boundary separating us from the outside world, the mucous membranes that line our digestive, respiratory and reproductive tracts are orders of magnitude greater in area. The notion of an 'extended' self (or organism, or *phenotype*) further blurs the boundaries between self and non-self. The fact that organisms may modify their environment (say, by constructing dens or burrows) for their own energetic and protective purposes – in order to harness environmental energy flows or protect themselves from energy loss or predation – makes the distinction between self and non-self all the more complex.

This threefold understanding of the intrinsic reflexivity of selfhood – as self-production, self-reproduction and self-containment – echoes Tom Cavalier-Smith's idea of living organisms as a 'mutualistic symbiosis between genes, catalysts and membranes'.[104] Cavalier-Smith defines organisms in terms of three deeply interdigitating systems: a genetic system, a structural system (based fundamentally on membranes) and what he calls an assimilatory system comprising trophic, metabolic and bioenergetic subsystems, responsible for channelling the flow of energy and matter to create structure and information. All organisms, he writes, depend on this 'three-way cooperation of a genetic and an assimilatory system, integrated into a discrete structure capable of integrated growth, division, and infinitely mutable inheritance'. All three systems are equally vital to the self-perpetuation of living selfhood.[105]

The self-generation of the boundary plays a similarly important role in autopoietic theory. The self-producing metabolic system and the boundary that contains it exist in a relationship of circular interdependency. As Thompson puts it, 'a cell stands out from a molecular soup by creating the boundaries that set it apart from what it is not and that actively regulate its interactions with the environment. Metabolic processes within the cell construct these boundaries, but the metabolic processes themselves are made possible by those very boundaries. In this way, the cell emerges as a figure out of a chemical background. Should this process of self-production be interrupted, the cellular components no longer form a unity, gradually diffusing back into a molecular soup'.[106] The membrane is produced by the metabolism, but it is also the very precondition for the metabolic network that produces it. It creates both a spatiotemporal 'unity' in the form of an internal milieu – a self-sustaining homeostatic environment that persists in time – and a thermodynamic separation from the 'outer' world. To 'contain' is to 'control', and this self-containment is what makes it possible to control the energy flow so it will perform the 'work' necessary to keep inside and outside properly segregated.

At the same time, a number of questions are raised. These, again, will be the focus of Chapter 6. Autopoietic systems are sometimes distinguished from what have been called 'autonomous' systems in that the former presuppose a material boundary, such as a semi-permeable lipid membrane in the case of cells, whereas the nature of the boundary is unspecified in the latter. In the case of metazoans such as worms, fish or humans, the 'containment' might be considered to take the form of the *epithelium*, which – along with connective tissue, muscle tissue and nervous tissue – constitutes one of the four basic types of animal tissue and includes the epidermis, the mucous lining of the gastrointestinal tract and the linings of body cavities. But how important is it for this containment to be a material boundary? Our immune system can also be considered a form of boundary or containment, operating rather like a system of border guards that distinguish 'self' from 'non-self' and neutralize the latter. In more or less all animals, it seems, any intruder that breaches the physical boundary of the epithelium is confronted with an innate immune system comprising elements such as the single-celled 'macrophages', amoeba-like white blood cells found under the skin. These so-called 'sentinel' cells recognize the characteristic 'non-self' molecules of the most frequent pathogenic invaders and duly ingest the microbes in question. In this case, the boundary is not so much material as behavioural.

This in turn raises the question of how important it is for the boundary to be not only semi-permeable but also 'active',[107] in other words not simply a passive 'wall' separating the inner environment from the outer environment while allowing entrance to the necessary nutrients, but an agent *working* to maintain the thermodynamic separation of inside and outside. Even among material boundaries, there can clearly be different types. More rigid or inflexible support systems (as provided by *cell walls*) contrast with the fluid, flexible and permeable boundaries provided by cellular plasma membranes. In the case of *cell membranes*, additional work (in the form of ion pumps) may be required to keep the inside and the outside separate. Gram-negative bacteria such as *E. coli* have not only a fluid plasma membrane, but also a tough cell wall made of *peptidoglycan* and a *lipopolysaccharide* layer facing outwards, clearly performing different functions of separation, structuration and protection. A similar diversity of function and form is found among animals. By contrast with the skin of amniotes such as reptiles, birds and mammals, the amphibian epidermis is in many cases not even waterproof and provides no obstacle to water loss through evaporation. The skin of many frogs plays a key role in respiration and thermoregulation. Such a fragile boundary is clearly distinct from defensive armour such as the bony osteoderms of reptiles, dinosaurs and even some mammals (such as armadillos). Yet even these have a function in energy regulation.

Equally important is the question whether the boundary really has to be *self*-generated. Provided that the functions of control and containment are performed, does the origin of the boundary really matter? What about a symbiotically engendered boundary? This might represent an incursion on our autonomy, but it is not obvious how far this would diminish our selfhood. What if our skin were provided by the environment in some way? It sounds almost unthinkably excruciating, presumably because we humans are so deeply attached to our self-generated skin. Material *allo*-containment of this sort would also put a severe brake on the capacity of an organism for self-movement, effectively precluding directed motility. Yet such considerations seem less relevant to non-material forms of containment. Consider, for example, how closely our microbiome – the collective of microbes we harbour in our gut – seems to be involved in our innate immune system.[108] What if our entire innate immune system consisted of an army of (genetically distinct) macrophages that had started out as an invasion of amoebae but had entered into a symbiosis with us whereby they did us the favour of recognizing and disposing of invasive non-self in return for the food or safe haven with which our bodies provided them? Would this affect the question of selfhood? The resulting self might best be viewed as the symbiotic whole (as in the case of human plus microbiome). A self need not necessarily be as unitary a phenomenon as we may like to imagine. What about a *man-made* immune system comprising a throng of nano-robots that swam through our bodies recognizing and eliminating bacteria, viruses and cancerous cells?

There is uncertainty too regarding the role of cellular compartmentalization at the origins of life. While 'naked DNA' theories have stressed the chronological primacy of replicators which *subsequently* learnt how to provide themselves with a boundary, the autopoietic school of thought has prioritized the self-generating boundary as essential to the very possibility of life. As we shall see in Chapter 5, others have suggested that the environment itself might have covered the earliest needs for compartmentalization, whether in the form of a 'surface metabolism' structured on clay or pyrite or through the rocky labyrinths of mineral 'cells' available at alkaline vents. Such 'semi-cells' imply a lesser element of *auto*-containment; these proto-selves would have been partly *allo*-contained. As such, perhaps, they would have only been 'semi-selves', on their way to full selfhood.

It seems likely, moreover, that such inorganic compartments would have provided a context in which genetic material would have been able to mix and recombine, evolving as a collective self rather than as individualized membrane-bound entities. There would have been less continuity of lineage, less genealogical persistence, and less functional integration and interconnectedness; instead there would have been greater modularity of cellular componentry and a constant exchange of elements via horizontal gene transfer. It was perhaps only once membrane-wrapped cells separated themselves off from the 'communal ancestral gene pool'[109] that individual as opposed to collective selfhood emerged. The significance of self-containment is that it is concomitant with the capacity to differentiate self from non-self. It grounds the possibility of an entity's self-delimitation or self-definition as the entity that it is.

We are contained or defined not only by our spatial boundaries. As biological individuals we are contained in time too, and to the extent that our birth (or conception) and our death are 'ours', we may be said to be temporally *self-contained*.[110] In these terms, the unit of selfhood is a *life cycle*, itself in many cases an ongoing process of pre-programmed self-transformation. The analogy between self-containment in space and self-containment in time is suggestive. Its applicability is clearest, perhaps, in the case of unicellular organisms, where each individual self may be considered to last from the fission that produced it to the fission by which it becomes two. In other cases, the boundary between being alive and no longer being alive is less clear-cut, whence the commonplace that we are dying even in the fullness of life.[111] While in evolutionary terms the limits for multicellular organisms such as fruit flies or humans might be considered to be constituted by the single-celled bottle-necks at the beginning of each successive life cycle, the end of the individual coincides not with the appearance of the next generation but with the demise of the organism. At the same time, the self-maintenance of multicellular organisms is built upon the exquisitely controlled death and regeneration of their component cells, a constant process of cellular dying and rebirth. This measured intrusion of 'death' into the living organism – essential to its continued functioning – can even be considered analogous to the semi-permeability or differential porosity of our membranous or epithelial boundaries. The ambiguity inherent in the concept of self-containment entails that the borderline between a living self and its 'other' (in this case its own non-existence) is unlikely ever to be straightforward.

Self and Self-Interest: Self as an End in Itself

So far we have identified three features fundamental to selfhood: self-maintenance (which may take the form of, or incorporate, a range of subcategories such as self-organization, self-production and self-adaptation), self-reproduction (or self-replication) and self-containment. The principle underlying these three interrelated features is that of intrinsic reflexivity. There may be those who object to the 'systematizing' implications of any attempt to 'reduce' the living universe to a single concept such as 'selfhood' or 'intrinsic reflexivity'.[112] A 'postmetaphysical' thinker such as Michael Marder thus objects to the Spinozan concept of *conatus* – the striving of every self to keep going in its selfhood – as 'a totalizing, metaphysical concept that casts life in the terms of a desire to stay alive, factored into every living being'.[113] In the present case, however, the inherent dependence of selfhood upon what is 'other', in conjunction with the necessarily problematic and ambivalent nature of self-containment, offsets any tendency to turn 'selfhood' into some sort of vacuous metaphysical absolute. The fact that each particular self has fuzzy boundaries – i.e. there is a point at which self coincides with non-self – underscores the importance of looking at each instance of potential selfhood on its own empirical terms, analysing in the greatest possible detail in what sense and to what extent a human being, fruit fly, nematode worm, quaking aspen, paramecium or *E. coli* bacterium can be said to produce itself and to contain itself, and even considering how far this may apply to 'selves' of more contentious status such as whirlpools, self-steering automobiles, viruses, biospheres or even the universe in its entirety.

However, a number of general points remain to be touched upon before turning to more specific considerations: first, the relationship between selfhood and the possession of interests; second, the relationship between selfhood and numerical identity or unity; third, the relationship between selfhood and the energetic flow that is required to sustain a self-perpetuating process. These will be the focus of the remainder of this Introduction.

The first question – how far selfhood is necessarily bound up with the possession of interests – brings us back to the inextricable relationship between self-maintenance and self-adaptation. As noted above, the capacity of a system to maintain itself in a dynamic environment hinges upon it being able to adapt itself to the changing conditions. This applies even to relatively simple self-organizing or dissipative systems, to which Prigogine and Stengers (among others) have attributed something akin to a 'prebiological adaptation mechanism'.[114] Far- from-equilibrium systems such as whirlpools, convection cells and chemical clocks persist for as long as they are 'coupled' to their environment; once they become 'uncoupled', they rapidly cease to maintain themselves as self-ordering entities. Maturana and Varela likewise regarded autopoiesis in this light[115]; in their view, autopoietic systems owe their ability to perpetuate themselves through time to the 'selection' of the appropriate 'nutrients' from the environment. To the extent that a metabolic system necessarily depends upon an interaction with the environment by which it selects those metabolites that have fostered its continued existence in the past, it is an adaptive system, and its adaptation takes the form of a 'structural coupling' with the environment.[116] One might put it thus: if selfhood is taken to consist in intrinsic reflexivity – in the intrinsically reflexive relationship that a self has to itself – then this also implies an intrinsic relationship to the non-self to which it is structurally coupled, i.e. to the non-self that 'matters' or is 'meaningful' to it. By adapting to or coupling itself selectively with what is around it, a self successfully works in its own interests. A self that *fails* to couple itself with non-self – that fails to work in its own interests – will quickly cease to be a self. Another intrinsically reflexive way of expressing this is that a self is *an end in itself*. The 'aim' or 'end' of the adaptive work it performs is to perpetuate itself. The idea is an ancient one: the Aristotelian notion of *entelechy* as a defining attribute of 'soul' likewise contains the idea of an entity that works for an end intrinsic to itself.[117]

More complex forms of selfhood may use specialized information and control systems – such as the nervous system, the immune system or the endocrine system of hormones – as mechanisms fostering the self-regulation of the body, signals from one part of the organism eliciting an appropriate response in another part or in the organism as a whole. Homeostatic self-adjustments of this sort can be regarded as forms of internalized self-movement, i.e. adjustments of self *caused by* self *within* self. It makes sense for an onlooker to say that it is in the organism's interests to regulate itself in this way. By contrast, it is with the *externalized* self-movement of locomotion that an 'interest' becomes something that is not only attributable by an onlooker but can be 'pursued' by the self in question.

Self-movement, or motility, thus represents a rather special mode of self-adaptation in that it is with the emergence of a capacity to move that the world takes on *meaning* for the self that inhabits it. This is exemplified by the case of a bacterium swimming towards glucose or aspartate or away from a noxious heavy metal. Only if an organism has some sort of capacity to assess its surroundings (as better or worse for itself) can it actively *behave towards* the world in a way that represents its own interests. In its simplest form, this opens up a dichotomy of attraction or repulsion and the associated behavioural options of approach or withdrawal. From this moment onwards, the world is imbued with 'value', where value reflects what is better or worse for the self in question. In these terms, a self is an entity that not only has interests but also the wherewithal to pursue them – the most fundamental of these interests being to persist in its selfhood over time.

Philosopher Daniel C. Dennett describes the decisive step in terms of what has here been termed 'self-containment' rather than self-movement. Talking about 'minds', Dennett explicitly links this original creation of value to the establishment of boundaries: 'as soon as something gets into the business of self-preservation, boundaries become important, for if you are setting out to preserve yourself, you don't want to squander effort by trying to preserve the whole world: you draw the line. You become, in a word, *selfish*. This primordial form of selfishness (which, as a primordial form, lacks most of the flavors of *our* brand of selfishness) is one of the marks of life'.[118] It is by putting a boundary around oneself and thus 'defining' oneself and one's interests that 'good' and 'bad' (or at least 'better' and 'worse') enter the world:

> *Consider a simple organism – say, a planarian or an amoeba – moving non-randomly across the bottom of a laboratory dish, always heading to the nutrient-rich end of the dish, or away from the toxic end. This organism is seeking the good, or shunning the bad – its own good and bad ... Seeking one's own good is a fundamental feature of any rational agent, but are these simple organisms seeking or just 'seeking'? We don't need to answer that question.*[119]

From this point on, we can speak of a point of view or perspective (here and now) to which and from which the world *appears*, always coloured or structured by something akin to value. In a deep sense, the world is never neutral, never a matter of indifference, to a cognitive or *selfish* system of this sort.

If interests, perspective and the emergence of a world permeated with value can be ascribed to single-celled entities, this raises the question of 'consciousness' and the accompanying conceptual minefield, which will be intermittently touched upon in the present work and examined in greater depth in a forthcoming study. Suffice it to say, for the present, that there is no *a priori* justification for denying some rudimentary form of consciousness to unicellulars. Yet while some thinkers are prepared to countenance the notion of microbial or unicellular consciousness, most are reluctant to confer upon an amoeba or dinoflagellate the very attribute that sets humans apart from the plodding masses of less exalted creatures.[120] To be sure, if consciousness is restricted to 'reflective' consciousness, i.e. an internal, conceptually articulated self-dialogue, then it must be limited to animals endowed with language. If taken in a broader sense connoting a range of phenomena such as wakefulness, alertness and attention, there is good reason not to be so exclusive in our ascriptions.

The 17th century philosopher John Locke provides a particularly insightful definition of selfhood that shows up the link between consciousness and intrinsic reflexivity: self, he writes, is 'that conscious thinking thing (whatever substance made up of, whether spiritual or material, simple or compounded, it matters not) which is sensible or conscious of pleasure and pain, capable of happiness or misery, and so *is concerned for itself*, as far as that consciousness extends'.[121] Locke is referring to human consciousness, of course, but the important point in this context is the relationship between the intrinsic reflexivity of self-concern and the possibility of consciousness, however brief its 'extension'. The fundamental association of consciousness with value (as 'better' or 'worse', more or less pleasurable or painful) reflects the fact that conscious selfhood is at root an expression of one's care for oneself, the care that prompts one to seek what is good and shun what is bad (for oneself). As Robert Nozick has argued, moreover, such self-care[122] is both reflexive and fundamental: I care about myself not because I like myself (I may *not* like myself), but because this is who I am:

> Note ... that the special caring of the self for itself is a self-reflexive caring. It is not that the self cares especially for itself as a bearer of some non-self-reflexive property, as an especially sterling example of some general property P that it happens to have. The self cares especially for itself as itself; I care especially for myself as me. In contrast, self-hatred ... always is based on the self's possession of some denigrated property that is non-self-reflexive ...; in self-hatred, the self does not hate itself as itself, but as a possessor of some undesirable (non-reflexive) trait.[123]

Nozick too is referring to human self-care as a foundation for specifically human self-synthesis, but again there is no reason to restrict such reflexive self-concern or self-care to the single species that happens to be ours.

To the extent that consciousness is grounded in self-care, it too is structured by intrinsic reflexivity. Such reflexivity has been recognized by the phenomenological approach to consciousness. One of the shared insights among phenomenologists has been that all awareness of the world presupposes and entails a form of *self*-awareness. This view contrasts with the commonly encountered idea that consciousness of the world (sometimes referred to as 'primary' consciousness) comes first, followed subsequently by consciousness of a self or self-awareness as a 'higher'-level development, an addition or contingency as opposed to an intrinsic feature of consciousness. According to the phenomenological view, subjectivity itself is inherently characterized by a tacit or pre-reflective self-awareness, and disclosure of the world from a first-person perspective necessarily goes hand in hand with co-disclosure of the self.[124] This self-awareness is not to be confused with reflective self-consciousness, i.e. with my narrative sense of autobiographical selfhood, with my linguistic ability to refer to myself correctly using the first-person pronoun, or with my ability to adopt the perspective of others towards myself. These are complex modulations of conscious selfhood, specific to the human case or limited at most to certain mammals and birds. The pre-reflective self-awareness that accompanies all consciousness is not consciousness of self as an object (i.e. as one object among a whole world of other objects).[125] Rather, it arises because the first-person point of view is an essentially *tendentious* perspective, involving a dynamic relationship between self and non-self and informed by my self-interested, self-concerned, self-maintaining bodily presence; my perspective is always tacitly shaped by my hunger or satiety, my alertness or tiredness, my pain or comfort, and so on. The world as perceived in consciousness is structured by intrinsically reflexive self-care.

But does this tacit self-awareness really imply the existence of a *self* that is aware of itself? Are we justified in this case in making the leap from the reflexive to the substantive? Philosophers are quick to bristle at any hint of conceptual laxity. Galen Strawson, for example, has recognized that self-awareness is a structural feature of all awareness, but is understandably loath to 'misuse' the reflexive pronoun. Commenting on the reflexivity inherent in awareness, Strawson proposes the formulation that 'all awareness comports self-awareness – so long as one is clear that the occurrence of "self" in "self-awareness" is merely reflexive ... and does not imply any awareness of something called a self'.[126] Strawson is right to urge caution; such self-awareness should not be taken to mean consciousness of one's own identity as a persisting narrative subject, the protagonist of an ongoing autobiographical story. In his caution, however, Strawson overlooks the minimal self – i.e. the tacit, pre-reflective self, the self as defined by its care for itself – which is prior to and a precondition for the possibility of any reflective consciousness of a self, however fleeting or persisting. It is this self-caring self that lays the foundations for the possibility of consciousness.

To the extent that selves are not always conscious, however, it is evident that there is no simple or one-to-one relationship between selfhood and consciousness. If the self were equated with consciousness alone, then it would flit out of existence every time I fell asleep, or even – depending on how consciousness is defined – every time I drifted into automatic mode or interrupted my internalized self-dialogue (which is most of the time). Such a view leaves out of account the underlying spatiotemporal continuity of any self-maintaining self, without the foundation of which these successive selves can only be *different* selves. This oversight led Strawson to his well-known vision of a succession of discrete selves strung out over time 'like pearls on a string'.[127] This counter-intuitive proliferation of selves – resulting in me being a distinct self each time I return to consciousness – is a consequence of a failure to ground consciousness in the intrinsic reflexivity of self-care and self-production. In fact, it is an ongoing bodily process of self-adaptation to our medium that generates the very possibility of our consciousness of world and self alike. We naturally tend to privilege consciousness as essential to ourselves because it is only by means of consciousness that we have reflective *access* to our self and our selfhood: I am only ever *conscious* of myself as *conscious*. Nonetheless, my bodily self-perpetuation is essential to myself in a way that consciousness is not.

In the terms laid out here, a self is something that is *selfish*, tautologically so. This notion of 'selfishness' will come under closer scrutiny in Chapter 3. Yet even at this point it is important to emphasize that the intrinsically reflexive self-concern of selves does not preclude morality and altruism. As Nozick puts it, the self's care for itself 'need not be greater than its care for all other things. The theory of the self does not entail egoism. The self's care about itself is special, not in its unique magnitude but in its distinctive reflexiveness; each of us can say "I care about myself simply for being me". We care specially about our current and future selves because they are us; we care about identity because we care about ourselves'.[128] Not only is intrinsically reflexive self-care *not* opposed to altruism and morality, it provides the very foundation for it. When I behave morally and care for others, part of the point is that what I do *matters to me*; I care about what I do. I cannot act morally if I am unconcerned about myself or my acts.

Self, Sameness and Unity

In its constant striving to pursue its interests and perpetuate itself, the self-adapting, self-concerned self exists in an intrinsic relationship to relevant or meaningful non-self. To this extent, the self is perpetually reaching beyond itself, transcending itself, seeking and targeting what is good for itself. The concept of 'self-transcendence' denotes a rather special sense of intrinsic reflexivity, seemingly contradicting the tautological and static law of identity 'I = I'; the 'I > I' of self-transcendence can only make sense as part of a temporal process. In fact, it is merely the converse of the 'I < I' of self-containment. In the ongoing process of containing itself, a self must necessarily transcend itself. This Janus-faced ambiguity is embodied in the selective porosity or permeability of our self-containment, which allows the highly tailored exchange of energy and matter with our environment and incorporates the whole range of sensory apparatus through which we 'open onto' the world. This dialectic of self-containment and self-transcendence may be viewed as the counterpart to that of self-maintenance and self-adaptation.

Just as self-transcendence only makes sense within a context of permeable self-containment (in that the transcending of limits presupposes the limits that are transcended), some sort of unity is likewise entailed within a process of self-adaptation. Even in the case of the more radical category of self-transformation, the idea is that self transforms self into self: *I* transform *myself* into *myself*. While the verb implies progression, change or difference, the numerical identity – or at least continuity – is logically certified by the repetition of the first-person pronoun. Understood thus, selfhood does not imply an unchanging 'core' or 'essence' so much as the continuation of a process. It implies unity, perhaps, but it is fuzzy unity.

The vitiation of sameness or identity is most acute in the case of self-reproduction. Strict numerical identity is fractured both by binary fission, where a single cell splits to form two, and by fusion, where two unite to become one. Instead of self becoming self, such processes involve self becoming selves, or selves becoming self, with the principle of identity undermined by the grammatical move from singular to plural, or from plural to singular. On the one hand (and from a personal point of view), these episodes are of great significance, in that such breaches in numerical identity furnish the temporal boundaries to biological individuality. On the other hand (on a transpersonal level), the identity of the reproducing with the reproduced self/selves can be left as indeterminate, insofar as it is the continuity – e.g. that of the lineage – that is taken to matter.

As shown by this dialectic of self-maintenance and self-transformation, some degree of sameness – whether expressed as continuity or identity – forms an essential part of a self. Locke famously conflated the identity of a self with the consciousness of this identity, seeing memory as the basic criterion of personal identity (being the 'same self'). The implication was that a self is an entity that remembers itself, and indeed *is constituted by* its memories of itself in that its selfhood extends as far back in time as these memories extend. As Derek Parfit has pointed out,[129] one of various problems with Locke's view of memory as the criterion of selfhood is that it does not allow that same self to forget anything he or she has done: if I cannot now remember performing my ablutions this morning, I am no longer the same self.[130] In fact, suggests Parfit, the relationship between memory and selfhood need not be as absolute as Locke claims. I may not now have any of the same memories as my five-year-old self; there may be no 'core' of essential recollections that guarantee the 'identity' of my present self with my past self. Yet while Locke limits identity to direct psychological connectedness through memories, Parfit argues that it might be enough for there to be a *continuity* of memory consisting in an overlapping chain of direct memories. Accordingly, even though I do not remember any of my experiences on this date 40 years ago, every day over the last 40 years I have remembered *some* of my experiences from the day before.[131] There may also be other types of connection such as plans or intentions formed in the past and executed in the future, or there may be constancy in my hopes, beliefs and skills.

Whether 'memory' really is a necessary feature of selfhood or an attribute only of certain 'higher' selves will of course depend on how it is defined. While a narrative autobiography (my memory of my life story) is seemingly restricted to selves armed with concepts and language,[132] it is also undeniable that *any* self-adapting self resides in an essentially temporal dimension, striving to survive into the future on the basis of self-adjustments made in the past. In other words, memory is a matter not just of episodic recollection but of 'knowing how' (as in remembering how to capture prey or ride a bike), i.e. *assimilating* and *appropriating* adaptations that allow us to repeat in the future patterns of behaviour that have worked well on previous occasions.

Such memory may be either ontogenetic (acquired within the individual lifetime) or phylogenetic (inherited from one's ancestors). Accordingly, although most of the cells making up my body have come and gone over the years, there is a collective memory – or continuity over time – at the cellular level that is inherent in the genetic memory of my DNA and the structural memory embodied in lasting features of each cell's cytoskeleton and plasma membrane. Essential biological processes and activities relating to metabolism and replication are 'remembered' from generation to generation, even while genetic recombination provides us with individual specificity. The genome in turn remains largely the same throughout the individual lifetime, providing each organism with an immunological identity that effectively 'defines' the individual self, warding off microbial non-self, causing the rejection of incompatible transplants and even (perhaps) influencing one's choice of sexual partner.[133] At the same time, this very genome – the embodiment of inherited memory – controls a series of metamorphoses that catapult humans from infancy via puberty to adulthood, lepidopterans from caterpillars to chrysalises and then butterflies, and cellular slime moulds such as *Dictyostelium discoideum* from single-celled amoebae to multicellular 'slugs' and then fruiting bodies containing encapsulated spores.[134] Such pre-programmed self-transformation does not undermine the unity of the self. On the contrary, self-transformation belongs to the essence of selfhood. Self-change *within* the life-cycle of the individual self is a trans-generationally stable feature of the lineage.

Sameness and constancy – memory in the broadest possible sense – thus come to light on the most disparate of levels of selfhood. Core biological processes curb phenotypic variation and put a brake on evolution; many of the fundamental life-processes are constrained to such an extent that most changes would be deleterious or non-adaptive.[135] DNA sequence conservation is so substantial that over half of the coding sequences of yeast are recognizable in mice and humans. And although we may be ignorant of the enduring trans-individual identity we share, say, with fungi (i.e. the shared genetic memory inherited from a most recent common ancestor that lived possibly over a thousand million years ago), on an individual level we *cling to* identity, taking comfort in our possession of a potpourri of persisting character traits and a 'personality' that accompanies us through our life, fostering the reassuring sense of an immutable essence (the *real* me).

Of course, it is in fact a conjunction of stability and flexibility, self-preservation and self-adaptation, which prevails on all levels. The specificity of the animal brain is complemented by its plasticity,[136] and the capacity for self-change endows an otherwise static personal identity with behavioural versatility. Likewise, self-transformation is an essential feature of the collective selfhood of evolutionary lineages, as the genetic inheritance of organisms evolves from generation to generation. It has been suggested that 'evolvability' is a quality that may itself be selected for. Under conditions of stress, bacterial genomes harbour a capacity for adaptive *mutagenesis* or hypermutation that provides them collectively with increased flexibility and improved chances of survival.[137] The logic of bacterial hypermutation is clearly multicellular, for the wellbeing of the individual cells– which perish unless they chance upon the mutation suitable for the particular circumstances – is sacrificed to the increased overall possibility of finding a beneficial adaptation as a collective. There is evidence of 'evolvability' in eukaryotic multicellular organisms too, which have been shown to undergo a greater rate of mutation and higher levels of genetic recombination during sexual reproduction in stressful or extreme conditions, thus tending to produce more variable offspring than those not exposed to such conditions.[138] Here too there is a collective logic at work, for while the heightened variability may result in the evolution of a better-adapted species, the majority of the mutations will prove detrimental to the offspring that are lumbered with them; these will be selected against and weeded out. The implication again is that the 'selfhood' in question – the unit of selection – may be less at an individual level than at a higher level, that of the clade or species.

The phenomenon of evolvability – self-transformation as a lineage-level 'strategy' – is also manifest in such developments as a segmented body plan, a modularization of the body such that parts and systems are repeated serially along its length. As described by Dawkins,[139] such segmentation seems to have arisen independently in *arthropods*, vertebrates and annelids. The transition from non-segmentation to segmentation cannot have been easy for the first segmented animal, descended from non-segmented progenitors and surrounded by non-segmented mates. Yet the success of the individual organism is not the point: 'what is important about the first segmented animal', writes Dawkins, 'is that its descendants were champion *evolvers*. They radiated, speciated, gave rise to whole new phyla. Whether or not segmentation was a beneficial adaptation during the individual lifetime of the first segmented animal, segmentation represented a change in embryology that was pregnant with evolutionary potential.'[140]

The key feature of segments is not just that they can be added or subtracted, as in millipedes and annelid worms, but that they lend themselves to differentiation and thus to specialization, producing a whole range of newly designed animals, as has happened in the case of vertebrates. Dawkins makes the point that such modularity is a form of organization comprising 'self-contained' and relatively autonomous subunits. As other examples of modularity, he cites sexual reproduction, with its concomitant recombination of essentially modular DNA, as well as multicellularity. Once evolution has produced mechanisms such as cell adhesion, cell communication and cell differentiation, the permutations for joining cells together and generating new designs are unlimited. The relative independence of the 'modules' allows for experimentation and the possibility of failure, but also opens up new dimensions of inventiveness. At the same time, however, modularity and species-level evolvability may also be associated with less than fully integrated selfhood, in that the occurrence of 'self-contained' subunits suggests the presence of subselves within selves. In its various guises,[141] modularity thus raises the question of the extent to which selfhood should be equated with organic unity, i.e. with synchronic as opposed to diachronic unity. How far can a self tolerate, and to what extent is it undermined by, the presence within itself of a potentially autonomous subself? Must a self be an organism?

Kant's above-mentioned definition of an organism highlights the common ground shared by the concept of an organism and that of a self. For Kant, an organism is a self-organizing entity in which each part reciprocally depends upon and helps produce all the others; in other words, every part exists both because of and for the sake of every other part and the whole. In an organism, the components of which it consists are not causally independent or chronologically prior to the whole, but are themselves produced by the whole and determined by their function in it; the whole in turn exists by means of the component parts. Recently, moreover, John Pepper and Matthew Herron[142] have pinpointed three frequently cited definitional criteria of organisms: continuity and persistence; autonomy and homeostasis; and functional integration, or what has been termed a 'teleological' nature. In particular, it is the notion of an organism as a 'discrete package of functional integration' – as implied by its definition as a 'complex structure of interdependent and subordinate elements whose relations and properties are largely determined by their function in the whole'[143] – that is most relevant in this context. While the concept of 'functionality' in itself implies direction towards an end or goal, the functional integration of an organism-self entails that this end is not merely an *extrinsic* goal shared by all the component parts of the organism in question (as in the case of a machine, where the goal is to perform the task for which it has been designed); rather, it is an *intrinsic* goal, namely the sustenance or perpetuation of this very system of integrated functionality. The functional integration of the parts of a self ensures that the integrated whole – i.e. the continued integration of the whole – is an end in itself. To repeat a circular formulation used above, a self is an end in itself; its end *is* its self.

Despite all the complexity, in other words, there is a unity of interest, manifest as a *unitary selfishness* (in the sense of the self-care encountered above). It is this unitary selfishness that defines the organism as a self. Again in circular terms, a self is the unit of self-interest.[144] This cohesive self-care, it has been suggested, further generates a self-reinforcing circular dynamic in evolutionary terms: 'natural selection is focused on organisms, rather than on their parts or on their groups, because it is organisms that are functionally integrated. At the same time, natural selection has the effect of creating functional integration of the entities ... it selects among'.[145] Positive feedback of this sort may well tend to make intermediate levels of integration unstable as evolutionary endpoints, fostering maximum levels of functional integration and independence as exemplified in 'paradigm' organisms such as vertebrates.

Seen in these terms, there is no contradiction between controlled or contained modularity and organic selfhood. While on the lineage level there may be selection for mechanisms of modularity to foster variability, adaptability and evolvability, the selection of individual selves will focus on organic wholes, each of whose component modules in practice succeeds in realizing the interests of the organism, i.e. forming part of a unitary 'self' that successfully pursues its own good. It is obvious that natural selection will not favour a lobster with the most sophisticated of claws if these have a mind of their own and a tendency to sever the lobster's own head. By contrast, modular hind parts with enough autonomy to keep on copulating even after one's head has been bitten off by a hungry or overenthusiastic mate may indeed serve a valuable purpose for the lineage, if not the individual.

Related questions, such as whether I form a single self with the microbiota that inhabit my intestines, will be explored in Chapter 6, which will analyse the implications of symbiosis for selfhood and more generally the often fuzzy boundaries that separate self from non-self. My dependence upon my resident bacteria – or rather our mutual interdependence – means that our interests, and thus our selfhood, may be judged to coincide. Nor is this an unusual state of affairs; almost all plants and animals[146] host microbial symbionts that affect their fitness and together with which they collectively form a 'unit' of self-interest. On a different level, the complexity of the specifically human self has resulted in the generation of subselves that may prove insubordinate. Severance of the corpus callosum in treatments for epilepsy is well known for producing situations in which the patient's right hand may obstruct or struggle with the left hand or even attempt to strangle the patient.[147] The hypnotic therapist Morton Prince in 1924 wrote of the 'composite nature of man, and ... the many selves of which the mind is composed', suggesting that all of us have 'as many selves as we have moods, or contrasting traits, or sides to our personalities'.[148] In evolutionary terms, the drawbacks resulting from fragmented selfhood that does not always behave in its own interests can be presumed to be offset by advantages associated with flexibility. Human self-division of this sort will not be a focus in the following study.[149] Such conflicts of interest are frequently opened up by the dimension of time and the failure, for example, of my pleasure-seeking present self to identify with the future self that will have to suffer the consequences.

Self and Flow

Self-Assembly

The self consists of the unity of a self-perpetuating process. Indispensable to this process is a throughflow of energy permitting the self-maintenance of a far-from-equilibrium system. This embodies what we have termed intrinsic reflexivity.

However, there is one form of what sounds (grammatically at least) like intrinsic reflexivity that plays a vital role in life on Earth and yet is to be distinguished from the forms of intrinsic reflexivity encountered so far. This is a phenomenon known as self-assembly. By analogy with concepts such as self-organization and self-production, self-assembly sounds like intrinsic reflexivity to the extent that 'self' has a double function as subject and object, cause and effect, assembler and assembled. Yet whereas in the case of self-organization (for example) self organizes self organizes self organizes self (and so on …), in the case of self-assembly self assembles self (full stop). The difference is that while self-organization implies a continuing process driven by an ongoing lack of equilibrium, self-assembly tends to be a spontaneously occurring process[150] that results in stable or at least metastable structures (a state of equilibrium) with no further dynamic tendency. As a consequence, there is no ongoing set of physical or chemical transformations. In thermodynamic terms, self-assembly is the end of the story (at least for the time being). There is no need for further self-maintenance, no need for work to be done in order to sustain the structure in the face of the threat of disorder. To the extent that we are left with a product rather than an ongoing process, a self-assembled entity is no longer constituted by intrinsic reflexivity, i.e. by reflexive activity that is intrinsic to the entity in question in the sense that the entity ceases to exist if the activity ceases to occur.

By contrast with self-assembly, therefore, selfhood involves the persistence of an (intrinsically reflexive) process, not merely the persistence of the product of such a process. It is the self-producing system that persists, not the self-produced product. Accordingly, selfhood is dynamic and processual and can never be 'complete'; completion implies stasis and thus the end of selfhood. Whereas self-organization – whether in the form of flames or whirlpools, convection cells or chemical clocks – is founded on energy-driven flow, self-assembly involves the spontaneous generation of static structure as typified by the formation of crystals, with molecules associating together in accordance with the dictates of geometry and chemistry. Of course, here too flow is necessary. The components that assemble must be mobile so as to be able to move in relation to one another, and accordingly self-assembly usually takes place in fluid phases or on smooth surfaces. Boundaries and templates are also significant, reducing defects and controlling the structures that form.[151]

Self-assembly may indeed seem self-like. Crystals are sometimes said to 'reproduce' themselves, seeding the growth of further crystals. It may be misleading, therefore, to suggest that self-assembly is simply the end of the story. In the appropriate circumstances, crystals may spread like the self-propagating 'wildfire' we shall encounter in Chapter 2. Like the replication of genetic material, moreover, such crystal self-replication may even be flawed, for crystals naturally contain defects. What distinguishes crystals from genes is that the information contained in these imperfections is not heritable; the mis-replications are not fed back into the system; and, like wildfire, crystals thus fail to provide a foundation for Darwinian evolution.[152]

While crystals are sometimes taken to be the very antithesis of life, their self-assembly may accordingly make them *akin* to living entities.[153] In fact, self-assembly plays a vital role in the formation of many of the large molecules and molecular aggregates that are essential to life.[154] The folding of proteins, which underlies their function as catalysts, is an archetypal product of self-assembly.[155] The protein's three-dimensional conformation and its resulting biological activity are implicit in the sequence of amino acids that compose it. If a protein – say, the enzyme ribonuclease – is 'denatured' (or unfolded), it will tend spontaneously to refold itself into its native configuration and in the process recover its catalytic capacities.[156] This process of protein refolding may require a catalyst (a chaperone), but no further energy source is needed.[157]

Self-assembly has also come to the public attention in a variation on the theme of protein folding. A signal exception to the notion that the native conformation of a protein is determined entirely by its amino acid sequence is provided by prions, which are stable *mis*-foldings. Given an appropriate supply of proteins, self-propagating prions can also spread 'like wildfire' (and crystals).

Unlike either wildfire or crystals, moreover, inheritable structural variations, or adaptive 'mutations',[158] may be introduced into initially identical populations of normal proteins, bringing prions even closer to the realm of the living. Yet they remain a product of static self-assembly rather than an ongoing process characterized by the performance of work or self-sustaining metabolism.

One of the most spectacular products of self-assembly is the *ribosome*, responsible for carrying out protein synthesis in all known life-forms from bacteria and archaea to single-celled and multicellular *eukaryotes*. This supramolecular complex consists of two subunits, between them comprising over 50 proteins assembled on a scaffolding of three or sometimes four species of RNA. Again, if these constituent macromolecules are experimentally disassociated, they can be induced in test-tube conditions to reassemble spontaneously into functional ribosomes. This occurs with little or no input of energy or information from external sources, the requisite information being provided (in large measure) by the molecular constituents themselves.[159] Self-assembly involving the protein flagellin is central to the generation of bacterial flagella, the whip-like appendages used for propulsion, just as eukaryotic cells are characterized by the self-assembly of tubulins and *actin* into the microtubules and microfilaments of the cytoskeleton, which functions not only as a mechanism of structural support but as something akin to the cell's circulatory and nervous system.

Self-assembly is even involved in something as basic as self-containment, for the lipid bilayers of which the plasma membrane is composed form spontaneously from a suspension of lipids in water, and the most stable configuration for such an assembly is a closed *vesicle*.[160] Yet although the growth of the lipid membrane can be considered a type of molecular self-assembly, things are again not quite so simple. Most importantly perhaps, cellular membranes – like chromosomes but unlike ribosomes and microtubules – do not form *de novo*, but always by growth and division or fusion of pre-existing membranes. Moreover, just as DNA replication is based on information from a pre-existing template, membrane growth too requires information from pre-existing membranes for its unique composition of proteins and lipids, and insertion of the membrane proteins is energy-dependent and thus unable to take place without work being performed by the cellular context.[161] Similar considerations apply to the lipopolysaccharide membrane, the outer envelope of Gram-negative bacteria, the basic structure of which can be produced by self-assembly in a test-tube but which in practice depends upon an energy gradient and scaffolding provided by the peptidoglycan wall.[162]

The role of self-assembly in so many aspects of biological organization – including lipid membranes, folded proteins and complex molecular machines such as ribosomes – led Joshua Lederberg in the 1960s to formulate the dictum:

'make the macromolecules at the right time and in the right amount, and the organization will take care of itself'. As cell biologist Franklin M. Harold argues, however, this idea is 'popular, seductive, potent and true up to a point – yet fundamentally wrong'.[163] It overlooks the extent to which such cellular self-assembly depends upon the environment provided by the cell – typified by the highly specific conditions required for ribosome and plasma membrane synthesis – and the extent to which it is directed in space and time by the precise specifications of the self-organizing and self-maintaining self. 'Cells make themselves,' writes Harold, 'but not by self-assembly of pre-formed molecules; they grow, thanks to a generative biochemistry that produces a restricted subset of molecules within a confined and structured space. If complex systems are to arise from raw chemistry, hold out against the forces of decay and multiply themselves in space and time, energy must supply the driving force'.[164]

Self and Stasis

At the heart of living selfhood is an ongoing, controlled flow of energy and matter. This is what fuels the self-maintaining, self-reproducing, self-containing activity of any self. In practice this controlled flow is inseparable from the presence of liquid water, though in theory a variety of other non-aqueous solvents might provide a feasible framework for living selfhood to occur.[165] It is water that provides the medium in which the chemical reactions of metabolism can take place in a contained manner, allowing sugar to be oxidized and the energy inherent in its chemical structure harvested in a measured way that contrasts with what happens when sugar is merely exposed to air (no reaction) or is thrown onto a fire (uncontrolled combustion). Yet not all water is linked with flux; some of it plays a structural role. A proportion of the water in every cell (18 percent) is known as 'bound water', limited in its movements by its association with proteins and other macromolecules structuring the cell.

Despite the multiple significance of water in cellular structure and flow, it seems to be a general feature of prokaryotes and some eukaryotic systems that, if dried under the proper conditions, they can withstand more or less complete dehydration. Freeze drying is a standard procedure in the preservation of prokaryotes; upon being re-hydrated, normal functionality is resumed. Clearly, in such conditions all processes cease and the system in question is reduced to pure structure, yet the requisite biological information must be retained if the condition is to be reversible. This raises some important questions about the relationship between water and living selfhood, pertaining in particular to the status of a reversibly desiccated or reversibly ice-bound self where flow is arrested. The following section will briefly look at some of the borderline cases where fluid water is absent and the dynamic self-maintenance of living selves comes to a standstill.

As U.S. biophysicist Harold J. Morowitz points out, 'there is nothing in the operating condition of living cells to suggest a priori that they will survive drying or cooling to very low temperatures. The structural nature of biological information is clearly a property of living cells, but is it a necessary property? Could we envision a cellular life for which the structural generalization was not operative? Perhaps the climatic fluctuations of the Archaean era were so severe that only those evolving systems that could stand drying and freezing were fit enough to survive'.[166] This structural aspect of life is embodied above all in the 'quasi-inert molecular structures' of DNA, an informational storage system that is largely off-line, i.e. uncoupled from the messy business of metabolism.[167] Whether or not such structuration is a necessary condition for life in general, it clearly provides an adaptive robustness that will have helped overcome the challenges posed by extreme and inhospitable environments. Yet structural information *in itself* is not sufficient for living selfhood. The complete absence of function – the *lifelessness*, albeit reversible – of desiccated bacteria reminds us that information must be combined with catalytic reflexivity.

The capacity of certain organisms to undergo more or less complete desiccation (also known as anhydrobiosis or xerotolerance) thus leaves one wondering what 'happens' to selfhood in the absence of water and flow. A brief answer is that a severe reduction in the body's chemical activity amounts to a *deceleration* of metabolism, subduing the processes required for self-maintenance, self-production and self-adaptation. Such fluctuations in metabolism may occur to varying degrees and for a variety of reasons of which desiccation is only one. They may take the form of regular biological oscillations or one-off responses to extreme conditions. Specialists have drawn a distinction between dormancy (also known as hypo-metabolism) and what has been called 'latent life' or cryptobiosis (ametabolism), where the latter refers to 'the state of an organism when it shows no visible signs of life and when its metabolic activity becomes hardly measurable, or comes reversibly to a standstill'.[168] Whereas cryptobiosis is generally understood to consist in the depression of an animal's metabolic rate to less than one percent of resting levels, in dormancy the metabolic rate is less rigorously specified, typically lowered to somewhere in the range between five and 40 percent of resting levels.

The process of self-maintenance can vary in the rate at which it takes place, yet there are limits to such variability. While anhydrobiosis is known to occur in prokaryotes and microscopic invertebrates such as adult rotifers, nematode worms and tardigrades (as well as in the embryonic cysts of some crustaceans, plant seeds and even some 'higher' plants known as 'resurrection plants'), there seems to be an upper bound to the size of animals capable of complete desiccation. Few animals bigger than midge larvae[169] or the encysted embryo of the brine shrimp *Artemia* can survive it. Some earthworms can withstand the loss of 83 percent of the water from their bodies. Whereas certain frogs can lose 50 percent and camels 30 percent, humans may die if they lose 14 percent of their bodily water.[170]

Anhydrobiosis involves a more or less complete suppression of metabolism, a cessation of flow and process; it might be called 'suspended' selfhood, or selfhood 'on hold'. There can be no activity, growth or reproduction. A persistent methodological question is whether ametabolism can ever be *known* to be complete. Experiments have shown cases where if metabolism is occurring at all, it must be at least 10,000 times slower than the resting rate, yet it remains impossible to prove the absence of a rate.[171] Minimal metabolism – in the form of radically curtailed self-maintenance – may still be going on. In animal dormancy the reduction in metabolism is less drastic than this. When humans (like many other mammals and birds) sleep at night, we become inactive and there is a drop in body temperature, yet even this minor reduction in oxygen consumption (10 percent) and body temperature (1–2 °C) yields energy savings of 7–15 percent for an endothermic animal.[172] The sleep of animals, which can be interrupted by the slightest of disturbances, thus lies at one extreme of a scale of dormancy that leads at the other extreme to complete ametabolism. Further along we find the torpor or deep sleep of brown and grizzly bears, which spend their winter months in dens but are easily aroused from their dormancy. Deep hibernation, by contrast, as practised by European hedgehogs and ground squirrels, involves a reduction in body temperature to just a few degrees above ambient temperatures, and body temperatures down to freezing have been recorded. In addition to this bodily cooling, the animals' heart rate and metabolic rate fall, and they do not drink, defecate or urinate. Again, this 'slowing of self' leads to major energetic savings, with the energy consumption of hibernating hedgehogs some 96 percent below that of active hedgehogs.[173]

While the sleep, torpor and hibernation of animals is a regular process repeated on a daily or annual basis, microbial cryptobiosis may well be open-ended. Microbiologists thus profess to have 'reawakened' ancient bacteria preserved in a sample of amber from a sleep that dates back some 25 to 40 million years,[174] while other claims go back as far as the Mesozoic, when dinosaurs flourished. With the suspension of all flux, time – and the accompanying ageing process – is effectively suspended too; biologically speaking, nothing happens. The zoologist David Wharton has thus proposed a distinction between the chronological and physiological age of an organism; while nematode worms normally complete their life cycle in a matter of weeks, they have been known to survive for decades in a state of extreme desiccation. Yet even though microbes, nematodes and tardigrades may be sleeping beauties waiting for an environmental 'kiss', the proportion of organisms that recover from such long-term dry storage slowly declines, possibly due to the destructive effects of oxygen and the lack of metabolism to carry out the necessary repair work. 'Slow self' thus merges seamlessly into death.

Microbes and multicellulars have several types of strategy for dealing with long-term dormancy or cryptobiosis, i.e. for resisting the tendency of ordered structures to fall into disorder in the absence or near-absence of self-maintaining work driven by an input of energy. These extreme responses throw considerable light on the nature of self-maintaining and self-containing selfhood. One way of coping involves the longer-term maintenance of cellular structure by sustaining a *minimal* metabolism for reparation work. It has been suggested in the case of the embryonic brine shrimp (during protracted oxygen deprivation) that a minimal free energy flow and metabolism may be kept up in order to support the energetic requirements of molecular chaperones whose function is to repair proteins that have become denatured or unfolded.[175] Studies have shown that for certain types of bacteria over timescales of roughly half a million years, low-level metabolic activity with DNA repair is a more effective survival strategy than complete ametabolism.[176]

In the context of desiccation, a common way of preserving cellular structure from within involves the use of certain sugars to replace the water, most notably trehalose. This has been found to occur in unicellular organisms, nematodes, tardigrades and rotifers. Not only does trehalose immobilize the cell's internal organization and protect the cell's macromolecules and membranes (through 'vitrification', or the formation of amorphous glasses); it also replaces the 'bound water' involved in structural functions. In this sense, trehalose serves as a substitute for water, but arresting the element of flow: as Clegg succinctly expresses it, 'the same mechanisms that preserve cell structure also prevent their function'.[177]

A different sort of general strategy available for long-term cryptobiosis involves modification of the cell's mode of self-containment, i.e. its protective boundary or more generally its interaction with the environmental non-self. This is most clearly manifest in endospores, the tough capsules produced by certain sorts of Gram-positive bacteria (e.g. Firmicutes such as *Bacillus*), which are endowed with as many as four different protective layers (the core wall, spore cortex, spore coat and exosporium) and are resistant not only to desiccation and extreme cold, but also ultra violet radiation, toxins and a variety of anti-bacterial agents. Other classes of *cryptobiotic* bacteria form what are known as 'exospores' or microbial cysts, which are not generally quite as tough as endospores.[178] Whereas micro-organisms resort to cryptobiotic mechanisms such as endospore formation or encystment, the resistance adaptations of animals are likely to involve behavioural elements (coiling up in the case of nematodes or withdrawing their legs into their bodies to form a barrel-like 'tun' in the case of tardigrades) or the construction of burrows and dens, which serve as enclosed 'containers' not unlike endospores in that the aim is to dispense with a throughflow of energy (as far as possible), and instead seal off and protect the animal.[179] Even sleeping humans may manipulate the environment to save on metabolic expenses: wrapped up (tun-like!) in blanketed beds within human-built houses, we likewise form a multilayered cocoon, a protective extension of the homeostatic unit that is our body.

Yet this is not all. Dormancy and cryptobiosis are accompanied by a modified form of *sensory* self-containment, which amounts to being 'dead to the world'. Just as an endospore can do without an entrance and egress for nutrition or waste (for ametabolism means no energetic throughflow), there is no need for the sensory organs that usually 'open out' onto the world *in search of* nutrition. The same principle of sensory closure is graphically illustrated by insect metamorphosis, where the pupal stage between larval and adult forms may involve not only the spinning of a cocoon, but also the death of most sensory neurons and the degeneration of motor neurons (as their target muscles disappear). Despite this outward closure, many of the interneurons of the central brain may persist, and some moths have been shown to remember what they learn as caterpillars.[180] This sensory shutting-down and unplugged motor system are reflected even in mammalian sleep. Yet such closure cannot be absolute. In the case of sleep it is regulated by the body's circadian rhythms, which are broadly aligned to the availability of light. We wake up if an external disturbance is acute or persistent enough. For cryptobiotic micro-organisms, the question of resuscitation is vital: dormancy can only be a viable adaptive strategy if the cell can subsequently be reanimated when conditions improve.

So how does it remain 'alive' enough to know when to return to the fray?[181] It seems that even in a dormant state many spores and cysts have surface receptors that respond to the presence of low-molecular-mass compounds such as amino acids and sugars, the princely kiss that arouses the sleeping beauty. Another hypothesis, the 'scout hypothesis', involves what is known as quorum sensing; here the idea is that 'scouts' – randomly resuscitated individual cells – test whether the external conditions are good or bad for growth, emitting a self-reinforcing signal to wake their dormant kin if the going is good enough. In this way, the microbial colony as a whole can be considered to be collectively 'keeping one eye open'. The point in all these cases is that even when selfhood is 'suspended' (in sleep, dormancy or cryptobiosis) mechanisms of self-adaptation persist, at least potentially. Like its metabolism, the entity's 'openness' to the environment may be reduced but not jettisoned completely. Just as a sleeping animal, though 'dead to the world', can still be aroused if circumstances so dictate, a dormant cyst cannot afford to shut itself away entirely.

Apart from desiccation, the other major class of cryptobiosis is cryobiosis, or cold-tolerance (also known as psychrotolerance). As Morowitz writes, 'many biological systems have been held at temperatures near absolute zero for various periods of time. On re-warming, many of these systems continue their biological activity unimpaired. It appears to be a generalization of cryobiology that if a system survives the trauma of ice-crystal formation, either on freezing or on thawing, then its function is unchanged by taking it to temperatures near absolute zero'.[182] As with full desiccation, a reduction of the temperature to near zero Kelvin amounts to a reversible yet complete cessation of process and function; the system is reduced to pure structure. Yet there is an important difference in the case of cryobiosis, for whereas biological macromolecules are unstable at ordinary temperatures and thus more susceptible to thermal degradation, near absolute zero these processes of degradation grind to a halt and the information-storing structures are indefinitely stable. Not only is there no flow of energy or matter, but time itself comes to a standstill (no degradation), again allowing the self to enter a state of suspension. The paradigm creature in this context is the tiny panarthropod known as the tardigrade, or water bear, which can survive temperatures almost down to absolute zero, i.e. minus 273 °C, again in a desiccated state based on vitrification.[183]

These cold, dry, slow selves are borderline cases of selfhood and are thus invaluable for defining or delimiting the concept. While most living things are identified by a range of activities and processes including ingestion and excretion, movement, respiration, growth, reproduction and responsiveness to stimuli, cryptobiotic selves do (almost) none of these things, leading some biologists to propose that there are not two but three states of biological organization: alive, dead and cryptobiotic.[184] Analysis in terms of intrinsic reflexivity, however, reveals enough continuity to ensure that the 'self' prior to cryptobiotic suspension is the same one as the subsequent 'self' and thus warrant the ongoing ascription of selfhood. Although a cryptobiotic self such as an endospore shows no growth and is not capable of self-reproduction, a degree of active self-maintenance is in most cases likely to persist, albeit at minimal levels (for purposes of DNA and protein repair). Self-containment is reinforced, with differential porosity largely sacrificed for the sake of increased and generalized protection, thus maintaining the structural continuity of a single self. At the same time, minimal openness to the environment and powers of self-adaptation must be retained for eventual resuscitation. In the case of the ultra-hardy tardigrade persisting at temperatures near absolute zero, metabolism is neither possible nor necessary even for purposes of structural repair. To the extent that time itself is taken to slow down and even stand still (as at absolute zero), there can be no breach, but just a deceleration of selfhood.

II.

Flux, Fire and Auto-Mobiles

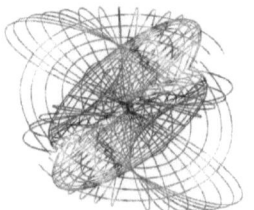

Fluid Flow

In the Introduction it was proposed that various forms of intrinsic reflexivity are jointly necessary but not individually sufficient conditions of 'full' or living selfhood. The phenomenon of self-organization was pinpointed as one such form of intrinsic reflexivity. Entities defined *solely* in terms of self-organization seem to lack some key ingredient to qualify as selves in the full sense. The present chapter will focus on non-living but life-like[185] phenomena such as flames and flowing water in an attempt to establish just why we may be reluctant to ascribe full selfhood to them.

There is no doubt that the idea of self-organization captures some of the most basic features of life and selfhood. Shapiro and Feinberg's thermodynamic definition of life as an organized system of matter and energy that uses a flow of free energy to maintain or increase its own organization has the advantage that it applies to life as a whole (the biosphere) yet without restricting life to the specific biochemistry it happens to have on our planet. It highlights the dependence of any living self on its non-self, i.e. on an external source of free energy that can be used to do the job of maintaining its structure. To be a self, in other words, involves an input of energy and the performance of work. It is the work of self-organization that allows the self to resist the tendency of all physical systems to fall back into disorder or thermodynamic equilibrium. Seen in this light, selfhood entails a necessary confrontation with the Second Law of Thermodynamics, which dictates that whenever energy is used to perform work some fraction of that energy will be dissipated in the form of heat or random molecular motion: the more energy that is frittered away as heat, the less that can be used for the work of self-organization.

This thermodynamic framework is certainly essential to living selfhood at the level of both the biosphere and the individual organism. Deprived of an external source of energy to perform the work of self-maintenance, self-organized systems will soon become disorganized and will cease to exist as such. Yet while self-organization may be a necessary condition for selfhood as we understand it, it is not sufficient as a condition.

Take autocatalytic systems such as the Belouzov-Zhabotinsky (BZ) reaction.[186] There is certainly something life-like about these chemical clocks, where the 'order' takes the form of a regular oscillation between two colours. Theoretical biologist Art Winfree described the BZ reaction as sharing 'many of the features that make living systems interesting: chemical metabolism (oxidation of organic acids to carbon dioxide), self-organizing structure, rhythmic activity, dynamic stability within limits, irreversible dissolution beyond those limits, and a natural lifespan'.[187] At the same time, however, such systems are without two of the three forms of intrinsic reflexivity identified in the Introduction, lacking a capacity to reproduce themselves (to multiply or replicate) and the ability to contain themselves within a boundary of their own making. Although self-organization falls within the broader category of self-maintenance (and thus meets, at least partially, one of the criteria of selfhood), more is required for full selfhood.

Even within the category of self-maintenance, indeed, a 'merely' self-organizing system fails to tick all the boxes. While such a system may be said to maintain itself over time (and Winfree refers to 'dynamic stability within limits'), there is relatively little capacity for self-adaptation; the system is more or less passive in relation to environmental contingencies. As soon as the scientist cuts off the input of chemical ingredients, the reaction stops and order disappears. As Ruiz-Mirazo and colleagues put it, it might be said that

> in pure self-organizing phenomena it is already possible to start speaking about 'self-maintenance' (in so far as the generation of the macroscopic pattern contributes to its own maintenance by means of its continuous constraining action on the microscopic dynamics). However, in that case, we would be using the term in its weakest sense. A more significant self-maintenance cannot take place until a system starts producing some of the constraints that are crucial to control the matter-energy flow through it and, in this way, it begins to develop the capacity to maintain its organization in the face of external perturbations (i.e., a primitive kind of 'organizational homeostasis').[188]

Not only is such a system limited in its ability to modify itself according to circumstances, but there is no element of self-containment or boundary (other than the receptacle in which the reaction takes place). The flow of energy is not harnessed for construction work, i.e. the work of self-construction; it is not controlled or channelled into the creation of structures that might serve to perpetuate the existence of the system (most basically, an outer membrane). In short, it is best viewed as a case of *energetic* self-maintenance rather than *structural* self-production. Furthermore, there is no self-replication, no heredity and no history. Such systems are not part of an evolutionary lineage, but the product of a rather haphazard meeting of molecules. By contrast, the biochemistry of living organisms is a highly specific product of evolutionary fine-tuning. In living systems the constituent molecules – and the processes they participate in – have been selected to give rise to a self-organizing system capable of both maintaining and transforming itself through generations.

The case of self-organizing hydrodynamic systems makes these points clearer. The word 'hydrodynamics' implies the involvement of water, the archetypal fluid associated with life on Earth. Indeed, the hydrosphere itself is not only a vital matrix, nutrient and transport system for terrestrial life-forms, but also a self-organizing self on a whole hierarchy of levels.[189] The thermohaline circulation of the oceans – the ordered flow of ocean currents driven by differential temperature and salinity levels – is just one example of the self-organizing flow of the Earth's waters. Such orderly flows make watery bodies inherently life-like (compare the circular flow of our haemoglobin-carrying bodily seawater),[190] and oceans and rivers lend themselves to personification. A biography has recently been written of the Atlantic – 'surely a living thing'[191] – a roaring, thundering behemoth endowed with moods and psychological attributes and a predictable life span. The oceans are themselves metabolic systems, ceaselessly recycling matter and energy through the trillions of microbes they contain; they are a pullulating matrix of genetic material that is constantly being shuttled around amongst host microbes by the 10^{30} viruses currently estimated to inhabit the world's waters.[192] The metabolic activity of rivers such as the Ganges endows them with seemingly miraculous powers of self-transformation and self-purification. Animism apart, however, the consensus is that flowing bodies of water are not 'in themselves' alive, or are only metaphorically so. While they may have beds and banks, the absence of *self*-containment makes these self-organizing waters difficult to pinpoint as individual entities with selfish interests. River waters flow wherever geographical or topographical contingency takes them.

Of course, self-organizing flows need not involve water. Hydrodynamics refers to any sort of fluid flow, and the equations that govern it (in simplified form) apply to any fluid: what matters is the ratio of forces driving the flow (such as the flow velocity or the temperature gradient) to those resisting it (such as viscosity). Indeed, one of the most striking areas of pattern-forming flow involves granular substances such as sand, as manifest in the creation of sand dunes. Though individually hard, crystalline and patently antagonistic to life, collections of sand grains develop a property known as liquefaction, resulting in the liquid-like ripples and waves characteristic of windswept beaches and the dunes characteristic of deserts. Positive feedback causes tiny random bumps or irregularities to self-amplify by capturing more and more grains of sand from the air; at the same time, these ripples or mounds shelter the leeward ground and thus prevent other ripples from forming within that area. In conjunction, these two processes keep the gradually self-amplifying ripples at a roughly constant wavelength. Yet such patterns are far from static. As one of the early specialists in dune formation, R. A. Bagnold, wrote in his 1941 book *The Physics of Blown Sand and Desert Dunes*, 'vast accumulations of sand weighing millions of tons move inexorably in regular formation, over the surface of the country, growing, retaining their shape, even breeding, in a manner which, by its grotesque imitation of life, is vaguely disturbing to an imaginative mind'.[193] More recent computer simulations of dune activities and movements have shown how dunes may 'cannibalize' one another and how 'baby dunes' may be spawned from the horns of bigger dunes.[194]

These sandy shapes may consume and grow and even propagate, but a great deal is still missing for them to be called living. Their reproduction does not involve heredity, for a start, since the persisting characteristics of any baby dunes will be determined wholly by the environment, i.e. the air-currents and sand and geography that shape them. More importantly, perhaps, there is no self-containment or functional integration of components: they are just fleeting aggregations of sand particles that may come and go with the wind.

By contrast with sand dunes, the element of 'containment' does seem to be present in one of the most commonly studied branches of fluid pattern formation, the convective self-organization produced by temperature gradients. When a shallow pan of oil is gently heated from below, a pattern of hexagonal shapes is formed, with the warmer, less dense fluid rising and the cooler, denser fluid sinking. These shapes are known as Bénard cells or more generally as convective cells, a usage that goes back to the German physician Heinrich Quincke, who had referred to the *tourbillons cellulaires* he observed.[195] The notion of a cell, which has its etymological roots in the enclosures of monastic life, thus suggests an element of confinement or constraint: while on the one hand it is the interactions of the molecules that create the convection cells, the cells that are formed in turn govern the motions of the molecules that constitute them, drastically curtailing the degrees of freedom they would otherwise have. In a relationship of circular causality, the component molecules generate a higher-order or global organization, and this global organization in turn constrains the behaviour of the individual components. In physically forming a 'cell', the components themselves constitute the 'boundary' that encloses and contains them.

Such convection cells can be seen not only in kitchen saucepans and laboratory receptacles, but in the dappled patterns of clouds that are produced when atmospheric temperature gradients cause warm air to rise and cool air to sink. They are also manifest in larger-scale phenomena such as the vast atmospheric convection cells that are caused by latitudinal temperature differences. The Hadley cell, for example, circulates between the equator and a latitude of roughly 30°, powering the air currents commonly known as the tropical trade winds; other such globally acting thermal loops are the Ferrel cell and the polar cell. The thermohaline circulation of the oceans is also convective in nature, although – as the name suggests – this is driven by differential salinity as well as temperature gradients.[196]

In the controlled conditions of a laboratory, such cells are reasonably predictable. A parameter known as the Rayleigh number[197] determines the threshold at which convective patterns appear (i.e. at which convection replaces conduction as the primary means of heat transfer). The cells also show a certain degree of adaptability. If the temperature gradient is increased so the Rayleigh number rises *beyond* the threshold level of 1708, the cells initially maintain their form – even though their constituent molecules are endowed with higher levels of energy. However, once the Rayleigh number reaches a certain value, there is an abrupt state transition or bifurcation; the system becomes more complex, with a new set of rolls forming perpendicular to the first set. If increased still further, the patterns become transient and irregular, and the system degenerates into chaos. The structures that are formed when the temperature gradient reaches such levels – with the Rayleigh number in the tens of millions – are too fleeting to acquire an identity as persisting entities. Such convective turbulence is a feature of the Earth's mantle[198] and the 500 km-thick layer of hydrogen gas at the surface of the sun.

Such self-organizing cells are at the mercy of the temperature gradient – the energy flow – that drives their formation. If it is too little, no cell will form in the first place; if too great, pattern formation will be obliterated by the onset of turbulence, as structures flit into and out of existence in an inherently unpredictable way. Something rather similar happens with the formation of self-organizing vortex structures.

Vortex formation occurs when flowing liquids (such as rivers) encounter obstacles (such as bridge pillars) that obstruct their flow and – if the circumstances are right – produce patterns of swirling vortices in their wake. The drag induced by the pillar gives rise to a rotating tendency called vorticity on either side, the two flows feeding back into one another to create a single regular train of whorls called a Kármán vortex street.[199] Just as the Rayleigh number makes it possible to predict the behaviour of convective cells as the energy input increases, for channelled flow too there is a universal parameter called the Reynolds number that likewise specifies the ratio of forces driving the flow (the flow velocity) to those resisting it (such as the fluid viscosity and the size of the obstacle), thus allowing predictions to be made about when the transition will be made from a smooth, laminar flow to an undulated patterning and how this patterning will further develop in complexity as the velocity is increased. Again, once a certain level – in this case a Reynolds number of 200 – is exceeded, the self-organizing regularity of the vortices vanishes and the flow degenerates into turbulence. Such is the case with the major rivers in nature, which generally have a Reynolds number of over a million and thus produce a pandemonium of momentary eddies and whirls rather than an orderly vortex street.

A related phenomenon is the shear instability[200] produced when two adjacent layers of fluid flow past one another at different speeds or in opposite directions, generating a shear force at the boundary between them. Random irregularities that may appear at this interface are magnified by a process of positive feedback,[201] causing tiny bulges to self-amplify into increasingly pronounced undulations and then roll over into whirling vortices, before eventually dissolving into turbulence. Like the graceful patterns of the Kármán vortex street, the self-organizing waves caused by shear instability will persist as long as there is a sufficient input of energy. Moreover, the swirling waves created by shear instabilities can eventually close round on themselves to produce fully-fledged vortices in the guise of whirlpools, cyclones and tornadoes. When this happens, they may acquire a self-contained autonomy that makes them much more life-like and more fully self-like.

This manifests itself for a start in their susceptibility to personification. Perhaps the best-known example is the whirlpool-figure of Charybdis encountered by Odysseus on his voyages, a voracious mouth capable of swallowing any ship that passes too close to it in negotiating a narrow channel (on the far shore of which is the equally fearsome monster Scylla). Since 1953, hurricanes too have been personalized and identified – in other words endowed with a persisting and individual identity – by being given names such as Mitch, Katrina and Sandy. More recently, typhoons have also been named. Tornadoes, by contrast, are perhaps considered too short-lived to be personalized with names, and are referred to in terms of the places they hit.

So how far can this analogy between a vortex and a living organism be taken? J. Scott Turner asks this question about a permanent eddy in the Niagara River, located at a sharp turn just downstream from the Niagara Falls.[202] Known simply as The Whirlpool, it shows all the trademark characteristics of a self-organizing system, using an influx of energy to perform the work of creating and maintaining a pattern (the pattern that it *is*) and dissipating frictional heat (its waste) in the process. The question of self-containment, however, is rather harder to answer. Turner himself describes eddies as 'highly organized' and 'self-contained'.[203] Like convective cells and supercell thunderstorms, the circular self-enclosure of eddies suggests a type of entity that also provides its own boundary. Yet Turner is quick to qualify his initial assertion: by contrast with an organism, the boundary of which can be cut open with a knife, The Whirlpool in fact lacks a distinctive demarcation separating whirlpool from NOT-whirlpool. If there is a boundary, indeed, the most valid candidate might be the riverbanks themselves, which contain and channel both the eddy and the energy flux that feeds it. But wouldn't this mean that the river was the 'self' in question? Or perhaps this is the wrong *sort* of boundary?

According to Turner, the difference between an eddy and an organism is that an eddy such as The Whirlpool disappears if the source of potential energy driving it is turned down (which can be done if the New York Power Authority decides to divert water away from the Falls). If the potential energy driving matter and energy through an organism is reduced, by contrast, the organism will respond by modifying its boundary in such a way as to maintain that flow. 'It is not the boundary *itself* that makes an organism distinctive', he writes, 'but what that boundary *does*. In other words, the boundary is not a thing, it is a *process*, conferring upon the organism a persistence that endures as long as its boundary can adaptively modify the flows of energy and matter through it.'[204] The idea of the boundary – or of self-containment – as a process is certainly an attractive one: to contain oneself in this sense is an activity, not a finished state of affairs. Yet it is still not clear that the distinction between an eddy and an organism is absolute: as a self-organizing 'cell', The Whirlpool too provides itself with a boundary, and this will likewise persist as long as it can adapt itself so as to make use of the available flows of energy and matter. The difference resides above all in the *degree* of adaptability. A whirlpool shows relatively modest powers of adaptation, whereas an organism has an enormous capacity for modifying either its internal milieu (by homeostasis) or the outside world (by acting on it). This ability to act on or modify the environment is undoubtedly one of the most remarkable characteristics of selfhood and life, yet it too has its limits. If you cut off its oxygen supply, even the most adaptable of (aerobic)[205] animals will not last long.

Asking what it would take to make a whirlpool behave more like a living thing, therefore, Turner's suggested answer focuses on adaptability:

> *Suppose ... that one night, when the New York Power Authority engineers divert water away from the Falls, The Whirlpool effects a change in the shape of the riverbed surrounding it, perhaps by forcing the riverbed downstream to sink in response to the diminished potential energy upstream. In this fanciful scenario, The Whirlpool might persist even in the face of the changing field of potential energy. In other words, if The Whirlpool could persist by adaptively modifying structural features of the environment surrounding it, the distinction between The Whirlpool and an organism – the adaptive control of the flows of energy and mass – would disappear. Could The Whirlpool then fairly be said to be 'alive'? Well, that would be stretching the analogy further than even I am comfortable with ...*[206]

Part of the problem by this stage has to do with the limits of our imagination. It is hard to conceive of a whirlpool undertaking any such manoeuvre, even by a skilled manipulation of the river's water flow. If such a modification of the environment were indeed to happen, it would be considered fortuitous: a mere 'event', not an 'action' pursued with intentionality. If it happened various times, or in varying contexts, one might perhaps start to speak of adaptive self-maintenance and flexibility. But it would have to be shown that the whirlpool was in some way responsible for the operation, and this remains a 'fanciful scenario'.

One of the features that epitomise the apparent gulf between eddies and living creatures is the lack of motility of the former, which remain entrenched within the confines of their own niche (a narrow channel of running water). Hurricanes such as Andrew or Mitch or Sandy, by contrast, go blustering around looking for trouble. They are self-moving entities, steered by the wind system of which they form a part and eventually dying when they run out of energy. Yet not all hurricanes are so mobile. The Cassini spacecraft has provided evidence of an enormous hurricane – with a width of some 8,000 km and wind speeds of up to 550 km/h (350 mph) – at Saturn's south pole, believed to have been 'trapped' there by the atmospheric conditions for a period of time that can only be speculated.[207] A rather smaller one, equally immobile, has since come to light at the north pole of Saturn.

Even bigger and better-known than Saturn's polar hurricanes is the huge vortex on Jupiter known as the Great Red Spot, a self-organizing giant produced by atmospheric shear instabilities at the boundary where two of Jupiter's zonal jets flow latitudinally in opposite directions. The Great Red Spot is known to have sustained itself for well over a hundred years since it was first observed in the 19th century, and it is sometimes claimed that Robert Hooke first noted its existence in the 17th century.[208] Like The Whirlpool, therefore, it has certainly persisted 'long enough for cartographers to put it on their maps'[209]. However, the tendency of such vortices to come and go raises doubts about their identity over time. Philip Ball suggests that the Great Red Spot may be a fundamental and recurrent feature of the turbulence of Jovian skies and that 'even if the present spot dissipates, another can be expected to emerge'.[210] This raises the question of whether – if it re-emerges in the same location – it will still be the selfsame spot (reawakening as after a period of dormancy). What if it re-emerges at a slightly different location? Does it make sense to speak of identity or continuity in such a situation? Or is its identity as indeterminate as that of a reproducing amoeba in relation to its offspring? Or as a shifting dune that merges with, then emerges from, a larger dune?

A possible analogy with reproducing organisms is also apparent. Fascinated by the parallel between the Great Red Spot and living beings,[211] theoretical biologist Stuart Kauffman notes how it 'in some sense persists and adapts to its environment, shedding baby vortices as it does so',[212] though – as with the 'breeding' dunes encountered above – this is clearly a case of reproduction without heredity. As such, there is no possibility of evolution, and no 'species self' with the potential for self-transformation over time or for learning how to manipulate non-self so as to perpetuate self. In fact, a more commonly encountered image is of the Great Red Spot 'feeding' on smaller eddies, first trapping them within its pull and then swallowing them, sustaining itself by incorporating their energy. Laboratory simulations too have shown how larger vortices tend to 'prey' on smaller ones, while two equally large vortices rotating in the same direction simply merge into one.[213]

The clearly 'cellular' nature of the Great Red Spot provides it with a degree of self-containment; there is a sense in which the system itself constitutes its own boundary. One might conceive of throwing some sort of wrapping round it – say, an enormous protective membrane – to make it more self-like, but this would have to be endowed with differential permeability, i.e. capable of letting nutrient energy in and waste out.[214] If it merely sealed off the interior, it would only be a matter of time before the container reduced the contained to the lifelessness of thermodynamic equilibrium.

Combustion

Wild Fires, Tamed Fires

The self-organizing flows characteristic of liquid or liquefied systems show some remarkable aspects of proto-selfhood, but clearly fall short of full selfhood. They conform to the category of self-maintaining systems, yet the element of self-adaptation or self-transformation is minimal. They lack anything approaching informational self-replication and the possibility of an evolving or self-modifying lineage, and the self-containment present in 'cellular' phenomena such as convective systems is only a vague foreshadowing of the self-containment of living organisms such as bacteria, amoebae or metazoans. Apart from autocatalytic systems such as the BZ reaction alluded to at the outset, moreover, they are physical rather than chemical systems. However, only chemical systems are likely to be specific enough to generate constraints and control mechanisms that are not only global (like the macroscopic patterns of dissipative systems) but also local and molecularly selective, thus giving rise to complex structures in which certain components of the system act as checks or controls on the activity of certain other components.[215] Only in this way is it possible for energy to be channelled to produce not just orderly patterns but also interacting components that can perform the further work required to perpetuate a self-constructing self. In turning to a realm of such chemical reactions, the following section will focus on oxidation, i.e. on fire and self-organizing systems associated with combustion.

Of course, fire in itself – the oxidation of usually carbonaceous fuel – is not strictly a self-organizing phenomenon. It is better described as self-generating or self-propagating, akin to a chain reaction. Though heat is required to pass a critical threshold and set it alight, once the fire has started, the heat it generates is enough to keep it going. To this extent it is a self-sustaining process and will persist as long as it has fodder for consumption. Richard Dawkins provides a powerful description of the parallelism between fire and life:

> *Fire rivals breath as imagery for life. When we die, the fire of life goes out. Our ancestors who first tamed it probably thought fire a living thing, a god even. … Fire stays alive as long as you feed it. Fire breathes air; you can suffocate it by cutting off its oxygen supply, you can drown it with water. Wild fire devours the forest, driving animal prey before it with the speed and ruthlessness of a pack of wolves in (literally) hot pursuit. As with wolves, our ancestors could capture a fire cub as a useful pet, tame it, feed it regularly and clear away its ashy excreta. … Wild fires would have been observed giving birth to daughter fires, spitting sparks and live cinders up on the wind.*[216]

For a thinker such as Dawkins, what distinguishes a forest fire from biological life is that although wild fires might be said to reproduce – he imagines our forefathers conceiving of a 'pedigree of descent among domestic fires traced from a glowing ancestor brought from a distant clan'[217] – they lack true heredity. Fires may vary, but variations among fires, whether in terms of flame colour or speed of propagation, are all determined entirely by environmental factors such as the supply of fuel and oxygen rather than the nature of the spark that lit them. Lacking true heredity, fires do not evolve, and they thus lack the adaptive complexity conferred by the process of natural selection.[218]

For Maynard Smith and Szathmáry too, this is the crux of the matter: excluded from natural selection, fires have no chance of evolving complex systems that comprise organs – hearts, livers, eyes, etc. – with functions ensuring growth, survival, reproduction and adaptation. This is certainly part of the truth. The faculty of self-replication or (evolving) self-reproduction is an essential element of the triad of intrinsic reflexivity we pinpointed in the Introduction. Equally important, however, is the factor of self-containment, which is notably absent in forest fires. Wildfires are pure dissipation, all heat and no work. In a living creature, by contrast, self-containment means that the energy that enters the system is 'contained' or 'channelled' or 'controlled' in such a way that it can be used for work, creating structures that will in turn foster the self-perpetuation of a self-perpetuating self.[219]

In the form of respiration, the flame of life is a process of controlled or *contained* combustion. As early as 1790, Lavoisier recognized that the purpose of respiration – the use of oxygen[220] to degrade organic substances and generate energy – is a 'slow combustion of carbon and hydrogen similar in every way to that which takes place in a lamp or lighted candle'.[221] This constant combustion is one of the fundamental features of cellular life, providing the normally unnoticed and unquestioned background to our living selfhood. The very word 'respiration' betrays a deep-seated link to 'spirit', the underlying principle or force traditionally understood to infuse all living things. As multicellular beings obliged to provide our constituent cells with the oxygen they need, we lead a life that extends from our first inhalation to our final exhalation. Dawkins notes that the breath of life is as universal an image as the flame. To respire is to fan the flame of life. Yet it is only upon reflection (or in meditation) – or when something goes wrong, as with asthma or apnoea – that we become conscious of the physiological processes designed to deliver oxygen to the lungs for further distribution and subsequent combustion.

Strangely, however, the whole point of this process of combustion is primarily to avoid or delay generating heat. After all, it would do us no good at all if we were to burst into flame like a parched shrub (in this sense it helps being so watery). When glucose or any other carbohydrate is burnt directly, all the energy stored in the configuration of its molecules (its potential energy) is immediately dissipated as heat and thus wasted before it can create order or structure. When an organism's metabolism burns glucose, by contrast, this energy is used to perform work. Yet the energy released by the combustion of glucose can only be made to work if it is *coupled* to a process that requires energy in order to take place, i.e. a process that has to be 'pushed up the thermodynamic hill', away from equilibrium. Known as '*endergonic* reactions', such processes include protein biosynthesis, the transportation of molecules across a membrane or against a concentration gradient, the generation of physical force or even the accurate transmission of genetic information.[222] This coupling of the exergonic or energy-releasing process of respiration to endergonic or energy-requiring operations such as macromolecule biosynthesis is essential to the ongoing growth, reproduction and repair – the self-maintenance and self-production – of organisms, and it relies on the presence of a universal energy currency, an intermediary or go-between that transmits the energy from glucose to the biochemical reaction that requires the energy. The universal energy currency that drives life on Earth is a molecule called adenosine triphosphate, or ATP.

This molecule can perhaps best be conceived as akin to a pent-up spring, carrying energy in the bonds that link the phosphate molecules to the nucleoside adenosine. When ATP donates energy for the performance of work such as macromolecule biosynthesis or locomotion, it is in the process broken down to adenosine diphosphate (ADP) and inorganic phosphate; the currency is 'spent'. One of the underlying functions of cellular metabolism – whether respiratory or photosynthetic – is thus to provide the energy to ensure a constant *resynthesis* of ATP from ADP and phosphate and in so doing to maintain the supply of available energy that can perform work.[223] What is remarkable about ATP is that it not only constitutes the basis for the exergonic-endergonic coupling that allows chemical energy to perform work, but it also permits chemical energy to be *stored* (in phosphate bonds) to be used subsequently as and when required. This capacity to store chemical energy is a key aspect of the control and containment of the process of combustion. It is as though a flame were being hoarded and ignited flicker by flicker.

The Second Law of Thermodynamics nonetheless dictates that whenever energy does work, some portion of that energy will be dissipated in the form of heat; the transformation of energy into order-creating work is never complete. To this extent, the performance of work is always, inescapably inefficient, producing 'useless' heat as well as creating 'useful' order. A value known as the 'total conversion efficiency' measures the efficacy with which the energy in food is converted into new organism, in other words how efficiently it is converted into ATP and this ATP is then used to power the reactions needed for growth.[224] Warm-blooded animals such as mammals and birds, which expend substantial quantities of energy on the *deliberate* production of heat, tend to score rather low marks in this respect. Keeping a constant body temperature means generating heat as rapidly as it is lost to the surroundings, making temperature regulation one of the major metabolic costs for such organisms. As Turner points out, the use of what he calls the 'metabolic energy stream' – in the form of the precious energy currency of ATP – for heat production is pure profligacy, 'akin to heating your house by burning dollar bills'.[225]

There are various broad strategies for combating this inefficiency, again 'containing' our combustion to make it more useful and less profligate. Such mechanisms involve adaptive modifications – either physiological or behavioural – to the boundary between self and non-self. A striking example is provided by male Emperor penguins, left by the females to incubate their egg in the freezing cold of the Antarctic winter. During this nine-week incubation they are unable to feed, since abandoning the egg is not an option. Yet they are wonderfully insulated by feathers and a layer of fat beneath the skin, and by huddling tightly together in 'crèches' they succeed in reducing their exposed surface area by up to five sixths. Even though they do resort to their food reserves to generate heat, therefore, the efficiency of their heat retention mechanisms means that they only lose 15 percent of their body weight over the entire period of incubation.[226] In this way, physiological and behavioural modifications of self-containment (feathers and fat; communal huddling) ensure that the energy released by the combustion of food is used as economically as possible.

Other strategies involve actively manipulating one's environment in order to harness external energetic flows or minimize energy loss. The construction of dens, burrows and houses adds a new dimension to self-containment, creating what Turner has called an 'external physiology' in addition to the 'internal physiology' of our body and again making the boundary between self and non-self less clear-cut than is often thought.[227] Humankind has gone even further in appropriating environmental energies in order to regulate its external physiology. Metabolic combustion has thus been augmented not only with the 'taming' of wood fires but the extraction and incineration of fossilized carbonaceous fuels stemming from the luxuriant forests of the Devonian and Carboniferous over 300 million years ago. This ancillary burning of fuel amounts to an externalization of combustion, an outsourcing of metabolism, for the purpose of helping to maintain a steady body temperature. One might equally refer to an 'extended self', a term we shall reencounter in Chapter 6. Either way, the boundary between self and non-self is manipulated in the interests of the self in question.

It is not merely a matter of providing a supplementary means of keeping warm. Just as importantly, the use of fire in cooking has functioned as an externalization of our digestive processes.[228] Indeed, it has been persuasively argued that some of the key steps in the emergence of the genus *Homo* and the species *Homo sapiens* coincided with the taming of fire – the containment of combustion – and the advent of easily chewed and digested cooked meals, allowing less energy to be spent on running a metabolically expensive gastro-intestinal tract and freeing up more energy to power the metabolic luxury of a big brain.[229] Much more recently, contained combustion – the use of machines such as the steam engine to convert heat into work – powered the Industrial Revolution, producing an explosion in the amount of work that could collectively be performed by the labour force in newly industrialized nations and transforming the capacity to produce and transport goods.[230]

Notwithstanding the ingenuity of big-brained humans in inventing ever new mechanisms for the control of combustion, even at a most rudimentary level a living self is a process of self-contained combustion. The way in which a single cell or a multicellular organism performs the work of self-containment – the way it regulates the boundary between self and non-self – in turn determines its metabolic needs and the energy available for work. Stuart Kauffman has referred to a 'work-constraint (W-C) cycle' in which 'work begets constraints begets work'.[231] In other words, the work performed by a self-producing system of this sort generates the self-containment that in turn makes further work possible and so perpetuates the process. Whereas in a wildfire it is dissipated heat that drives the self-sustaining process, therefore, in a living self it is the *containment* of energy flows and the performance of work that makes combustion self-perpetuating.

Auto-Mobiles and the Containment of Combustion

The notion of self-contained, self-maintaining combustion is certainly illuminating. But is it really sufficient for an understanding of living selfhood? What is the nature of this 'containment'? A nuclear explosion is a self-propagating and self-feeding chain reaction; a nuclear reactor 'contains' this autocatalysis and makes it do useful work. Yet a nuclear reactor is not normally considered to be alive or a self.[232] Perhaps a brief thought experiment will help shed further light on the strengths and limitations of the idea.

Take the following notoriously front-heavy steam engine, the *fardier à vapeur* or steam dray designed by Nicolas-Joseph Cugnot in the late 1760s. Here we have a case of combustion that was certainly 'contained'. By being contained, moreover, it could be made to do work, powering the reciprocating motion of a piston and thus by extension the circular motion of the wheels. Despite the technological teething troubles, the result was arguably the first self-moving vehicle: an *auto-mobile*.

Figure 3: Nicolas-Joseph Cugnot's automotive contraption

The *fardier à vapeur* suggests an immediate association between the containment of combustion[233] and the capacity to move (oneself) that has traditionally been attributed to entities regarded as living or endowed with a 'soul', i.e. animated. Recognition of a special network of relationships between fire, movement and soul goes back to the ancients. It is present in Democritus, who is derided by Aristotle for his conception of soul as a 'sort of fire or hot substance' that generates movement in animals.[234] An understanding of soul in terms of self-movement (though not fire) is found in Plato's *Phaedrus*, where Socrates tells his eponymous interlocutor that 'every body which derives motion from without is soulless, but that which has its motion within itself has a soul, since that is the nature of the soul'.[235] And one of Plato's less illustrious successors as head of the Academy in Athens, Xenocrates, defines soul more cryptically as a 'self-moving number'.[236]

This association of soul with (possibly combustive) locomotion or self-movement has an intuitive appeal, yet a logical consequence in more modern times may be the ascription of souls to 'automobiles', from Cugnot's trundling steam dray to the most aerodynamically sophisticated of racers. It is telling, indeed, how the German noun *Auto*, a reflexive prefix that has succeeded in throwing off its root word and acquiring lexical autonomy,[237] seems to hint at distilled or epitomised selfhood; in other eras and other circumstances, a self-moving vehicle might well have been called simply *Selbst* (or how about Suso's *Sich*?). Of course, the selfhood of cars is illusory. A car is ultimately 'selfless' in that it performs all its work for its human drivers. As with other forms of externalized combustion devised and exploited by humans, one might subsume the would-be selfhood of cars within the 'extended selfhood' of their drivers. Or is it going too far to speak of symbiosis? Whatever the case, in its own ecological niche – the autobahn – it is often questionable who really is in charge.

A traditional car is like an organism in that it needs fuel to move itself, yet unlike any motile organism in that it is completely unable to fuel *itself*. So how about if we were to imagine that the burning wood[238] in Cugnot's car (now appropriately weighted so as not to fall flat on its oversize nose) not only powers its wheels but also a sizeable yet easily manoeuvrable saw? As the car moves, it fells and dices the trees in its path and shovels them into an aperture or maw that leads straight to its furnace. In this way, it stays 'alive', keeping itself going as an automotive 'self' until it runs out of trees or falls apart. It can now be called 'self-like' in that it has a metabolism of sorts, a mechanism of controlled combustion that keeps itself going as long as its surroundings let it. It is now also 'self-ish' to the extent that all it does is chop down trees for its own subsequent consumption.

Yet we may still hesitate to call this self-maintaining *proto-auto* a self. Perhaps this is partly because it is made of metal rather than something more 'squishy' (to recall Gerald Joyce's phrase), i.e. its non-biological nature. A second objection to any ascription of selfhood may be its implausibly idealized environment. As described above, the car just saws and shovels away at whatever it happens to find in front of its nose, and it is thus dependent on the presence of an extended row of trees ready and waiting to be felled. In principle, a simplified environment need not be an issue. All living beings depend on being structurally coupled to their environment, and there is a sense in which the less adjustment is necessary, the better. This is exemplified by endosymbiotic cells – such as '*Candidatus* Carsonella ruddii', whom we shall encounter again in Chapter 4 – which live inside other cells in conditions of the utmost stability. However, the lack of any capacity in Cugnot's *auto* to sense its environment and adapt its behaviour accordingly – for example by steering – may be deemed a serious shortcoming. If it contained a sensor that could identify trees and a steering system that could orient the car in their direction, it would certainly *seem* more like a self; even more so if it fed not on trees but on (presumably slow-moving) animals, the sight or scent of which would prompt it to 'give chase'. Such animals might hide or freeze at the sight of it, keen not to become fuel to its flames. If *we* were those slow-moving animals, our attribution of selfhood (or not) to Cugnot's carnivore would be deeply irrelevant in the face of our more pressing urge to elude its attentions. Our behaviour would be the same (avoidance) whether we referred to it as a self or as something that merely *resembled* a self in its self-perpetuating activity of pursuing, consuming and combusting the nutritious prey that provide it with the energy required for the perpetuation of such activity. Nevertheless, there may remain a nagging suspicion that it could still be made *more* self-like.

Considerable experimental work has been done on such artificial selves (or robots), focusing in particular on what has been called their 'energetic autonomy',[239] i.e. their ability to generate energy for themselves from their environment. A notable example is a robot called 'SlugBot', described as 'the world's first artificial predator',[240] which forages for organic prey in the shape of slugs (plentiful and above all slow-moving garden pests that lend themselves to fermentation and are felt to be ethically inconsequential to the extent that they are subject to lethal control measures anyway). These are caught by a long arm with a sensor and a grabber at the end, which picks them up and puts them in a watery pocket. When SlugBot's pockets are full or it needs to recharge its batteries, it returns to its recharging station and offloads its collection of slugs into a 'digestive system', which turns them into a bio-gas. Fed into a fuel cell, the bio-gas generates the electric energy that will power the robot on its future excursions. SlugBot thus performs work that channels environmental energy in such a way as to power further work. In this sense, it may be considered a prototype of Cugnot's locomotive self in its 'advanced', carnivorous guise.

However, there are limits to SlugBot's energetic autonomy: for a start, the fermentation vessel and fuel cell are not themselves part of the robot, but are located externally to it. SlugBot will feed them and in turn be fed. In itself, this need not represent a serious infringement of its autonomy.[241] As the designers point out, it is a strategy used by certain social insect colonies, whose members forage for leaves they cannot digest, which they have to bring home to a 'fungus farm' in the nest: they then eat the fungus. The problem is that this 'digestive system' – like the ants' fungus farm – will in turn require energy in order to fulfil its function, and it seems unlikely that SlugBot will be able to cover both its own energetic requirements and those of its digestive system.[242] We thus have a mobile system that is unable to provide the energy its digestive system needs to be able to provide *it* with energy. Such problems can perhaps be considered *practical* teething troubles, but at this stage at least SlugBot's energetic autonomy is still very much a provisional form of autonomy, for its self-maintaining metabolic combustion is crucially dependent on a rather elaborate manmade infrastructure.

Of course, energetic autonomy can fall back on other, less flesh-based energy sources. Solar vehicles of all sorts use photovoltaic material contained in panels to convert solar energy directly into electric energy used for propulsion. But such vehicles – self-moving 'souls' though they may be – seem even less self-like than carnivorous self-movers such as SlugBot. After all, they go wherever they are driven, and they remain critically reliant on explicit or implicit human intervention. So how about providing them with 'intelligence'? One might hybridize them with the sort of driverless cars being designed by research teams at Google and elsewhere, which sport features such as artificial intelligence, video cameras and sensors, GPS receivers, radars and lasers. These certainly appear to 'sense' the environment and use this sensing to behave appropriately. One might envision a 'phototactic' driverless solar car that is programmed to drive to wherever there is sunlight, i.e. to track its energy source.

Such a project is unlikely to get much in the way of funding.[243] In itself, it is flagrantly pointless, although this pointlessness is perhaps the point; the thing about selves is that they have no point, or rather they are *their own* point. As implied by their intrinsic reflexivity, selves are ends in themselves. In fact, such a driverless solar car would bear a striking functional resemblance to a beautiful living creature known as *Volvox* – a hollow, spherical colony of algae comprising as many as 50,000 cells each endowed with a simple eyespot and two flagella that protrude like oars. The flagella beat in the dark, but stop beating in sunlight, thus steering the whole sphere towards the sun and tracking the optimal conditions for photosynthesis. Equally notable is the single-celled dinoflagellate *Euglena gracilis*, which uses its eyespot to detect and swim towards the light, where it can photosynthesize. Where light levels are lower, it survives by eating as an animal does, thus evoking a cross between a driverless solar vehicle and a carnivorous version of Cugnot's car. Yet despite any similarity to such self-moving photosynthesizers – indeed despite their information-processing sophistication and 'intelligent' behaviour – it might still be felt that sun-seeking, solar-powered driverless cars would lack some feature required for us to be able to ascribe full selfhood to them. They may be behaviourally very similar to simple biological selves; they may share their self-like 'pointlessness'. But they wouldn't be full selves, would they?

The question remains: what is missing for us to be willing or able to ascribe selfhood to these various forms of *auto*? One of the most obvious answers is simply that *we made them*. Instead of being the result of a process of self-reproduction (perhaps involving informational self-replication), they are the fruit of *allo*-production. They are not self-made. Yet it is not obvious to what extent the genesis of an entity (how its parts were originally put together) should be considered to affect what that entity actually *is* (how its parts work together now). Equally, it is not clear whether this stipulation – a self must be not only self-maintaining (in the present) but also self-made (in its origins) – is something that just happens to apply to all biology as we know it (which it does) or whether it is a more general condition of full selfhood. Importantly, even if the nature of an entity *does* depend upon the history of the 'lineage' of which it forms a part, it is not self-evident that this history – the story of how it has evolved by natural selection – necessarily involves either macromolecular self-replication or cellular self-reproduction.

For one thing, robots may assemble *other* robots. Indeed, a 'mother' robot has recently been developed that is able to 'select' its most efficient 'offspring' in a way that mimics natural selection. The mother, a robotic arm, creates its offspring by combining a small set of motorized cubic modules; it then observes which of the resulting 'baby' robots – each with its own 'genome' embodying the requisite construction parameters – moves the furthest distance during a test period, mutating or recombining the less successful ones and retaining the fastest ones for the next 'generation'. Over a sequence of generations, a marked improvement in performance is noted, with the quickest individuals in the final generation moving more than twice as fast as those in the first.[244] In such a scenario, however, the mother (the robotic arm) is producing offspring (locomotive agents) that are very different from itself both in structure and function; this hardly counts as *self*-reproduction. There would perhaps be something more akin to continued selfhood if the mother robot were producing progeny whose efficiency or 'fitness' involved not merely locomotion but also an ability in turn to assemble *further* progeny, which were in turn capable of both locomotion and producing yet *further* progeny. From the point of view of the original human designer, this would combine currently unfeasible complexity with exquisite pointlessness. But who is to deny that a team of small robots might soon be able to operate (and maintain) a highly automated assembly line dedicated to the production of further generations of small robots, whose multiple functions would include the operation (and maintenance) of such assembly lines?

Indeed, other mechanisms of evolution are possible. David McFarland thus predicts that a form of 'marketplace' natural selection will come to prevail in the evolution of *task-performing* robots, involving a system of trial and error and survival in a competitive market. To this extent, the evolution of robots will throw up parallels with the evolution of animals: such robots 'will be bought and sold and will have to compete in the marketplace against other robots and against humans willing to carry out the same tasks. This ecological competition will lead to the evolution of certain attributes, among them robustness, speed of reaction, self-sufficiency and autonomy'.[245] Clearly, such robots will exist in a 'symbiotic' relationship of mutual dependence with their human users,[246] albeit less so where energetic autonomy is achieved. Above all, this will manifest itself as a form of *reproductive* symbiosis, which will depend on their success in satisfying users in terms of (for example) reliability, flexibility and energetic efficiency; only those robots that *do* satisfy their users will generate demand, and only those for which there is demand will emerge from the production line. Yet this raises the more general question of how far symbiosis encroaches upon selfhood? To the extent that the self-perpetuating existence of such robots depends upon their usefulness to humans, they are no longer 'ends in themselves'.[247] As will become clear in Chapter 6, however, symbiosis may be regarded as a form of *shared selfhood*, each partner 'using' the other for their mutual benefit. Such reproductive symbiosis is in this sense no different from other kinds of symbiosis.

In the light of McFarland's considerations, we might thus imagine a scenario in which Cugnot's car (in its more advanced version with sensors) not only provides *itself* with energy but utilizes this energy to do something useful, possibly something dangerous or unpleasant that humans are unable or reluctant to do, or perhaps merely something commercially viable. This would be the equivalent in evolutionary terms of an animal's reproductive work; the work is performed to please its human user and thereby ensure its survival (with possible modifications) into the next generation. One example of such an activity is the slightly less than life-threatening task of mowing the lawn. A Virginia-based company called EcoMow Technologies has accordingly designed a self-guiding lawn mower (EcoMow) that uses the grass cuttings it accumulates to create a grassy biomass from which it draws its energy. What is noteworthy about this particular contrivance is that EcoMow's self-fuelling activity coincides entirely with the task it performs to satisfy its human user (its 'reproductive' activity). EcoMow does not have to 'decide' what to do: by eating grass it 'satisfies' both itself and its user.[248]

In other scenarios, an engine's need to provide itself with energy may fail to coincide so conveniently with serving and satisfying its reproductive symbiont (its user), giving rise to a 'choice' between different sorts of activity.[249] This is exemplified by (as yet hypothetical) on-demand driverless cars, which may soon transform day-to-day human transportation. Such vehicles will need to 'know' not only how best to take their customers to a specified destination, but also where, when and how to refuel themselves, or at least *get themselves refuelled* by the requisite manmade infrastructure. The vehicle is faced with two underlying goals: 'self-maintenance' (providing itself with fuel) and 'self-propagation' (satisfying a user). McFarland thus distinguishes energetic autonomy from what he calls 'motivational autonomy'.[250] As with animals, he suggests, self-sufficiency is 'largely a matter of balancing one vital requirement (e.g. foraging / refuelling) against another (e.g. reproductive activities / doing useful work). This balancing act is sometimes called behavioural stability'.[251] To attain autonomy of this order, such a robo-car would have to make decisions about the best behaviour for it to pursue:

> *[It] must be able to decide for itself when to break off work and seek fuel. Like an animal, the robot must be able to manage its motivational alternatives in a way that makes best use of its time and energy. Somehow it must be able to assess the costs and benefits of the alternative activities open to it. In the long term, the costs and benefits relate to whether the robot is doing the 'right thing', that is, staying alive and pleasing the customer. Similarly, for an animal the right thing amounts to survival and reproductive success.*[252]

To this end, such a robo-car needs to be able to assess – among other things – the state of fuel or food within its own body (i.e. its 'hunger' and 'thirst'), as well as the availability and accessibility of fuel in the environment, while at the same time keeping a record of the amount of work accomplished so as not to get into arrears with its user-pleasing task-performance.[253] In robotics research, this process of 'weighing up' various behavioural alternatives on the basis of a set of parameters is known as the action-selection mechanism.

Once endowed with this capacity, our *auto* will be exhibiting complex and not always predictable self-maintaining and self-propagating behaviour. It may not be long before we find ourselves tempted to engage in empathy, i.e. to regard it fully as a self, capable of feeling not just 'hunger' but hunger. But would we really want to remove those scare quotes? Can this high-tech version of Cugnot's car really be said to feel anything? Does it make sense to ascribe sentience or consciousness to it? To rephrase Nagel's much-quoted question: is it like anything to be Cugnot's car? We have not yet established the nature of the relationship between selfhood and consciousness, though we have ascertained that the two cannot simply be equated. Provisionally, a self might be characterized as the sort of entity that *can* be conscious, or that provides a foundation from which consciousness *can* emerge. Does our motley array of cars and robots provide such a foundation? If not, why not? The remainder of this section will touch upon a few preliminary considerations in anticipation of a more exhaustive discussion of consciousness to come. This will involve looking, once again, at the concepts of self-containment and self-production and their implications for the possibility of directed self-movement in response to environmental stimuli.

The notion of self-containment is crucial. This does not merely refer to the physical vessel, whether the reinforced furnace in which the combustion is contained or some sort of protective outer coating that shields the whole vehicle against the scratches of trees or the bites of recalcitrant prey and that we might visualize as self-assembling and self-healing by analogy with lipid membranes.[254] Self-containment is deeply linked to the notion of functional integration, for the greater the degree of organic interconnectedness among the components of a system, the less the need for an actual physical boundary to hold them together. In this sense, to be self-contained is to be composed of a set of organically interrelated components (none of which can benefit by becoming independent). This brings us back, of course, to Kant's definition of an organism as a self-organizing entity in which each component both depends upon and helps produce all the other components and the organism as a whole. Ruiz-Mirazo and colleagues use the concept of a 'component production system' to refer to what they describe as one of the most characteristic properties of a living organism: 'in particular, its capacity to build and rebuild continuously all the components and constraints that are responsible for its organization and behavior, together with the capacity to adaptively modify that internal organization (plus the actual relation with the environment) as a response to external changes'.[255] Self-containment is to this extent inseparable from integrated self-production.

The problem with Cugnot's poor car, therefore, is not that it does not reproduce itself; it does not even *produce* itself.[256] We are here brought back to the distinction between energetic self-maintenance and structural self-production, with self-fuelling cars ensconced firmly in the former category. If the piston or the furnace or the information-processing system is removed, they can be replaced with other similar ones with no loss of function, but the car is *not itself* able to produce or perform this replacement. Cells, by contrast, are constantly generating the proteins that are vital to them as structural elements. Multicellular organisms are in turn generally able to replace individual cells that are lost, although this capacity varies with cell type (it is curtailed in the case of most neurons, for example) and diminishes with age. To be sure, whole organs are more difficult to regenerate from within,[257] but the principle is shown by the master of such self-production, the planarian worm (a non-parasitic flatworm of the class Turbellaria), which – if its head is cut off – grows a whole new brain within seven days,[258] while the severed brain grows a new hind part and likewise shuffles off, raising the 'amoeba' question of which of the two planarians is the original. The equivalent would be for Cugnot's car (if its furnace were removed) not only to regenerate its furnace, but for the removed furnace to regenerate the rest of the car. However, this is likely to be taking the reader's suspension of disbelief a step or two too far.

A living self's higher level of integrated self-containment is also manifest in the sensory organs and transmission channels by which we are 'open' or 'closed' to the world and which form an indispensable part of the boundary between self and non-self. Here again the contrast with a computer-run robot or car is striking. As Dennett points out, 'in a computer there is a nice neat boundary between the "outside" world and the information channels'[259] that is lacking in living beings. Input devices such as microphones or video cameras transduce information into a common, electronic medium in which it is transmitted, stored and eventually converted into output. In theory the medium of information transmission is irrelevant: whether it is a flow of electrons in a coaxial cable, light in an optical fibre or wireless radio waves, the information is the same; it is 'media-neutral'. As a consequence, information-processing systems 'can be readily interchanged with no loss of function'.[260] Yet this is not the case either in the nervous system of an animal (as Dennett argues) or in the control systems of single-celled prokaryotes or eukaryotes.

This is because the internal transmission channels of bacteria and amoebae are intricately intertwined with the structural information embodied in the cell as a whole, the inherited wisdom of its self-maintaining metabolism. The circuitry of individual cells is now known to be protein-based in that cellular proteins are computational units, capable of performing logical operations and thus collectively forming biochemical networks. Because of their capacity to 'flip' between alternative states with different properties (on the basis of the short-term addition or removal of phosphate groups), proteins can function analogously to transistors in electronic circuits, acting as molecular switches that guide the cellular processes in one direction or another. At the same time, however, they are vital structural elements and catalysts. The 'wiring' of the cell – its biochemical circuitry – thus depends intrinsically on the very proteins that form the dense potage of the cell's cytoplasm. In this sense, the wiring *is* the cell, and the message is inseparable from the medium through which it passes.[261]

Unlike a computer-run robot, therefore, the control system cannot be disentangled from the system being controlled. The information-transmission channel that relays a signal – generated by an internal or external stimulus such as fuel levels or the presence of prey – to a motor effector so as to give rise to appropriate locomotion cannot be excised from the entity as a whole. As a result, the cognitive activity of a living self, its ability to 'behave' in its own interests in response to changes in its inner state or outer conditions, is not merely a question of media-neutral signal transmission, but involves a process that is integrated within and inextricable from the cellular system as a whole, a self-caring self that exists in an intrinsic relationship to the meaningful non-self upon which its continued existence depends. The question remains open, for the present, to what extent we might or might not be justified in referring to an *E. coli* bacterium or a predatory *protist*, unlike Cugnot's carnivore, as *hungry* rather than just 'hungry' and as *aware* of its potential prey rather than just 'aware' of them.

III.
Selfish Genes and DNA

Selfishness

It was proposed in the Introduction that a self is something that is selfish, tautologically so.[262] The self is the unit of selfishness, or of self-interest. In the present chapter I want to examine this relationship between selfhood and selfishness in the context of 'selfish genes' and 'selfish DNA'. After distinguishing two uses of the term 'selfish', this will involve looking at Richard Dawkins' early notion of 'selfish genes', the possible self-like attributes of informational macromolecules, the apparent autonomy of 'cosmopolitan' genes, and finally the concept of 'selfish DNA' as applied to 'rogue' genes that may or may not be endowed with some sort of 'mobility'. The next chapter will then move from genetic material in its nakedness to genetic material enclosed in a protein capsid, i.e. to viruses.

Such a notion of 'selfishness' is liable to be misunderstood, so clarification is called for. To claim that a self is intrinsically selfish in this way is not to make a claim about human or animal psychology.[263] The claim is not that humans (to take one category of 'self') are *in reality* necessarily selfish (in the usual sense of greedy, grasping or self-seeking) and that this is generally disguised beneath a mere *display* or *semblance* of benevolence or moral care; it is not that if you scratch away at our moral mask, a selfish core will come to light; it is not that the apparent selflessness or altruism we may show is merely feigned or fake.[264] The claim is rather that any human or non-human self by definition exhibits a distinctive intrinsically reflexive self-care (of the kind described by Nozick); this is what a self does, by virtue of being a self. This self-care *provides the foundation* for meaningful and coherent behaviour, whether morally engaged or morally indifferent. The cardinal point is that the world in which we live and our – egoistic or altruistic – actions within this world *matter* to us. We may choose to lead a life pursuing the well-being of others and we may aspire to be 'selfless', but this presupposes *self-interest* in the sense that we care about what we do and who we are.

This is not to suggest that selves always *do* behave in their own interests. Human selves are a particularly complicated case, made up as we are of less than perfectly integrated *subselves* that may have manifold and conflicting interests. The difficulties of knowing what is good for us and of predicting the effects of our behaviour, the unreliability of indices of well-being such as 'pleasure' or 'happiness', as well as the existence of abstract ideals such as freedom, self-fulfilment or self-sacrifice, may make it difficult for an observer (including ourselves) to perceive the underlying self-care that drives our behaviour.[265] In practice, human beings are opaque, fragmented, multiple selves rather than beacons of rational transparency, and our interests may be correspondingly fragmentary, multiple and contradictory. Given such complexity, the notion of 'self-interest' makes more sense as a regulative criterion of rationality than as an analytical truth about selfhood: what each self has most reason to do is whatever would be best for himself or herself, or in his or her own interests.[266] This is an idealization insofar as it presupposes unity of selfhood, axiological monism (i.e. a unitary conception of what is of value or good, i.e. what 'in one's own interests' actually means), and the possibility of perfect or near-perfect knowledge.

We may thus identify a number of variations on the original formulation of the relationship between selfhood and selfishness. A self is a being that cares for itself, or is selfish (as we first put it), or that acts in its own interests, or that *tends* to act in its own interests (to the extent that it can), or that acts in its own interests insofar as it knows what these are and is successful in assessing their relative weight. Or, given the difficulty of the above, a self is a being that *has reason to* ascertain its own interests and act in accordance with them; tautologically, the rational course of action is for a self to act in its own interests.[267] It is clear, however, that we are not using the word 'selfish' in the way in which it is generally used, charged with negative connotations, but rather in a neutral sense that implies mere conformity with one's own interests. Such double usage has been a recurrent feature of philosophical discourse on selfishness through the ages.

Aristotle, for example, famously distinguishes between the rapacious selfishness of the 'vulgar' and the measured, rational self-love of the 'wise'. In approaching the question of whether self-love is blameworthy or legitimate, he stresses the importance of terminological precision: 'the present difficulty may be cleared up', he suggests, 'if we can discover what meaning each side attaches to the word "self-love"'.[268] While the term of reproach refers to 'those who assign to themselves more than they are entitled to in money, public distinctions and bodily pleasures', the term of approbation refers to the 'good' man, who excels in rationality and moral beauty: 'it follows that such a man will be self-loving in a different sense from that attached to the word when it is used as a term of reproach. From the vulgar self-lover he differs as far as the life of reason from the life of passion, and as far as a noble purpose differs from mere grasping at whatever presents itself as an expedient'.[269] By contrast with the greedy and covetous self-love of the vulgar, the self-love of the rational man is the very foundation for morality and noble self-sacrifice. Though Aristotle's description of rational self-love ends up bringing it perilously close to smug self-righteousness, the underlying principle that self-love – in the sense of being good to oneself – provides us with a platform from which we can be good to others has retained its relevance through to today.

A similar distinction has been drawn more recently between a moral principle usually known as 'ethical egoism' and the selfishness of those who pursue their own interests at the expense of the interests of others. As the English moral philosopher G. E. Moore put it:

> *Egoism, as a form of Hedonism, is the doctrine which holds that we ought each of us to pursue our own greatest happiness as our ultimate end. The doctrine will, of course, admit that sometimes the best means to this end will be to give pleasure to others; we shall, for instance, by so doing, procure for ourselves the pleasures of sympathy, of freedom from interference, and of self-esteem; and these pleasures, which we may procure by sometimes aiming directly at the happiness of other persons, may be greater than any we could otherwise get. Egoism in this sense must therefore be carefully distinguished from Egoism in another sense, the sense in which Altruism is its proper opposite. Egoism, as commonly opposed to Altruism, is apt to denote merely selfishness.*[270]

The theory of 'ethical egoism' as laid out both before and since Moore[271] has confused generations of moral philosophers, who have struggled to cope with the contradiction between this theoretical egoism (which tells us we ought to aim at our own maximum well-being) and moral principles such as utilitarianism (which tells us we should aim at the well-being of all). In fact, 'egoism' – in this neutral, theoretical sense – is not an ethical principle at all; it is a principle of rational selfhood. We do not *need* to be told to act in our own interests as a matter of moral guidance. Accordingly, altruism (or moral benevolence) and rational self-interest do not stand opposite one another as two mutually contradictory moral positions. Rational self-interest is not a moral position, but dictates what we have *reason* to do, namely behave in accordance with what we judge to be our best interests. This behaviour will be altruistic or otherwise depending on how we evaluate these interests. If it is altruistic, this altruism will be founded on rational self-interest precisely to the extent that our own interests are judged to coincide – in some way or other – with the interests of others.[272]

The question of precisely *why* in practice moral benevolence or altruism may be judged to be in our own interests (and thus rational) deserves a study in its own right. Various systems of carrots and sticks may be involved, whether divine, social or neurophysiological: it might be the prospect of a Dantesque inferno or paradise that makes moral behaviour seem to coincide with self-interest; it might be the esteem and social prestige that comes with being seen to be good, or the pragmatics of reciprocal back-scratching; or we might simply get a kick out of treating people kindly (it might make us happier to see a smile than a frown).[273] It also seems likely that there is a collective logic at work: there is reason to believe that a community of morally cooperating people will all 'do better' for themselves than an aggregation of warring individuals each pursuing their own interests. As Hobbes recognized,[274] men are by nature motivated to act in their own interests, yet this can lead to moral behaviour because prudential morality is in the interests of everyone.

The Selfishness of Genes

This ambiguity in the use of the concept of 'selfishness' as applied to human beings has also structured discourse on the selfishness of sequences of nucleotides, or genes. One of the charges commonly brought against the 'neutral' or 'philosophical' meaning of the word is that it rules out the possibility of any meaningful or empirically testable distinction between selfish and selfless behaviour: while you are *obviously* selfish if you cynically purloin the life savings of a little old lady, you are still *ultimately* selfish if you give away your own life savings to alleviate the suffering of the dispossessed (seeking to enhance your reputation, assure yourself of a cushy afterlife, or simply enjoy a buzz from benevolence). The term has been emptied of all content and practical applicability. Alternatively, such empirically vacuous claims can be taken as making an affirmation or proposal about language use. In this case, the deeper claim is that this is what a self is: a being or person who – on some level – acts in his or her own interests.

The same criticism might be levelled against Richard Dawkins' use of the term 'selfish gene'; Dawkins himself would probably endorse it. Taking the definition of a gene as 'any portion of chromosomal material that potentially lasts for enough generations to serve as a unit of natural selection',[275] Dawkins argues in effect that such an entity – to qualify as a gene rather than just a random stretch of DNA on a chromosome – must behave in such a way as to last for generations. Its 'genehood' is defined in terms of its ability to persist, and this it achieves by replicating more successfully and manipulating the world to better advantage than the alleles with which it is competing. Indeed, Dawkins defines the gene as 'the fundamental unit of natural selection, and therefore the fundamental unit of self-interest', explicitly drawing attention to the analytic nature of his claims: what he has done by means of this definition, he contends, is to *define* the gene in such a way that he 'cannot really help being right!'[276] A few pages later, the term he uses is the 'basic unit of selfishness': 'any gene that behaves in such a way as to increase its own survival chances in the gene pool at the expense of its alleles will, by definition, tautologously, tend to survive'.[277]

To the extent that Dawkins is operating with the philosophical, neutral sense of 'selfish', the concept can here be understood as equivalent to 'successful for itself', a notion that likewise embodies the necessary reflexivity. The gene is the archetypal 'self' precisely insofar as it is also the most elementary 'unit of selfishness'. In corroboration of its more or less unitary nature, it comes close to what Dawkins refers to as 'the ideal of indivisible particulateness'.[278] As such, it is not plagued by the conflicting interests of complex human selves: it has a single 'interest', and that interest is to get itself replicated.

Admittedly, in *The Selfish Gene* Dawkins rather muddies the waters by mixing this philosophical sense of 'selfishness' with its more derogatory, psychological usage. As a consequence, he ventures disconcertingly into the realm of gene personality: 'at the gene level', he notes, 'altruism must be bad and selfishness good'.[279] Just as disconcertingly, he extrapolates from a misleading assertion about genes to an even more misleading assertion about human nature: 'Like successful Chicago gangsters, our genes have survived ... in a highly competitive world. ... [A] predominant quality to be expected in a successful gene is ruthless selfishness. This gene selfishness will usually give rise to selfishness in individual behaviour'.[280] The waywardness of this argumentation has been much criticized. Since the publication of *The Selfish Gene,* the deep-seated importance of cooperation has become increasingly manifest on all levels; even coexistence on a chromosome requires collaboration. Cooperation, it is evident, is anything but an evolutionary afterthought in an originally or inherently selfish world. Nonetheless, the *tautological* point about selfishness as an inherent attribute of selves retains its validity. As Dawkins himself subsequently expressed it in *The Ancestor's Tale:*

> *My first book,* The Selfish Gene, *could equally have been called* The Cooperative Gene *without a word of the book itself needing to be changed. Indeed, this might have saved some misunderstanding. ... Selfishness and cooperation are two sides of a Darwinian coin. Each gene promotes its own selfish welfare, by co-operating with the other genes in the sexually stirred gene pool which is that gene's environment, to build shared bodies.*[281]

Among the earlier book's most vehement critics was the philosopher Mary Midgley. In a scathing review of it, Midgley takes issue not so much with the tautological nature of Dawkins' claims about selfhood as with his ascription of the concept to an entity to which she feels it cannot conceivably apply: 'genes cannot be selfish or unselfish', she writes, 'any more than atoms can be jealous, elephants abstract or biscuits teleological'.[282] What Dawkins claims, according to Midgley, 'is both meaningless and absurd, since he has linked the notion of self-interest quite gratuitously to a kind of subject for which it can make no sense at all. The only possible unit of self-interest is a self, and there are no selves in the DNA'.[283] The implication is that Dawkins' application of the notion of 'selfishness' to genes is a category mistake.[284] However, this in turn rests upon a dogmatic and unexamined understanding of selfhood, for Midgley does not make it clear what sort of entities selfhood *can* be ascribed to, or why. The job of *critical* philosophy is not to claim that you can or cannot describe a gene as selfish, but to call into question both the claim that you can and the claim that you cannot. Practical science, meanwhile, will opt for the terminology and the assumptions that provide it with the greatest predictive power.

Elsewhere, Midgley is willing to grant that calling genes selfish is a metaphor,[285] which is not necessarily the same thing as a category mistake. Like similes, of course, metaphors can vary in the perceived aptness or absurdity of the comparison that they implicitly or explicitly draw. If 'selfishness' is indeed a metaphor, an analytical approach would thus be to consider the points of similarity and difference between 'genes' on the one hand and 'selves' (however they may be defined) on the other hand, i.e. to ask whether the metaphor 'works' and to what extent. This could be a perfectly productive and enlightening procedure, revealing previously undisclosed similarities between genes and (perhaps human) selves. Yet this is not the path Dawkins chooses to follow in his reply to Midgley. Though he had initially conceded that his language was at times metaphorical,[286] he now argues that the notion of 'selfishness' forms part of the conventional scientific terminology: 'when biologists talk about "selfishness" or "altruism" we are emphatically not talking about emotional nature, whether of human beings, other animals, or genes. We do not even mean the words in a *metaphorical* sense. We define altruism and selfishness in purely behaviouristic ways'.[287] His concern, he reiterates, is simply with the effects of a gene's behaviour on the survival prospects of the gene in question. Of course, this in turn raises the question of whether it is appropriate to designate whatever it is genes 'do' – whatever it is that produces these 'effects' – as 'behaviour'.[288]

In fact, however, the reference to technical terminology does not rule out rhetoric (scientific terminology is replete with metaphor), and the terminology here – whether Dawkins likes it or not – certainly seems metaphorical to the extent that it relies on a juxtaposition of similarity and difference with respect to 'normal' usage. In a nutshell, the similarity between 'everyday' and 'genetic' selfishness lies in the idea of the identity of the *ultimate* cause or producer of certain beneficial effects (here defined in terms of chances of survival) with the *beneficiary* of those effects; a major difference resides, for example, in the *proximate* cause of such self-benefiting effects, which in everyday discourse is presumed to be psychological or grounded in intentionality, etc.

Granted that the selfishness of genes is 'only' metaphorical, in other words, a fundamental question is what exactly separates genes from the sort of entity that can be considered selfish in a literal sense. Dawkins himself provides some of the answers. He stresses that genes are endowed neither with consciousness nor purposefulness.[289] This is significant because the ascription of selfishness – with the theory of moral value it tacitly presupposes[290] – normally implies intentionality on the part of the agent: unintended harm is not usually deemed blameworthy (except perhaps on the grounds of thoughtlessness) any more than causing the well-being of others involuntarily is thought to deserve moral praise. Though there is a sense in which genes might be considered to have the 'goal' of self-replication (to 'want' to get themselves replicated), the ascription of such intentionality to a sequence of nucleotides would generally be dismissed as an anthropomorphic projection.

Yet this begs the further question of *why* we refuse to attribute intentionality to a gene. Is it merely the lack of explanatory value of any such ascription (in that the presence or absence of a putative 'intention' does not provide us with any additional information about a successfully self-replicating gene)? Is it Ockham's razor at work? Or perhaps it is because the notion of a goal in turn implies 'interests' in the entity in question. But in what sense can it be said to be in the interests of a macromolecule to get itself replicated? What are the benefits – and to whom – of proliferation? How can it be in the interests of a selfish gene to multiply, to increase the number of replicas of itself in the world? The very suggestion provides Midgley with another opportunity to vent her spleen: 'in short', she fumes, 'because a gene cannot perpetuate *itself* but only likenesses of itself, the language of selfishness is so crashingly wrong that even Dawkins sees he will have to hide it under the table for a bit'.[291]

However, Midgley's argument fails to do justice to the ambiguous logic of selfhood we encountered in the Introduction. Here it emerged that selfhood – to the extent that it is understood merely in terms of self-replication – is best viewed as a collective phenomenon, comprising a population of entities; the individual unit cannot be separated from the lineage of self-replicating, evolving units from which it has emerged and which it in turn will be perpetuating. Within the context of an overarching 'lineage self', indeed, the replication of individual units can be regarded as a *mode* of self-maintenance; the lineage maintains itself through the replication of its component parts. Seen in this light, the question of the identity or non-identity of self-replicat*ing* molecules with the self-replicat*ed* molecules – of progenitor with progeny – remains undecidable; even allowing for mutation and change, it is simply a matter of words whether or not we choose to say that the original gene is 'the same as' its subsequent replicas. Dawkins himself, as we have seen, is ambiguous in the matter.

But perhaps the reason for our reluctance to ascribe intentionality to a gene is that the notion of a goal implies not only 'interests' but an ability to move oneself (to 'behave') in the *pursuit* of these interests. It is hardly surprising that we are disinclined to attribute self-movement and behaviour to a string of nucleotides. After all, the macromolecule in itself is just an inert, passive medium that lends itself to information storage (in both biological and non-biological contexts). In interacting with its environment (the cell that houses it), of course, it may be said to 'manipulate' the world to its own advantage. Some genes – characterized as 'jumping genes' – even seem to exhibit a form of mobility. But it remains to be seen whether this is really the sort of self-movement we are after.

Equally, perhaps, the question revolves around the extent to which it makes sense to speak of interests where there is no pleasure or pain, well-being or suffering. Here we are brought back to the distinction between entities that feature all three of the forms of intrinsic reflexivity analysed in the Introduction and those – like self-replicating macromolecules – that only feature one of these forms. As will become clearer in later chapters, it is only with self-maintaining, self-containing, self-transcending organisms – organisms capable of *actively* manipulating self and non-self for their own benefit – that meaningful non-self and the possibility of good and bad or better and worse (as evaluated by self and for self, not by a spectator or observer external to the system) start to become conceivable. The precise stage at which 'pleasure' and 'pain' are judged to come into being – perhaps with the emergence of directed behaviour, motility and choice – can remain unspecified for the time being. The point is that the self-replication of an informational macromolecule does not in itself seem to be a sufficient foundation for the appearance of interests in a world imbued with value.

Self-Like Macromolecules

Naked genes may fail to comply with the criteria for full selfhood (the three types of intrinsic reflexivity), yet they are selfish and self-like by virtue of their powers of self-replication. Their selfishness is best described as metaphorical insofar as they lack interests and intentions, as well as (arguably) the self-movement or 'behaviour' that grounds interests and intentions as something that can be *pursued*. Likewise, their selfhood is best described as metaphorical in that – even for self-replication – they are dependent upon the controlled conditions of the system of which they form a part, a self-contained microenvironment that they themselves help create and maintain. They lack the autonomy normally demanded for genuine selfhood. Without the living cell that houses them, they are simply quasi-inert molecular structures, with a tendency to degrade over the course of time.

But wait a minute: isn't this a rather overhasty dismissal of DNA? Mightn't the genome be regarded as the informational hub of cellular life in the way that the brain is the informational hub of animal life?[292] Just as one might be tempted to pinpoint the brain as the core location of the human self (arguing that you can replace an arm or transplant a liver, but if the brain were to be transplanted, the self would follow hot on its heels, like a shadow), so perhaps the genome is the true locus of cellular selfhood.

To assess this suggestion, we need to look a little more closely at the analogy between brain and DNA. Life on Earth has been described as a 'two-biopolymer' system, comprising both a genetic biopolymer (consisting of nucleic acid in the form of DNA) and a catalytic biopolymer (consisting of proteins). On the brain-DNA analogy, the genetic-catalytic dichotomy would correspond to the brain-body dichotomy. The importance of the genetic biopolymer is (at least) twofold: on the one hand, it stores information and bequeaths this information to progeny; on the other hand, it directs the biosynthesis of the second biopolymer, protein, which is responsible for most phenotypic traits involving structure, motion and catalysis.[293] Unlike DNA, however, the brain is itself a self-maintaining and ceaselessly self-modifying entity, in constant dynamic interaction with the rest of the body and the rest of the world: it needs to be fed with energy and nutrients to keep on functioning. By contrast, DNA is in large measure metabolically 'off-line',[294] decoupled from the muddle of metabolic self-maintenance. Although it has now been shown to have limited catalytic activity, it is generally considered 'a passive molecule, ideally suited for carrying genetic information but structurally monotonous and therefore functionally impoverished'.[295] The 'lifelessness' of an informational macromolecule makes it more akin to a book than a brain.

However, this analogy too is far from perfect. If the genome is a book, it is an interactive book from which the constituent paragraphs can on occasion be deleted and restored – switched off and on – as a function of the circumstances in which the book finds itself. Within a cellular context the expression of particular genes is thus 'regulated', for example, by mechanisms of chemical DNA modification (such as methylation). Given the prevalence of such gene regulation, DNA is not nearly as immutable, static and 'dead' as the 'book' metaphor might imply. As a consequence of its inherently modular nature, moreover, it is endowed with a remarkable capacity to undergo mutation without losing its physical identity. As Steven Benner has argued, a genetic biopolymer must be able to 'search "mutation-space" independent of concern that it will lose properties essential for replication. If a substantial fraction of the mutations possible within a genetic information system cause a biopolymer to precipitate, unfold, or otherwise no longer be recognizable by the catalyst responsible for replication, then the biopolymer cannot evolve'.[296] In this respect, the contrast with proteins is marked: 'the physical properties of proteins (including their solubility) can change dramatically upon point mutation within the mutation space allowed by the 20 standard amino acids'.[297] Unlike the great majority of organic molecules, a mutant of a DNA sequence generally maintains all the physical qualities that allow it to dissolve in water, replicate and serve as a basis for protein biosynthesis, endowing it with the potential to change but still persist – in other words, to *transform itself*. Adaptive flexibility of this sort may be regarded as a form of 'learning', but it is learning at the level of the population of evolving entities rather than the individual organism. This again evokes a notion of higher-level selfhood.

In our two-biopolymer world, catalysis and genetics seem to impose contradictory demands on the kinds of organic molecules that are required.[298]

Yet what about a molecule capable of both? We have already come across RNA as a macromolecule that can not only store and bequeath information but is also capable of catalytic biological activity – and that is conjectured to have paved the way for DNA in the early evolution of life. Embodying the reflexivity that allows it to catalyse its own self-replication, perhaps such molecules can be considered a form of minimal self in a way that does not apply to the relatively lifeless molecules characteristic of DNA. Indeed, a recent set of experiments has seen Tracey Lincoln and Gerald Joyce produce just such a minimally self-like system, in which RNA enzymes – known as *ribozymes* – are shown to catalyse the replication of RNA molecules, including the RNA enzymes themselves, from component oligonucleotide substrates.[299] The result is not merely a molecule that self-replicates but a system that sustains and indeed amplifies its self-replication, provided it is 'fed' with a steady supply of substrates. This is achieved by what is known as a 'serial transfer experiment' in which a portion of a completed reaction mixture is transferred to a new vessel with a fresh supply of substrates.

Despite their self-sustaining, self-replicating nature, such test-tube systems are unlikely to be considered living selves. The authors describe the system they have created as non-biological. To attribute this simply to the artificiality of the experimental set-up is to beg the question. It is not obvious why it might not be possible to generate a living self within a laboratory setting. The point, it seems, is rather the lack of any element of *self-containment*, for the 'containment' required to prevent the dispersal of the components – to channel the creation of order – is provided by the idealized 'vessels' in which the reactions all take place. The self-sustaining system is reduced to pure replication, indeed, since there is no need for it to encode the proteins involved in the provision of cellular membranes, viral capsids or any other biological structures or functions. The system's 'nutrition' – the substrate required for the production of the RNA molecules – is supplied by the experimenter, so there is no possibility or need for evolution on the part of the system, other than towards ever more frenetic replicative efficiency. Once the experimenter stops providing the substrate, the self-replication will gradually peter out. For such an RNA-based genetic system to come closer to living 'selfhood', it would have to encode functions beyond mere self-replication and harbour possibilities for discovering novel function.[300]

A major critique of an approach to life centred on genetic material has come from the proponents of autopoietic theory. In a penetrating analysis, Evan Thompson explicitly raises and then dismisses the possibility that replicative molecules such as RNA – in the form of the ribozymes that can catalyse their own replication – might be considered a form of minimal life:

> *Ribozymes are remarkable because they have both catalytic abilities like enzymes and the template specificity of nucleic acids. In a test-tube they rapidly evolve self-replicating patterns. If such molecules deserve to be described as living, then autopoiesis is not necessary to characterize a system as living. ... This line of thought presents a problem, however: it shifts tacitly from the individual, here-and-now account of life to the population and genetic-evolutionary account. A single RNA molecule does not catalyze its own replication and evolve by natural selection. Autocatalytic replication requires a large family of molecules, and evolution by natural selection requires a reproductive population.*[301]

Thompson is dealing with a different question from the one that is of prime concern here: his interest is life rather than selfhood, whereas the issue in the present context is *primarily* selfhood and the light that this can *secondarily* cast upon the nature and origin of life. Yet whatever our feelings about the aptness of the term 'life' as applied to such a system of ribozymes, what is evident is that it constitutes a chemical system that – if provided with the requisite 'food' and energy – is able not only to replicate its components but also to sustain itself as a self-replicating system. As such, it exhibits two of the three categories of intrinsic reflexivity required for full selfhood. Essential is that the system is endowed with the necessary double functionality incorporating both template-based replication and self-catalysis, and that the ensuing self-replication is sustained through time. Thompson's cavil is that 'life' would be ascribed, incipiently if at all, to the *evolving population* of ribozymes rather than to the individual molecules, whereas the autopoietic viewpoint he favours focuses on the *individual* cell in the here-and-now. To the extent that living selfhood may be considered both in terms of individual organisms and the overarching biosphere that both comprises and is presupposed by those same individual organisms, however, it seems dogmatic to restrict it to a single level of organization: say, to individuals as opposed to evolving populations of individuals. What is relevant on either level is the degree and form of intrinsic reflexivity.

A deeper problem, perhaps, is the failure to take into account the factor of self-containment and the unity of interest to which this gives rise. The experimental set-up provides a strange form of *allo*-containment in which the reactive vessel produces an artificial micro-universe whose molecular contents have no possibility of contact or interaction with other micro-universes unless the experimenter mixes them up. By contrast, if a free-living system of such molecules somehow came not only to catalyze its own replication but also to encode, for example, a differentially porous lipid membrane that could be thrown around itself to segregate itself from other such systems and allow the entrance and egress of nutrients and waste, we would have a much more self-like entity. And if this self-contained system then started *competing* with other self-contained systems in order to appropriate the oligonucleotide substrates necessary for its own nourishment, we would have behaviour akin to proto-selfishness. The practical plausibility of originally 'naked' genetic material subsequently 'learning' to throw a protective coat around itself will be examined when we look at various scenarios for the origins of cellular life.

Thompson's attack on genocentrism concentrates mainly on DNA rather than RNA; many of his most critical remarks are aimed at the doctrine's over-reliance on a vague and metaphorical concept of 'information' as an abstraction that pre-exists its actual expression or embodiment:

> *The deepest fault of the metaphor of DNA as program or information-store is that it implies a dualist framework of matter and information, one homologous to the computationalist and functionalist dualism of the mind as informational software and the brain as hardware. In both cases, processes that are intrinsically dynamic (temporally orchestrated), embodied (somatic and organismic), and embedded (necessarily situated in an environment or milieu) ... are projected into the reified abstractions of a genetic program in the cell nucleus or a computer program in the brain.*[302]

Thompson regards this dualism of matter and information as a surreptitious reincarnation of the age-old metaphysical dualism of body and mind, with the disembodied, informational, quasi-mental essence of the self now conceived as residing in a genetic program.[303] The roots of this new form of dualism have been traced back to the end of the 19th century, when August Weismann drew a distinction between the germ line and the *soma*. According to Weismann, the genetic material, which forms a continuous lineage dating back to the very dawn of life and is in principle immortal, orchestrates the synthesis of the visible organism through the application of the information it contains; the organism itself – the soma – is a mere vehicle, mediating between the germ line and the environment but with no significance beyond the propagation of the mutating but fundamentally timeless genome.[304]

At the heart of this view is the 'causal asymmetry doctrine', according to which 'extragenetic elements and processes in the cell depend on the genes, but the genes are not similarly dependent on them'.[305] In fact, it is now beyond question that genes – or genetic material – cannot be considered causally or logically *prior to* the cell in which they are housed and whose biosynthesis they orchestrate. DNA could not replicate itself without its specific cellular environment (most obviously, the crucial enzyme DNA polymerase), and there would be no cellular environment without the cellular membrane that holds self apart from non-self. Nor is DNA the only form of inheritance, as Weismann contended. So-called epigenetic inheritance systems include methylation patterns, structures such as the cytoskeleton,[306] and cell membranes.[307] So while it is true that these membranes (for example) could not exist without the genetic encoding of the products that constitute them, genes in turn could not exist without the membranes that enclose or contain the microenvironment they require – membranes that are themselves constituted on the basis of information not only from DNA but also from pre-existing membranes. The causality is not so much asymmetrical as characterized by the circularity of a self-synthesizing and self-containing organism.

The information-matter dualism that Thompson associates with genocentrism is in part a product of the virtues of DNA as an information storage system that is largely 'off-line' and uncoupled from metabolism and that maintains its structural integrity even in some of the most extreme conditions possible. This apparent exemption from material contingency may have mistakenly been taken to suggest some form of abstract or Platonic 'purity'. In fact, it is the foundation for its reliability as a mechanism of inheritance. So while life and selfhood are certainly conceivable without DNA inheritance mechanisms, DNA provides a conjunction of robustness and open-ended evolvability that contrasts with the fragility that would beset any system where compositional information was embodied solely in the persisting structures of the organism. Removed from a cellular context, of course, informational macromolecules may be as lifeless as desiccated bacteria, lacking any hint of an intrinsically reflexive process. In themselves they do not embody or impart living selfhood. For this, we also need the catalytic reflexivity that gives rise to self-maintaining structure and function.

Cosmopolitan Genes

Despite these misgivings about interpreting genetic material as a model or a mainspring of living selfhood, the impression of autonomy is made graphically manifest in the concept of 'cosmopolitan' genes,[308] a notion that conjures images of culturally versatile globetrotters in contrast with the provincial hillbillies tied to a genomic home community. A crucial idea underpinning the cosmopolitanism of these genes given to 'wandering among bacteria (or archaea) as environmental pressures dictate' is that of horizontal (or lateral) gene transfer *(HGT)*. This has been defined as 'the non-genealogical transfer of genetic material from one organism to another'.[309] In other words, HGT denotes a process in which one organism incorporates genetic material from another without the latter being the progenitor of the former; it contrasts with vertical gene transfer, in which genetic material is passed from progenitor to progeny.

HGT is believed to be rampant among viruses, as a result of which the integrity of viral genomes is in many cases especially fleeting. Such is the prevalence of HGT that a particular set of genes co-existing at a particular time in the form of a particular viral genome is unlikely to remain together for more than a few generations.[310] After this, the genome's identity as a persisting entity will have been undermined by the constant coming and going of genes in accordance with environmental exigencies. Given this modular fluidity of viral identity over the generations, the individual genes – or perhaps clusters of genes[311] – thus seem to be more 'self-like' than the vehicles they transiently inhabit, at least in the sense of being endowed with an enduring identity through successive self-replications.[312] This impression is underscored by the sheer wealth and diversity of viral genes.[313] Most of the world's genes are not stably ensconced within the microbial or metazoan genomes of the biosphere, it seems, but form a fluid part of the virosphere. The question of whether the virosphere in turn constitutes a self in its own right, or perhaps forms part of an overarching biospherical self, must be put on a back burner for the present.

Within the microbial world too, HGT is a pervasive and extremely influential force, mediated via three main mechanisms: transformation (naked DNA uptake from the surroundings); transduction (virus-mediated DNA transfer); and *conjugation* (the transfer of DNA between two cells, for example via *plasmids*). It is a powerful tool of adaptability, on occasion conferring upon the recipient cell benefits such as antibiotic resistance or the ability to take up new metabolites. 'In the wild', write Nigel Goldenfeld and Carl Woese, 'microbes form communities, invade biochemical niches and partake in biogeochemical cycles. The available studies strongly indicate that microbes absorb and discard genes as needed, in response to their environment. ... It is becoming clear that microorganisms have a remarkable ability to reconstruct their genomes in the face of dire environmental stresses, and that in some cases their collective interactions with viruses may be crucial to this'.[314] An early study calculated that between 1.6 and 32.6 percent of the genes in microbial genomes have been acquired by HGT rather than vertical gene transfer. Taking account of the cumulative impact of HGT on lineages, however, a network analysis of shared genes among 181 sequenced prokaryotic genomes has revealed that on average more than two thirds of the genes in the genomes in question have been involved in HGT at some stage in their history.[315] More specifically, it has been claimed that *E. coli* has acquired 18 percent of its genes by HGT from external sources since its divergence from its closest relative (*Salmonella enterica*) roughly 100 million years ago. Assuming a homogeneous rate of HGT per gene over time, this would imply that virtually the entire vertical phylogenetic signal in the *E. coli* genome would be wiped out every 500 million years.[316] HGT has also been shown to take place between organisms that are only distantly related, with substantial transfers (of as much as a quarter of the genome) occurring in both directions between bacteria and archaea.[317] Transfer is even known to have taken place between prokaryotes and eukaryotes, exemplified by one of the major enzymes involved in *glycolysis* in *E. coli*, which is believed to have an ancient origin in animals.[318]

However, not all genes are equally cosmopolitan, or inclined to partake in HGT. A distinction has thus been drawn between the 'core genome' of a species, which contains the genes common to all the strains of that species, and the 'dispensable genome', which comprises those present in just a subset of strains or even unique to a single strain.[319] Taken together, the core genome and the dispensable genome constitute what has been termed the 'pan-genome' – the total of all genes ever found in the species – which in many cases is thought to be orders of magnitude greater than any single genome. Most strains of *E. coli*, for example, harbour some 4,000–5,000 genes, whereas the pan-genome now stands at 16,000 genes,[320] and mathematical modelling suggests that it will continue to grow indefinitely – in other words, that each time a new strain is sequenced, new genes belonging to the dispensable genome will be found.[321] Whereas the core genome includes the genes responsible for the 'basic aspects of the biology of a species and its major phenotypic traits', the dispensable genome is taken to encode 'supplementary biochemical pathways and functions that are not essential for bacterial growth but which confer selective advantages, such as adaptation to different niches, antibiotic resistance, or colonization of a new host'.[322]

An alternative distinction that has been drawn is between operational genes (those involved in cellular 'housekeeping') and informational genes (those involved in transcriptional and translational processes).[323] Throughout evolution the former have been much more likely to be horizontally transferred than the latter. A theory called the 'complexity hypothesis' has been proposed to explain this discrepancy: whereas the products of the operational genes involved in cell maintenance are members of small assemblies that undergo few interactions with other molecules, the products of informational genes typically participate in large, complex systems comprising multiple molecular interactions.[324] In *E. coli*, for example, the process of translation requires the coordinated interactions of at least 100 gene products, and ribosomal subunit proteins typically interact with four or five other ribosomal gene products. Operational gene products, by contrast, may interact with just one other gene product. Since the probability of successful HGT will be strongly influenced by the number of successful interactions that a given protein must undergo, the fewer the number of proteins that a gene product has to interact with, the greater its chances of success will be. This is borne out by evidence showing ribosomal proteins to be among the most transfer-resistant genes.[325]

A key implication of the 'complexity hypothesis' is that the degree of HGT is closely linked to the degree of modularity of the gene product. As we saw in the Introduction, modularity is a mode of organization consisting of relatively 'self-contained' or autonomous subsystems that can be added to or subtracted from the organization of an entity without violating the integrity of the entity as a whole. Where the gene products are comparatively self-contained and thus interchangeable in relation to the whole, therefore, the gene itself is endowed with a greater licence to come or go according to the circumstances. Where the gene product forms a part of a complex subsystem, by contrast, the gene will be obliged to stay put, renouncing the possibility of cosmopolitanism.[326] The greater the autonomy of the gene product, the greater will be the autonomy of the gene.

It is not only genes that vary in their predisposition to engage in HGT; different types of bacteria and archaea themselves exhibit a variable inclination to swap genetic material horizontally. The 'open' pan-genome characteristic of genomically diverse species such as *E. coli* has thus been distinguished from a 'closed' pan-genome, where the sequencing of additional strains rapidly ceases to unearth any further genes. An open pan-genome is associated with 'species that colonize multiple environments and have multiple ways of exchanging genetic material', whereas the closed pan-genomes of (for example) *Bacillus anthracis* and *Mycobacterium tuberculosis* are typical of species that live 'in isolated niches with limited access to the global microbial gene pool'.[327]

The closed pan-genome is taken to an extreme in the context of endosymbiosis. This phenomenon is exemplified by the case of *Buchnera aphidicola*, an obligate intracellular symbiont that lives *within* the cells of greenflies, or aphids. The genomes of these bacteria are characterized by a number of features. On the one hand, they show enhanced mutation rates and a process of ongoing gene reduction, as the genome divests itself of functions that are provided by the host cell and are no longer required (including the genes for DNA repair that would put a brake on the mutation rate).[328] On the other hand, they display extreme stability or constancy in their genomic architecture, i.e. the structure and organization of the genome. Indeed, the *Buchnera aphidicola* genome has shown no chromosomal rearrangements or gene acquisitions over the last 50–70 million years, whereas the genomes of the closely related free-living bacteria *E. coli* and *Salmonella typhi* have been shown to be more than two thousand times more labile.[329] This resistance to change is itself a result of the elimination of sequences that facilitate the uptake and recombination of foreign DNA,[330] genes such as the *com* genes involved in transformation and the *rec* genes that mediate genome rearrangements. The protein machinery encoded by these genes provides the genetic flexibility or malleability that is indispensable for any autonomous or free-living cell, but is less important for an intracellular symbiont tucked away in an optimally stable environment inside its host. To renounce the ability to gain new genes in this way is to rule out the acquisition of new biosynthetic functions or metabolic diversity, irreversibly forfeiting the ability to adapt to a changing environment or annex new niches and thus relinquishing the possibility to associate with a new host or return to an extracellular existence.[331] In these circumstances it is the genome itself – or perhaps the species whose identity is determined by the genome – that comes to the fore as a stable unit of self-maintaining selfishness, dispensing with the adaptability and evolvability conferred by itinerant or cosmopolitan genes.

In spite of such cases, the prevalence of HGT has led to a questioning of the concept of 'species' in a prokaryotic context.[332] Whereas among eukaryotes the mechanisms of reproductive isolation (which prevent a human from successfully mating with a chimpanzee or a gorilla) provide a form of 'self-containment' that keeps the gene pool of different species separate and thus allows a species to be regarded as a form of unitary self,[333] among most prokaryotes HGT effectively undermines such self-containment, perforating the barriers that separate one species from another. Instead, multi-species communities of interacting microbes may be considered a basic functional unit of self-maintaining selfhood, while a broader view focuses on the domain of prokaryotes *in its entirety* (more or less) as sharing a common gene pool and thus behaving as a self with a seemingly unitary set of interests. As Sorin Sonea and Leo Mathieu put it, 'the entire prokaryotic genetic patrimony is thus available to most cells, resulting in a global biological communication system: a world-wide web of genetic information at the disposal of prokaryotic cells'. The outcome is what they describe as a 'global prokaryotic superorganism',[334] which flourishes on the basis of HGT between complex communities or consortia of bacteria, with constant selective pressures generating the best mixture of phenotypes available for the conditions in question. In such a situation, ask Goldenfeld and Woese, 'how valid is the very concept of an organism in isolation? It seems that there is a continuity of energy flux and information transfer from the genome up through cells, community, virosphere and environment'.[335] The world of prokaryotes harbours mutually inextricable levels of selfhood, ranging from the globetrotting gene to the individual bacterium, and from the microbial consortium to the prokaryotic domain in its totality. It is surely dogmatic and reductionistic to collapse selfhood into any particular rung on the scale.[336]

Selfish DNA

A gene may be as cosmopolitan as it likes – swapping host cells as the need arises – but when it comes to self-replication it will never be cosmopolitan enough to do without *any* cell whatever. The cell in turn depends upon the activity encoded in the entire genome, which not only has to be able to replicate, repair and package itself but is required for the continuing self-maintenance of the organism. The genome *as a whole* may thus be considered a more apt metaphor – or synecdoche – for unitary selfhood than the individual gene. At least for the duration of the individual lifecycle, the individual genes pull together for a common cause. Or do they? The notion of 'selfish DNA', which is not to be confused with the tautologically 'selfish' genes made famous by Richard Dawkins' early work, suggests otherwise. The 'selfishness' of such selfish DNA will be the focus of the remainder of this chapter.

One of the earliest papers on the subject, by Leslie Orgel and Francis Crick, defines selfish DNA in terms of two properties: 1) it arises when a DNA sequence spreads by forming additional copies of itself within the genome; 2) it makes no specific contribution to the phenotype.[337] Referring to selfish genetic elements, a more recent definition modifies this definition somewhat: 'First, the elements must have a transmission advantage relative to other DNA encoded in the organism. Second, the elements must be neutral or deleterious to organismal fitness'.[338] Selfish DNA is DNA that tends to replicate faster than the rest of the DNA in the genome, fulfils no apparent function for the cell and may actually be detrimental to it in some cases. Indeed, as the potential damage caused by selfish DNA has emerged over the years,[339] selfish elements have increasingly come to be understood as working, or as seeming to work, against the interests of the host organism and thus of the rest of the host genome.

The idea is that such DNA has not learnt the Hobbesian lesson that the best way to pursue one's own interests is to cooperate. This is selfishness not in the neutral, philosophical sense (which may manifest itself as altruism), but in the everyday sense of systematically putting 'self' before 'other' (regardless of whether or not this is a good idea). Dawkins refers to such elements as 'replicating fellow-travellers', 'rebels' and 'outlaws'.[340] They are rogue DNA.

Of course, if selfishness undermines the well-being of the host organism, it might indeed prove a somewhat risky strategy, indirectly subverting the element's own interests. As the tautological bottom line is that DNA cannot *ultimately* act against its own interests without sooner or later consigning itself to the dustbin of extinction, there are three main possible explanations for its persistence. The first is that the selfish element 'goes unnoticed' in the sense that its deleterious effects are not substantial enough to produce a selective disadvantage against the organism. This was the proposal put forward by Stephen Jay Gould, who claimed that 'self-centered DNA'[341] survives 'only because it makes no difference to bodies'; once it proliferates sufficiently to become a burden to bodies, the bodies in question will soon find themselves at a disadvantage in natural selection and take their self-centred DNA with them when they die or fail to reproduce.[242] The second possibility is that the organism – or the host genome – is successfully able to defend itself against the freeloading intruder, perhaps by developing mechanisms of immunity against DNA recognized as 'foreign'. A third possibility is that the 'selfish' element is not *really* – or with time *ceases* to be – selfish. The host organism may thus acquire a selective advantage by appropriating the beneficial effects of the selfish element's presence, 'taming' or 'domesticating' the initially wild outlaw. As Orgel and Crick put it, 'slightly harmful infestation may ultimately be transformed into a symbiosis'.[343] We shall look into these three alternatives after introducing some of the most prominent genetic rogues and rapscallions.

Selfish DNA may be put into three broad categories.[334] These are summarized in Table 1 below. A first category comprises what are termed 'allelic outlaws', amongst which are the 'segregation distorter' or 'meiotic drive' genes as well as so-called homing *endonuclease* genes and (arguably) green-beard genes. A second category refers to non-genomic or cytoplasmic DNA, i.e. genetic material that resides within the cell but not within the host genome. Such material, which includes mitochondrial DNA and plasmids, may pursue interests potentially at variance with those of the genome or the organism. A third category encompasses what Dawkins calls 'laterally spreading outlaws', also known as 'jumping genes' or 'mobile elements', where the gene's mobility consists in an ability to get itself replicated into new loci elsewhere within the same genome. This mobile DNA will be the main focus here, in part because 'mobility' is a trait that is closely associated with life and selfhood and that may be regarded as conferring a characteristic 'self-like' quality upon these sequences of nucleotides.

Category	Examples
Allelic outlaws	• Segregation distorters (meiotic drive genes) • Homing endonucleases • Green-beard genes (?)
Cytoplasmic DNA, non-genomic DNA	• Plasmids • Mitochondrial DNA
Mobile DNA, jumping genes, laterally spreading outlaws	• LTR retrotransposons: e.g. endogenous retroviruses • Autonomous non-LTR retrotransposons: e.g. LINE-1 • Non-autonomous non-LTR retrotransposons: e.g. *Alu* • DNA transposons: e.g. P element • Mobile bacterial retroelements: e.g. group II introns

Table 1: Overview of the main categories and examples of selfish DNA treated in the text

To start with the first category, a segregation distorter refers to a gene that has a 'positive selection coefficient at its own locus'.[345] In other words, two different *alleles* at a locus on a *diploid* individual's two chromosomes are not transmitted 'fairly' to the gametes (the sperms and eggs) produced by meiosis, but rather one of the alleles will be transmitted to a disproportionate number – more than half – of the offspring. Such a gene, or gene complex,[346] has been shown to exist in the genome of the fruit fly *Drosophila melanogaster*, as a consequence of which a fly inheriting the segregation distorter gene from one parent (i.e. on one chromosome) and the normal allele from the other parent (i.e. on the other chromosome) will transmit the segregation distorter to 95 percent of its offspring, instead of equitably to 50 percent. Such genes tend to proliferate quickly within a population in spite of the deleterious effects they may have upon the organism (for example by reducing fertility), resulting in a patent conflict of interests between the segregation distorter and the rest of the genome. In the context of such intragenomic conflict, it is thus in the interests of the genes in the rest of the genome to *suppress* segregation distortion, which they do by 'modifying' the phenotypic effects of the rogue gene. Indeed, genes endowed with the capacity to mitigate the outlaw's harmful effects on the organism can be expected to be favoured by natural selection. The result is what Egbert Leigh termed 'a parliament of genes': each gene 'acts in its own self-interest, but if its acts hurt the others, they will combine together to suppress it'.[347] The metaphor of 'parliament' (etymologically a place of speech or parlance) is of course as misleading as it is enlightening. It is instructive in its association with majority rule and the idea that for most possible selfish genes there will be many more genes whose collective interests are best served by curbing this selfishness. Yet it must not be taken to imply any sort of conscious choice or volition.[348]

The presence of segregation distorters has also been ascertained on sex chromosomes, resulting in a sex-ratio bias in the progeny of the individual that carries the gene. In describing the phenomenon, Matt Ridley portrays a scenario in which a gene on the *X chromosome* encodes a toxin lethal only to sperm carrying Y chromosomes; a man with this gene would have as many children as otherwise, but they would all be daughters. The gene would swiftly spread (for all his daughters would carry it), only easing off 'when it had exterminated so many males that the very survival of the species was in jeopardy and males were at a high premium'.[349] As a case of such 'sex-chromosome drive', Ridley cites a species of butterfly of which 97 percent of the population is female, but many other such examples are known, particularly among insects. In humans, the antagonism between the sex chromosomes – manifest in the greater potential of X chromosomes to evolve genes that are deleterious to Y chromosomes than vice versa[350] – has led to the much-announced shrinkage of the Y chromosome.

Unsurprisingly, such antagonism has lent itself to at times humorous anthropomorphism. Ridley himself does not conceal his amusement at the following depiction of the conflict in a 'sober and serious' academic journal: the mammalian Y chromosome, we are told, is 'likely to be engaged in a battle in which it is outgunned by its opponent. A logical consequence is that the Y should run away and hide, shedding any transcribed sequences that are not essential to its function'.[351] The martial imagery is unquestionably playful in tone, taking delight in the disorderly retreat of the wimpish Y chromosome. What underlies the metaphor is a statistical flourishing of one set of selfish entities at the expense of another, with the decline of the latter caused more or less directly by the flourishing of the former. Unlike human hostilities, however, this is a contention in which there are no intentions to kill or maim, no pain, anger or fear, and no pleasure in victory.

In addition to segregation distorters, two further kinds of allelic outlaws should be mentioned. The first consists of the homing endonuclease genes, which simply replace their rival allele with a copy of themselves. They do this by expressing an endonuclease – a pair of enzymatic 'scissors' capable of cleaving apart a sequence of nucleotides – that creates a break in their allelic counterpart; they then use their own nucleotide sequence as a template to repair the break. Particularly remarkable is another type of allelic outlaw, the so-called green-beard genes. These are of special note because they embody what has been termed 'gene self-recognition'.[352] For this to occur, the gene must exhibit 'pleiotropy', which means that it must code for multiple phenotypic traits: in this case, it must code for 'some perceptible feature of the organism' (say, a green beard, as whimsically proposed by Dawkins),[353] the perception or recognition of this feature, and a tendency to behave preferentially towards others in whom the feature is recognized. Though such a gene was originally deemed too complex to exist in nature, various versions of it have now been found. One striking example is a gene called *csA* which encodes a homophilic *cell-adhesion molecule* (CAM) anchored in the surface membrane of the cellular slime mould *Dictyostelium discoideum*, the species of social amoebae we encountered in the Introduction. Amoebae possessing this CAM not only 'recognize' one another (thanks to the *homophilic* nature of the CAM), but engage in cooperative streaming when they enter their social or multicellular phase, binding to one another and pulling one another along into the aggregation – and thus leaving the amoebae that lack this gene lagging behind.[354] As a result, amoebae with the gene are better at combining into aggregates than those without; the 'selfish' gene thereby fosters cooperation and generates 'altruistic' behaviour, albeit only among cells that share the gene and to the exclusion of those that do not.[355]

The second of the three categories of selfish elements is non-genomic (or cytoplasmic) DNA, in other words the DNA present in organelles such as mitochondria and in plasmids. Plasmids are circular DNA elements, thousands of which may reside in the *cytoplasm* of bacteria, as well as (less frequently) archaea and eukaryotic organisms. They are able to replicate independently of the host cell's chromosomal DNA and at the time of cell division they are distributed between the two daughter cells; they can also be transmitted from one host to another via horizontal gene transfer. Plasmids are considered selfish insofar they 'exploit the cell's metabolic machinery for their own reproduction'.[356] By way of recompense, they may provide their host with benefits such as antibiotic resistance, useful toxins and in general increased versatility. Unlike viruses, however, plasmids comprise *naked* genetic material and do not even encode the encasement proteins required by viruses for transfer between hosts. They are thus best viewed as entirely parasitic in terms of 'containment', relying upon their host cell for a suitable environment. Despite the apparent autonomy bestowed upon them by their capacity for HGT, they are no more (or less) *self-like* than any other successfully self-perpetuating sequence of naked nucleotides.

Mitochondria are membrane-enclosed organelles responsible for the provision of energy in the form of ATP in most eukaryotic cells; they are known as the cell's 'powerhouses'. They are widely believed once to have been free-living bacteria which subsequently entered into an endosymbiotic relationship inside what were to become eukaryotes, now residing within the cytoplasm of the cell.[357] Eukaryotic cells may contain many thousands of mitochondria, yet mitochondrial selfishness is largely restrained by the fact that all the mitochondria in an individual cell are genetically identical, inherited only from one parent, namely the mother in animals and the higher plants. This in itself, however, is not without further consequences, especially in plants. Since most flowering plants are hermaphroditic (i.e. produce gametes from both male and female reproductive organs) but the mitochondria are only transmitted via the egg cells, it is in the interests of mitochondrial genes to arrest the development of the male organs of the flower and redirect the resources used in making pollen towards the production of egg cells. As a consequence, mitochondrial genes have provoked 'cytoplasmic male sterility' in over 150 plant species, the best known of which is perhaps *Thymus vulgaris*, wild thyme.[358] Of course, male sterility is not in the interests of the chromosomal genes, which can be transmitted either by male or female gametes. The 'parliament' of chromosomal genes in *Thymus* thus conspires to suppress the effects of the mitochondrial genes, resulting in the restoration of male fertility.[359]

By comparison with plants, examples of selfish mitochondrial DNA (mtDNA) in animals are relatively few and far between, possibly because metazoan mtDNA is generally only a tenth the size of plant and fungal mtDNA. Even so, they are not unheard-of. In the nematode *Caenorhabditis briggsae*, deletion-bearing mutations of mtDNA have been shown to spread through natural populations despite the deleterious effects they clearly have on the organisms in which they occur.[360]

For those with qualms about attributing selfishness to mere sequences of nucleotides, it might make more sense to interpret this conflict – a conflict between intracellular subselves with divergent interests – in terms of the selfhood or self-interest of the mitochondrial 'cell' as a whole, as opposed merely to the DNA it contains. Selfishness would accordingly be ascribed to the mitochondrion rather than to the mtDNA within. After all, to the extent that mitochondria have their origins as membrane-bound (i.e. self-contained) endosymbionts, they are in many respects akin to other bacteria-derived symbionts such as *Buchnera*, which continue to be classifiable as cells in their own right. One might ask what *practical* difference might be associated with one interpretation as opposed to the other. We shall return to the issue of mitochondrial selfhood in Chapter 4.

Mobile DNA

Selfish DNA has so far come to light in the guise of allelic outlaws and cytoplasmic DNA. Allelic outlaws are 'selfish' in their propensity to multiply, yet they do not actually *do* anything except passively express a protein (i.e. get themselves transcribed) and get themselves replicated. The absence of anything akin to 'behaviour' or 'intention' keeps the notion of selfishness well within the realm of the metaphorical. The selfishness of cytoplasmic DNA seems less metaphorical through its association with intracellular subselves such as plasmids and mitochondria. The last of the three broad categories of selfish DNA may also seem more self-like, consisting as it does of mobile elements or 'jumping genes' that are able to proliferate 'laterally', i.e. by getting themselves replicated into new loci elsewhere in the genome that harbours them. Here I shall look briefly at some of the main types of mobile elements. These are referred to by the following (somewhat daunting) technical names:

- LTR (long-terminal-repeat) retrotransposons (also known as endogenous retroviruses, or ERVs)

- non-LTR retrotransposons, both autonomous (such as LINE-1) and non-autonomous (such as *Alu*)

- DNA transposons (such as the P element)

- group II introns, a class of mobile bacterial retroelements.

In each case, particular attention will be paid to their mobility, since this seems crucial to whether or not they appear 'alive' or 'self-like' and may well have a bearing upon our temptation to anthropomorphize or attribute volition to entities that nonetheless remain ultimately bereft of 'interests' or 'intentions'.

LTR Retrotransposons

A first prominent category of alien selves – mobile units of genetic selfishness – that have infiltrated the human genome is provided by LTR *retrotransposons*. These are believed to have their origins in retroviruses, which are RNA viruses (such as HIV) that replicate in the host cell through a process called reverse transcription: the retrovirus employs a *reverse transcriptase:* (RT) enzyme to convert its own RNA genome into a DNA copy, which it then incorporates into the host's genome (as the 'provirus'). Once in the host's genome, the viral DNA will either remain latent or – under certain circumstances – be transcribed by the cell as though it were the cell's own DNA, producing new RNA genomes as well as the viral proteins that serve to prepare and package the viral RNA for release from the cell as new virus particles; these *'virions'* are protected by a capsid and enclosed within an envelope composed of lipids acquired from the host cell's *plasma membrane.*

Retroviruses typically contain three genes, *pol, gag* and *env*: *pol* codes for enzymes such as reverse transcriptase and the integrase that allows its genetic material to be integrated into the host genome; *gag* codes for the structural protein components of the viral capsid; while *env* encodes specific cell-surface receptors for the membrane envelope, enabling the virus particle to bind to and then enter its subsequent target host. The parasitic or non-autonomous selfhood of viruses will be the focus of the next chapter. For the present, suffice it to say that a retrovirus shows what might be called *indirect* intrinsic reflexivity in that it *finds itself* a self-maintaining and self-containing microenvironment (albeit provisionally), *gets itself* replicated, and even *procures itself* a capsid and a lipid membrane endowed with its own cell-surface receptors, granting it the mobility to leave the cell with a view to 'reinfecting' a new cell. In these terms, the selfhood of a retrovirus might be termed *secondary*. It is parasitic upon the primary selfhood of the cell it infects.

Retroviruses usually infect somatic cells (exemplified by the HIV virus, which targets cells of the immune system), but from time to time germ-line cells such as gametes are also affected. On rare occasions, the organism in question may survive germ-line infection of this sort, thus incorporating the retroviral genome as an integral part of its own genome. This process of 'endogenization' converts what was an exogenous retrovirus (XRV) into an endogenous retrovirus (ERV) that will in turn be inherited by the organism's own progeny.[361] Human ERVs (HERVs) – i.e. the relics of such retroviral infections – make up between five and eight percent of the human genome, comprising some 98,000 elements,[362] more than four times the number of protein-coding genes.

In theory, ERVs have the ability to replicate either via an extracellular or an intracellular pathway, i.e. either as viruses or as transposable elements.[363] The former is known as 'reinfection' and involves the ERVs using the *env* gene to exit their present host cell and re-enter another. The latter is associated with the mutation and inactivation of the *env* gene and involves retrotransposition, a process by which the DNA element transcribes itself into RNA and then uses reverse transcriptase to convert the RNA back into DNA that can be re-integrated at a *new locus* within the genome of the original host cell. Such elements are known as LTR-retrotransposons. Notably, it is the presence or absence of a functional *env* gene that determines the form of the element's mobility, i.e. whether it moves from cell to cell – from host to host and even from species to species – like an infectious virus or whether it restricts its movements to within the cell, hopping from one locus on the genome to another. The evidence suggests that there is a general progression over time from reinfection to retrotransposition.[364] The latter is possibly a more efficient mechanism, permitting the mobile element to bypass the risks and contingencies of a hostile extracellular environment and evade some of the organism's innate antiviral defences. The safety and predictability of the cellular environment may make the transition from inter-host (and possibly cross-species) mobility to intracellular mobility a worthwhile evolutionary gamble.

The other main tendency over time is the increased mutation caused by host DNA replication, as a consequence of which most sequences of retroviral origin are degenerate, lacking both the *env* and *gag* genes required for reinfection and the *pol* gene required for reverse *transcription*. Noteworthy is the frequent use of the metaphor of 'life' and 'death' in descriptions of the phenomenon. The implication is that ERVs capable of reinfection or retrotransposition are in some sense *alive*; perhaps it is the element of mobility – whether intracellular or interhost – that confers the impression of a living entity.[365] By the same token, it is only when they are actively 'jumping' that *retroelements* can be termed 'selfish' in the sense of possessing a transmission advantage over the rest of the organism's DNA. Once inactivated, by contrast, they cease to be alien 'selves' within the host genome, becoming mere 'corpses' – or possibly acquiring a function within the larger genomic self.

Whatever form its movement may take, mobile DNA is understood by some to be 'quick' in the etymological sense of functionally active and animated. As John Goodier and Haig Kazazian note, 'the seminal discovery that genomes contain pieces of DNA capable of moving to new locations challenged prevailing notions of genes as static "beads on a string" passed essentially unchanged from one generation to the next'.[366] The question whether one should speak of *self-moving* elements confronts us with further logical conundrums of the sort we have already encountered. Mobile DNA does at least *partially* cause its own movement (it encodes the reverse transcriptase and the integrase), though strictly speaking the 'movement' it causes is the movement of an identical replica. Once again, the degree of qualitative or numerical identity of the nucleotide sequence(s) in question is best left as indeterminate.

Non-LTR Retrotransposons

A second category of mobile DNA is composed of the strictly intracellular non-LTR retrotransposons, which are present in even greater measure than HERVs within the human genome and date back to the origins of multicellularity some 600 million years ago[367]. Having multiplied spectacularly over the last 160 million years of mammalian evolution, they now occupy roughly a third of the human genome, i.e. over ten times more than protein-coding genes. The only currently active – or selfish – autonomous non-LTR retrotransposon in humans is L1 or LINE-1 (standing for 'long interspersed element'): this is the most successful mobile element in the human genome by mass, with more than half a million copies of it constituting approximately 17 percent of the total genome.[368] A very sizeable proportion of our genome thus has its origins in parasitic non-self that has selfishly used the cellular setting provided by our genome as a vehicle for its own proliferation.

A full-length L1 element is roughly six *kilobases* long, though most such elements have been rendered inert – bereft of active selfhood – by mutations, truncations and internal rearrangements. While the vast majority of the half million copies of L1 are no longer active, however, an average human genome is estimated to contain approximately 80–100 elements that are 'retrotransposition-competent', six of which (known as 'hot L1s') are presumed responsible for most cases of currently occurring L1 retrotransposition. As a result of these few highly active L1s, retrotransposition in the human germ line occurs at an estimated rate of rather less than one event per 20 births. By contrast, mice are thought to have as many as 3000 active L1 elements in their genome.[369] In general, there are greater controls on L1 transcription and retrotransposition in somatic cells (to minimize the harm caused to the host organism), whereas these control mechanisms are less strictly enforced in the germ line.[370] At the same time, there is also evidence of a reactivation of L1 retrotransposons in a variety of human cancers.

Because LINE-1 encodes the enzymes required for its retrotransposition (specifically a RNA-binding protein for transport and chaperoning, an endonuclease, and a reverse transcriptase), it is described as 'autonomous'. As a parasite, of course, this autonomy or self-sufficiency is severely limited; it depends on the environment provided by the host, and it is likely to depend on host proteins to complete retrotransposition.[371] In its autonomy, however, it contrasts with what are known as *non-autonomous* non-LTR retrotransposons (also SINEs or 'short interspersed elements'), the most prolific of which is the *Alu* element. This is the most successful mobile element in the human genome in terms of copy number; there are over a million *Alu* copies in human DNA, amounting to 11 percent of the genome. *Alu* retrotransposition events are thought to take place at a rate of one per 30 births and to have resulted in over 20 known cases of genetic disorders.[372] Yet the typical *Alu* element is just 300 bases long, and as it does not encode proteins – and thus cannot produce its own endonuclease or reverse transcriptase – it is forced to rely on the enzymatic machinery provided by L1 in order to achieve mobility. It is for this reason that *Alu* has been referred to as 'a parasite's parasite'.[373] With its autonomy reduced to a minimum, its 'selfhood' – if the term can be used – amounts to a disposition to get itself multiplied, i.e. transcribed and then reverse-transcribed to a new location in the genome.

DNA Transposons

The mobility of the selfish 'retroelements' encountered so far entails being transcribed into an RNA intermediate, then reverse-transcribed back into DNA and reintegrated into the genome, thus consisting of a so-called 'copy and paste' mechanism. DNA transposons, by contrast, are excised from one site and integrated into another by a 'cut and paste' mechanism of transposition, which requires the operation of a so-called transposase enzyme encoded by the transposon.[274] The transposase removes the transposon from its original site and inserts it into the target site, which tends to be reasonably close to the original one (less than 100 kilobases away), whence the term 'local hopping' (though more distant hops are also possible). When they jump in this way, DNA transposons leave behind a double-stranded DNA break that is mended by the cell's own DNA repair pathways, which in most cases involves replacing the missing sequence at the newly vacated site with homologous material.[375] The net result is an increase in the number of copies, allowing the element to spread rapidly through a population. Again, mobility is associated with multiplication; it is as though I were to make an identical replica of myself – or have one made – and dispatch either 'it' or 'myself' (whichever is which) to a new location elsewhere.

DNA transposons constitute roughly three percent of the human genome, but are believed not to have been active or mobile since the early days of primate evolution some 37 million years ago.[376] However, the proliferation of which transposons are capable is exemplified by an element some 3000 bases in length, called the P element, which has spread through the fruit fly species *D. melanogaster* within a matter of decades. Such elements are patently selfish in that they proliferate with respect to the other genes in the host genome, yet provide no apparent benefit to their host organism and can even have damaging effects such as partial sterility.[377] Indeed, they may even prove to be *too selfish for their own good*, replicating themselves out of existence. This is known to occur in small populations, where rapid invasion of P elements usually ends up with the extinction of the stock. In larger populations, some form of negative regulation of the transposition activity generally prevents this extreme from coming to pass. Maynard Smith and Szathmáry propose two possible regulatory mechanisms.[378] The first is the existence of parasites-within-parasites, akin to *Alu* in their embodiment of ever more indirect, streamlined, minimalistic selfishness. The *D. melanogaster* genome thus contains not only autonomous P elements, but also *non-autonomous* elements that do not code for the transposase required for transposition. On their own, these elements do not 'jump', but they can still be mobilized if there are functional elements that encode transposase elsewhere in the genome. The presence of such parasites-within-parasites reduces the ability of the autonomous selfish element to amplify, thus indirectly helping the host organism.

A second, more important mechanism limiting the proliferation of selfish DNA, suggest Maynard Smith and Szathmáry, is a product of selection at the level of the organism itself.

> *A selfish element that is too successful at multiplying within a cell will kill its host, and kill itself at the same time: it has killed the goose that lays the golden eggs. This can cause selfish elements to evolve mechanisms that limit their own growth. The process can ... be illustrated by the P element.*

> The element codes for two proteins: the transposase and a regulator protein that limits transposition. In the absence of the regulator, transposition is so frequent that it kills or sterilizes the fly, and in so doing destroys the P element it carries.[379]

Aided by natural selection, it seems, the selfish P element collectively 'learns' the lesson that unrestrained selfishness is not in its own interests. Successful selfishness – the tautological or philosophical selfishness of a self that persists in time – is self-regulated selfishness.[380]

Mobile Bacterial Retroelements

Retroelements such as retrotransposons are found in nearly every eukaryotic species, and in many cases they make up a considerable proportion of the genome: over 40 percent of the human genome, and more than 60 percent of the maize genome. Most bacteria, by contrast, do not contain a reverse transcriptase, and when they do, the RT-containing elements usually represent less than one percent of the genome as a whole. In general, this reflects lower overall levels of mobile DNA in bacteria. Three families of bacterial retroelements are currently recognized. Only one of these families – group II introns[381] – clearly displays the autonomous mobility characteristic of genetic selfishness.

Group II introns are selfish elements comprising a reverse transcriptase encoded within a catalytic RNA unit, or ribozyme. They are found in bacterial genomes, as well as in the mitochondrial and chloroplast genomes of lower eukaryotes and higher plants.[382] The term 'intron' (derived from 'intragenic region') refers to a sequence of DNA within a gene (or the corresponding RNA transcript) that is removed by a process called splicing when the mature RNA is being produced. In other words, it is a non-coding sequence that splits genes up into fragments in the genome. In eukaryotic cells, introns are removed by a complex of macromolecular machinery called the spliceosome. The group II introns found in bacteria, by contrast, are *self-splicing*; that is, the intron-containing RNA molecule has the catalytic ability to splice *itself* out of the RNA sequence, effectively functioning as a pair of scissors that can excise itself from the surrounding RNA. As well as being a self-splicing ribozyme, however, the group II intron is also a retroelement capable of the retrotransposition that enables it to become more widely dispersed in the genome.[383]

These extraordinary self-splicing retroelements are selfish to the extent that their mobility as retrotransposable elements lends them a certain tendency to propagate within the genome. In practice, this mobility seems to be moderate, and studies of various strains of *E. coli* have suggested that cellular mechanisms may actively impede it. The introns themselves also incorporate mechanisms that regulate transposition and minimize the damage done to the host. An example is their apparent tendency to insert themselves in 'benign' sites, i.e. *between* as opposed to *within* genes (unlike eukaryotic introns), or within other mobile elements,[384] where they are unlikely to cause harm by disrupting a major function. Indeed, one theory of the origin of group II introns – i.e. how the retroelement and the self-splicing ribozyme came together in partnership – is that they arose when a retroelement incorporated self-splicing activity in order to reduce to a minimum the detrimental effects of its transposition on the host, effectively splicing itself out of harm's way.[385] Whatever the measures they have taken to mitigate the effects of their selfishness, they have certainly been successful in pursuing their own interests over hundreds of millions of years. Genome sequencing has revealed that approximately a quarter of bacterial genomes house group II introns.[386]

The Containment of Alien Selfishness

Despite their antiquity, group II introns are a far less pervasive presence in prokaryotes than retrotransposons in eukaryotes.[387] Even though only a few score of the half million L1 copies in humans are retrotransposition-competent and just a handful are 'hot', the effects of L1 have been particularly significant. Comparisons of the human genome with the chimpanzee genome suggest that over 10,000 species-specific insertions of transposable elements have taken place since the species diverged six million years ago, most of which have either been L1s or non-autonomous elements trans-mobilized by L1s.[388] Such mobile elements are considered selfish insofar as they act in their own 'interests' (in the limited sense of self-multiplication) but against the interests of their host. In what remains of this chapter, I shall ask whether these elements are necessarily so harmful and selfish or whether their selfhood – and thus their selfishness – may come to be subsumed *within* that of their host. Perhaps they are not as rascally as they seem, but confer overt or covert benefits upon the organism; perhaps they allow themselves to be domesticated in order to serve the 'evolutionary interests'[389] of the genome that carries them.

Certainly, their potential deleteriousness was what was first emphasized by researchers and commentators. An apparently straightforward consequence of the ongoing accumulation of mobile elements is an increase in genome size. L1 and *Alu* elements alone are estimated to have contributed roughly 750 megabases to the human genome, including over eight *megabases* since our divergence from the chimpanzees. It is not clear whether (or to what extent) a big genome is *in itself* necessarily a bad thing, putting organisms at a 'metabolic disadvantage'[390] relative to those with smaller, 'junk'-free genomes. The case of the single-celled eukaryote *Amoeba proteus*, endowed with a colossal genome over 100 times bigger than our own,[391] suggests that size is neither an insurmountable handicap nor a particular benefit.

Other effects are more obviously detrimental. One such effect is insertion mutagenesis,[392] which is known to produce genetic disorders and occurs when elements such as LINE-1 or *Alu* transpose themselves or are transposed into protein-coding or regulatory regions of the genome. Roughly 0.3 percent of all human mutations are thought to be attributable to insertions of L1 elements or non-autonomous elements such as *Alu*. An equally considerable threat to genomic stability is posed not by retrotransposition itself, but by the endonuclease protein, i.e. the molecular 'scissors' required by L1 elements for reinsertion into the genome, which can wreak havoc by causing breaks in chromosomal sequences. Further effects are insertion-mediated deletions and a heightened risk of chromosomal rearrangements.[393]

At the same time, cells themselves are endowed with a variety of control mechanisms that prevent or restrain L1 transcription and retrotransposition, and that thus keep in check the threat of the selfish subselves they harbour. For a start, selfish elements seem to be 'contained' in the sense of restricted to certain parts of the genome, or excluded from others. In most vertebrates, for example, they are conspicuous by their near-absence from what are known as *Hox* clusters, i.e. areas of the genome rich in the *Hox* genes that play a critical role in the embryonic development of metazoans. Other regions with development-related genes also show a robust correlation with the exclusion of selfish elements.[394] Seemingly 'refractory' to invasion by selfish elements, such regions are perhaps simply *too important* to permit an accumulation of potentially unruly intruders.[395]

Where present, it is the *activity* of the selfish retroelements that needs to be curbed. Foremost among the control mechanisms for suppressing such activity is a process called cytosine methylation, which involves attaching a methyl group (consisting of carbon and hydrogen atoms) to cytosine, one of the four main bases in DNA and RNA. By methylating the *promoter* of a selfish element (i.e. the part at which transcription is initiated), the element is effectively 'switched off', meaning it can no longer be transcribed. Methylation has traditionally been thought to serve as a way of switching off genes that are not required in specific tissues at specific times and thus as a device for differentiating one cell from another within an organism, but the evidence now suggests that its primary function may have been the suppression of parasitic nucleotide sequences.[396] This raises the question how elements such as ERVs or L1 copies are 'recognized' as non-self and earmarked for suppression,[397] for it is not clear by what means the epigenetic information embodied in the methylation pattern is passed from generation to generation. Self-defence mechanisms normally presuppose the possibility of distinguishing 'self' from 'non-self', yet there is a sense in which endogenized retroviruses and retrotransposons – selfish though they may be – can be considered to have become part of the host 'self'.

Notable in this context is that cancer – itself an archetypal manifestation of rebellious 'selfishness' perpetrated by cells that proliferate counter to the interests of the organism as a whole – is associated with a *de*methylation of L1 sequences, unshackling the selfish DNA and giving it free rein to 'express' itself. Here too, however, retrotransposition appears not to be as frequent as more general chromosomal instability. It may be that not even cancer cells can survive with retrotransposons fully unfettered.[398] If one of the few retrotransposition-competent or 'hot' L1s is demethylated, a gene called *TP53* is likely to step in as a second line of defence to induce apoptosis, i.e. programmed cell death. In *somatic* cells, it is only if *TP53* is mutated – mutation of this gene being one of the hallmarks of cancer[399] – that L1 really does 'come back from the grave'.

In addition to methylation and apoptosis, a further self-defence mechanism used for the control of transposable elements is RNA-induced silencing. This process subjects selfish DNA to post-transcriptional regulation, using short (ca. *22*-nucleotide), non-coding RNA molecules such as so-called microRNAs (miRNAs) as templates to recognize and bind with complementary sequences in the messenger RNA (mRNA) transcribed from selfish elements.[400] Once these small RNAs have recognized a specific sequence in an mRNA molecule and have bound to their target site, they repress the translation of this mRNA into protein, possibly by promoting its degradation.[401] Regulatory miRNAs of this sort are themselves thought to have their origin – at least in part – in transposable elements,[402] which have thus been 'tamed' or 'domesticated' to perform the function of identifying similar tell-tale sequences of nucleotides. What were initially selfish elements are appropriated for the good of the whole, serving as a device for the detection and subsequent neutralization of kindred selfishness.[403]

Two of the three broad explanations for the persistence of selfish DNA in host organisms have already emerged. The first is that – although such DNA is indeed selfish and harmful to its host – it is not harmful enough to be 'noticed' by natural selection. The case of the blindly selfish P element replicating itself into oblivion illustrates the point; the P element has to curb its selfishness to serve its own interests. A second, closely related alternative is that the putatively selfish DNA *would* be selfish if not 'contained'[404] *by the organism*, which uses an array of cellular mechanisms to keep it in check. One might even picture the selfish element as 'allowing' its selfishness to be restrained in this way – for the sake of the host, but ultimately for its own sake too.

The third (related) alternative is that selfish DNA is *in fact* not really selfish, i.e. that 'selfish' is no longer the right word except in the tautological sense in which any replicatively persisting or proliferating element must in some way be successfully pursuing its own (purely replicative) 'interests'. On this view, apparently 'selfish' DNA may end up benefiting its host, providing it with otherwise unavailable functions and increasing its evolutionary options. To the extent that transposable elements and host genes may seem to have forged a relationship that is 'symbiotic'[405] or mutually beneficial, the word 'selfish' is no longer strictly accurate, for symbiosis implies that their interests – and thus their 'selfishness' and their 'selfhood' – are *shared*. As Goodier and Kazazian write,

> *the notion of transposable elements as merely molecular parasites, benign at best and powerful mutagens at worst, that hijack cellular mechanisms for their own selfish propagation, [has] seemed incomplete to some biologists. Given that evolution tends to dispose of that which is useless and harmful for a species, it was curious that the genome should be cluttered with so much 'junk.' Now we understand that genomes have coevolved with their transposable elements, devising strategies to prevent them from running amok while coopting function from their presence. Repetitive DNA, and retrotransposons in particular, can drive genome evolution and alter gene expression. Evolution has been adept at turning some 'junk' into treasure.*[406]

Of course, there must be no temptation to imagine a narrative progression from initially selfish elements to reformed altruists, who – like the stock misers of comic drama – come to see the error of their selfish ways and the benefits of benevolence. There is no decision involved, let alone loyalty, gratitude or sense of justice; there is simply the self-evident truth that *ceteris paribus* mobile elements that happen to help their host will fare better (collectively or statistically) than those that do not, while hosts that chance upon a way of making use of their guests will also fare better than those that do not. But how is this done? While it is clear that transposable elements depend upon host genes for transmission from one generation to the next, how have the host genes benefited from the association?

In fact, originally selfish elements can exert a wealth of beneficial effects on host genes and genomes. They are particularly prominent in gene regulation. We have already seen how mobile elements may be exapted as non-coding genes in the case of the small RNA molecules (e.g. miRNAs) that function as translational repressors. These regulate the activity not only of other transposable elements but also of host genes. Nor is this the only role that such elements play in the control of gene expression. A considerable proportion of the promoter sequences (i.e. stretches of DNA that initiate transcription of a particular gene) in the human genome contain sequences derived from transposable elements (TEs),[407] and hundreds of human genes are thought to be regulated by elements generated by the insertion of TEs. Retrotransposons have been associated with the repair of DNA damage as well as with possible roles in coping with stress produced by heat, radiation, heavy metals and poisons.[408]

In addition to these and other general benefits conferring regulation and flexibility, ancient retroelements are also known to have provided specific protein-coding sequences that now perform vital physiological functions.[409] One possibly TE-derived enzyme of remarkable significance is telomerase, which in most eukaryotes is responsible for replication of the ends of germ-line telomeres, the protective buffers of apparently meaningless nucleotide repeats at the termini of chromosomes. In the absence of telomerase, each time a cell duplicates, the ends of its telomeres are shortened, eventually leading to cell senescence and mortality (once the protective buffer is worn away). This is what happens, to varying degrees, in most somatic cells. In the germ line, by contrast, the enzyme telomerase regenerates the telomeres, thus repairing the chromosomal termini and endowing germ cells with the 'immortality' that enables them to reproduce generation after generation through the eons.

The enzyme in question is a ribonucleoprotein, or RNA-protein complex, the protein component of which is similar in sequence and function to reverse transcriptase, while the RNA subunit acts as the template for synthesis of the telomeric DNA. Though not universal, the presence of telomerase is widespread in eukaryotes (e.g. in protozoa, fungi and mammals), suggesting that its use for telomere maintenance may date back at least to the earliest eukaryotic cells. At present, however, one can only speculate on the precise phylogenetic relationships between telomerase and other categories of retroelements such as retroviruses, retrotransposons and group II introns.[410] One theory is that telomerase itself *gave rise to* parasitic retroelements or shared a common ancestor with them, while another equally feasible phylogenetic tree situates non-LTR retrotransposons as the oldest elements, with telomerase and retroviruses diverging from this lineage. This interpretation has been taken to imply that 'in early eukaryotes the important cellular function of telomere maintenance was fulfilled by recruitment of an RT [reverse transcriptase] gene from a parasitic mobile element'.[411] It seems that an originally selfish element may have ended up bestowing 'immortality' upon the eukaryotic germ lines in which it has taken up residence.[412] In the process, it has also rather cannily bestowed 'immortality' upon itself.

The acquisition of transposable elements may also be associated with various forms of combinatorial flexibility and versatility, conferring patent benefits not upon individual cells but upon multicellular aggregations of cells (such as humans). Three such forms have attracted special attention. A first example relates to the possible contribution of L1 retrotransposition to the genomic plasticity of neurons. Such a phenomenon, recently observed both in mice and humans, challenges the notion that L1 mobility is restricted to the germ line (to enhance its proliferation) and excluded from somatic tissues such as the brain (in order to minimize potential harm to the host). Indeed, while retrotransposition-competent elements are in general heavily methylated and transcriptionally inactivated in most somatic cells, there is evidence that in some neurons L1 retrotransposition occurs at relatively high levels of frequency both during embryonic development of the central nervous system and subsequently during adult *neurogenesis*. It may be stimulated by environmental factors such as voluntary exercise and mediated by a mechanism that transiently releases the L1 promoter from epigenetic suppression.[413]

The high level of L1-induced mutagenesis in neurons implies the possibility of genotypic diversity among neurons, broadening and diversifying the range of behavioural phenotypes available. It is noteworthy that the hippocampus – a region of the brain associated both with memory and adult neurogenesis – seems particularly predisposed to L1 retrotransposition,[414] which reinforces this conjectured link with neural plasticity. Restricted to somatic cells, of course, adaptive L1-induced mutations will not be inherited by an individual's offspring. However, if the mechanism that generates this diversity has an effect on fitness, it is the diversity-generating mechanism – i.e. controlled L1 retrotransposition – that will be subject to natural selection; if the effect is noticeably positive, this domestication of alien selfishness will flourish.

Another mechanism of combinatorial diversity – this time within the adaptive immune system of vertebrates – is also thought to have its origins in a mobile selfish element. Current consensus has it that the roots of our highly flexible adaptive immunity go back to a DNA transposon that 'hopped' (perhaps from a microbe or virus) into the genome of an ancient jawed vertebrate several hundred million years ago.[415] Characterized by its ability to 'cut and paste' DNA, this jumping gene is presumed to have inserted itself within one of its host's genes, possibly a gene already involved in the immune system. With time, it would have endowed subsequent generations with the ability to shuffle their DNA about, giving rise to the technique of 'V(D)J recombination' responsible for generating the diversity characteristic of the body's B cells, each with its own specific antibody.[416]

The trick is that the genes encoding the variable regions of the B cell's antibody proteins comprise multiple copies of three different types of gene segment (known as V, D and J), one of each of which is 'chosen' and the rest of which are excised and discarded; the 'chosen' segments are then pasted together to form the mature B cell (now with its 'personalized' antibody). The proteins involved in excising the superfluous segments and helping repair the remaining ones are coded by two transposon-derived genes known as the recombination-activating genes, RAG1 and RAG2. Significantly, in their diversity-generating function, RAG1 and RAG2 no longer undertake to reinsert the DNA they have excised (they no longer 'paste' it elsewhere). This ability has presumably been suppressed by modern cells in the course of taming the original transposon and preventing it from causing undue harm.[417] As with the microRNAs encountered above, therefore, the 'containment' of alien selfishness involves a process in which (a) self is invaded by foreign self, i.e. by exogenous selfish genetic material; (b) this foreign self is integrated or endogenized into the host self, resulting in the convergence of its selfish interests with those of the host; and (c) it eventually becomes part of the host self's self-defence apparatus.[418]

One further case of TE-derived diversity stems from mobile group II introns. As noted above, these are present in relative moderation in bacteria and are endowed, moreover, with the capacity to splice themselves out of the RNAs that contain them. Their presumed eukaryotic descendants, by contrast, are a much more obtrusive force. The coding sequences of most animal and plant genes are interrupted by a profusion of introns, and no fully-fledged eukaryote is known to be completely without them.[419] Each human gene contains an average of seven introns, which far exceed the protein-coding regions in their total length.[420] Known as spliceosomal introns, they are thought to date back to the origin of eukaryotes,[421] when the endosymbiotic fusion between an archaeon and the bacterial ancestor of the *mitochondrion* would have resulted in the subjection of the archaeal genome to an invasion of mobile introns from the bacterium. Today's eukaryotic introns are no longer either mobile (they must have eventually 'calmed down' for the host to survive) or self-splicing. The splicing is now carried out by a cellular system called a spliceosome, which may itself derive from – or share a common ancestor with – the splicing equipment of group II introns. Like other selfish elements, therefore, jumping introns have been 'tamed' with the passage of time, and this domestication has opened up a whole new dimension of biological complexity and versatility. 'As soon as jumping genes no longer posed a threat,' writes Nick Lane, 'the introns themselves turned out to be a boon. One reason is that they enabled genes to be cobbled together in different and novel ways, giving a "mosaic" of potential proteins, a major feature of eukaryotic genes today. If a single gene is composed of five different coding regions, the introns can be spliced out in different ways, giving a range of related proteins from the same gene'.[422] More than 70 percent of human genes are known to encode at least two proteins.[423]

In all these cases of diversity and versatility, the mobile element is not primarily 'helping' the individual cell; it is at a collective level that help is being provided. In the case of the combinatorial immune system, for example, the heterogeneity of the individual B cells yields 'cognitive' benefits at a systemic level, in the form of a heightened capacity to 'recognize' possibly antagonistic non-self. Likewise, the apparent activation of transposons in response to stress produces benefits at a collective level. As Goodier and Kazazian put it, 'with so many ways that insertions of transposable elements can influence genes, a modest increase in transposition could drive evolutionary change at a rate not possible by random nucleotide mutation. This could advantage a species faced with a deteriorating environment and the need to adapt or die'.[424] In these terms, the logic underlying the transposition of selfish elements is akin to the adaptive mutagenesis or hypermutation shown by bacteria in challenging conditions; the welfare of individual cells is sacrificed for the sake of a possible adaptation that will either benefit the multicellular organism or augment the survival chances of the species. The 'evolvability' generated by such genetic mobility thus brings us back to the dialectic interplay of self-maintenance and self-change that is essential to selfhood. The counterpoint, of course, is provided by the stress-free life 'enjoyed' by endosymbionts such as *Buchnera aphidicola*. Given an environment as unchanging as an intracellular one, self-change may become an unnecessary risk, so self-seeking intruders should be kept at bay.

Mobile elements have accordingly been described as achieving 'a balance between detrimental effects on the individual and long-term beneficial effects on a species through genome modification'.[425] There is a temptation to ask whether the evolutionary success of selfish elements – typified by the proliferation of L1 in the human genome – should be attributed to the advantages they confer upon a genome, cell, organism or species (suggesting that they are not *really* selfish), or regarded as a phenomenon achieved *despite* their underlying selfishness. This false dichotomy alerts us once again to the dangers of applying the concept of 'selfishness' in any sort of quasi-psychological sense. The tautological bottom line is that a successful retrotransposon is one that has succeeded in pursuing its own selfish 'interests' (and continues to do so); circumstances will have dictated whether this in fact involved a greater or lesser degree of cooperation with its host.

These conceptual difficulties are partly a result of ascribing the notion of selfishness to entities – sequences of nucleotides – that fulfil, at most, only one of our three criteria of full selfhood, namely self-replication, while failing to comply with the criteria of metabolic self-maintenance and self-containment. These are not entities capable of taking action (of genuinely moving themselves) in response to a world suffused with value, thus making the attribution of 'interests'[426] inherently problematic. The question remains how far 'blind' proliferation – bereft of any awareness of this proliferation, any pleasure taken in it or pain endured as a result of it – can be said to be in the interests of anyone or anything. Or perhaps one should reverse the perspective. Perhaps replication is *the* primordial interest, and pleasure and pain merely ancillary by-products, carrots and sticks subsequently 'designed' by natural selection with a view to fostering the survival and replication of selfish entities. This might at least be what a virus would claim. So how far can a virus be said to be any more self-like than a selfish gene or sequence of DNA?

IV.

*Viruses and other
Selves-Within-Selves*[427]

Coat-Wearing Genes

Preliminary Considerations

A virus may be thought of as a selfish sequence of nucleotides that encodes its own coat. This coat is not just any old coat, but a protein coat specifically encoded – made-to-measure – by and for the sequence of nucleotides that wears it. Known as a capsid, the viral coat constitutes a form of self-containment, (arguably) fulfilling a second of our three categories of intrinsic reflexivity[428] and making a virus seem much more self-like than mere selfish DNA. By means of its capsid, viral genetic material in some sense knows how to protect itself from the elements. As we shall see below, however, there are important differences between capsids and cellular membranes, and the existence of virus-like entities that go naked through life (viroids and plasmids, as well as the capsid-less RNA viruses that seem to have mislaid their coat) undermines any straightforward association between capsids and selfhood: why should merely donning a capsid turn a sequence of nucleotides into a more fully-fledged self?

The underlying question is how far viruses really do satisfy our criteria of intrinsic reflexivity. While they may be characterized in terms of an ability to get themselves replicated or proliferate, the absence of a metabolism *of their own* seems to rule out what we have termed self-maintenance (in the form of self-production and adaptive self-modification), which requires an ongoing input of energy and in turn grounds the possible possession and pursuit of 'interests' beyond mere replication or proliferation. But are such considerations in themselves enough to disqualify viruses from full selfhood?

After making a number of introductory points on the intrinsic reflexivity of viruses, the present chapter will examine the notion that viral selfhood might best be viewed as collective in nature rather than inhering in the individual viral particle; it will look at some of the most minimalistic viruses currently known to exist; it will consider the role of the capsid in viral identity and identifiability; and it will analyse the extent to which the parasitic dependence of a virus on its cellular host for replication and maintenance precludes the ascription of living selfhood. It will ask, in other words, how far and in what senses viruses can be said to be or have selves.[429] It will then turn to examine other self-like entities – both pathogens and mutualists – that reside within and depend upon host cells.

A first major difference between viruses and the minimal self-maintaining selves (cells) we encountered in the Introduction is that viruses fall into the category of self-assembling rather than self-organizing entities.[430] What this means is that in the appropriate (aqueous) conditions certain viral particles can *spontaneously assemble themselves* from their molecular RNA or DNA and the protein subunits that make up the capsid. No 'fuel' (in the form of ATP) is required for this self-assembly to occur; it is simply the system naturally gravitating towards its state of lowest energy. Once the particles are assembled, moreover, no further energy is needed for their structure to remain intact. In a classic series of experiments undertaken in the 1950 s,[431] the tobacco mosaic virus (TMV) was shown to reconstitute itself from a solution of its purified RNA genome and the protein subunits that comprise its rod-shaped capsid; the reconstituted virus particles were indistinguishable from the original virus in terms of both morphology and infectivity. Self-assembly has also been demonstrated in various 'spherical' plant viruses, which spontaneously tend to form a capsid that is often – though not always – icosahedral in form.

Seen in this light, a virus may seem little more self-like than any other self-assembling crystal, an inert and lifeless aggregation of dumb molecules. Other things being equal, its persistence is not in jeopardy (immediately at least), and it does not need to perform any work – it does not need to *strive* – to maintain itself against the threat of entropy. Yet the distinction is not as clear cut as this. For a start, self-assembly also plays an essential role in cellular structure, and even *phospholipid* membranes have been shown to be capable of forming by such a process.[432] Nor can *all* viral assembly be explained solely in terms of straightforward self-assembly. While all the information required for the relatively simple cases of self-assembling rods or icosahedrons is contained in the protein subunits, other viruses such as *T4 phage* – which infects *E. coli* bacteria – require additional 'morphopoietic factors' encoded by the viral genome to generate an astoundingly complex structure that incorporates a head, neck and tail, as well as tail fibres and a base plate (see image below).[433] Furthermore, viral existence is not just a matter of self-assembly (followed by a full stop; end of story) as in the case of a crystal. Functional viral particles are endowed with *infectivity*, which embraces a capacity to move (or at least get themselves moved), 'recognize' a host and deposit their genetic material inside the host for replication. Once in place within their host (and having duly divested themselves of their coat), these lifeless assemblies of molecules turn into insatiably self-replicating intruders, rapacious parasites that usurp the host's 'self' for their own ends. This duality of almost robotic or machine-like (un-'squishy'[434]) lifelessness and the misappropriation of host 'self' makes viruses deeply disquieting. The consensus, nonetheless, is that life is cellular, and that viruses are not strictly alive. Parasitic as they are upon host cells, their ontological status is secondary or subordinate.

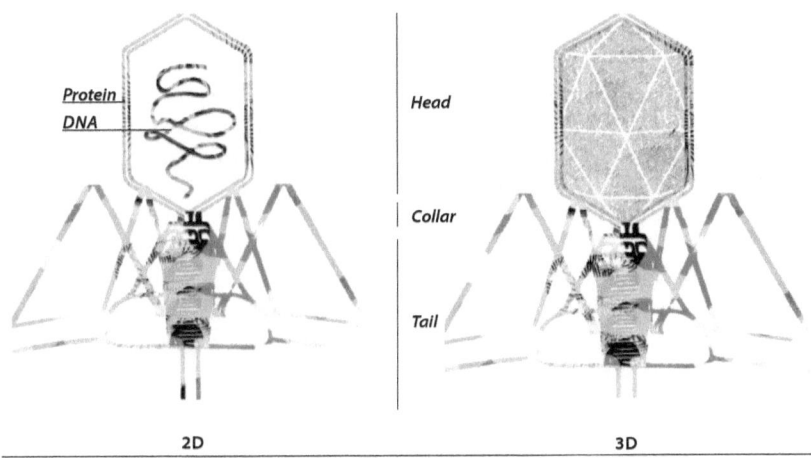

Figure 4: T4 phage

If life is understood in autopoietic terms, for example, viruses are located emphatically outside the realm of the living. Evan Thompson thus argues that a virus fails to fulfil the autopoietic criteria for being alive:

> It does not produce from within itself its own protein coat or nucleic acids. Rather, these are produced by the host cell in which the virus takes up residence. ... Viruses are not dissipative systems or metabolic entities. They do not exchange matter or energy with the environment. Outside of a host cell a virus is completely inert and is entirely subject to the vicissitudes of the environment. Inside a cell it makes use of the cell's metabolism, but it has no metabolism of its own. A virus is thus a fundamentally different kind of physicochemical entity from both prokaryotic cells or bacteria and autocatalytic proto-cells.[435]

Such 'cytoplasmic' schools of thought emphasize the self-organizing and self-maintaining nature of living entities. Lacking any form of carbohydrate metabolism or protein synthesis, it is claimed, viruses cannot be considered alive. Even when they have genes that encode such functions, these are believed to have been obtained by horizontal gene transfer,[436] implying a chance acquisition or even something poached or purloined as opposed to inherited from the ancestral lineage.

Proponents of a 'nucleocentric' or gene-centred point of view, by contrast, counter that viruses comply with a conception of life that is based on replication, heredity, adaptation and evolution.[437] To put it in terms of selfhood, viruses can be regarded as living selves precisely to the extent that they selfishly proliferate and collectively evolve, differing from the selfish elements encountered in the last chapter only in their coat and the extracellular life-cycle this permits. In itself, such a definition may be understood to open the door to computer viruses, which can also be designed to produce evolving copies of themselves. Essential to RNA and DNA viruses, however, is their inextricable association not with computers (which – as things stand – are neither selves nor living entities) but with the cells of the biological world (which *are* selves and living entities), an association manifest in the shared nucleic acids, proteins, lipids and complex sugars of which they are composed. It is through this association with living selves that viruses vicariously come to selfhood and life. Of course, such an argument in turn undermines the *primacy* of viral selfhood, which betrays itself as conditional upon the living cells with which it is necessarily associated.

At this point, the insistent cytoplasmist may thus respond with a grammatical twist: viruses neither self-replicate nor evolve, but *are evolved* by cells (in the way that human technology is evolved by humans).[438] By the same token, viruses have been said to be 'produced but not self-produced'[439]; more recently, it has been posited that viruses are 'not living, but lived entities'.[440] With this grammatical switch from reflexive activity to passivity (i.e. from producing oneself to being produced, from *auto*-production to *allo*-production), viruses are seemingly denied the intrinsic reflexivity that I am here proposing as essential to selfhood. But perhaps this is excessively drastic. An alternative grammatical description of what is going on instead involves a switch from direct to indirect reflexivity: a virus may not replicate on its own, but it *gets itself* replicated; once in a cell, it *gets itself* maintained; prior to leaving the cell, it *gets itself* coated. The reflexivity – and thus the selfhood – is indirect rather than direct, but we would be missing something out if we insisted that it was not there at all. Grammatically speaking, a purely passive voice omits any form of *agency*.

Yet can we really speak of agency in the case of a virus? Does a virus 'act'? The causative verb 'get' in the notion of a virus 'getting something done to or for itself' is worryingly vague. Can the notion of agency be stretched to include the encoding of instructions in a genome, plus the coupling of these instructions to an environment in which they are 'appropriately' followed? It is certainly true that the individual viral element does not need to bring about any change *within itself* in order to achieve the effect in question. It gets itself replicated (or coated, etc.) simply by *being what it is*, for example by its possession of certain conformational or configurational attributes. This may seem a very strange form of agency, tenuous enough to be indistinguishable from the purest passivity. Yet it perhaps implies the occurrence of a 'directed' interaction between the viral particle and its circumstances, as opposed to the random dance of a feather at the mercy of the wind. Or perhaps the agency occurs at a collective level? Perhaps the versatile appropriateness of the virus's conformational attributes manifests the agency of a *viral lineage* or *community* adapting itself to its constantly changing environmental circumstances?

The question of agency can also be broached in terms of a virus's mobility, the power of self-movement that is such a widespread feature of living selfhood. This proves to be equally indeterminate in viruses. Though unable to fly or propel itself through its environment, the viral particle, or virion, relies on being able to *get itself moved*; newly made virions have to be able to find, recognize and infiltrate a host to have any chance of further replication. This does not involve the ATP-powered activation of motor proteins such as *myosin* or kinesin characteristic of individual cells, or the contraction of muscles that underlies animal movement. Yet the example of small RNA plant viruses that need to move beyond their site of synthesis to find new cells for replication shows the tenuousness of the distinction between activity and passivity. These RNA viruses encode so-called 'movement proteins' that bind to the genetic material itself to construct *ribonucleoprotein complexes*; these in turn attach themselves to specific host proteins that otherwise serve to move endogenous macromolecules from one cell to another within the plant. The host's own transport molecules thus provide the virus with the mobility on which it depends.[441]

Some RNA viruses also encode 'coat proteins' which – by mechanisms as yet unknown – are thought to regulate and facilitate longer-distance trafficking through a plant's vascular system.[442] Again, the relationship between host and virus is parasitic: the viruses are effectively 'hitching a lift' on the host plant's internal communication system. This enables them to get from A to B without any requirement for combustive fuel to power themselves. Such mobility involves neither work (on their part) nor self-propulsion; there is no reason or need to postulate consciousness, choice or planning. Yet their selfhood, however indirect it may be, depends upon this genetically embodied capacity or disposition to *get themselves moved*, a disposition that is essential to their continuing existence as self-replicating entities. Viruses that fail to encode the requisite 'movement proteins' will rapidly cease to be self-perpetuating selves. Viral lineages that consist of such viruses will peter out.

Irrespective of these grammatical niceties, we may still harbour a residual feeling that viruses are simply too small – or that they lack the necessary complexity – to be regarded as selves in any interesting sense. Such a view is partially undermined by recent discoveries of giant viruses such as mimivirus, pandoravirus and pithovirus, some of which exceed many bacteria in terms not only of their size as viral particles but also their genome size and the number of genes they possess. Even so, lacking genes for virtually anything except making new copies of themselves and helping those new copies of themselves to make yet more new copies, viruses in general seem to be microscopic distillations of the purest replicative selfishness, bereft of the metabolic 'flame' that keeps itself ablaze within even the simplest self-maintaining cell.

Collective Viral Selfhood

As with the selfish genetic elements examined in the last chapter, one response to such considerations may be to view viral selfhood as a collective phenomenon. In these terms the individual, capsid-wearing virus particle is inseparable from the lineage of self-perpetuating and rapidly mutating viruses that it is perpetuating and of which it is a perpetuation. Noteworthy here is the transitory nature of viral identity, which is constantly sapped by the high levels of genetic recombination and horizontal gene transfer (HGT) – both among viruses and between virus and cellular host – characteristic of the viral world.

We have already seen how the prevalence of HGT subverts the notion of 'species' in the context of bacteria and archaea.[443] Whereas eukaryotic species can be regarded as unitary entities that are in large measure 'self-contained' by the reproductive isolation that prevents the members of one species from successfully producing offspring with members from another species, the HGT that prevails among prokaryotes undermines the identity that connects ancestors to descendants over the course of generations. For viruses too, if enough genes or gene clusters have been swapped with other lineages, it becomes impossible to establish whether any particular virus particle belongs to the 'same' lineage as a potential progenitor virus from which it might seem to have inherited many of its other genes. As transient assemblages of genes that come and go at the environment's behest, viruses have been deemed unlikely to maintain any particular assemblage for more than a few generations,[444] and such viral lineages may be felt not to endure long enough to qualify as a 'self', i.e. as an entity that maintains itself through time. Of course, it is beyond question that viruses *do* form identifiable lineages; officially recognized taxa are characterized by 'similar suites of genes'.[445] The point is that the selfhood of a self-transforming self may be a function of continuity, which allows of gradations, rather than numerical identity, which is all or nothing. Our ignorance of the *degree* of continuity in a rapidly evolving viral lineage does not mean that there *is* no continuity, but reflects our own cognitive limitations. Given these practical difficulties, however, a more meaningful unit of self-maintaining selfishness is perhaps to be found at a higher level.

As with bacteria, in other words, one might posit the existence of selfhood – i.e. of a unitary and in some sense self-maintaining, self-reproducing, self-contained entity – less at the level of the individual particle or the 'lineage' or 'species', than at the level of a global viral superorganism encompassing the 'virosphere' in its entirety.[446] The idea would be of a vast, common genetic pool accessible (either directly or indirectly) to all viruses, the ubiquity or 'cosmopolitanism' of viral genes implying that it is the environment that selects what is where, and when.[447] But things are not quite as straightforward as this. For a start, it might be more accurate to refer to distinct *pools* accessible to all viruses of a particular *class* or *family*, given that viruses can indeed be categorized according to various criteria, including not only their genetic material (DNA or RNA), but also the single- or double-strandedness of this genetic material and its linearity or circularity. Further distinctions can also be drawn in terms of replication mechanisms, genome size and host range (most fundamentally: bacterial, archaeal or eukaryotic). Virologists have thus differentiated a number of putatively monophyletic groups of viruses, i.e. groups all of whose members are descended from a single ancestral virus and comprising all the descendants of this ancestor. These include positive-strand RNA viruses, which are common mainly in animals and plants; small DNA viruses and plasmids; tailed bacteriophages or *Caudovirales*, which are hosted by bacteria; nucleocytoplasmic large DNA viruses (NCLDVs), such as poxvirus and mimivirus; and the retroid viruses, amongst which are many of the retroelements discussed in Chapter 3.[448]

At issue, therefore, is the unit of selfhood: is it the viral world as a whole, or is it the various subsets of viruses or viral genes within it? Most notably, the genes of the tailed bacteriophages are believed to constitute a single pool in their own right,[449] and there are other viruses, such as certain thermophilic archaeal viruses, that seem to be 'disconnected from the rest of the virus world',[450] apparently having no genes at all in common with any other viruses. So can we really speak of a 'selfish' virosphere – where 'selfish' incorporates the notion of a self-perpetuating unity – if this seems to consist of a number of varyingly-sized genetic puddles rather than a single pool?

One answer emerges from the work of Eugene Koonin and colleagues, who have highlighted the existence of what they term 'viral hallmark genes'. Even though there is no universal gene common to all viruses in the way that genes for ribosomal RNA are universal among cellular organisms, the hallmark genes are essential genes spread among the most widely dispersed viral lineages and categories. One of the most widespread such genes encodes the so-called jelly-roll capsid protein, which forms the main subunit of many viral coats; this protein 'crosses the boundary between RNA and DNA viruses and spans an astonishing range of virus groups, from some of the smallest positive-strand RNA viruses to the nucleo-cytoplasmic large DNA viruses'.[451] The hallmark genes are associated with the most basic aspects of viral existence, such as replication and the formation of the virion, and date back, it is conjectured, to a pre-cellular stage in the evolution of life, when a primordial gene pool would have provided a framework in which intense gene mixing could take place among divergent groups of virus-like selfish elements.

Of course, this is only one of various hypothesized scenarios for the origin of viruses and the origin of life.[452] As Koonin and Valerian Dolja have put it, however, the most parsimonious explanation for the existence of these hallmark genes – which possess only distant homologues in cellular life-forms yet compose a network spanning much of the viral world – is that they became isolated from cellular genomes at an early stage in the evolution of life. Ever since, they have 'comprised the framework of the temporally and spatially continuous, expanding virus world'.[453] Understood in these terms, the hypothesis of a primordial gene pool provides today's fragmentary virus world with a unitary, selfish origin from which it has evolved in self-transforming continuity.

Questions still remain. Even granted the existence of a selfish virosphere, does it make sense to conceive of it as an entity separate from the biosphere, which after all provides each virus with its ecological niche and host? More generally, how should we characterize this relationship between virosphere and biosphere? Various options come to light. The first is that the virosphere and the biosphere together form the true, overarching global self, for their quasi-symbiotic interdependence is too deep-seated for either one to be singled out at the expense of the other. Considered thus, the ultimate unit of selfishness is the 'biosphere + virosphere'.[454] In genetic terms, indeed, the biosphere may even seem to be the subordinate partner, playing second fiddle to the heaving viral behemoth. This is suggested by the sheer abundance of the viral world as measured by the number of nucleic-acid-containing particles that compose it, which is currently believed to exceed that of prokaryotes approximately fifteen-fold.²⁵⁵ The global population of tailed phages alone is thought to be more than 10^{30}, this group of viruses in itself constituting an absolute majority of the organisms on Earth.⁴⁵⁶ Most of the genetic information in the bio-virosphere is thus present in viral rather than cellular genomes, with cellular genes seemingly awash in a sea of viral genes. Miniscule as viruses are, however, their *biomass* amounts to only five percent of the prokaryotic biomass.⁴⁵⁷

It might alternatively seem as though the biosphere and the virosphere form not one, but two conflicting selves, their relationship one of relentless antagonism. Viral lysis – the mechanism by which lytic, or virulent, viruses rupture the membrane and break out from the cell in which they have replicated themselves to satiety – is estimated to eliminate over one fifth of the bacteria inhabiting the world's oceans every day.⁴⁵⁸ Yet this destructive parasitism is not the only strategy available to viruses: so-called temperate viruses pursue a 'lysogenic' strategy, whereby the phage's genetic material is integrated into the host bacterium's genome in the form of a 'prophage'.⁴⁵⁹ Persisting viruses of this sort replicate *with* the host bacterium, together with which they thus form a stable association that – as we shall see – may confer lasting benefits on the bacterial identity (though the threat of lysis may remain). By the same token, the horizontal gene transfer that is mediated by viruses constitutes a crucial mechanism of adaptive flexibility, a flow of genetic information that enhances the ability of prokaryotic communities to respond to environmental contingencies in an appropriate and versatile way. Seen in this light, the relationship between virosphere and biosphere is one of complementarity rather than competition. The two components of the global self cooperate to further their shared interests as a single entity.

Such talk of a self-perpetuating or self-maintaining self at the level of the bio-virosphere is beset with controversy. Not only is any such global self a singularity, thus lacking the repeatability required for scientific experiment and analysis, but we are *part of* this singularity, depriving us of a view from outside or above.⁴⁶⁰ Given these epistemological limitations, we simply cannot know whether the apparent self-regulation of the bio-virosphere is merely a fleeting accident (which will last until it stops) or an intrinsic property of the system itself (which carries the teleological implication of a self that in some sense *seeks* or *tends* to perpetuate itself, i.e. a universalized *conatus*).⁴⁶¹ Having briefly touched upon the theoretical possibility of this global viral self, therefore, it is time to turn to other, more down-to-earth ways in which viruses may be, or have been, deemed self-like. The first relates to viruses in their minimalist form as mere 'selfish elements'; the second involves the capsid as a manifestation of viral selfhood; and the third concerns the virus as part of a virus-host 'symbiotic' self.

The Streamlined Selves of Small Viruses and Viroids

Most simple viruses may be considered selfish genetic elements endowed with an extracellular stage during which they don a capsid and in some cases a lipid membrane envelope or two. The clearest conceptual link between the selfish elements analysed in the last chapter and capsid-encoding viruses is provided by retroviruses, the RNA viruses that replicate in the host cell by converting their own RNA genome into a DNA copy and then inserting this into the host genome. The retroviral strategy is then for this viral DNA, or *'provirus'*, to get itself transcribed as part of its host's genetic material, generating new RNA genomes as well as the viral proteins required for packaging the newly made viral RNA into capsid-protected and membrane-bound virions for subsequent release.

Essential to the successful activity of retroviruses is possession not only of genes encoding reverse transcriptase and the structural proteins necessary for the viral capsid, but also a gene called *env*, which codes for specific cell-surface receptors in the membrane envelope, allowing the virion to recognize and bind to its new target host and penetrate the cell by a process of membrane fusion. A functional *env* gene is what endows the retrovirus with infectivity and distinguishes it from selfish retroelements such as the LTR-retrotransposons, which dispense with the extracellular stage and adopt retrotransposition as their mode of proliferation. In effect, the latter have merely modified their mechanism of mobility, avoiding the uncertainties associated with extracellular transportation and reinfection and limiting their movements to intragenomic hopping. In both cases, we are dealing with *minimalist* forms of proto-selfhood, devoid of 'interests' other than brute proliferation; there is no need to invoke pleasure, pain or the faintest spark of consciousness. In the case of viruses with an extracellular stage, however, the pursuit of these proto-interests does demand what might seem to be a 'search' – albeit one based on a strange form of *indirect* or even *passive* mobility – for a new site where proliferation is possible.

The logical simplicity of such minimal selfhood is demonstrated by the case of Rous sarcoma virus (RSV), which is not only a retrovirus but was also the first known *oncovirus*, causing sarcomas – i.e. cancers of the connective tissues – in chickens.[462] RSV has just four genes. Three of them (*pol*, *gag* and *env*) code respectively for reverse transcriptase, capsid proteins, and the specific envelope glycoproteins that enable it to infect new host cells. However, it is additionally endowed with a gene called *src* (pronounced 'sarc' and short for 'sarcoma'), which codes for an enzyme called a tyrosine *kinase*.[463] The kinases are a class of enzymes that function as molecular switches within a cell, modifying other proteins by attaching phosphate groups to them; attachment of such a phosphate group to a protein is equivalent to an 'on' switch, effectively activating the protein's function. In certain cases, a cascade effect is produced, as one kinase activates another kinase, which in turn activates yet others (and so on), and on occasion a chain reaction of kinase cascades can end up provoking the unregulated mitosis of the cell, causing it to split into genetically identical daughter cells. The enzyme encoded by *src* is just such a kinase, unleashing a 'volley of phosphorylation'[464] and a cascade of activation. The result is cancerous cell proliferation.

By inducing accelerated mitosis and causing cells to switch from a non-dividing to a dividing state, the retrovirus is effectively circumventing the need to 'search' for a new host in which to replicate; it simply gets the host cell to multiply, and the new copies of the cell will of necessity include new copies of the parasitic virus. As with retrotransposition, therefore, the unpredictability associated with an extracellular stage of viral existence is at least partly avoided. A similar strategy – accelerating the rate at which a host cell divides into daughter cells – is pursued by another oncovirus, human papillomavirus (HPV), which infects human epithelial cells (i.e. skin and mucous membrane) and has come to the public attention as a cause of cervical cancer in women.[465] Essential to its capacity to cause cancer is not only that it speeds up cell division, but that one of the proteins it encodes inactivates the gene known as *TP53*, the tumour suppressor gene that induces *apoptosis* (cell suicide) in cells recognized as damaged or abnormal. By indirectly promoting the 'immortality' of its host, HPV thus selfishly promotes its own immortality.

The four genes of Rous sarcoma virus (by contrast with the more than 20,000 genes in the human genome) represent a near-minimum for viral selfhood. Equally abbreviated selfhood is also embodied by the *bacteriophage* MS2, a single-stranded RNA virus endowed with a genome that is a mere 3.6 kb in length. The four genes that constitute this impeccably streamlined proto-self encode a capsid protein, a lysis protein, a *replicase* protein, which associates with three host proteins to form an enzyme that catalyses the replication of RNA from an RNA template, and a protein called A2, which is needed to enable the virion to attach itself to the *E. coli* bacterium that it targets as its host. The 'selfhood' of MS2, in other words, consists in finding and getting itself into its host, replicating itself, donning its coat, and wasting as little time as possible in getting itself back out again, with a gene earmarked for each function.

In fact, the streamlining can go even further. One of the smallest viral genomes known at present is the single-stranded DNA porcine circovirus (PCV), two types of which are known, PCV1 and PCV2, the latter associated with a newly emerging wasting disease that infects pigs. PCV boasts a genome of less than 1.8 kb and just two major protein-coding sequences, *rep* and *cap*, which carry out, according to Annette Mankertz, 'the two elementary functions of a virus, genome replication (rep) and packaging (cap)'. These mini-viruses can be regarded as a 'paradigm for the reduction of the molecular equipment to the absolute essentials'.[466] Other commonly encountered viruses are scarcely bigger: the human rhinovirus responsible for the common cold is provided with just ten genes, yet this 'haiku of genetic information'[467] is enough to enable it to invade our bodies, outwit our immune system, and produce a runny nose and a hawking cough for further dispersal.

One of the best known of these highly streamlined viral selves is the RNA bacteriophage Qβ, a parasite of *E. coli*. This phage also has four genes, which between them code for a replicase (which combines with three host-encoded proteins to form the RNA-dependent RNA polymerase required for viral RNA replication), a coat protein and a protein responsible for host lysis as well as host recognition and entry. Yet as a series of experiments by Sol Spiegelman and co-workers has famously shown, even this is not the most streamlined viral self possible. What Spiegelman and his colleagues did was to put the phage Qβ, together with its own specific replicase and some raw materials (RNA nucleotides) and energy, into a series of test tubes and monitor the reaction.[468] The result was not only the *replication* that occurred as the phage used the supply of nucleotides to make more copies of itself. Over the course of a sequence of test-tube generations,[469] the RNA was seen to *evolve*, becoming faster and faster at replication and shorter and shorter in length. As it evolved, the Qβ phage was mutating into a slimmer, more 'efficient' version of itself.

This happened because the ideal world of test-tube experimentation (i.e. a world of spoon-fed *allo*-containment) had created conditions in which the sequences required for functions such as capsid manufacture and host recognition and entry had ceased to be necessary. The effect of natural selection was to reduce the size of the virus to a new minimum, as genes encoding proteins became superfluous and the new, streamlined sequence was trimmed back to the smallest possible unit of self-replicating selfhood. As the authors put it, the question being asked was in effect: 'what will happen to the RNA molecules if the only demand made on them is the Biblical injunction, *multiply*, with the biological proviso that they do so as rapidly as possible':

> *The outcome is what might have been expected on* a priori *grounds. The smaller the polynucleotide chain, the shorter the time required for its completion. Consequently, if the initial Qβ-RNA molecules possess sequences which are dispensable under the conditions of the experiment, their elimination could confer a selective advantage. In accordance with this expectation, it was found that as the experiment progressed, the multiplication rate increased and the product became smaller. By the 74th transfer, 83 per cent of the original genome had been eliminated.*[470]

This tiny genome – comprising just a sixth of the original length of the Qβ phage – replicated 15 times faster than the ancestral virus. After just five test-tube generations, however, it had ceased to be 'biologically competent', characterized as it was by a 'very high affinity for the replicase but ... no longer able to direct the synthesis of virus particles'.[471]

Spiegelman's Monster, as it has since come to be known, was subsequently reduced to a length of just 50 nucleotides, a length that represents the *binding site* for the replicase enzyme. Further experiments have demonstrated that in the appropriate conditions a test tube with no viral RNA at all, but merely energized RNA bases plus the Qβ replicase, can end up spawning similar versions of this apparent quintessence of self-replicating selfhood.[472] Spiegelman and his colleagues described their monster as 'the smallest known self-duplicating entity',[473] yet the intrinsic reflexivity implied by 'self-duplication' is perhaps slightly misleading. Quite apart from the idealized conditions that make all self-containment superfluous, the very process of replication relies on a non-stop supply of Qβ replicase that is not encoded by the monster itself.[474] Nor is the monster capable of the self-movement that might enable it to seek or maintain this supply. Outside the sanctum of laboratory life, Spiegelman's mollycoddled monster would not really be much of a self at all.

In fact, nature has itself produced virus-like elements akin to Spiegelman's Monster in their concision and simplicity. First identified in the late 1960s, so-called viroids differ from viruses in that they exist in vivo as non-encapsidated or naked RNAs that do not code for *any* proteins. Their single-stranded circular RNA genomes are just 246–401 nucleotides in length and comprise fewer than

10,000 atoms, yet these tiny genomes provide them with the wherewithal to reside and get themselves replicated 'autonomously'[475] in susceptible plant cells – though this replication of course involves the skilled subversion or misappropriation of the transcriptional machinery of their host nuclei and chloroplasts.[476]

Unlike Spiegelman's selfish monster, however, getting itself replicated – i.e. providing a template for replication – is not the viroid's only trick. The roughly 30 known viroids belong to two major families, the *Pospiviroidae* (e.g. *Potato spindle tuber viroid*) and the *Avsunviroidae* (e.g. *Avocado sunblotch viroid*), the former accumulating in the plant cell nucleus and the latter in the chloroplast. The latter have attracted particular attention on account of their capacity to engage in or undergo self-cleavage, which here denotes a process by which the longer-than-necessary strands of newly replicated RNA (synthesized with the help of the host machinery) prune or splice themselves to their 'proper' length.[477] The fact that in the case of *Avsunviroidae* this process is self-catalysed entails that the viroid is also a *ribozyme*; in other words, it is a dual-natured RNA enzyme that embodies both information in the sequence of its nucleotides and biological function in its distinctive folded structure. This conjunction of template properties with enzymatic capabilities prompted Theodor Diener, the discoverer of viroids, to describe them as 'the only biological macromolecules that can function both as *genotype* and phenotype', testifying to the possibility of 'Darwinian selection and pre-cellular evolution at the RNA level in the absence of DNA or protein'.[478] According to Diener, indeed, viroids are the best candidates available for consideration as 'living fossils' dating back to the pre-cellular RNA world hypothesized to have existed prior to the emergence of DNA and protein.[479]

Again unlike Spiegelman's Monster, moreover, viroids are endowed with a certain sort of context-derived mobility. Such mobility is essential to the viroid's infectious cycle, which – in the absence of an obliging experimenter armed with fresh test tubes – requires them not only to enter the host cell nucleus (for the *Pospiviroidae*) or the chloroplast (for the *Avsunviroidae*), but (after replication) to exit these organelles, move from one cell to the next via microscopic intercellular channels called plasmodesmata, enter the plant's vascular system for long-distance transportation within the plant, and eventually leave the vascular tissue to infect new cells.[480] As with viruses, of course, this is not the truly 'active' mobility associated with motor proteins and muscles; it is a question of the viroids *getting themselves moved* rather than moving themselves. Unlike viruses, however, viroids complete their infectious cycle without encoding either a capsid or any form of 'movement protein' that would enable them to 'recognize' and bind to appropriate host molecules for transport from cell to cell or through the plant's communication system. Instead, they rely on information embodied in the shape of their constituent RNA itself to interact with the cellular proteins that will get them from place to place. Though the precise mechanisms are still unclear, it is thought that specific RNA sequence motifs – i.e. three-dimensional RNA structures – allow viroids to ride piggyback on the RNA trafficking system used by the host plant to carry out physiological processes such as immune defence, the regulation of growth and development, and nutrient allocation.

Lacking encapsidation, viroids are naked RNA molecules that seem able to do without any form of 'self-containment'. To the extent that the term is deemed permissible in the absence of metabolism and flow,[481] perhaps it is the host cell or host plant that provides the requisite containment, protecting them from environmental contingency. Or perhaps their compact, self-enclosed, circular form and complex three-dimensional structure make them self-contained enough per se. As with Spiegelman's Monster, it has been claimed that viroids are 'the smallest self-replicating genetic units known,'[482] yet they go considerably further in the intrinsic reflexivity they embody. Self-contained or not, their hitch-hiking 'self-movement' and the self-cleaving catalytic activity shown by some of them clearly make them more complete paradigms of minimal quasi-selfhood – notwithstanding all those residual doubts about *indirect* forms of intrinsic reflexivity, i.e. the extent to which metabolic, replicative and even locomotive parasitism undermines the autonomy required for full selfhood.

In this sense, their closest (though slightly bigger) rivals are perhaps the capsid-less RNA viruses,[483] a family of ssRNA viruses – including the hypoviruses, the endornaviruses and the tiny narnaviruses – that are frequent inhabitants of fungi and plants and are thought to have evolved from ancestors that have lost, or dispensed with, the ability to produce capsids. With a genome that varies from a mere 2.3 to 3.6 kb in length, the two genera of the *Narnaviridae* family – *Narnavirus* and *Mitovirus* – have thus reduced their armoury of genes to just one, a gene encoding the RNA-dependent RNA polymerase (or replicase) that catalyses the replication of RNA from an RNA template. Of course, this again leaves the question of (self-)containment unanswered. In practice, it seems that the loss of the capsid is associated with a loss of virus transmissibility via extracellular routes, which means that the viruses – unable to venture forth from the safety of their host – are deprived of their 'infectivity'[484] and thus restricted to vertical transmission from host-generation to host-generation. With the virus effectively confined to its host cell, an element of 'containment' is thus already provided. Viruses of the genus *Mitovirus*, which reside in fungal mitochondria, seem to be further *allo*-contained in host-derived lipid vesicles. This may be for the sake of the host cell rather than the virus.

Also worthy of note in this context are the (considerably larger) plasmids we came across in the last chapter, which most commonly make themselves at home in the cytoplasm of bacteria in the form of circular, naked double-stranded DNA molecules. Plasmids too are 'selfish' in their capacity to capitalize on the host cell's metabolic machinery while replicating independently of the host cell's chromosomal DNA, yet they may also bestow advantages upon their host, providing them with useful genes associated with antibiotic resistance, toxin production and in general the flexibility that goes with HGT. It is significant that plasmids may encode their own 'mobility' in the form of the mechanism underlying their own transmission from one cell to another during bacterial conjugation. More specifically, they may code for a hair-like appendage known as the conjugative ('sex') pilus, which is required for the plasmid DNA to pass between the two cells. Bacterial conjugation is a complex manoeuvre that involves not only recognizing a mate, but also ensnaring and reeling in the recipient bacterium, creating direct contact in the form of a mating bridge and generating a pore or channel through which the DNA can pass into the cell. So-called conjugative plasmids themselves provide the genes encoding the cell surface proteins that will enable their present host cell to recognize a potential *new* host cell and carry out the complex mechanics of conjugation.[485] In this way, they make it possible for their host to do all the hard work required for their own movement.

You Are What You Wear

The question of self-containment is deeply relevant to virus selfhood, or the lack of it. Unlike viroids and the jumping genes of the last chapter, most viruses encode a protein capsid that protects them during their extracellular stage and in certain cases provides cover inside a hostile host as well.[486] Yet viral capsids differ in many ways from the plasma membranes characteristic of cells, raising doubts about whether they really comply with the criterion of self-containment required for full selfhood. For a start, the fact that viroids also have an extracellular stage yet get by perfectly well *without* a capsid may be taken to suggest that a capsid is more contingent and less essential to a virus than a lipid membrane is to a cell, for there can be no cell without its membrane. Admittedly, viroids are distinct entities from viruses; they are not degenerate or derived forms of viruses, i.e. viruses that have somehow 'lost' their coat in the way that the careless lineage of narnaviruses has. On the contrary, they are 'structurally, functionally and evolutionarily different' from viruses.[487] Even so, the entity and its container do seem to be more *inextricably* integrated in the case of the cell than the virus, as suggested by the experiments in self-assembly showing how the tobacco mosaic virus can not only be dissociated into its constituent proteins and RNA (e.g. by agents such as concentrated acetic acid, urea, heat and pressure), but will spontaneously reconstitute itself, unscathed, into its original form.[488] It is difficult to conceive of a cell divested of its membrane subsequently being put back together in this way.

Whereas viral capsids can be envisioned as 'protecting' something inert (a 'lifeless' informational macromolecule), cell membranes serve as a 'container' for a metabolic space, a space of energetic flow, where 'containment' implies not only enclosure but also control. A cell's plasma membrane thus serves to channel or guide a flux rather than protect a structure. It is characterized by the selective or differential permeability that is a precondition for ingestion and excretion, sentience and mobility, as well as for communication (though a capsid too has its part to play in host recognition and penetration). It is constantly maintained in a process of dynamic interaction with the ongoing self-maintenance of the cell as a whole, rather than merely assembled and 'worn'; it fits as snugly as skin as opposed to the pre-designed and seemingly disposable viral wrap.

To be sure, many viruses also have lipid membranes, frequently worn outside the capsid. These are usually derived from the membranes of the host cell, comprising host proteins and phospholipids as well as the virus's own specific glycoproteins. Yet these viral envelopes do not serve as 'containers' of flow (there is no flow), but rather as mechanisms of subterfuge. One of their main functions is to provide a means of recognizing and binding to the membrane of a host organism and then fusing with it to gain entry to the cell, effectively adopting its host's identity in order to become 'one' with it. This is unlikely to be the only function of viral envelopes, moreover, for they are sometimes present *inside* the capsid. Such is the case with certain large DNA viruses: mimivirus, for example, is endowed with two membrane layers within a capsid protein shell covered with a dense matrix of closely-packed fibres.[489] It is surmised that – once inside the host cell – one of these inner membrane layers fuses with the membrane of the *phagosome*, the cellular compartment within which foreign particles are enclosed and subsequently digested; this fusion of membranes presumably provides the particle with a conduit through which it can escape from the phagosome to the cytoplasm, thus steering clear of degradation by the host's digestive enzymes. The other viral membrane is thought to form a vesicle containing the mimivirus genome once it has made it to the host cytoplasm.[490]

A further point that has been made – as one of a series of arguments seeking to exclude viruses from the tree of life – is that viral lineages lack the structural continuity that specifically cellular membranes confer upon lineages of cells. Whereas the *cytoplasmic membrane* characteristic of a cell is inherited from its precursors (formed by the splitting of pre-existing membrane)[491] and thus perpetuates an unbroken sequence stretching back to the earliest cells of primeval life, such continuity is lacking in viruses, whose constituents – including the lipid membranes of certain viral families – have to be synthesized *de novo* with the help of the host cell as part of each viral infection cycle. The question once again is how far, if at all, the continuity of a lineage is relevant to the selfhood of the individual members of that lineage existing in the here-and-now. It is not self-evident that the individual virion is any less self-like just because its constituent capsid and membrane had to be synthesized *de novo* rather than emerging as a seamless continuation of its predecessors.

Whatever the case, the capsid has played a major role in considerations of what viruses are. One recent proposal, put forward by Didier Raoult and Patrick Forterre,[492] has involved dividing biological entities into two classes of organisms: ribosome-encoding organisms, which include all prokaryotic and eukaryotic organisms (in other words cellular life), and capsid-encoding organisms, which encompass all viruses but exclude viroids and plasmids. According to this system of classification, a virus is defined as 'a capsid-encoding organism that is composed of proteins and nucleic acids, self-assembles in a nucleocapsid and uses a ribosome-encoding organism for the completion of its life cycle'.[493] It should be stressed that these authors are not concerned with the notion of 'selfhood', but with the status of viruses as biological organisms. What is of interest in the present context, however, is that they should focus on a possible (even if problematic) manifestation of self-containment as a defining feature of one of their two fundamental categories of living being.

Raoult and Forterre base their classification on the fact that the genes that code for ribosomal proteins and ribosomal RNA and that are thus indispensable for the synthesis of proteins are among the few genes that are common to *all* cellular organisms, even tiny intracellular parasites.[494] By contrast, *no* virus is known to encode ribosomal proteins. Unlike the realm of ribosome-encoding organisms (REOs), indeed, there is no single protein that is common to the entire virosphere. Even the most prevalent virus-specific proteins – the 'hallmark' proteins pinpointed by Koonin – are not universal, although they are spread among a wide range of diverse lineages. What *is* common to all viruses, or at least all viruses with an extracellular stage in their life cycle, is expression of the capsid that is required for them to propagate themselves outside the host REO and locate and infect new ones. The proteins of which the capsid consists may vary greatly. The jelly-roll capsid protein is one of Koonin's hallmark genes, found in no cellular organism yet present in the capsids of the most varied viruses,[495] whereas the tiny bacteriophage MS2 sports its own tailor-made protein coat that is at present thought to be structurally unique within the virosphere.[496] Yet *some* capsid – whether unique or commonplace – is still required.

One consequence of such a classification is that viroids and plasmids are left out in the cold as 'orphan replicons', along with mobile elements such as transposons.[497] Raoult and Forterre suggest that such orphan replicons fail to qualify as organisms because 'the term organism implies at least a minimal level of integration (the association of several organs into a functional unit)' and is thus reserved for biological entities equipped *both* with 'genes that are involved in their replication (a replicon cassette) *and* genes that encode either ribosomes or capsids', to the exclusion of those entities whose genes encode neither ribosomes nor capsids.[498] It may seem somewhat arbitrary that the presence or absence of a self-assembling protein coat (albeit a self-encoded protein coat) should serve as the criterion for distinguishing whether a sequence of nucleotides constitutes a living organism or not. What are we to make of the narnaviruses that have 'lost' their capsid? Have they slipped out of the realm of the living simply by dispensing with their overcoat? From a practical point of view, of course, it is not *just* a question of capsid-loss, but of the *effect* of this loss in terms of the renunciation of 'infectivity' and extracellular transmissibility. The capsid is what makes infectivity possible, and a capacity to infect cells has tended to be regarded as one of the relatively few positive characteristics of viruses.[499] Perhaps it is ultimately just a matter of semantics whether capsid-less, non-infectious viruses are classed as 'true' viruses and thus as organisms as opposed to 'mere' genetic elements.[500] It is certainly tempting to view them as 'renouncing' any claims to selfhood to the extent that they become a permanent part of their host. Noteworthy is that Raoult and Forterre are not alone in focusing on the capsid. Indeed, they cite the work of Dennis Bamford and colleagues, who have used the term 'viral self' to designate the identity conferred by a capsid on the virus that encodes it.

In this context, the concept of viral selfhood is a response to the difficulty of establishing long-term evolutionary relationships on the basis of the constantly changing viral genome. The aim has been to ascertain what is lasting or phylogenetically 'conserved' in particular viruses: the term 'self', as employed by Bamford and colleagues, thus denotes something akin to an essence, something unchanging that is passed down from generation to generation:

> *Conservation is expressed in association with structures essential for carrying out core viral functions, such as particle assembly and genome packaging, whereas functions linked to specific interactions with the evolving host cell are much less conserved. This observation leads to the idea that there are distinct viral 'self' functions and structures that can be used to trace viral lineages in spite of the 'noise' caused by the more rapidly evolving host-related phenomena.*[501]

Rather than resorting to the sequence information embodied in the genome, therefore, the idea has been to use the structural information embodied in the capsid as an approach to analysing the relationships among viruses. This approach has focused, for example, on the similarities in the arrangement of the capsid proteins in the bacteriophage PRD1 (a virus that infects Gram-negative bacteria) and adenovirus (a virus that infects vertebrates), as well as – more tentatively – certain large eukaryotic viruses that infect ciliates.[502] Given the diversity of their hosts in conjunction with the structural similarities that the viruses are nonetheless found to share, Bamford's controversial proposal is that the viruses in question have a common ancestor that dates back to a period before the division between the prokaryotic and eukaryotic domains of life.

Doubts have been raised about the suitability of capsid structure for resolving phylogenetic uncertainties: it could be the case that most viral capsids adopt a limited number of geometrical architectures because structural convergence as it were 'picks out' the most robust or efficacious form available.[503] The near-ubiquity of the jelly-roll protein fold across so many lineages is another problem. As Bamford and colleagues themselves acknowledge, its pervasiveness 'largely precludes its use as a diagnostic for viral lineages,'[504] making it impossible to tell whether it indeed represents a faint vestige of an 'urvirus progenitor'[505] common to a range of lineages or whether it came into being independently in different viral lineages. A further, terminological point – relevant in the present context – relates to the use of the word 'self'. What Bamford and colleagues are pursuing is something lasting or static, something perdurable through the eons, an essence that defines a lineage.[506] Selfhood as defined in terms of intrinsic reflexivity, by contrast, is inseparable from self-production and the possibility of self-change: what unifies the lineage is not simple *identity* (capsid$^{\text{time 1}}$ = capsid$^{\text{time 2}}$) but the *continuity* of a self-synthesizing entity (though possibly an indirectly self-synthesizing entity in the case of a virus), as manifest in its constant self-adaptations and transformations.

The viral 'self' spotlighted by Bamford is not so much a self as a means of *identifying* a self. It is a matter of *viral identity* rather than *viral selfhood*. In the case in hand, this identity is embodied in the ancestral coat that has been handed down from viral progenitors. This is not to deny or belittle the importance that identity – in the sense of *identifiability* – holds for selfhood.[507] As a basic component of viral identity, the capsid represents the nearest thing a virus has to a face or to dress sense or a personality: it is a point of interface or interaction between 'self' and 'non-self', a medium through which self 'identifies' meaningful non-self (host) and may in turn be 'identified' (by a host's immune system, or by Bamford and colleagues).[508] Nonetheless, a more integrated notion of viral selfhood requires an approach that attempts to account for all three categories of intrinsic reflexivity, incorporating not just the factor of containment (including mechanisms of identifiability and self-protection), but also the facilities for self-replication and self-maintaining metabolism provided by an unwitting or unwilling host.

Selfhood Recruited or Hijacked

One of the factors that impelled Raoult and Forterre to reclassify viruses as biological organisms was the recent discovery of mimivirus, a virus so big (a gargantuan 750 nm) that it was initially mistaken for a bacterium: 'the size of Mimivirus challenges the definition of a virus', they wrote, 'and even the definition of a microorganism as a living entity'.[509] Its 1.2 Mb genome was more than twice the size of the largest viral genome then known and larger than those of many of the smaller cellular organisms, such as the typhus-causing parasite *Rickettsia* we shall reencounter below. It contained well over a thousand genes, again more than many small parasitic or symbiotic prokaryotes (even humans only have twenty times as many; MS2 and Qβ have four genes; narnavirus, one). Particularly remarkable was that some of these genes were associated with protein synthesis, a feature previously unheard-of in viruses, which generally appropriate host translation machinery for the purpose.

Since the discovery of mimivirus, a clutch of closely related viral giants of similarly impressive proportions have come to light. The fact that one of these – known as mamavirus – is itself known to 'fall ill' when infected by another virus, its own 21-gene 'virophage' by the name of Sputnik, has been taken to provide further support for the idea of viruses as biological organisms: 'there's no doubt this is a living organism', claims virologist Jean-Michel Claverie; 'the fact that it can get sick makes it more alive'.[510] The idea of viruses being infected by viruses – parasites-within-parasites – again suggests an ongoing recursion of selves-within-selves (within selves...). At the same time, the sequence of newly discovered viruses is revealing a progression of giants of increasingly Rabelaisian proportions. The two strains of pandoravirus that made the news in 2013, the saltwater form *Pandoravirus salinus* and the freshwater form *Pandoravirus dulcis*, have genomes of at least 2.5 and 1.9 megabases, respectively.[511]

In themselves, these large DNA viruses (known as *NCLDVs*[512]) still lack many of the features – such as metabolism and responsiveness to stimuli – generally considered to be defining characteristics of living selves. Despite the impressive size of the genome and virion and the abundance of proteins they encode, they fail to encode the ribosomal proteins common to all cellular organisms. Perhaps it is misguided, however, to focus on the viruses 'in themselves'. For when viruses such as the NCLDVs enter their host, they do not simply disperse at random within the cytoplasm; rather, they form a spectacular complex, an intracellular compartment called a virus factory that takes in raw ingredients and spits out new DNA and proteins and all in all 'looks and acts remarkably like a cell'.[513]

Such virus factories are elaborate cytoplasmic structures established in the host, providing a protective framework within which virus replication and assembly can occur. Their formation leads to deep changes in the structure of the host cell, including the recruitment of organelles such as mitochondria and the exclusion of host proteins. They may be, but are not necessarily, surrounded by a membrane. The case of mimivirus, for example, seems to involve a structure similar to a cellular defence mechanism called an aggresome,[514] a cage made of cytoskeletal proteins called vimentin filaments normally used *by the cell* to circumscribe and confine potentially toxic proteins prior to subsequent degradation. Such a structure thus generates a form of 'containment', both enhancing replication efficiency (by concentrating the requisite components) and conferring a safe context for viral activity. Relatively safe, that is. As we have seen, virophages such as Sputnik may be able to infiltrate the virus factory and hijack the machinery for their own replicative purposes. In an ironic twist, the parasite is out-parasitized, undermining its ability to proliferate.

Viral factories may take a variety of forms. One of the best-characterized factories pertains to the Vaccinia virus (VV), a large *dsDNA* virus that encodes roughly 250 genes and belongs to the poxvirus family. The VV factory[515] is a highly dynamic structure, transforming itself several times over the course of an infection. While the early replication complexes are enclosed by cellular membranes (usurped from the host's *endoplasmic reticulum*), the onset of virus assembly produces a dramatic change in the mode of containment, with a switch to the aggresome-like 'cage' characteristic of mimivirus and other NCLDVs. Subsequently, the assembled virions are transported to a cellular membrane structure called the *Golgi apparatus*, where the virions are wrapped in a double membrane, before being further dispatched to the plasma membrane for release.

Other classes of viruses organize their factories around different sets of membrane-bound compartments inside the host cell, using structures such as *lysosomes* (a sort of cellular 'stomach' normally responsible for degrading waste materials and debris) to provide protection and spatial coordination for RNA replication and possibly also capsid assembly.[516] Underlying the diversity of forms, however, such viral factories seem to share a number of core features: first, they are composed of some sort of enclosure, framework or scaffold, whether provided by aggresomes or by cellular membranes derived, for example, from the endoplasmic reticulum or from host lysosomes; secondly, they rely on the recruitment of mitochondria to supply the energy for replication and/or assembly; thirdly, they employ host trafficking mechanisms to connect viral genome replication with the subsequent assembly and concluding exit of the mature virions.

The viral factories thus provide the functional unity and 'self'-containment within which a self-maintaining process of viral self-replication and self-assembly can take place. Again, however, the 'self' in self-containment is best placed in scare quotes, given that the containment (the endomembranes or the vimentin cage) is not furnished by the virus but by the host cell; the same goes for the mitochondria that power the processes of replication and assembly and the trafficking systems that keep things moving. One of the terms most commonly used by virologists in this context is 'recruitment': the host membranes or cytoskeletal elements and above all the mitochondria are said to be 'recruited' by the virus.[517] The implication is that viruses do not 'own' or 'possess' a body (a metabolism, a self?), but rather hire or mobilize the parts they need as and when they need them. A presumably inadvertent connotation of 'recruitment' is that there is an element of 'choice' on the part of the recruitees, with the mitochondria seemingly unmasked as a band of hirelings or mercenaries, faithlessly switching their allegiance from host cell to virus.[518] Another habitual metaphor implies coercion: the host machinery is said to be 'hijacked' by the virus, underscoring that the poor mitochondria never really had an alternative anyway. Whether recruited or hijacked by the virus, the bottom line is that the mitochondria are induced to behave against their own interests, for the virus has 'usurped' or 'commandeered' the selfhood of the host organism. The conventional association of selfhood with unitary ownership (the notion that a self has one owner: itself) is subverted by parasitism.[519] The host organism is no longer unitary precisely to the extent that host and parasite – cell and viral factory – are pursuing divergent interests, namely the replication of different genomes.

Again inspired by mimivirus, Jean-Michel Claverie has indeed suggested that the key to the nature of viruses is not the virion, but rather the virus factory. On such a view, it is this complex assemblage of viral components – together with an array of 'recruits' or 'hostages' including mitochondria, cytoskeletal proteins and miscellaneous cellular membranes – that should be regarded as the 'actual virus organism'. The virus factory would thus be the virus soma, whereas the virion would be equivalent to the germ line, i.e. the 'continuous immortal lineage responsible for carrying one generation to the next'. In other words, suggests Claverie, 'interpreting the virion particle as "the virus" is very much like looking at a spermatozoid and calling it a human'.[520] Or to express it in terms of 'selfhood': the merely *potential* selfhood inherent in the virus particle is *brought to full selfhood* by the combustive metabolism and containment it recruits-hijacks to serve its own replicative interests. The viral self is constituted by the conjunction of viral parasite and cellular host, or at least certain recruited-hijacked parts of the cellular host.

An alternative vision of merged parasite-host selfhood comes to light in the behaviour of temperate viruses, which have a markedly different reproductive strategy from virulent viruses. Whereas the *lytic* cycle of the latter comprises a destructive sequence of replication, assembly and exit from the cell by lysis, the *lysogenic* cycle of the former either entails the integration of the viral DNA into the host bacterium's genome as a provirus or prophage, or the generation of a genetic element akin to a plasmid that can exist and replicate freely in the cytoplasm without lysing the host cell. Lysogeny does not result in the creation of new viral particles, therefore, but in the spread of the viral DNA through the reproduction of the host, with both daughter cells (normally) containing new copies of the prophage as part of their genetic material. In this way, a stable association is formed between host and parasite.[521] Persisting viruses thus *become one* with the cell, 'colonizing'[522] their host and in the process establishing a new, lasting virus/host identity. To the extent that the virus has 'become one' with its host and the host has 'become one' with the virus, their interests can be understood to have merged and they have become a single self (though this unity may be precarious; such viruses can turn virulent again).

As Luis P. Villarreal and others have argued, however, such an association would tend to disintegrate quickly over evolutionary timescales if the parasite did not succeed in making itself 'indispensable' to the host cell, as it were 'forcing' the stable association to be maintained. The prophage must thus be endowed with a mechanism that prevents its host from getting rid of it. One such mechanism is the so-called 'addiction module'. This notion was developed to explain the enduring relationship between the *E. coli* bacterium and the P1 phage that inhabits it persistently as an extrachromosomal genetic element (similar to a plasmid) and that programmes the death of any daughter cells in which it is lacking.[523] By encoding toxins that kill any bacteria in which the P1 phage plasmid is absent and antitoxins that save those in which it is present, the phage ensures that its host is 'addicted' to its own continued presence. The plasmid addiction module has been described as a sort of time bomb: 'the charge, a stable toxin; the timer, a labile antidote. Detonation occurs when the ratio of antidote to toxin becomes too low. In the plasmid-free cell, neither antidote nor toxin is replenished and the antidote is eliminated more rapidly than the toxin, leaving the latter to exert its lethal potential'.[524]

Moreover, the infection or 'colonization' of *E. coli* by the P1 phage generates not just addiction but a collective or group identity, since the addiction module eliminates not only cells that lose or get rid of P1 but also cells that get infected by competing phages such as P1's lytic rival T4 phage, described with conspicuous understatement as 'the *T. rex* of the phage world'.[525] When P1-colonized bacteria are infected with T4, the antitoxin gene is destabilized, allowing the toxin gene to eradicate any T4-infected cells in the P1-colonized population and thus preventing T4 from extending to uninfected P1-harbouring populations. This can be considered a form of programmed cell death, an induced suicide response that restricts T4 replication and transmission and thus protects the P1-colonized population in its entirety. The logic, as so often, is collective: the individual T4-infected bacteria are sacrificed – or sacrifice themselves 'selflessly' – for the benefit of the community as a whole. At the same time, the collective association of P1 and *E. coli* reasserts itself as a group identity by 'recognizing' T4 as a variety of non-self that is to be excluded and neutralized. At the level of the collective, the addiction module functions as a method of immune defence.

In their capacity as the immune system of a collective self, such toxin/antitoxin (T/A) modules also function as a way of distinguishing self from closely related strains of prokaryotes, i.e. phylogenetically neighbouring non-self.[526] Indeed, the word 'lysogenic' was first coined (in the 1920s) to denote a phenomenon sometimes observed when two closely related strains of bacteria are grown together and one of them lyses the other. Only subsequently did it emerge that such 'lysogenic' strains of bacteria contain a silent prophage that can infect and kill the other strain without itself being harmed in the process (due to their possession of the requisite 'immunity').[527] Similar phenomena have been discerned among certain strains of archaea, which are found to generate toxins that are only detrimental to closely related strains, but do not harm either bacteria or eukaryotes.[528] As Villarreal argues, 'the main purpose of these toxins cannot be to poison competing but phylogenetically distant species. They are mainly intended to limit competition by related species. Put another way, we can think of these toxin/antitoxin modules as identity modules'.[529] By conferring upon its host a highly specific collective identity and the capacity to recognize deviations from it, the prophage thus provides it with a self/non-self discrimination mechanism, i.e. the hallmark of an immune system. This can be conceived of as a form of self-containment precisely to the extent that the boundary between self and non-self is defined, and non-self is recognized as such and excluded.

Other Intracellular Selves

Rickettsia *and Mitochondria*

We have looked at a range of viruses and virus-like entities with a view to ascertaining the extent to which they can be considered self-like and the ways in which they may fail to meet the criteria for selfhood. The conventional wisdom is that their parasitic nature – their dependence on a host cell – deprives them of the autonomy required to be a self. In these terms, their selfhood comes across as vicarious or indirect, or perhaps as borrowed, recruited or hijacked. However, there are other, clearly cellular entities (which can safely be viewed as autopoietic, living systems) that may also lead a parasitic existence within a host cell. As intimated by the lifestyle of intracellular pathogens such as *Rickettsia prowazekii* (which causes epidemic louse-borne typhus in humans) and intracellular mutualists such as *Buchnera aphidicola* (which inhabits a specific type of cell in aphids), matters are not as clear cut as they might initially have appeared, and the conceptual boundary between selfhood and its absence is as porous as a plasma membrane. Such creatures and their relatives will be the focus of the remainder of this chapter.

Like a virus, the obligate intracellular parasite *R. prowazekii* – notable for having infected and killed millions of human beings in the aftermath of the two World Wars – is only able to multiply inside living eukaryotic cells. With a genome of 1.11 Mb containing 834 protein-coding genes, it is 'smaller' than some of the large DNA viruses we encountered earlier in the chapter.[530] In themselves, of course, these features are far from providing grounds for dismissing *R. prowazekii* as being too 'virus-like' for full cellular selfhood to be ascribed to it. According to the classification proposed by Raoult and Forterre, it is unambiguously a ribosome-encoding organism as opposed to a capsid-encoding organism, possessing the foundations for autonomous protein synthesis. It also has a capacity for energy metabolism: despite using a membrane-spanning transport protein called ATP-ADP translocase to import energy in the form of ATP from its host early in its infectious cycle, it is able to synthesize its own ATP by *aerobic* respiration once the pool of host ATP has been exhausted.[531] However, while its metabolic capabilities are similar to those of free-living proteobacteria, it depends on a supply of *cofactors* from a cellular host for them to be expressed. As a result, *Rickettsia* rapidly loses its metabolic activity outside a cellular environment (for example, in a salt solution), though it can survive for hours if certain nutrients are provided, and its metabolism will resume if ATP is added. Unlike a virus, it must remain 'metabolically competent' for at least short periods of time outside the cytoplasm, since it is transferred from host to host by arthropod vectors such as lice and metabolic activity is required for infection of the new host.[532]

Rickettsia also shows a striking resemblance to Gram-negative bacteria in its self-containment, endowed as it is with their characteristic three-layer structure comprising an innermost plasma membrane, a rigid cell wall made of peptidoglycan and an outer coat of lipopolysaccharide. This provides the parasite with a clear boundary in relation to its host, as well as with the protection that allows it to live unconstrained within the potentially 'hostile, uninviting environment' that is the host cytoplasm.[533] At the same time, this very cytoplasmic environment yields a cornucopia of biosynthetic ingredients that are not usually encountered in such plenty by free-living bacteria, and *R. prowazekii* has evolved a capacity to import vital metabolites across its membrane, allowing its genome to dispense with genes for functions such as the production of amino acids and nucleotides.[534] The selective permeability of its boundaries thus permits the parasite to remain a separate entity – a distinct self – from its host, while hiding *within* it and assimilating or incorporating the nutrients it provides. Despite its profound dependence on its host, therefore, *Rickettsia* seems endowed with the metabolic and structural autonomy of a self, albeit a self-within-a-self.

The question of whether *Rickettsia* is more virus-like or cell-like has often been answered with reference to its ancestry: there is compelling genetic evidence, it is argued, that such endocellular pathogens, unlike viruses, 'have lost many of their metabolic functions as a result of reductive evolution from more complex, free-living ancestors'.[535] More specifically, *Rickettsia* is now believed to belong to a particular class of proteobacteria – the alpha-proteobacteria – that includes free-living soil microbes such as *Rhizobium* and *Agrobacterium* as well as an extremely broad range of other genera. Of course, the question of ancestry may be taken as contingent in relation to the question of selfhood in the here and now; it is surely possible, even at a lineage level, that selfhood might simply 'peter out', rather like a hurricane or whirlpool gradually running out of steam. Aristocratic ancestors are no guarantee of enduring nobility.

What is certain is that in making the change from a free-living bacterium to an intracellular parasite, *Rickettsia* has largely sacrificed its motility, its facility for self-movement. It has changed from being an active to a fundamentally passive being.[536] Such intracellular existence – a life of cytoplasmic abundance – excludes the need to search for prey or flee from predators, making it difficult to conceive of *value* (hunger or fear, pain or pleasure) in the world of such parasites. It is hard to imagine that it is 'like anything' to be an individual *Rickettsia* cell, residing immobile within its host. Though it seems acceptable to ascribe selfhood to such a self-maintaining, self-replicating, self-contained entity, therefore, the intrinsic reflexivity it embodies is unlikely to be associated with even a glimmer of what we might call 'consciousness'.

Rickettsia is far from being the only obligate intracellular pathogen,[537] yet it is relevant not only as a paradigm exemplifying some of the issues relating to the selfhood of parasites, but especially because it is thought to descend from an alpha-proteobacterial ancestor that is also the ancestor of the mitochondria we encountered in Chapter 3. Indeed, phylogenetic analysis suggests that of all microbes analysed to date *R. prowazekii* is the one most closely related to the membrane-bound organelles that power eukaryotic cells from within.[538] Evidently, the kinship of the parasite and the organelle is almost unimaginably remote, with their shared progenitor dating back to the origin of eukaryotes some 1,500 to 2,000 million years ago. Yet comparison of the genome sequences of *Rickettsia* and mitochondria reveals both similarities in their procedures of energy metabolism (ATP synthesis) and shared deficiencies in the manufacture of key macromolecules such as amino acids and nucleosides. In both cases, many genes indispensable to free-living bacteria appear to have been supplanted by homologues in the nuclear (i.e. host) genome.[539]

In terms of selfhood, however, mitochondria present a rather different scenario from *Rickettsia* bacteria. Unlike pathogens, mitochondria have made themselves indispensable to the eukaryotic cells in which they have set up home, working to their hosts' advantage and merging their interests with their own (thus forming a unitary 'self' in the sense of a single unit of self-interest). Their relationship can thus be termed mutualistic rather than parasitic,[540] where the distinction between *mutualism* and parasitism reflects the degree to which functional interests are shared and selfhood is integrated into a harmonious unity.

Indeed, this integration seems virtually complete in the case of mitochondria, which have in large measure 'handed over' their autonomy as embodied in the informational macromolecules that direct their reproduction, metabolism and self-containment. Most of the genes governing mitochondrial activities are now found in the nucleus of the host cell; in the case of humans some 900 mitochondrial proteins are encoded by the nuclear genome for subsequent import into the mitochondria.[541] Mitochondrial genomes are in this respect reduced to just a shadow of their former selves, though there is remarkable diversity in their genome size and coding capacity: the size of mitochondrial DNA (mtDNA) varies from a diminutive 6 kb (just under twice the size of the genome belonging to the tiny phage MS2) in the malaria-causing obligate parasite *Plasmodium* to 490 kb in rice (*Oryza sativa*) and a massive 3.9 Mb in the flowering shrub *Amborella trichopoda*.[542] The coding capacity ranges from just five genes in *Plasmodium* to almost 100 genes in a class of single-celled eukaryotes called the jakobids.[543] These genes are associated with a handful of basic processes, always including energy metabolism and translation, and sometimes also protein import and transcription.[544] The 'transfer' of the rest of the mitochondrial genes to the host nucleus would have depended crucially on the development of molecular machinery allowing the requisite proteins to be imported from the host cytoplasm back across the mitochondrial membranes into the mitochondria.

Despite this drastic loss of informational autonomy the mitochondrion continues to retain its integrity as a self-contained unit, losing its cell wall but maintaining both its outer membrane and the inner membrane that provides the apparatus for the generation of energy. As the microbiologist Franklin M. Harold muses, 'a curious aspect of all these transfigurations is that, while genes are subject to transfer and proteins come and go, membranes are commonly preserved; it is not at all clear to me why that should be so'.[545] The element of self-containment once again emerges as a foundational aspect of living selfhood, albeit in this case a residual selfhood that has been gradually surrendering its autonomy over the eons. Of course, insofar as the membranes and the proteinaceous pores they incorporate are now encoded by genes in the host nucleus rather than the mitochondrion, we could equally well speak of *allo*-containment instead of *auto*-containment. In turn, however, the genes encoding the plasma membrane of the host eukaryotic cell are themselves thought to be mitochondrial in origin (though of course now also located in the host nucleus), the original archaeal membrane having been replaced by bacterial membrane.[546] To ask which cell 'contains' the other thus becomes increasingly redundant. To the extent that symbiont and host now *share* their selfhood, the very distinction between *auto*-containment and *allo*-containment is rendered largely irrelevant.

Any notion of unitary containment (of each mitochondrion being enclosed within its own membranous 'container') is further undermined by the co-existence in each eukaryotic cell of hundreds[547] of mitochondria subject to a constant dynamic of fusion – a process involving the coordinated merging of both the inner and outer mitochondrial membrane – and subsequent fission. According to David Chan, 'any given mitochondrion is not a discrete, autonomous organelle. In fact, the identity of an individual mitochondrion is short-lived, because it will fuse with a neighbouring mitochondrion in the near future'.[548] This ongoing interplay of mitochondrial fusion and fission seems to be essential to the wellbeing of the cell, ensuring that ATP can be produced wherever energy is required within the cell (even in the most distal regions; even in the nerve terminals of neurons). The implication is that – in such cases at least – the mitochondria form a collective self, functioning as an active and highly flexible network. What matters is not the fleeting selfhood of the individual mitochondria, but the versatile energy supply they combine to provide for the sake of the cell as a whole.

We thus have the paradox of a self (or rather, a quasi-self, where 'quasi' expresses those nagging doubts about its lack of autonomy) that is at the same time more or less completely subservient to a larger self. As an organelle (the cellular equivalent of an organ), it is more akin to a heart or liver, or perhaps to a system of hearts that flit into and out of existence depending on where there is a need for blood-pumping activity, than to an entity considered alive or self-like in its own right. This raises the question of just why mitochondria have ceded so much autonomy, in genetic terms at least. One major reason doubtless has to do with the function of mitochondria as the ATP-generating 'powerhouses' of the cell, which makes them less than ideal as a storage place for genes. As Nick Lane puts it:

> *Mitochondrial membranes generate an electric charge, operating across a few millionths of a millimetre, with the same voltage as a bolt of lightning, a thousand times more powerful than domestic wiring. To store genes here is like depositing the most precious books of the British Library in a dodgy nuclear power station. ... Mitochondrial genes mutate far faster than genes in the nucleus. For example, in yeast, a handy experimental model, they mutate some 10,000 times faster. Yet despite this, it is critical that the two genomes (the nuclear and mitochondrial genomes) function properly together. The high-voltage force powering eukaryotic cells is generated by proteins encoded by both genomes. If they fail to function well together, the penalty is death – death for the cell, and death for the organism.*[549]

Given the risks and difficulties associated with coordinating a nuclear genome with a rapidly-mutating mitochondrial genome, the question indeed becomes why mitochondrial genomes are kept at all. One plausible answer – corroborated by the reticulate nature of mitochondrial selfhood – is that they provide a mechanism for the fine-tuning of cellular respiration, adjusting power to demand. Increasing flexibility in this way requires continuous feedback and thus local rather than 'centralized' (i.e. nuclear) control of gene activity.[550]

The existence of other organelles that are believed to share a common evolutionary ancestor with mitochondria but that dispense entirely with their genome adds a further twist to the matter, raising the question of whether the vestigial genome of a mitochondrion is really indicative of any more selfhood than no genome at all. There are varieties of anaerobic eukaryotes – including species such as *Trichomonas vaginalis* and *Giardia lamblia* – that lack mitochondria, but possess modified, often genome-free forms of the organelle: either hydrogenosomes, which continue to produce energy but use a different mechanism from mitochondria (the fermentation of organic fuels to release hydrogen), or mitosomes, which seem not to be involved in energy generation at all but are thought to have maintained other mitochondrial functions.[551] Like mitochondria, both hydrogenosomes and mitosomes are 'self-contained' in that they have maintained a double-membrane envelope, recalling Harold's musings on the tenacious preservation of membranes even as all other indications of living selfhood fall by the wayside. Like mitochondria, they divide by binary fission. Yet in the absence of a genome of their own, their persistence in the host organism can only mean that all the proteins required for their maintenance and reproduction are encoded by nuclear genes. Their intrinsic reflexivity is completely deflected via the selfhood of the host organism.

So what is left of the organelle's original selfhood in such circumstances? Does the presumed descent of mitochondria, hydrogenosomes and mitosomes from illustrious free-living bacterial forefathers suggest the presence of 'more' selfhood than in other membrane-bound organelles?[552] Or has their selfhood been extinguished or overwhelmed by the more forceful selfhood of the host, like a smaller whirlpool engulfed within a larger one? It might appear that mitochondria and their genome-free organellar cousins have been reduced to mere functionality in the service of a 'higher' self, a means to an end – no longer their own end, but another entity's. The concept of 'helotism' or slavery has been used to describe the conversion of symbiont to mitochondrion,[553] the metaphor of enslavement implying a loss of freedom or autonomy, coupled with restriction and immobility. This is perhaps underscored by an element of evolutionary *adhocism* that may also be at work, as epitomized by certain single-celled *dinoflagellates* called warnowiids which have 'recruited' (or perhaps 'hijacked', or even 'press-ganged') clusters of mitochondria to serve as the 'cornea' of complex eyes known as 'ocelloids', playing a structural rather than a metabolic role.[554] In the multicellular world, the same principle is shown by flatworms such as the parasitic *Entobdella soleae*, which has likewise shoehorned some of its mitochondria into optical use, in this case as a lens.[555] Such resourcefulness illustrates even more graphically how organellar selfhood may be 'subsumed' within the higher selfhood of the host organism as a whole.

Yet the metaphor of slavery betrays that – like a master over-reliant upon his slaves – the host organism may likewise come to be (more or less) dependent upon its constituent organelles/endosymbionts, the master in turn losing his autonomy. Evoking an almost Hegelian *verkehrte Welt*, Lewis Thomas questions who is really in charge:

> *The usual way of looking at [mitochondria] is as enslaved creatures, captured to supply ATP for cells unable to respire on their own.... This master-slave arrangement is the common view of full-grown biologists, eukaryotes all. But there is the other side. From their own standpoint, the organelles might be viewed as having learned early how to have the best of possible worlds, with least effort and risk to themselves and their progeny. Instead of evolving as we have done, manufacturing longer and elaborately longer strands of DNA, and running ever-increasing risks of mutating into evolutionary cul-de-sacs, they elected to stay small and stick to one line of work. To accomplish this, and to assure themselves the longest possible run, they got themselves inside all the rest of us.*[556]

There is a sense in which we eukaryotes are the slaves, or prisoners, of the mitochondria we hold within, which have flagrantly *used* us to perpetuate themselves through the tracts of time. Alternatively, the relationship might be characterized as a partnership of mutually dependent subselves as much as an assimilation of one by the other. The depth of this interdependence is suggested by the status of the mitochondrion as something akin to a defining feature of eukaryotes, whose presence dates back to the very origins of what eukaryotes are.[557] All extant eukaryotic cells – protozoan or plant, fungal or animal – are now believed to be descended from an ancestor that possessed a mitochondrion.

Of course, there are limits to this interdependence. For a start, as we have seen, there are the unicellular eukaryotes that lack the organelle but have hydrogenosomes or mitosomes instead. There are other mitochondria-free eukaryotes that harbour more recently acquired symbiotic *prokaryotes* within their cytoplasm. The giant freshwater amoeba *Pelomyxa* is a case in point, accommodating within its cytoplasm several types of aerobic bacteria that carry out the respiration required to furnish it with energy.[558] Though it was initially believed that *Pelomyxa* represented a form of primitive proto-eukaryote whose ancestors had branched off from the eukaryotic lineage prior to the acquisition of mitochondria, it is now believed by some to have 'lost' its mitochondria, confirming that they are metabolically 'substitutable' after all.[559] Perhaps the mitochondrial slave is not so indispensable to its master. Perhaps the slave is not such a perfect subordinate either. Perhaps it continues to exhibit signs of having a 'self' of its own.

Such signs may be discerned in its membranes, its ribosomes and in the genetic material it contains. Not only is the mitochondrion 'contained' by both an outer and an inner membrane and to this extent topologically distinct from its host; it also falls within the category of ribosome-encoding organism (REO) proposed by Raoult and Forterre, the implication being that – armed with (some of) the machinery required for protein synthesis – it is a living entity in its own right.[560] Mitochondrial 'selfishness' has also come to light in many plants, where the maternal inheritance pattern of the mtDNA has resulted in male sterility for more than 150 species. Through their DNA, the mitochondria seem to be pursuing their own immediate (replicative) interests in blatant conflict with those of the host organism.[561]

Equally remarkable is the apparently special status of mitochondria among organelles. Normally, dysfunctional and damaged mitochondria are subject to a process called mitophagy, whereby they are effectively 'eaten' by the cell of which they form a part: ailing mitochondria are enveloped in double-membrane vesicles called autophagosomes, which are transported to the perinuclear area of the cell (the area between the two membranes), where they fuse with lysosomes and have their contents degraded.[562] Given the tendency of mitochondria to mutate and malfunction, strict regulation of mitochondrial turnover is an essential feature of cellular homeostasis.[563] Impaired and potentially harmful mitochondria have to be 'eaten' in the interests of the cell as a whole. In fact, mitophagy is just one of various classes of autophagy (or self-eating) that are called into play in conditions of stress such as nutrient deprivation. Autophagy of this sort – to which organelles such as peroxisomes and intracellular bacteria are also subject – promotes cell survival when times are hard, allowing superfluous contents to be 'recycled' and thus replenishing vital macromolecule precursors such as amino acids, sugars and fatty acids. Mitochondria, however, seem to have a special capacity to 'resist' being consumed as a result of starvation-induced autophagy. Studies have shown that in conditions of nutrient deficiency mitochondria are able to transform their morphology to enhance their survival. Processes of elongation and hyperfusion turn the fragmented mitochondrial network into a tubular one that cannot be consumed by the cell.[564] Such 'tubulation' saves the mitochondria (other organelles are 'eaten' instead), but is also thought to benefit the cell by resulting in a more efficient form of ATP production.[565] By saving their own skin, the mitochondria also serve their host cell.

Perhaps the most striking reminder of vestigial mitochondrial selfhood and selfishness comes to light in one of the major cellular functions it performs today: namely, as the central regulator of apoptosis, or programmed cell death (PCD), a form of cell suicide without which complex multicellular life is difficult to conceive. One of the principal mechanisms of apoptosis is based on the activation of cascades of so-called 'caspase' proteases, a type of enzyme that carves up and degrades proteins. These enzymes are thought to have been part of the dowry bestowed by the proto-mitochondrion on entering the symbiotic marriage that resulted in eukaryotes.[566] Caspase cascades can be activated by external signals, as occurs in the immune response, but also by processes that involve the mitochondrion releasing specific proteins, among them the transmembrane protein cytochrome c, into the cytoplasm.[567] Once again, such cell suicide involves a collective logic, based on the 'selflessness' of a cell that – when damaged, infected or simply surplus to requirements – sacrifices itself for the good of the community of cells of which it forms a part; the interests of the individual self are subsumed within the interest of the global self. Apoptosis is thus a precondition for multicellular life forms,[568] where it is essential to developmental processes, homeostatic self-maintenance and immune defence.[569] All five lineages of independently-evolving multicellularity (animals, plants and fungi, as well as red algae and green algae) are armed with similar caspase enzymes as a mechanism of PCD.[570]

But what are the roots of this seemingly far-sighted, altruistic behaviour that ultimately led to a collective self and multicellularity? How did it emerge from the selfishness of an individual mitochondrion? Koonin and Aravind have put forward the hypothesis that the early alpha-proteobacterial endosymbiont might have secreted caspase-like enzymes to kill its host cell once this ceased to provide a hospitable environment, for example when nutrients were in short supply. Such a mechanism would have permitted the bacterium to make efficient use of the corpse of its murdered host (as nutrition) before moving on to another host.[571] Eventually, this aggressive selfishness would have been 'tamed' or 'domesticated' by the host lineage, which may well have added regulatory components to yield a controlled mechanism of programmed suicide. This, it can be presumed, would have ultimately redounded to the collective benefit of both parties. Just as bacterial 'selflessness' may be produced by parasitic genetic elements such as plasmids and *prophages* that induce 'altruistic cell death' in their host, so the eukaryotic 'selflessness' that ultimately led to multicellular life forms may have likewise been the product of an (initially disharmonious) union with a selfish subself.[572]

Buchnera *and* 'Candidatus *Tremblaya Princeps*'

A distinction is commonly drawn between organelles such as mitochondria and chloroplasts – which have undergone extreme genome reduction and now import most of their functional proteins from the host cell – and other bacterial symbionts such as *Buchnera aphidicola*, generally regarded as retaining 'more robust gene sets that are considered complete enough to support autonomous life'.[573]

As we have already seen,[574] *Buchnera* is an obligate endosymbiont that inhabits certain cells in greenflies and whose genome exhibits both enhanced mutation rates and ongoing genome reduction, gradually ridding itself of functions that are provided by its host. Just as the ancestral lineage of *Rickettsia* and mitochondria is believed to be traceable to a free-living alpha-proteobacterium, it is thought that the progenitors of *Buchnera* were similar to modern-day gamma-proteobacteria such as *E. coli* or *Salmonella*, which are its closest free-living relatives. Phylogenetic analysis has shown that the symbiosis between *Buchnera* and its host aphids was the product of a single bacterial infection of the common ancestor of all extant aphids that took place some 200–250 million years ago and led to the subsequent coevolution and cospeciation of host and symbiont.[575] Since their divergence from the enteric bacteria, the various strains of *B. aphidicola* have all undergone a massive reduction in the size of their genome. Whereas the genome size for *E. coli* ranges from 4.5 to 5.5 Mb, the *Buchnera* genome is usually little more than a tenth of the size (630–650 kb), and in one lineage it is just 422 kb.[576] The *Buchnera* genome basically comprises just a small subset of the *E. coli* genome, itself possessing only four genes that *E. coli* lacks.[577]

The recent discovery of the 422-kb genome of the strain of *B. aphidicola* associated with the aphid *Cinara cedri*,[578] and the ongoing genome reduction and gene loss characteristic of such endosymbionts, raises the question of how far such reduction can go. Possessing just 362 protein-coding genes, the strain in question has lost many of its metabolic functions,[579] and even relinquished the ability to produce the vital amino acids tryptophan and riboflavin for its host, though it is thought that these functions may have been assumed by a secondary endosymbiont, '*Candidatus* Serratia symbiotica', which is present in similar numbers. So what is happening to *Buchnera* as a self in such circumstances? Is the process best understood as a gradual fading away of what was once a free-living bacterium? Is there a cut-off point beyond which its selfhood can be taken to be snuffed out, like a candle? Or perhaps it is the *association* of host and symbiont as a whole (including the secondary symbiont as well, where present) that should be regarded as the living 'self'.

The answer to these questions – if there is one – will depend on the precise nature of the endosymbiotic relationship. In fact, *Buchnera* is one of a number of obligate intracellular symbionts whose shared features may help shed some light on the nature and extent of their selfhood. Similar associations between sap-sucking insects and primary endosymbionts include psyllids (jumping plant lice) with '*Candidatus* Carsonella ruddii', mealybugs with '*Candidatus* Tremblaya princeps', and whiteflies with '*Candidatus* Portiera aleyrodidarum'.[580] Carpenter ants, termites and cockroaches also harbour bacterial symbionts, while the blood-sucking tsetse fly hosts the much-studied *Wigglesworthia glossinidia*.[581] All these associations are mutualistic in that the relationship benefits both parties. The plant sap on which aphids, psyllids, mealybugs and whiteflies all feed is lacking in crucial amino acids, and one of the main functions of the endosymbiont is to synthesize the missing nutrients for its insect host; *Wigglesworthia* is thought to provide its tsetse fly host with the B vitamins needed to supplement the vertebrate blood that constitutes its diet. The benefits are mutual to the extent that the bacteria cannot survive outside their host, which provides them with a stable, nutritious and sheltered environment.

Two immediate points of comparison come to mind. Whereas the parasitism encountered in *Rickettsia* denotes the exploitation of one self by another with only one beneficiary, mutualism involves two selves helping one another to the advantage of both; effectively, it amounts to a sharing of interests and thus to a manner of *shared selfhood*. The relationship of organelle to organism, as exemplified by that of mitochondria to their eukaryotic host cell, might also be described in such terms, but arguably comes closer to the subsumption or swallowing of one unit of selfhood *within* another. Again, this is unlikely to be an all-or-nothing distinction, as suggested by Lewis Thomas's musings on the subtly wielded mastery of the apparently subservient organelle. The question, perhaps, is the degree of 'autonomy' – however this is to be interpreted – that remains in the subordinate self.

There clearly exists a certain asymmetry in the relationship between parasitic pathogen, mutualistic symbiont and an organelle such as the mitochondrion. Whereas both parasite and mutualist depend on their host,[582] the host is better off *without* the parasite but better off *with* the mutualist. It is difficult to conceive of an evolutionary route leading from parasitic pathogen to organelle without the pathogen being in some way 'tamed' or 'domesticated' so that its interests (and thus its self) come to coincide with those of its host. By contrast, the distinction between mutualistic symbiont and organelle is inherently fuzzy: one might imagine a seamless surrender of selfhood as the former evolves into the latter. It has been suggested that the presence of protein import machinery is a sufficient criterion to distinguish an organelle from an endosymbiont.

Only a few of the proteins operative in organelles are encoded by the organelle's own DNA; most are encoded by the nuclear DNA of the host, translated on ribosomes in the host cytoplasm, and imported into the organelle by means of protein import apparatus.[583] In this respect, the organelle may be regarded as *genetically dependent* upon the host cell. However, the distinction is again not watertight. Smaller endosymbionts such as '*Ca*. Tremblaya princeps' also lack many of the genes required to perform basic functions such as DNA repair, ATP synthesis and ribosome construction and thus to maintain themselves as cellular entities. The viability of these tiny organisms remains to be elucidated.[584] It is perhaps unnecessary to reduce the difference to a single factor when host-symbiont integration can occur on a variety of levels. Host regulation of the number of symbiont bodies and synchronisation of their division and segregation might thus be considered an equally valid criterion,[585] while a further possible distinction is that true organelles are present in almost all eukaryotic cells, and not just specialized host cells.[586]

Buchnera and relatives are clearly participants in a mutualistic association, therefore, but how great is their autonomy with respect to their host? The conversion of a symbiont to an organelle has been described in terms of enslavement,[587] perhaps conceived as a progressive relinquishment of genetic independence. Yet 'slavery' is in itself not a straightforward image, given both the master-slave dialectic broached above and the term's value-laden connotations. One is tempted to ask whether life as a mutualistic symbiont – a paid servant or well-nourished valet? – is really any 'better' than as an organellar slave. In both cases, there is a loss of *freedom of movement* with respect to a free-living progenitor. As with its mitochondria, indeed, the host cell might be portrayed as *imprisoning* its bacterial symbionts, almost all of whose motility is sacrificed for a life of carefree confinement. Yet in the near-absence of motility[588] (i.e. any ability to move oneself and thus to *behave* in response to an environment infused with value), there is little reason to believe that it is much 'like' anything – good or bad – to be *Buchnera* or its symbiotic relatives.[589] The privileged domestic service of an obligate intracellular symbiont would not 'feel' any different from the abject serfdom of a lowly mitochondrion, because in neither case would there be any 'feeling' at all.

The dimension of imprisonment comes to light even more strikingly in an example of self-within-self-within-self. The case in question[590] involves the sap-feeding mealybug *Planococcus citri*, which has an association with the bacterial endosymbiont known as '*Ca*. Tremblaya princeps'. Endowed with an extremely reduced genome comprising just 138 kb and 121 coding sequences, this beta-proteobacterium in turn harbours *within itself* a gamma-proteobacterium known as '*Candidatus* Moranella endobia'.[591] The tiny genome of '*Ca*. Tremblaya princeps' – smaller and with less coding capacity than the poxviruses and just a fraction the size of the pandoravirus genome – retains a relatively high percentage of genes involved in informational processing (translation, transcription and replication) and the amino acid biosynthesis required for its host, yet it is deficient in many major functions.[592] Despite its deficiencies, however, it retains enough selfhood – in structural terms at least – to play master to an internalized servant of its own. As with other secondary endosymbionts that 'support' primary endosymbionts, this may well compensate for some of its shortcomings, allowing gene loss and genome reduction to proceed further than would have otherwise been possible.

The imagery of imprisonment – and of prisons within prisons – returns us to the question of self-containment. After all, to be imprisoned is in a sense to be *allo*-contained, and there is certainly an element of *allo*-containment present in endosymbiosis that is absent in pathogenic parasitism. While pathogens have to elude detection and defend themselves against attack from the host immune system,[593] mutualistic symbionts thus tend to be tucked away within specialized protective environments. For a start, they are only present in a certain class of host cells called bacteriocytes, the location of which varies with the host insect. These bacteriocytes in turn aggregate to form 'organs' known as bacteriomes situated, for example, in the body cavity of aphids and the gut of tsetse flies. Within the bacteriocyte, moreover, further envelopment may or may not be provided: while *Wigglesworthia* cells reside directly in the cytoplasm of the host cell, *Buchnera* cells are enclosed within host-derived vesicles.[594]

Given so much protection and 'containment' from the host, it is hardly surprising that there is less pressure on mutualistic bacteria to 'contain' themselves. *Buchnera*, for example, has dispensed with many of the genes needed to produce peptidoglycan for its cell wall and all those required for lipopolysaccharides for its outer membrane.[595] It has been found to lack the genes associated with the biosynthesis of the phospholipids required for the cell membrane, presumably importing these from the host cell. Its cell surface is likely to be much less robust and flexible than that of bacteria such as *Wigglesworthia* that live freely in the host cytoplasm.[596] There are clearly varying degrees of autonomy even among endosymbionts. *Buchnera* and *Wigglesworthia* thus show functional discrepancies not only in the structure of their cell membrane but also in the flagellar apparatus necessary for motility, whose completeness in *Wigglesworthia* suggests a closer affinity to free-living or parasitic bacteria.[597]

At the same time, the permeability of the *Buchnera* cell envelope – in conjunction with its nutrient-rich environment – in turn allows further genes to be shed, since low-molecular-mass metabolites such as nucleotides and amino acids are able to pass through the membrane, making it unnecessary for them to be synthesized by the endosymbiont itself. Of one of the strains of *B. aphidicola*, it has thus been suggested that it comes close to being a 'free-diffusing cell' to the extent that 'most metabolites can be passively exchanged through a highly simplified cell envelope'.[598] Where non-self is so stable and full of easily accessible goodness, self-containment can be trimmed back to a minimum.

The reduction in the factor of self-containment associated with intracellular mutualism comes to light particularly clearly in the shape – or rather misshape – of '*Ca*. Tremblaya princeps', whose gnomic genome retains no genes involved in the biosynthesis of the cell envelope. As the genomes of such endosymbionts shrink in size, it seems, the genes required for the production of fatty acids, phospholipids and peptidoglycan are progressively discarded, permitting maximally reduced organisms such as '*Ca*. Tremblaya princeps' to dispense with a cell wall and presumably rely on the host or on a co-symbiont for their cell membrane. The progressive shrinkage of the genome and loss of key proteins, moreover, leads to a change in morphology from rod-shaped to spherical cells, before finally resulting in the highly irregular 'blob' characteristic of '*Ca*. Tremblaya princeps' or the irregular tubes exhibited by '*Ca*. Carsonella ruddii' and others.[599] The tiniest endosymbionts are somewhere between self-contained, other-contained and not contained at all.

Postscript: Minimum Genomes, Minimum Selves

The recent discovery of 'Ca. Tremblaya princeps' and other such genomically challenged organisms[600] has cast an interesting new light on the venerable question of how much genetic information is necessary for cellular life; or, in other words, the *minimum genome* that is required for a cell to maintain itself, replicate itself and contain itself. There are clear patterns to the gene retention in these tiny endosymbiotic genomes, most of the residual genes being associated on the one hand with informational processing (i.e. translation, transcription and replication), protein folding and stability,[601] and on the other hand with interaction with the host (i.e. the provision of amino acids or other nutrients lacking in the host diet). The genes most easily shed, it seems, are those relating to the biogenesis of the cell envelope (the effects of which can be counterbalanced by vesicles and other forms of 'containment' provided by the host), as well as to DNA repair and recombination.[602] Ever tinier symbiotic genomes will doubtless continue to be found, though John McCutcheon and Nancy Moran suggest a lower limit of some 93 genes (including eleven required for the synthesis of an amino acid to ensure the symbiont's usefulness to its host) and a 70–80 kb genome.[603]

The precise status of these tiny-genome symbionts is ambiguous. McCutcheon and Moran describe them as 'a conundrum of biological classification'[604]:

> *They have smaller genomics encoding fewer proteins than those found in some organelles and viruses, but they differ from these entities in that they retain many genes enabling the core processes for cellular life. They encode far fewer genes than most bacteria but represent one end of a continuum with no clear points of differentiation; known*

> *endosymbiont genome sizes range from 139 kb to more than 1,000 kb. ... [M]any of these symbiont genomes are missing genes that would widely be considered 'essential'.*

Others have gone further in dismissing them from the realm of living organisms. It has been argued – in reference to '*Ca.* Carsonella ruddii'[605] – that 'the extensive degradation of the genome is not compatible with its consideration as a mutualistic endosymbiont and, even more, as a living organism. The ability to perform most essential functions for a cell to be considered alive is heavily impaired by the lack of genes involved in DNA replication, transcription and translation'.[606] The implication is that such a genome fails to fulfil the criteria of a 'minimum genome' since it does not contain enough information to keep the cell 'alive' (self-maintaining, self-replicating and self-contained). It may even fail to provide the full quota of amino acids to the cell's needy host.

The search for the minimum set of protein-coding genes required to keep a cell alive has become something of a 'Holy Grail' for researchers, an effort to 'define the necessary and sufficient components for a living system'.[607] Initial studies focused on the genome of *Mycoplasma genitalium*, a parasitic Gram-positive bacterium that inhabits the genital and respiratory tracts of primates and that was for a long time regarded as the organism with the smallest genome. By comparing the genome of *Mycoplasma genitalium* (469 genes) with that of a small pathogenic *Gram-negative bacterium Haemophilus influenza* (1703 genes), Arcady Mushegian and Eugene Koonin were able to pinpoint a subset of 256 shared genes that encode such functions as transcription, translation and protein folding; DNA replication, recombination and repair; a reduced anaerobic metabolism, limited lipid biosynthesis and machinery for metabolite import.[608] With Gram-negative and Gram-positive bacteria believed to be separated from their last common ancestor by at least 1500 million years of evolution (i.e. they are exceedingly remote cousins), the idea was that genes conserved across such an enormous phylogenetic span are likely to be essential for the functioning of a cell. Another, complementary estimate of the minimum genome was undertaken by Mitsuhiro Itaya,[609] who ascertained the percentage of randomly selected genetic loci in the *Bacillus subtilis* genome that could undergo mutation without making the cell non-viable. By calculating the fraction of the actual genome that was 'indispensable', Itaya came up with a minimum genome size between 318 kb and 562 kb, corresponding to between 254 and 450 genes and seemingly corroborating the results obtained by Mushegian and Koonin.

There is, however, a certain ambiguity in the project. On the one hand, Koonin stipulates that the minimal gene set should comprise 'the smallest possible group of genes that would be sufficient to sustain a functioning cellular life form under the most favorable conditions imaginable, that is, in the presence of a full complement of essential nutrients and in the absence of environmental stress'.[610] What better description could there be of the life of an intracellular mutualist tucked away in a nutritious environment in a vesicle in a specialized cell in a specialized organ in an aphid that depends on it for its dietary supplement of amino acids? On the other hand, many studies have further specified it as a gene set that can be grown axenically, i.e. independently of any other living organism[611] (the term 'axenic' signifying the absence of what is 'foreign' or 'non-self'). In these terms, the focus should indeed be on such organisms as *M. genitalium*, which has the smallest genome of any bacterium that has been axenically cultured to date.[612]

Ultimately, however, the distinction is rather arbitrary. Parasitism, in a broad sense signifying the vital dependence of one self upon another self or other selves, is a matter of degree. Even *M. genitalium* is a parasite. In terms of autonomy, the laurels should perhaps go to a tiny marine bacterium named 'Ca. Pelagibacter ubique' – thought to be the most abundant cellular life-form on the planet, accounting for some 25 percent of all microbes – which is credited with the most diminutive genome (1.3 Mb) of 'any cell known to replicate independently in nature'.[613] In fact, all living organisms (i.e. selves) depend *in some way* upon other living organisms (i.e. other selves) unless they live directly on sunlight or the chemical energy of the planet. Such is the collective parasitism of *heterotrophs* on *autotrophs*,[614] the former feeding directly or indirectly on the labours of the mainly photosynthetic autotrophs that do the hard work of turning inorganic raw materials into organic molecules.[615] Notably, the ecological simplicity and relative self-sufficiency of autotrophs seems to go hand-in-hand with biochemical complexity: light-harvesting *cyanobacteria* such as *Synechococcus* and archaea such as *Halobacterium halobium* have genomes four or five times bigger than *M. genitalium*.[616]

The point, therefore, is that selves tend to be inextricably bound up with other selves; a laboratory might be axenic, but life is not. 'Ca. Carsonella ruddii' and 'Ca. Tremblaya princeps' have taken their dependence upon a host towards one end of what McCutcheon and Moran rightly call a continuum, but it is a continuum that might also be taken to include mitochondria, mimivirus and (why not?) even tiny viroids and capsid-less RNA viruses. In so doing, they may have surrendered most aspects of their individual selfhood, yet they have also united their interests with those of their partner in mutualism, forming a shared self. At the same time, they have found themselves a cushy number. There is no reason for them to go to the trouble of biosynthesizing vital compounds if they can hit upon and survive in an environment that provides them with those compounds.

V.

The Urself, LUCA and the Origins of Life

Urself and Überself

Although it was initially thought that cells with small genomes might represent ancestral or primitive organisms, the preceding chapter has made it clear that there is no *straightforward* correlation between simplicity and chronological precedence. The evolutionary path leading from free-living bacterial ancestors to intracellular descendants demonstrates that later selves are not necessarily more complex than their forerunners. Conversely, it is not self-evident that tracing selfhood back to its roots involves a search for what is smallest or simplest. The present chapter will thus explore the origins of selfhood more in terms of the *logical* preconditions for the urself that marked the transition from a world or universe devoid of selves to one inhabited by selves.

The first question is whether the question itself makes sense. Surely an urself is a contradiction in terms, for any self worth its salt is the work of a progenitor self. An understanding of the self as an entity that produces and is produced by itself (a self-begetting self, a self that always generates itself *out of* a pre-existing self and *into* a post-existing self) might be felt either to take us on an infinite regression to the dawn of time (whatever *that* is supposed to mean!) or suggest the ontological gymnastics of a Münchhausen hoisting himself into existence by his own bootlaces or periwig. Reassuringly, our evolutionary perspective allows us to entertain the idea of a gradual progression: on this view, selfhood is something that has come into existence through an ongoing concatenation of incremental physico-chemical steps. The conundrum of the self-begetting self is resolved by the fuzziness of its origins: we can put the earliest selves in inverted commas or attach a prefix such as 'proto' or 'quasi' to them in order to indicate that a self probably evolved seamlessly from something that was only self-like, and this in turn evolved from something that was even less self-like, and so on back to something so un-self-like that it can hardly be called a 'self' at all. To provide a brief overview of such narratives is part of the aim of the present chapter.

Yet even these Earth-bound narratives depend upon a bigger picture. At a deeper level, therefore, it might be the self-organizing universe[617] as a whole that is considered to be the urself.[618] One might see urselfhood in the galaxy that resolves itself into a self-perpetuating pattern, or perhaps in the star that feeds off gravitational energy to power its self-sustaining nuclear combustion through a stellar life cycle, or even in the atmospheric turbulence of a planet, which in turn draws sustenance from the flux of energy emitted by its star to form configurations of matter that persist in time. Biological selfhood may be understood to presuppose a universe characterized by disequilibrium and the energetic flow without which self-organization would be unthinkable, a universe powered by gravity or the cosmic expansion. A background lacking such imbalance and flux is incompatible with the possibility of stars whose life cycles result in the creation of elements such as carbon, oxygen and iron, and (in some cases) whose spectacularly explosive death throes disseminate these heavier elements across the interstellar environment, sowing the seeds for the subsequent emergence of the biology characteristic of our planet and possibly others. While such self-organizing cosmological urselves – or perhaps überselves is a more apposite term – may not in themselves comply with the complete set of criteria required for selfhood as expounded in the Introduction, they *lay the foundations* for the possible emergence of the living selfhood that is the focus of origin-of-life narratives. The 'full' selfhood that inhabits our planet has its ultimate roots in the überself[619] of which it forms a part and within which it is nested.

Against this dual background, the question of original selfhood can be broached from either or both of two directions, namely from the bottom up or the top down.[620] A bottom-up approach examines what conditions had to be fulfilled to permit the jump from 'merely' physico-chemical self-organization – from dissipative structures of the sort encountered in Chapter 2 – to the earliest system that might uncontroversially be called 'living'. It asks how this primal cell or organism, the first self to inhabit the planet, could have arisen and what form it would have taken. Key factors include the need for the flux of energy to be channelled or 'contained' within structures and boundaries such as membranes. This containment makes it possible for the energy flow to be used for work rather than dissipated as heat, in turn maintaining the structures and boundaries that allow work to be done, and thus perpetuating a cycle of work and containment. At the same time, the ability of the system to replicate itself and evolve through generations is generally considered to be equally crucial. Two questions have dominated the debates on how this transition came about: the first question is whether the first living system was 'metabolic' or 'genetic' in nature; the second, closely related question is at what point such living systems came to be enclosed within 'compartments' (such as cellular membranes). In essence, these two questions are a reflection and corroboration of the three-pronged intrinsic reflexivity of full selfhood, understood in terms of self-production, self-replication and self-containment. The attempts that have been made to pinpoint the relative logical and chronological primacy of these three modes of intrinsic reflexivity will be the focus of much of the present chapter.

A top-down approach, by contrast, focuses on the biochemical features common to all life actually known to exist – from bacteria, archaea and single-celled eukaryotes to many-celled animals, plants and fungi – which are taken to be jointly inherited from the last common ancestor that all living beings share. Every cell in every animal's body, every cell in every plant, every amoeba and every *E. coli* bacterium, is endowed with an array of stock characteristics that can be taken to date back to this 'cenancestor', the last universal common ancestor, aka LUCA. By analysing these features, a considerable amount can be inferred about this ancestral self, the great^{great}-grandparent from which my intestinal bacteria, my recently ingested banana and I all descend. LUCA is not to be confused with the primal cell or urself: the latter is reconstructed by tracing a hypothetical geochemical route from a lifeless world to one populated with the earliest living selves; LUCA is reconstructed by tracing a route backwards (or downwards[621]) from all extant selves, determining what they have in common with one another and thus also with their shared arch-ancestor. As Harold Morowitz has written, 'we envision the ur-cells as being very simple, whereas the universal ancestor must – by comparison to these – have been quite complex. Thus, the gap between the approach from above and the approach from below must be filled by an evolutionary path from the ur-organism to the universal ancestor. ... When the universal ancestor finally evolved, it outcompeted the rest of ur-life, leaving many niches for the radiation of its descendants'.[622] The time it took for the urself to evolve into LUCA is generally considered to be relatively brief in comparison to the history of life as a whole, possibly less than 200 million years.[623] Whatever form it took, LUCA is commonly thought to date back to a time more than 3,500 million years ago.[624]

Despite this conceptual distinction, the two approaches complement one another. Speculations on the possible scenarios that might have led to the generation of self-reproducing cells are helpfully constrained by the form that life is in fact known to have adopted. There must be explanatory continuity, i.e. a feasible evolutionary pathway, leading from one to the other. Yet this raises the question of how far LUCA – and all living selfhood that descends from her –

is necessary and how far contingent in her characteristics. Could the urself have evolved in a different direction? How different could the course taken by evolution conceivably have been? Just how different might selfhood have turned out?

In drawing up a list of the most general characteristics that underlie and ground all current biology, Morowitz draws attention to the unitary yet highly delimited nature of Earth-based biochemistry, typified by the restricted set of low-molecular-weight organic compounds that are involved:

> Amid the enormous diversity of biological types, including millions of recognizable species, the variety of biochemical pathways is small, restricted, and universally distributed. All protein is made from the same group of amino acids, all RNA from the same group of ribonucleotides, all DNA from the same group of deoxyribonucleotides, all carbohydrates from a small group of sugars, and all phospholipids from a limited group of fatty acids. Thus, in most cases over 90% of cellular material can be accounted for by fewer than fifty compounds and polymers of these compounds.
>
> If one considers all low molecular weight compounds ... that can be made from carbon, hydrogen, nitrogen, oxygen, phosphorus and sulfur, the number is immense. Yet from this potential group, a very small subgroup is actually used by living systems.[625]

This limited set of relatively small organic molecules combines to produce just four major classes of macromolecules – proteins, lipids, carbohydrates and nucleic acids – which make up the great bulk of the non-aqueous part of living selves, raising the question of whether other macromolecules might not have served just as well.[626] Indeed, the commonality underlying all known life on Earth encompasses a range of basic features that seems not to be explainable *merely* in terms of biochemical necessity. Such features include the universal occurrence of ATP as a means of energy storage and transfer,[627] ribosomes responsible for protein synthesis, proteins constructed from a small set of amino acids, lipid membranes, the ATPases used in chemiosmotic energy generation, and – perhaps most fundamentally of all – the universally shared genetic code.

The hint of arbitrariness even hangs over the type of genetic material that happens to be characteristic of terrestrial selfhood, for it is far from certain that it really *had* to take the form that it has done, namely RNA and DNA. How inevitable was it, for example, that the sugars ribose and deoxyribose were used as the backbone structuring the long RNA and DNA molecules? Recent years have seen scientists develop alternative forms from different sugars, producing new genetic molecules such as ANA (based on arabinose) and TNA (based on threose). Collectively termed xeno-nucleic acids (XNAs), these new molecular species have already been shown not only to replicate, but also to evolve.[628] A further species of molecules, known as *peptide* nucleic acids or PNAs, is now known to utilize a peptide-based backbone to link its nucleobases rather than a sugar such as deoxyribose or ribose. Might one imagine a PNA-based form of living selfhood?[629]

Terrestrial selfhood could almost certainly have taken a different course in some of its most basic features; environmental contingencies might have led to divergent adaptations that would have proved to be not only less but also more efficient. The deep unity that *in fact* connects the cells in my body with all other prokaryotic and eukaryotic cells on the planet is generally taken as providing solid evidence not so much of the constraints of biochemistry as of the putative ancestor we all have in common.[630] Earth-based biology, it is argued, has turned out the way it has because of its origins in this single universal progenitor, which in its time was presumably able to fend off competition from other, less energetically or replicatively efficient rival proto-organisms. Biochemically speaking, all the selves on our planet since LUCA are veritable chips off the old block: like urmother, like child.

Yet our common origin in LUCA is unlikely to explain everything: other, possibly more profound explanatory principles may also be invoked. One of the best-known of the generalizations that Morowitz highlights as essential to biology is that all life is cellular in nature; i.e. it consists of cells or the products of cells.[631] This of course coincides with the factor of self-containment, a definitional feature of selfhood that goes *deeper* than the historical contingency of shared terrestrial origins. Relevant questions pertain to the requisite extent and limits of such self-containment. One wonders what sort of selfhood is possible in the absence, or near-absence, of self-containment and whether self-containment must indeed be 'membranous' or more generally 'cellular' in nature.

Another of the generalizations proposed by Morowitz is the predominance of the elements carbon, hydrogen, nitrogen, oxygen, phosphorus and sulphur (commonly abbreviated to CHNOPS in this 'origin-of-life' context) as the atomic components required for all functioning biological systems.[632] CHNOPS is certainly essential to the present biochemistry of our planet, and Morowitz indeed speculates that there might have been a pre-nitrogen stage involving just CHOPS.[633] Unlike the particularities of our genetic code and the importance of ATP, however, the reasons for the prevalence of CHOPS perhaps have to do less with evolutionary contingency (replicative or energetic efficiency in the environmental conditions that happened to prevail at a specific time on Earth) than with certain features intrinsic to the elements themselves, especially carbon: namely their inherent 'sociability' as elements that readily form bonds amongst themselves and with one another and are thus endowed with exceptional flexibility and variability in the molecular forms they can assume.

In this they diverge notably from so-called 'higher' elements (i.e. elements with higher atomic numbers), which are considerably less sociable. By contrast with specific biochemical features such as RNA or ATP (which have proved to be central to post-LUCA selfhood), therefore, it can perhaps be ventured that CHNOPS, CHOPS or simply carbon are more *intrinsically* associated with the possible emergence of living urselfhood. Carbon in particular seems to play an indispensable part in any such process, the stability of the carbon-carbon bond (at temperatures close to those on Earth) providing a scaffold on which complex biomolecules can be constructed.[634] Silicon is generally considered the only alternative biomolecular scaffold, yet it is neither as abundant as carbon in the universe nor able to match the unique variety of combinations carbon can undergo with elements such as hydrogen, oxygen and nitrogen.[635] Life on our planet is thus commonly described as carbon-based.

Or rather: water- and carbon-based. We have already encountered the dependence of life and selfhood upon liquid water,[636] which is not only a vital metabolite but plays a crucial role as a solvent facilitating the possibility of a controlled flow of energy. Morowitz himself pinpoints water as essential to functional living systems, the aqueous content of which varies from 50 percent to over 95 percent.[637] On Earth, life seems to be present wherever there is water and absent wherever there is not. Like CHNOPS, moreover, water can be assumed not to be a feature specific to LUCA and her descendants; its availability is likely to have been a prerequisite for the appearance of the very first primal self. Yet we have also seen that purely 'carbaquist' approaches to life and selfhood are vulnerable to accusations of parochialism: if we restrict our conception of selfhood to water and carbon-based entities, it is argued, this can only be because we lack the imagination to look beyond our own cosmological noses.

While it is true that some sort of liquid solvent[638] is required for the possibility of flow (allowing dissolved reactants to interact with one another), a variety of non-aqueous solvents have thus been proposed that might well do the trick equally efficiently. Advocates of a non-aqueous origin of life point to the corrosive nature of water as a feature that is deeply inimical to the emergence of living systems. As a result of water's characteristic reactivity, genetic macromolecules tend not only to dissolve in water, but to fall apart in it. It is only because of ongoing repair work that molecules such as DNA are now able to mend the breakages and thus maintain their integrity within a watery environment. To the newly emerging genetic material of the hypothesized RNA world, by contrast, water would have posed a possibly insurmountable challenge.[639]

In non-terrestrial contexts, alternative, non-aqueous solvents such as liquid ammonia have thus been proposed as conducive to or compatible with life, albeit life with a very different metabolic biochemistry from what is found on Earth.

Like water, ammonia dissolves a range of organic compounds and is liquid over a reasonably wide range of temperatures, though it would be gaseous at terrestrial temperatures and lacks some of water's more remarkable life-fostering properties.[640] Counter-intuitively, sulphuric acid has been suggested as another solvent that could sustain chemical reactions, while non-polar solvents such as hydrocarbons (methane, ethane, propane, etc.) and even supercritical fluids – substances above a critical temperature and pressure where liquid and gas phases are no longer distinct[641] – have been propounded as further alternatives. The term 'weird life' has been coined to refer to organisms that do not depend on water.[642] Within the Solar System, it has been speculated that weird forms of life might be present in the hydrocarbon lakes of Titan, the largest of Saturn's moons. Even if this were feasible, however, the biochemical complexity of such *weird selfhood* would be severely hamstrung by the scarcity of oxygen and the limited capacity of liquid hydrocarbons to dissolve macromolecules such as nucleic acids.[643]

In the context of terrestrial origins, by contrast, perhaps the most interesting variant is a non-aqueous solvent called formamide (CH_3NO), which would have been generated when the hydrogen cyanide (HCN) of the primordial atmosphere combined with water. Formamide contains the CHNO of CHNOPS[644] and also has the key property of being a liquid between 4 °C and 210 °C, its relatively high boiling point meaning that in an environment hotter than 100 °C it would become concentrated as the water boiled away.[645] Notably, many biomolecules susceptible to *hydrolysis* in water are spontaneously generated in formamide, which has been shown to provide a unitary framework for the origin of genetic polymers, a broad range of *carboxylic acid*s involved in metabolism, and the formation of *micelles* required for compartmentalization. Yet even allowing for formamide to play a role in a terrestrial origin-of-life scenario, the challenge posed by water would undoubtedly have to be met sooner or later. Explanatory parsimony perhaps suggests sooner rather than later.

Though not ruling out alternative scenarios, Iris Fry thus advocates a cautious *carbaquism*:

> *The strongest case for carbon as the major biogenic element and also for water as both constituent of life and its environment, not only on Earth but in the universe, is based on the conception of organisms as complex, self-organized, self-maintaining, and self-reproducing systems that are the products of evolutionary processes. For any system to perform all these functions and to evolve – first and foremost, to be able to pass information from generation to generation – it must possess molecules that are large, complex, stable and varied. Organic chemistry as known to us, based on carbon and water, provides a very sound basis for any such system.*[646]

In the light of these stipulations and our limited knowledge of what is chemically feasible, the presence of carbon and liquid water (with their attributes and abundance) can be taken to represent a *solid foundation* rather than a binding precondition for the possible emergence of living selfhood, at least in a universe endowed with the fundamental physical characteristics shown by ours. At the risk of parochialism, therefore, the rest of the present chapter will focus on the broadly carbaquist biochemistry of Earth-based selfhood (the only sort we know) and remain sceptically agnostic about the possibility of extraplanetary selves based on non-aqueous solvents or silicon as an alternative biomolecular scaffold.

Given the properties of carbon and liquid water, it has even been suggested that living selfhood may in fact be a rather *likely* consequence of their presence in conjunction with suitable energetic conditions. Noting that life on Earth arose more or less as soon as environmental circumstances permitted, Stephen Jay Gould famously argued that 'it is not "difficult" for life of bacterial grade to evolve on planets with appropriate conditions. The origin of life may be a virtually automatic consequence of carbon chemistry and the physics of self-organizing systems, given favorable conditions and the requisite inorganic constituents'.[647] The notion of a 'virtually automatic consequence' is a strong one in such a context. The question is whether a self-organizing universe furnished with elements such as CHNOPS merely provides the necessary framework within which living selfhood of an Earth-like variety *can* emerge (as a logical possibility), or whether it may naturally *tend to foster* its emergence (given the absence of certain limiting conditions such as protracted meteorite bombardment). Like claims about the self-complexification of biospheres, of course, such claims about natural tendencies are resistant to falsification and may have teleological connotations. This is not to say that they are either meaningless or wrong. The point is simply that from within the system in question – the only one with which we are acquainted – we cannot know them to be right.

Soups, Genes and Catalysts

Warm Ponds and Hot Soups

One of the earliest formulations of the role of water in the origin of life stems from the pen of Charles Darwin. In a letter dating from 1871 Darwin wrote speculatively of a 'warm little pond' containing ammonia and phosphoric salts, which under the influence of light, heat and electricity produced 'a protein compound ... ready to undergo still more complex changes'.[648] In general, Darwin claimed not to be concerned with the origin of the first life,[649] yet it was only with the rise of the Darwinian evolutionary worldview that the question could be wrested from the grip of Christian theology and Aristotelian natural philosophy and formulated in terms of a gradual, continuous, causally coherent narrative involving physico-chemical mechanisms rather than divine intervention or spontaneous generation.[650]

In the first half of the 20th century, Darwin's 'warm little pond' was taken up first by the American Leonard Troland, who in the 1910s proposed the fortuitous (and thus highly improbable) appearance in the primal seas of a primitive molecule with autocatalytic abilities, i.e. a 'genetic enzyme' with a capacity to catalyse its own formation and thus proliferate.[651] The following decade saw the appearance of two independently conceived papers both entitled 'The Origin of Life', one by the Soviet biochemist Alexander Oparin (1924) and the other by the British geneticist J. B. S. Haldane (1929). Both papers argued that the path towards the emergence of life on Earth necessarily involved a process of chemical evolution leading to the synthesis of organic compounds in the 'soup' of the primordial oceans, a proposal that has come to be known as the 'Oparin-Haldane Hypothesis'.[652] Under the influence of this hypothesis, scientists in the field of experimental prebiotic chemistry have since attempted to recreate this primeval soup, simulating the conditions in which the first living selves hoisted themselves into existence some 3.8 billion years ago. Most famously, Stanley Miller and Harold Urey in 1953 built an experimental system comprising an 'atmosphere' of methane, ammonia and hydrogen in conjunction with a pool of water; an electrical discharge was used to imitate lightning.[653] They found within a week that their pool of water had turned reddish and now harboured organic compounds, including (most significantly) amino acids, the building blocks of proteins. Subsequent work in the field has succeeded in synthesizing purines and pyrimidines, the building blocks of RNA and DNA.[654]

The 'primordial soup' hypothesis is encumbered with a number of problems. Serious doubts have been raised about the existence of the strongly reducing atmosphere (i.e. one high in hydrogen and low in oxygen) assumed by its earliest advocates. In the presence of an only *weakly* reducing atmosphere consisting of carbon dioxide rather than methane and nitrogen gas rather than ammonia, the yield of organic compounds is drastically diminished. A related issue is the sheer diluteness of the organic soup, raising the question of whether the biomolecules that were formed could have achieved sufficient levels of concentration for biological activity to occur. A further problem – already encountered above – is the tendency of water to cause hydrolysis, splitting long, chain-like polymers up instead of linking their constituent amino acids and nucleotides together. Water-based life faces a constant battle to resist being dismantled by the very medium on which it depends.[655] As pointed out by Nick Lane and colleagues, however, perhaps the most fundamental drawback of the 'primordial soup' hypothesis is its failure to provide a suitable flux of energy; soups imply homogeneity and a lack of the thermodynamic disequilibrium that is required for energy to be controlled, channelled or contained and thus made to do work. Ultraviolet radiation and lightning tend to destroy as much as they create, whereas what is required is a 'continuous and replenishing source of chemical energy'.[656] It is clear that at least some of these misgivings could be dispelled if the prebiotic scenario were conceived, not in free solution but in compartments of some kind: a soup *per se* fails to provide any form of 'containment'. It is only through (self) 'containment' that an entity in flux can hold itself apart from what is not itself.

An alternative response is to dismiss the 'soup' scenario altogether. Exogenous organic material is widely believed to have reached Earth from outer space in the course of the bombardment by comets and asteroids to which the planet was subject during its formation. The presence of the simplest of the amino acids, glycine, has been reported on comets and in interstellar gas clouds, and very small proteins such as a dipeptides and tripeptides (compounds comprising two or three amino acids) are also considered capable of forming in space.[657] If key compounds such as formaldehyde and a selection of amino acids really were delivered by impacting bodies during the Earth's early years, such a non-terrestrial source of prebiotic materials would have arguably rendered a primal soup superfluous. Yet this increasing awareness of the potential sophistication of interstellar chemistry may be conceived as *complementing* rather than supplanting the role of water-based chemistry in the origin of life,[658] since the problems connected with water still need to be addressed at some point. The fact remains that any organic material delivered from the skies would have had to face the various challenges posed by the 'soup' that awaited it on Earth: most significantly, the threat of being dismantled by hydrolysis, the need for energetic disequilibrium, and the requirement of a 'container' to counter the handicap of diluteness and the risk of diffusion and dispersal. The convenient delivery of ready-made ingredients is one thing, but the generation of complex chemical systems endowed with the capacity to use a controlled flow of energy to produce and re-produce themselves over a protracted period of time remains difficult to conceive without water – despite all the difficulties that this may entail. While the 'soup' metaphor may indeed have proved misleading or incomplete, a broadly water-based framework continues to be indispensable.[659]

Genetic and Metabolic Approaches

The debate on the origin of life has been characterized by a broad dichotomy between a genetic approach that ascribes chronological primacy to a genetic system and a metabolic approach that prioritizes an autocatalytic or metabolic system consisting of enzymes. This dichotomy goes back to the dual figures of Oparin and Haldane, for whereas Oparin envisioned the living systems that emerged from the primal oceans as complex multimolecular systems endowed with a metabolism, Haldane stressed the role of self-replicating molecules.[660] The divergence has been perpetuated in a lasting conflict between 'protein people' and 'nucleic acid people', i.e. between the advocates of metabolism-first and replication-first approaches.[661] As Iris Fry points out, the arguments wielded are partly empirical in nature, relating to the likelihood or unlikelihood of certain chemical processes taking place in the conditions that prevailed on the newly formed planet. Yet they also have to do with the very conception of a living system or self:

Is life basically a 'replication machine', and hence, did life start with the emergence of a self-replicating molecule, and only later, through mutation and natural selection, did 'all the rest' develop? Or should the first living systems be characterized as an integrated cycle of weak enzymes that sustained itself through the exchange of matter and energy with the environment under far-from-equilibrium conditions, with the later appearance of genetic material being only the consequence of this primordial metabolism?[662]

Each view gives antecedence to one of two contrasting forms of intrinsic reflexivity examined in the Introduction, focusing on a conception of life defined either in terms of metabolic self-maintenance or a capacity for self-replication. Neither alone can be taken to be sufficient for full selfhood, though both – in different ways – represent plausible *routes* to such a self. The two views are confronted with complementary conundrums. The metabolic view must face the question of whether (and how) it is possible for a self-maintaining, autocatalytic system to reproduce itself through generations and thus evolve *without* the template-based genetic material that it is retrospectively assumed to have acquired by a process of evolution. The genetic view must be able to answer the question of whether (and how) self-replicating molecules are able to engage in successful self-replication *without* forming part of some sort of self-controlled and self-controlling molecular microenvironment whose existence requires an ongoing process of metabolic and energetic self-production through time.

Metabolism-first theorists tend to postulate a two-stage origin of life and selfhood. A first stage involves the emergence of a primitive metabolic, cellular system that is based on protein-like enzymes and can grow and divide. At this point, the 'genetic information' is seen as embodied not in individual molecules, but in the structure of the system as a whole. Stuart Kauffman, for example, envisions the emergence of an autocatalytic set of enzymes that is capable of catalysing its own reproduction. Kauffman regards such autocatalytic systems as able to evolve *without* a genome, or rather as serving as their own genome. At the same time, he notes, 'the capacity to incorporate novel molecular species, and perhaps eliminate older molecular forms, promises to generate a population of self-reproducing chemical networks with different characteristics',[663] which would in turn be liable to natural selection. The transition from the first to the second stage would be from a systemic to a template-based system of heredity, presumably made possible by the incorporation of 'novel molecular species'. Freeman Dyson has proposed a transition based on the invasion of the original metabolic system by a parasitic RNA entity, which with time would become an essential component of the cell.[664] On such views, the urself would have been a self-reproducing enzymatic system that only *subsequently* incorporated a template-based mechanism of heredity.

The notions of pre-genomic metabolism and pre-genomic evolution imply that life and selfhood are not tied by logical necessity to informational macromolecules; self-reproducing networks embodying system-level 'genetic' information will do the trick. In practice, however, such proto-selves are beset with evolutionary limitations, rapidly reaching a bottleneck or dead-end in their development. Systems of this sort may already be said to have a certain capacity for heredity or a 'chemical memory', write Ruiz-Mirazo and Moreno, yet 'this is still very precarious: it is distributed over the whole organization and not really trustworthy because it is subject to unpredictable, random changes'.[665] In the absence of the template activity of nucleic acids, such systems lack reliable methods of inheritance and so cannot start a 'Darwinian evolutionary process'.[666] Purely metabolic or autocatalytic systems are thus incapable of evolving to more complex levels of selfhood *without* the mechanisms of template-based replication – the informational macromolecules – that bestow upon them an apparently unlimited potential for heredity and variation.

The genetic approach to the origin of life focuses on just such informational macromolecules, in recent years adopting RNA as its macromolecule of choice. As noted in the Introduction, indeed, the so-called 'RNA world' may in itself be taken to *resolve* the dilemma of metabolic or genetic primacy, overcoming the dichotomy thanks to the dual nature of RNA as both a biological catalyst and a repository-cum-transmitter of information. The problem was traditionally couched as the riddle of the chicken and the egg: given that every living cell known to us comprises highly complex nucleic acids (the DNA that carries genetic information) and highly complex proteins (the enzymes that determine the functionality of the cell), and given that their synthesis and activity are totally interdependent, how could one have arisen without the other? More specifically, how could the first proteins ever have arisen without the nucleic acids that direct their synthesis, and how could the first nucleic acids ever have arisen without the proteins that catalyse their replication and synthesis?[667] Characterized by the double-functionality that lends itself to intrinsic reflexivity (as subject and object), RNA solves the chicken-and-egg problem *by being both*, on the one hand embodying information in its sequence of nucleotides and on the other embodying biological function in its unique three-dimensional structure.

Of course, such duality poses a constant challenge insofar as it places competing demands on the structure of the molecules in question. While the template activity of an informational macromolecule is favoured by a uniform, linear morphology, catalytic activity calls for a diversity of three-dimensional configurations.[668] As a consequence of the intrinsic contradiction between these two goals and given the need for a structural compromise, it is argued, a single-biopolymer system such as the RNA world would be more 'fragile' and less 'robust' than the two-polymer system characteristic of life on Earth in its present guise.[669] Like pre-genomic metabolic systems, therefore, self-replicating RNA-based systems have also been conceived as coming up against a bottleneck[670] that would have only been surmounted by those proto-selves that made the transition to producing two distinct types of polymers, each of them more efficient in their respective functions: DNA molecules for more faithful and less error-prone replication, and proteins for more effective enzymatic activity. The intrinsic reflexivity previously embodied within a single type of molecule (the RNA that served as subject and object, chicken and egg) came to be shared, as it were, between the two interdependent macromolecular constituents of living selves.

In fact, RNA is not the only molecule endowed with this gene-catalyst duality. Given the catalytic attributes of single-stranded DNA (in conjunction with DNA's better-known virtues as a genetic template),[671] the occurrence of a 'DNA world' has also been posited. This too would harbour the potential to solve the 'chicken-and-egg' problem, with primeval DNA acting not only as a genetic macromolecule, but also – in its single-stranded form – as a catalyst. An RNA world is nonetheless considered the more plausible option. As Ronald Breaker and Gerald Joyce put it, the notion of an RNA world is grounded not only on the dual functionality of RNA, but also on the observation that 'RNA has a primitive role in many of the most highly preserved processes in biological organisms'.[672] For a start, RNA plays an integral role in nearly all the informational processes of the cell, for example in the form of the messenger RNA that transmits genetic instructions from the DNA to the protein-synthesizing ribosome, itself a molecular machine that is built out of RNA and protein complexes. RNA is required for the replication of DNA, as well as for the editing and splicing of genetic information prior to translation. As a type of cofactor called a 'coenzyme' (many of which are modified ribonucleotides), moreover, it also plays a pivotal support role in nearly all the most basic aspects of cellular metabolism, most notably in the guise of ATP, the universal energy currency.[673] The vestiges of the RNA world, it seems, pervade the informational and metabolic apparatus of modern life.[674]

In the light of such evidence, there is broad agreement not only that a network of RNA molecules *could have* produced a system endowed with a capacity for both autocatalysis and self-replication, but also that RNA is the candidate *most likely* to have actually done so. A system of this nature could have used a flux of energy to maintain itself, reproduce itself and also transform itself (or evolve) over an extended period of time. The intrinsically reflexive urself would thus have contained RNA as its main ingredient. To be sure, the afore-mentioned difficulties associated with a *watery* RNA world have prompted the suggestion that such a world may have been preceded by or accompanied by other biochemical scenarios – perhaps involving a genome-free or a nitrogen-free protobiology, clusters of inorganic minerals, or a more stable macromolecule such as PNA. What seems beyond question, however, is that the RNA world cannot have formed in free solution. It is not enough to postulate the presence of diverse small organic compounds dissolved in the vastness of the primal oceans and hope for a self-producing RNA world to schlep itself into existence. For a start, some form of containment or compartment is required to concentrate the prebiotic ingredients and foster cohesion and structure.

It has tended to be the metabolic approach to the origin of life that has laid greater emphasis on the need for a cell-like structure – often provided by a membrane – to prevent the dispersal of the system's components and to separate and protect the self-maintaining network from its environment. The genetic approach, by contrast, has been more willing to posit the emergence of 'naked genes' in a primordial soup,[675] and the RNA world has sometimes been understood as a precellular stage of evolution.[676] The early Manfred Eigen and co-workers, for example, reasoned that 'organization into cells was surely postponed as long as possible. Anything that interposed spatial limits in a homogeneous system would have introduced difficult problems for prebiotic chemistry. Constructing boundaries, transposing things across them and modifying them when necessary are tasks accomplished today by the most refined cellular processes'.[677] In general, however, both empirical and conceptual considerations – the empirical implausibility of a completely 'uncontained' stage in incipient life no less than the conceptual characterization of all modern life as a 'mutualistic symbiosis between genes, catalysts and membranes'[678] – make the emergence of 'containment' one of the most pressing concerns in attempts to grasp the origins of selfhood. The nature and extent of compartmentalization and 'self'-containment in the emergence of life and selfhood will be the focus of the remaining part of this chapter.

Microdroplets and Membranes

The notion of some sort of partition between proto-self and non-self goes back to the earliest metabolic theory. Oparin had referred to microdroplets called 'coacervates' that are known to be produced by intermolecular forces when a specific concentration of polymers such as sugars or proteins is reached in a solution. Such coacervates were shown to be able to absorb small organic molecules from the external solution, and Oparin believed that they could have harboured a primitive metabolism. Increasing in size as it absorbed more and more molecules, the 'parent cell' would eventually divide into two 'daughter cells'. A related line of thought was subsequently pursued by Sidney W. Fox, who posited the formation of similar spherical particles called 'microspheres' from a solution of protein-like polymers in specific environmental conditions.

The Oparin-Fox tradition of non-membranous microspheres continues to be seen by some as a viable way of circumventing a number of problems – in particular the problem of impermeability – connected with the complex phospholipid bilayers characteristic of modern cell membranes. Shogo Koga and colleagues,[679] for example, propose the spontaneously accumulating microdroplets that form in solution from a mixture of nucleotides (such as ATP) and low-molecular-weight peptides as a model for such membrane-free protocells. These 'compartments' are capable of the partitioning and preferential 'sequestering' of certain essential small biomolecules such as light-sensitive porphyrins and can serve as platforms for catalytic activity involving inorganic nanoparticles and enzymes; the presence of high accumulations of ATP suggests the possibility of coupled metabolic energy transformations. The notion of '(self-) containment' throws up some interesting questions in a membrane-free context. Such microdroplets are the product of self-assembly based on electrostatic attraction[680] rather than self-organization, allowing the entity to persist as a unit without the need for an explicit 'container' or active 'containment': in effect, the system 'contains itself' simply by holding itself together, 'spontaneously' generating and maintaining a distinction between inside and outside, self and non-self. One practical drawback of this mode of 'containment without a container' could be a deficiency of the sort of *structure* that is a precondition for directed locomotion. Other possible limitations include an inability to fine-tune or control the selective permeability that is essential to a cell's capacity to absorb nutrients and expel waste while holding vital macromolecules within.

In many metabolism-first approaches to the origin of life, the compartment is basically passive in nature, a means of holding together and preventing the diffusion of what really matters – the autocatalytic network of enzymes.[681] Other researchers and theorists, by contrast, have stressed that the membrane is itself inseparable from the self-producing metabolic system that it encloses.[682] On such a view, membrane and metabolism exist in a relationship of circular interdependency; the membrane is (in part) a product of the metabolism, but also a precondition for its very possibility. While this may sound disconcertingly like another case of chickens and eggs (which came first: membrane or metabolism?), the case for the primacy of membrane is boosted by the well-documented formation of simple lipid vesicles through processes of self-assembly. It is thus conjectured that lipid membranes could have self-assembled to form enclosed vesicles on the newly formed Earth, fostering the emergence of living selves by providing a surface where primitive metabolism could have taken place and in turn lending themselves to self-division and multiplication. As Iris Fry puts it, membrane-first theorists 'consider the emergence of an entity separated from its environment by a membrane as the defining stage in the transition from nonlife to life'.[683]

For such membrane theorists, the 'containment' provided by the lipid vesicles of the primordial Earth is to be viewed as a process or activity, as opposed to the passivity implied by a mere receptacle or vessel. According to the account given by Harold Morowitz in *Beginnings of Cellular Life*, the lipid bilayer of the minimal protocell would have incorporated a primitive pigment system – or chromophore – capable of absorbing light energy that would have been stored in the form of a proton gradient across the membrane.[684] This transmembrane proton gradient would have given rise to a so-called 'chemiosmotic' energy reservoir available to perform work, the flow of protons back across the membrane (i.e. down the gradient) being coupled to the generation of the energy currency ATP.[685] This would have in turn driven the production of new membrane material and powered the ongoing metabolic processes within the cell, causing the vesicle to grow and eventually leading to its spontaneous fission. The phenomenon of chemiosmosis – the use of a proton gradient across a membrane to drive the synthesis of ATP – plays a fundamental and universal role in providing modern-day cells with power.[686] Transmembrane proton gradients are ubiquitous in bacteria and archaea and drive the work of chloroplasts and mitochondria in eukaryotes. In the model proposed by Morowitz, the emergence of the lipid membrane is indissolubly bound up with the possibility of channelling and controlling and thus 'containing' the energy required in order for living selfhood to perpetuate itself. The urself emerged with, and was grounded upon, the membrane-based partitioning of the world into self and non-self and the use of this partition to power self-sustaining metabolic networks.

The scenario developed by Morowitz was crucially influenced by the research work of biochemist David Deamer and colleagues on how the self-assembly of closed membranous vesicles from amphiphilic lipids – i.e. lipids containing both hydrophilic and hydrophobic poles – might have set the scene for the origin of life. Such compounds could have either been delivered exogenously[687] or produced by the synthetic pathways that are presumed to have existed in the prebiotic environment of the young planet. Deamer contrasts his scenario with the RNA world, which he regards as hugely improbable in the absence of a concentrating mechanism such as lipid vesicles to promote the polymerization of nucleotides into molecules of sufficient length. He also opposes his vesicles to the coacervates and microspheres of Oparin and Fox, which would have lacked a true boundary able to serve as a selective permeability barrier.[688]

However, the question of selective permeability remains a constant challenge for membranes as well. A fundamental problem is how the macromolecules that were necessarily incorporated into the vesicles en route to the creation of living systems came to permeate the boundary in the first place. Deamer suggests that the initial encapsulation of polymeric molecules could well have occurred through the sort of hydration-dehydration or freeze-thaw cycles produced by the evaporation or freezing of a lagoon: 'molecules as large as DNA can be captured by such processes. For instance, when a dispersion of DNA and fatty acid vesicles is dried, the vesicles fuse to form a multilamellar sandwich structure with DNA trapped between the layers. Upon rehydration, vesicles reform that contain highly concentrated DNA'.[689] A freshwater lacustrine environment, Deamer contends, would have been conducive to membranes of sufficient stability.

Yet boundaries, by their nature, are mechanisms both of inclusion and exclusion, and the life of a cell and a self represents a constant trade-off between the two. A boundary membrane impermeable enough to keep *in* – to contain – the constituent macromolecules of the cell runs the risk of concomitantly keeping *out* the nutrients that are essential for growth. Modern-day cells, such as bacteria and archaea, are armed with a sophisticated array of protein pumps specialized in transporting specific nutrients across the lipid bilayer. Such complex proteins, however, can be assumed not to have existed in the early days of life, and any hypothetical scenario must minimize its reliance on such molecules. The ur-membranes must have thus been relatively permeable. One solution proposed by Deamer is that primitive membranes made of simple amphiphiles were significantly shorter, allowing 'molecules as large as ATP to cross the permeability barrier at a useful rate, while still maintaining macromolecules in the encapsulated environment'.[690] But more impermeable membranes also have their advantages: the transition from the simple, single-chain lipids with which ancestral cells would have been endowed to modern phospholipids would have furnished clear benefits in terms of membrane growth and stability.[691] The ensuing evolution of more robust but less permeable phospholipid membranes at the expense of more rudimentary membranes would have thus resulted in selective pressure for the emergence of either a more complex *internalized* metabolism or primitive forms of transmembrane channel or pump to compensate for the diminished permeability.

Another such dilemma faced by the relatively free-diffusing urself (with its comparatively permeable boundaries) pertains to the creation of a proton gradient and the capacity it confers to harness energy for the performance of work. The catch is that the thin membrane of an urself would have let protons through as well, precluding a chemiosmotic function; conversely, a membrane impermeable enough to produce a proton gradient for the containment of potential energy would have also excluded ions, nutrients and metabolites.[692] If the urself did indeed start out with such permeable boundaries, therefore, it could not have evolved chemiosmotic energy generation – whether using the energy from sunlight or the contained combustion of nutrients – until *after* the emergence of a more complex metabolism or transmembrane transport system had made it possible to have longer and more stable phospholipids. Yet another case of chickens and eggs? One possible solution to the puzzle is that other forms of energy generation such as fermentation – traditionally seen as a primordial source of energy[693] – could have played a role in powering the urself on its path to becoming a more self-contained self. Nevertheless, there are good reasons for viewing fermentation as a derived rather than a primitive mode of energy production. By contrast, the ubiquity of chemiosmosis in all cells since LUCA[694] suggests an early role for proton gradients and the 'containment' they appear to presuppose. Perhaps the answer is to look at other forms of self-containment that might have participated in the primordial days of selfhood.

Hemi-Cells and Semi-Selves

Mineral Surfaces

One of the most trenchant critics of membrane-first scenarios has been the organic chemist Günter Wächtershäuser, who has highlighted the problem of membrane impermeability and the ensuing 'self-suffocation' to which this would give rise.[695] Observing that all modern cells have metabolism, genetic machinery and cell envelopes, he agrees that *one* of these subsets of cell componentry can indeed be assumed to be 'logically and phylogenetically prior to unicellular organisms' and thus to represent 'the primordial form of life'.[696] But he disagrees with membrane theorists and RNA world advocates about which of the subsets it is.[697] Wächtershäuser has sought the solution to the complementary problems of self-suffocation (membrane impermeability) and self-diffusion (an excessively dilute prebiotic broth) in the idea of a two-dimensional surface metabolism. Here we shall briefly examine the notion of a primordial surface metabolism before turning to two alternative forms of *semi*-containment[698] that have been proposed as stages en route to the full, self-encoded self-containment characteristic of all modern cells.

In fact, the idea that a two-dimensional surface might solve the problem of the diluteness of the primordial consommé goes back at least to the Irish biophysicist and crystallographer J. D. Bernal, who in 1951 posited that prebiotic evolution occurred not in the open waters but on the surface of the clay minerals that would have been abundant on the ocean bed. Such minerals would have concentrated organic compounds by adsorbing them on their surface, as well as favouring the synthesis rather than the degradation of polymers such as *oligonucleotides* and peptides (i.e. linking the *nucleotides* or amino acids through polymerization rather than breaking the links through hydrolysis).[699] A more radical version of such a mineral-based origin-of-life scenario has since been proposed by Graham Cairns-Smith. According to Cairns-Smith, the first 'organisms' – though not yet 'living entities' – were indeed *constituted* by mineral crystals such as clays, which can be envisaged as 'crystal genes' owing to their ability to embody and replicate information in the form of the specific distribution of electrical charges on their surface. In the course of time, these self-assembling clays would have 'learnt' how to synthesize organic molecules on their surfaces, the organic compounds eventually taking over from the mineral 'scaffolding', which was thus discarded without trace.[700] Yet the drawback of such a notion is its lack of continuity with present-day life forms. 'Contemporary organisms, with their universal features', writes Morowitz, 'show no vestiges of cellular clay inclusions or structures that can be directly related to clays'.[701]

The appeal in both cases is that inorganic minerals provide organizational or structural scaffolding that serves as a foundation for biogenesis. Wächtershäuser's theory of a bi-dimensional surface metabolism has the same attraction, as well as the additional advantage of providing an autotrophic model, i.e. a primal organism that could manufacture its own nourishment.[702] According to Wächtershäuser, the surface in question would have been pyrite, a mineral consisting of iron disulphide and commonly known as 'fool's gold', which is synthesized from a reaction between hydrogen sulphide and iron salts that also releases hydrogen and energy; the setting would have been the hydrothermal vents or submarine volcanic sites that are indeed known to consist largely of pyrite. The free energy available from the synthesis of the mineral would have permitted the reduction of carbon dioxide to the organic metabolites necessary for life to get started. 'Containment' would of course have been essential to prevent such metabolites from being lost by diffusion, but this would have initially been provided not by lipid vesicles – with the attendant risk of cellular self-suffocation – but by a mixture of electrostatic and covalent association with the pyrite surface. At the same time, the possibility of metabolism (i.e. the transformations and interactions of the various chemicals) would have been ensured by the tendency of the molecules to migrate yet remain constantly bonded to the mineral surface.[703] It is telling that Wächtershäuser himself describes his two-dimensional metabolism in terms of interiority: 'the surface organism', he notes, 'constitutes an irreversible flow-through reactor with (*i*) an input of inorganic nutrients; (*ii*) an "internal" surface metabolism of surface-bonded organic constituents, generated on the surface and adhering as ligands to the surface; and (*iii*) an output of surface-detached organic products of decay'.[704] The pyrite crystal surface would act both as 'container' and 'catalyst', eventually generating membranes that would lead to cellularization and the opportunity to cast off the shackles of two-dimensionality.[705]

Wächtershäuser's ideas are vulnerable to criticism from various quarters. As with Cairns-Smith's clay surface, Morowitz detects an infringement of his criterion of continuity, a lack of evidence linking the pyrite scenario with the subsequent evolution of living entities.[706] Others have questioned the chemistry, i.e. whether the formation of pyrite would indeed drive the synthesis of organic compounds.[707] The surface chemistry that powers Wächtershäuser's primordial life forms arguably takes insufficient account of the factor of chemiosmosis as a universal feature essential to the powering of modern-day cellular selfhood.[708] On a different level, Cavalier-Smith objects to the inclusion of a 'surface metabolism' and the resultant 'semi-cell' within the realm of living entities:

> *The terms 'surface metabolism' and 'semicells' ... are misnomers. Metabolism is a biological concept: the interconversion within a cell of organic precursors of the macromolecular constituents of the cell – its genome, membranes, and catalysts. Chemical reactions on a surface in the absence of replicators, membranes, or encoded catalysts are not biological processes at all, but simple geochemistry.*[709]

Wächtershäuser's surface-bonded molecules are not organisms at all, says Cavalier-Smith, but merely chemical entities, lacking both replicators and the organismal discreteness or individuality that would enable them 'to reproduce as a unit and experience higher-level selection allowing the evolution of complexity'.[710] Leaving aside the question of chemical feasibility, this is of course *partly* a matter of terminology. If biology has its roots in geochemistry, how dogmatic must we be in severing the growing plant from the roots that underpin it? Cavalier-Smith seems right to define life in terms of catalysts, genomes and membranes, just as full selfhood requires the triad of self-maintenance, self-replication and self-containment. But – on the road to full selfhood – might it not be permissible to extend the notion of 'self-containment' to incorporate a relatively robust metabolic system stably coupled with a cluster of pyrite? Or must we wait until the formation of lipids that detach themselves from the surface and make themselves independent? To be sure, a great advantage of the latter is that it implies the possibility of the spatial autonomy associated with locomotion, a key characteristic of many (though not all) living selves.

The phenomenon of self-containment is clearly complex and heterogeneous and can be present to varying degrees. 'Perfect' self-containment is indeed tantamount to self-suffocation. Alternative models of primordial (semi) self-containment are required to shed further light on the matter.

Inside-Out Cells

A first alternative is the notion of 'obcells' – or inside-out cells – propounded by Cavalier-Smith himself. While broadly assenting to a 'naked gene' scenario in which chronological primacy pertains to what he calls a 'nucleic acid' (NA) world,[711] Cavalier-Smith also lays particular emphasis upon the structural role played by membranes in the earliest organisms. The emergent NA world, he conjectures, would have consisted of 'nucleozymes' (chains of nucleotides capable of acting both as templates and catalysts) that were attached to catalytic phosphate surfaces, but it would only have been by associating with lipid membranes that these replicating molecules could conjoin to become proto-organisms.[712] Initially, the nucleozymes and membranes would not have formed a unitary entity, but Cavalier-Smith suggests that some of the first peptides coded by RNAs would have served to anchor ribosomes and replicating molecules to the *outside* of the membranes, giving rise to the strange inside-out constructions he terms obcells. Such a scenario, he claims, would have had a distinct advantage over surface-metabolism theories: 'the capacity of lipid vesicles for growth and division means that replicators on the surface of vesicles can evolve as a discrete proto-organism, in a way that those on a mineral surface cannot'.[713] Further integration would have involved the originally uncoded lipid membranes being brought under increased control in terms of growth and division.

Membranes would have evolved, in other words, not so much as mechanisms of enclosure, but as elements of structure and cohesion, points of attachment for the relevant sets of nucleozymes: 'mere encapsulation does not make a cell', writes Cavalier-Smith, stressing that replicators and ribosomes in all extant cells are *'physically attached* to membranes by specific proteins'.[714] Subsequently taking the form of what he dubs hemicells, such membranes would have also come to play a protective role, not only fostering the cooperative association of genes to produce small chromosomes but shielding the chromosomes and high-energy phosphates from predators and competitors.[715] Cavalier-Smith regards chemiosmosis as unlikely, as the membrane would have been too permeable. Instead he conjectures that inorganic phosphate fuels (ATP precursors such as polyphosphates) would have been viable sources of energy.[716]

Cavalier-Smith insists on an important distinction between these hemicells or obcells and a subsequent stage of double-membrane 'protocells', which would have been engendered by the fusion of two cup-shaped obcells. It would not have been until the appearance of such protocells, the first true cells, that an enclosed *cytosol* – an internal milieu separate from the environment – came into being, giving rise to a water-based metabolism and amino-acid biosynthesis.[717]

At this point, the function of the membrane would have ceased to be merely as a mechanism of attachment and integration and increasingly become one of enclosure and delimitation, holding self apart from non-self. Cavalier-Smith suggests that the distinction between obcell and protocell corresponds to that between the proto-organism and the cenancestor (LUCA).[718] In these terms, the obcell corresponds to the proto-organism (comprising a mutualistic integration of genes, catalysts and membranes), but it is not yet a true cell. It is the protocell that is the first cell, and it is ultimately the mode of self-containment that marks the difference.

So how does selfhood fit into the picture?[719] Can an obcell be designated a self, or must we wait until the truly cellular protocell for selfhood to emerge? Perhaps, once again, the best option is to envision a gradual progression of 'increasing' selfhood with 'increasing' self-containment, a continuous pathway from hemi-cells and semi-selves to the 'true' selfhood of protocells and their modern-day descendants.

Inorganic Microcompartments

A further model of primal containment involves geologically produced, abiogenic, three-dimensional compartments as opposed to two-dimensional surfaces or inside-out lipid vesicles. One of the most plausible origin-of-life scenarios – first proposed by geochemist Mike Russell in the early 1990s – is provided by a special type of hydrothermal spring known as an alkaline vent.[720] These hydrothermal systems are created when seawater reacts with a mineral called olivine (a magnesium-iron silicate), which is present in abundance in the ocean floor and would have been even more so in the planet's younger years. The reaction produces the mineral serpentine and in the process releases hydrogen, alkaline fluids and heat, but – most importantly in this context – the vents are characterized by a delicate maze of tiny micro-compartments, a fine porous scaffold that could have served the structural and organizational functions of proto-'containers'.

Russell's initial proposal has since been corroborated by the discovery of just such a hydrothermal system at 'Lost City', an active field of alkaline vents on the ocean bed just off the mid-Atlantic ridge, which appears to meet many of the criteria thought to be required for the emergence of life. In addition to providing a natural geological scaffold, the Lost City vents supply a source of hydrogen from the reaction of olivine with water, which would have reacted with carbon dioxide (albeit slowly) to produce organic compounds and energy; the resulting iron-sulphur bubbles would have catalysed primordial biochemical reactions; nitrogen compounds such as ammonia would have also been present in the vent fluids, fostering the synthesis of amino acids; further, fatty acids have been found to accumulate, resulting in the creation of cell-like membranes *within* the rocky pores.[721] Crucially, perhaps, the scenario is endowed with a natural proton gradient, which would have been created by the interface of the alkaline vent fluid with the acidic waters of the ancient oceans (dissolved carbon dioxide yielding carbonic acid): 'Alkaline fluids bubbling into an acidic ocean form catalytic mineral "cells" with a proton gradient across their inorganic membrane', says Russell. 'They're set up in the same peculiar way as all cells today'.[722] The iron-sulphide compartments of alkaline vents thus furnish at least three elements indispensable to emerging selfhood: a concentrating and limiting structure that prevents the diffusion of the biochemical ingredients; mineral catalysts that would have assisted the necessary chemical reactions; and a constant, nourishing source of disequilibrium with the possibility of a controlled energy flow in the form of a proton gradient, i.e. chemiosmosis.

This potential for chemiosmosis is of special significance.[723] Proton gradients are pivotal to cellular respiration and photosynthesis alike, and bacteria and archaea – the division between which is commonly considered the earliest branching in the tree of life – share this capacity to generate ATP through *chemiosmotic coupling* across a membrane. Such pervasiveness is compelling evidence that the machinery was inherited from LUCA, the last common ancestor of bacteria and archaea and thus of all life on the planet. In other words, just as the universal distribution of DNA, RNA, proteins, ribosomes and our specific genetic code has led scientists to conclude that these features would already have been present in LUCA, the equally widespread occurrence of ATP and the proton-powered protein required for *making* ATP suggests that LUCA would also have been powered by a proton gradient.[724]

Light is shed upon the nature of LUCA, however, not only by the features *common* to bacteria and archaea (and all cellular life on Earth), but also by certain key *differences* between the two prokaryotic domains. The most parsimonious explanation for such differences is that the features in question evolved twice – separately in the two domains – and had not yet appeared in LUCA.[725] In particular, archaea and bacteria exhibit profound differences in their cell membranes, which consist of unrelated lipids (ether lipids in the former, ester lipids in the latter) and are generated by non-homologous enzymatic pathways.[726] This divergence suggests that the two kinds of prokaryotic membrane must have emerged independently *since* the time of their last common ancestor, substantiating the hypothesis that LUCA was not 'contained' by a membrane of its own manufacture (which would have been bequeathed to both bacteria and archaea),[727] but by the sort of inorganic microcompartments that would have been created at alkaline vents. In other words, LUCA was *allo*-contained rather than *auto*-contained. True self-containment was subsequently invented – independently – in the two prokaryotic lineages on the pathway to modern cells and modern selves.

Yet this in turn presents an apparent contradiction. For while the lack of common ground between archaeal and bacterial membranes hints that these membranes arose *after* LUCA, the properties shared by archaea and bacteria – which were presumably already in existence *by the time of* LUCA – include the presence of the transmembrane enzyme *ATP synthase*. This nanoturbine is responsible for the generation of ATP from the potential energy inherent in a proton gradient, and its operation in turn presupposes the existence of a membrane. To judge by the differential inheritance of bacteria and archaea, therefore, LUCA seems simultaneously to *lack* a self-produced membrane and to *presuppose* the presence of a membrane. The solution proposed by Lane, Allen and Martin is that the proton gradient that occurred naturally at the interface between the alkali fluids and the acidic seawater would have initially been harnessed by an abiotically assembled 'membrane' made of the fatty molecules that are known to concentrate at hydrothermal vents, coating the iron-sulphur pores and forming cell-like bubbles.[728] The enzyme ATP synthase would then have served as a way of 'appropriating' these originally exogenous containers, furthering the interests of the incipient 'self' and making the containers a part of that 'self' – producing something more akin to 'self'-containment. With time, the simple lipids lining the mineral compartments would have been supplanted by more complex and stable phospholipid membranes encoded by LUCA's descendants.

Escape to Selfhood

Wächtershäuser's surface metabolism, Cavalier-Smith's hemicells attached to phosphate surfaces, and the inorganic microcompartments studied by Russell and Martin all involve something akin to *allo*-containment. It may well be the case that none of these three hypothesized modes of containment is an accurate representation of what actually occurred. The point is that they illustrate how far a search for the origin of life and selfhood is a search not only for the earliest possible forms of self-replication and metabolic self-maintenance, but also for the transition to genuine *self*-containment. The *allo*-containment associated with the above scenarios implies a manner of incarceration, or at least restriction; adaptive motility is no more an option than with the 'imprisoned' endosymbionts of Chapter 4. Koonin and Martin conceive of successful genetic elements as 'infecting' neighbouring compartments and of the compartments as 'growing' by natural geological processes.[729] At this stage, however, the compartmental contents fall short of full selfhood because – while they may be capable of maintaining and replicating themselves – they lack an adaptive and self-integrated 'boundary' or 'container'.[730] Failing to comply with the criterion of genuine self-containment, moreover, they are bereft of a capacity for appropriately directed mobility as opposed to mere growth.

In the case of the rocky alkaline vents, escape would have depended upon the evolution of genetic elements that encoded systems for synthesizing lipid membranes, allowing them to become/create their own containers and shift away from the fixity of the inorganic pores. As Nick Lane points out, moreover, it would also have relied upon the development of the machinery for chemiosmotic energy generation, permitting cells that ventured slightly further afield from the main vent axis – to where the naturally occurring proton gradient was weaker – to produce their own gradient and thus power the generation of ATP.[731] True self-containment would thus provide the foundation for the possibility of modifying and (as far as possible) controlling the relationship between self and non-self by mechanisms of self-adaptation and movement.

VI.

Cellf and Self-Containment

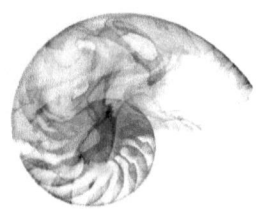

Introduction:
(More or Less) Containing One's Self

The nature of selves as self-containing entities has been a recurrent theme so far. Even some of the simple systems of self-organizing flow cited in Chapter 2 – the fluid patterns produced by temperature gradients or by shear instability spring to mind – display self-containment in the form of the 'cells' that seem to hold them together; convective flows are commonly described as 'cellular'. In the case of self-propagating forest fires, a mode of 'containment' is provided by the limits to the supply of dry carbonaceous fuel or by the geographical boundaries of the combustible fodder. Yet in neither instance can we speak of self-containment in the sense of a material barrier or mechanism of enclosure specifically generated by the system itself. We have encountered the self-encoded capsids worn by viruses in their extracellular stage, the membranes many of them sport as a mechanism of access to host cells or of protection once they are within those cells, and the virus factories some of them construct to concentrate the components needed for effective replication and provide themselves with a safe haven for their activities. In other instances (such as viroids and capsid-less RNA viruses), the host cell itself can be regarded as providing the requisite protection. We have seen the relatively insubstantial or defective membranes and walls with which parasites and endosymbionts enclose themselves within their hosts, and in exploring the origins of selfhood we have considered a number of hypothetical semi-cells and two-dimensional 'vessels' that have been posited as evolutionary stepping stones on the way to more complete forms of self-containment. Such 'full' self-containment, it is suggested, is attained by the free-living, single-celled organisms that belong to the three domains that make up the whole range of life on Earth: bacteria, archaea and eukaryotes. The term 'cellf' – *Zellbst* in German – might be coined to refer to these fully self-contained, membrane-bound cells, but this is such a woeful pun that I shall not labour the point.

First articulated by the botanist Matthias Schleiden and the physiologist Theodor Schwann in the late 1840s, cell theory is one of the unquestioned foundations of modern biology.[733] Schleiden and Schwann recognized that organisms such as animals and plants are composite entities that consist of countless individual cells; one recent calculation came up with a figure of roughly 37 trillion (i.e. 3.7×10^{13}) cells for an adult human, not counting the even greater number of bacterial cells that inhabit our body in a symbiotic association.[734] Such cells are the fundamental and universal units of life, showing the same basic organization whether they exist as unicellular microbes or are aggregated into multicellular organisms. Their unity is physically embodied in the form of the lipid membranes that contain them and thus delimit and define them as units. Of course, there is a sense in which any object – even a stone or a block of ice – may be considered 'self-contained' to the extent that the particles of which it consists are 'stuck' together, requiring energy to be pulled apart. Yet there is more to selfhood than this, for a self involves a *flow* of energy and matter that is contained *by itself* in such a way that this energetic flow performs the work necessary to perpetuate itself. The boundary is anything but marginal to selfhood.

Compartmentalization is essential, for example, for bringing and holding together an autocatalytic set of replicating molecules capable of cooperating for a common goal (the common goal of perpetuated cooperation); it prevents the dissipation and dispersal of these molecules and segregates them from the unwanted presence of non-participating and possibly parasitic elements. It is a necessary condition for selection among evolving ensembles of such genetic cooperatives, allowing for the evolution of ever more stable and efficient elements. As emphasized by autopoietic theory, however, the boundary of a self-producing system also exists in a relationship of mutual interdependence with what it contains. The metabolic work of a cellular self generates the boundaries that separate it from non-self, but this work is itself only made possible by the boundaries that it has generated; the container and its contents sustain one another in a process of self-perpetuating circularity, the container facilitating the creation of the contents that in turn create the container.

As Cavalier-Smith explains, membranes in fact play an integrative role in all three aspects of what we have termed the *intrinsic reflexivity* of the cellular self: self-maintenance, self-reproduction and self-containment. For a start, they are crucial to what Cavalier-Smith calls an assimilatory system, in other words the triad of trophic, metabolic and bioenergetic subsystems required for the import and conversion of organic nutrients and the provision of the energy that powers the cell. Secondly, they provide a point of attachment for replicating genetic material, and their growth and division is the foundation for cell reproduction. Thirdly, they provide the cell with structure and form, in bacteria anchoring and catalyzing the growth of the exosketeton (the cell wall) that gives the cell its structural strength, and in eukaryotes furnishing attachment sites for the endoskeleton (the *cytoskeleton*) that generates an even greater degree of organizational complexity and flexibility.[735] Such an integrative role lends itself to metaphor. If a cell is an orchestra and DNA the score, asks Franklin M. Harold, who or what is the conductor?[736] Resisting the commonly accepted notion that it is the genome that wields the baton, Harold proposes the plasma membrane as a more plausible candidate, in that it creates 'the enclosed and controlled space within which societal behavior emerges from the interactions among individual molecules'.[737] Despite its undoubted role in structuring cellular space, however, 'the organizing powers of the plasma membrane, and of a transient cytoskeleton, are obviously limited'. Harold suggests a concert-master as a more fitting metaphor than a conductor. This leaves Harold with the 'disquieting notion of an orchestra without a conductor'.[738] But such a notion should not be so disquieting. A self-contained cell is an orchestra that conducts itself – and that thus conducts its self.

The self-containment provided by a membranous boundary is not just that of a passive receptacle, therefore, but an active principle of organization, separation and segregation. Work is involved not only in keeping self apart from non-self, inside apart from out, but also – through an intricate manifold of pores and pumps – in maintaining the differential permeability that grants access to (appropriate) nutrients and egress to waste. Another metaphor is thus suggested by Adam Rutherford who, recognizing that cell membranes are not mere vessels but are in constant interaction with the surrounding environment, describes them as 'more akin to a customs house, an interface that monitors and controls the import and export of all the goods and messages that a cell needs'.[739]

The plasma membrane is not the only mechanism by which self-containment in the form of such border control is achieved. The immune system also plays a crucial role in defining and delimiting the boundaries of an organism, discriminating between self and non-self and eliminating the latter from the realm of the former. Immune defences of one sort or another are now known to be virtually ubiquitous features of both unicellular and multicellular organisms, virtually as indispensable as a membrane to a cell or skin to a human. Yet this still does not exhaust the breadth of the notion of self-containment, which may be understood not only in terms of membrane-based enclosure and physiological or immunological mechanisms of inclusion/exclusion, but also the *functional interdependence* that causes a diversity of components in a composite entity to remain attached both to one another and to the entity as a whole. Organelles such as mitochondria or organs such as livers will tend to 'stay put' within their respective unicellular or multicellular organisms because neither the components nor the organismal whole will normally survive or flourish in the wake of their separation. As a composite of such mutually interdependent parts, an organism can in this sense also be described as 'self-contained'. These various, often interrelated aspects of the phenomenon of self-containment are the subject of the present chapter.

The focus will not be exclusively on unicellular selfhood. One of the underlying presuppositions of this essay is that multicellular as well as unicellular organisms exhibit the three forms of intrinsic reflexivity considered necessary and sufficient for full selfhood: self-maintenance, self-reproduction and self-containment. An idea that will come to prominence in the present chapter is that the parallelisms and correspondences between their respective forms of self-containment – their physical boundaries, immunological defences and functional integration – will cast light both on single-celled organisms and on multicellular selves such as animals and plants. Full minimal selfhood[740] is a term that can be applied not just to the simplest or foundational organism (the cell), therefore, but also to more complex organisms insofar as they too are characterized by all three forms of intrinsic reflexivity. Indeed, the more 'sophisticated' forms of selfhood characteristic of animals such as humans presuppose, and are built upon, the underlying minimal selfhood provided by this threefold reflexivity. The term can even be applied to the more multilayered forms of selfhood displayed by super-organisms or species, though such entities must likewise have their own modes of self-containment if their selfhood is to be regarded as full.[741]

A recurrent feature of self-containment that will emerge in the following account is its inherently fuzzy nature, i.e. the blurredness of the boundaries that (half-)separate self from non-self. There are a number of reasons for this fuzziness. In the first place, it may be suggested, the very concept of a boundary embraces a certain ambiguity – a 'dual identity'[742] – as both a bridge and a breach between self and non-self. Secondly, to the extent that the self should be viewed not as a soup-filled balloon but as a dynamic throughflow of energy and matter, its containment must necessarily be differentially porous, characterized by the controlled regulation of entrance and exit. Things are further complicated by the fact that most animals are the shape of a doughnut or torus, with a topologically external boundary running 'through' us from mouth to anus, raising the question of whether what is inside the tube – though topologically external to the epithelium that contains us – is inside or outside ourselves. We tend to view the mouth as the relevant frontier between self and non-self and the gut as *inside* the body; indeed, this makes sound sense to the extent that entry into the gastrointestinal tract is generally irreversible and thus, as Paul Rozin and April E. Fallon put it in their study of disgust, 'represents de facto entry into the body'.[743] Yet it remains unclear where I begin and where I end and how far I am supposed to include the gaps and cavities that riddle me like a Swiss cheese, just as it is impossible to pinpoint at which moment, if at all, an ingested molecule (say, of sugar) starts being *me*. The 19th-century materialist Ludwig Feuerbach referred to the human body as 'nothing other than the porous I',[744] yet this porosity is exquisitely controlled, preventing us, as a rule, from bursting at the seams, spouting spontaneous leaks or ballooning up when we soak in the bath.[745]

There are other reasons for the fuzziness of our frontiers. The 'containment' in question cannot be pinned down to a single essential attribute or feature, but is more akin to a family of related and often overlapping concepts, including notions of enclosure, protection and defence; structure, cohesion and functional integration; and separation and differential porosity. It may coincide with concepts of individuality and identifiability. To ask whether the 'essence' of self-containment is to provide structure or enclosure is thus to ask the wrong question in that there *is* no single essence. Even a simple bacterium has not only an indispensable plasma membrane – across which it 'breathes' – but in many cases a cell wall located *outside* the membrane that endows the cell with its structural strength. If the cellular self is defined in terms of its plasma membrane (which no cell can manage without), how are we to classify the cell wall (which some groups of bacteria *can* and *do* dispense with)? Is it inside or out? Perhaps it is more akin to a snail's house? What about the many other bacterial components that are situated beyond the plasma membrane, components such as the outer lipopolysaccharide membrane and the flagella – the filamentous appendages used for locomotion? There is not necessarily a clear-cut answer to such questions.

Distinctions may also be drawn between passive and active (work-performing) conceptions of the 'container' and between different forms of work that are performed; these include energy-generation, thermoregulation and the osmoregulation by which the inflow and outflow of water and salts are regulated to maintain the homeostatic balance of the cellular contents and keep the composition of the fluids inside qualitatively distinct from those outside. As we shall see, moreover, insofar as one of the major categories of self-containment refers not to physical or physiological boundaries but to functional unity (where this unitary function is the continued self-maintenance of a self-maintaining self), the *location* of the constituents in question may be of secondary significance. The physical boundary is not what matters, for a self may appropriate what is ostensibly 'outside' itself – in the guise of tools or shelter or what has been referred to as external physiology – to serve this common function. Symbiotic relationships between mutually interdependent selves, such as my microbiota and me, throw up similar questions. Research is shedding ever more light on the inextricability of human selfhood and that of the roughly 100 trillion microbes that have colonized the human epithelium, and especially the gut, where they provide vital contributions to the host organism's digestive, metabolic and immune systems. I may balk at the idea that my bacteria-in-residence form part of my self, but without them I would be but a shadow of the self that our mutualistic cooperation allows me to be.

The present chapter thus focuses on a range of mechanisms by which selves – unicellular and multicellular – may both contain and reach *beyond* themselves. In the first section of the chapter ('Forms of Container'), this self-containment is examined as a form of protective enclosure, physically separating what is inside from what is outside. In the second section ('Functional Unity as Self-Containment'), it is analysed in terms of the functional integration of a unitary organism, focusing in particular on cases where such oneness is undermined or called into question; such cases include clonal fungi and plants, as well as other less-than-unitary forms of multicellularity, such as slime moulds. The problematic status of the self viewed not only as a self-bounded physiological individual and a self-integrated organism but also as a 'genetic individual' is then explored, paying special attention to examples of chimerism and symbiosis that infringe notions of genetic homogeneity or uniqueness.

The third section of the chapter turns to immunological self-containment. Contrary to certain recent proposals, the suggestion is that selfhood, properly understood, is indeed the best concept for understanding the nature of immune defence. The fourth section ('Managing the Interface of Self and Non-Self') looks at how forms of self-containment – in particular the dimensionality of the self/non-self interface as manifest in our organs of respiration, nutrient absorption and osmoregulation – can be modified to foster the homeostatic stability of a self-sustaining self, while the fifth section ('Extending One's Self') considers how the boundary between self and non-self may be blurred by modes of reinforced self-containment (such as housing and clothing) or by the use of tools as functional extensions of selfhood. The final section of the chapter ('Transcending One's Self') raises the question of how the sensory interface between self and non-self enables the self to engage in directed self-movement that is appropriate to its interests. This sensory dimension of self-containment and the guided movement it makes possible will be understood as laying the foundations for the possibility of consciousness.

Forms of Container

Membranes, Walls and Tests

Perhaps the most remarkable aspect of the cell membrane is its role in the harnessing of energy. The generation of a proton gradient across a phospholipid membrane and the use of the resulting influx of protons to drive the synthesis of ATP from ADP and phosphate – the process known as chemiosmosis – are ubiquitous in powering cellular life on Earth. The significance of the membrane resides in the creation and maintenance of differences of composition and charge between two aqueous phases, i.e. between 'inside' and 'outside', and the exploitation of the ensuing energy gradient for the performance of work. There are two main pathways by which cells drive the flow of protons that generates the ATP used to power their activities: oxidative phosphorylation, where it is the process of respiration – the combustion of organic substances by oxygen or other oxidants – that provides the energy to transport protons across the membrane; and photophosphorylation, where it is the absorption of light in photosynthesis that produces the transmembrane gradient. The generation of a proton gradient across their membrane is a feature shared by bacteria and archaea despite the 3,500 million years of evolution that separate them, and the two groups of prokaryotes likewise share remarkably similar forms of the transmembrane enzyme ATP synthase, the nano-turbine responsible for channelling the potential energy of the proton gradient to synthesize the molecules of ATP. As Harold Morowitz suggests, therefore, 'the necessity of thermodynamically isolating a subsystem is an irreducible condition of life'.[746] Equally important is the mechanism for tapping into the potential energy that is thereby created. This represents a notable point of contrast with respect to both the *capsids* and the membranes of viruses.

Yet it is not just prokaryotes that are powered in this way, for eukaryotes are in turn powered by *internalized* prokaryotes that are powered in this way. So while most eukaryotes likewise rely on transmembrane proton gradients to generate the energy that drives them, the membranes and the gradients are in this case provided by long-assimilated bacteria that persist in the guise of mitochondria and – for organisms powered by photosynthesis – chloroplasts. The originally symbiotic relationship with what are now regarded as cellular organelles has come to provide the host organism with a way of interiorizing, and thereby containing or controlling, the boundary responsible for its supply of energy. Having once been free-living microbes in their own right, the mitochondria thus function rather like domesticated or internalized non-self,[747] albeit a vestigial non-self which – as an *organelle* – is now such an essential component of its host that the distinction between self and non-self can scarcely be applied.

This interiorization is taken a step further in multicellular organisms such as animals and plants: the mitochondria are kept internalized in cells, and the cells are in turn 'internalized' in our bodies. It is notable that there is little division of labour or specialization in the production of energy. We have not evolved an *organ* of energy generation – some sort of macroscopic inner oven akin to the furnace powering Cugnot's car – in the way we have evolved lungs, kidneys and hearts for other aspects of self-containment (as we shall see). Individually provided with fuel, each of our constituent cells is called upon to transform this fuel into the energy it requires. Even red blood cells, which are bereft of mitochondria since their function involves carrying not consuming oxygen, have to generate their own ATP, resorting to the less efficient means of anaerobic fermentation as opposed to oxidative phosphorylation. This is not to suggest that our macroscopic boundaries do not perform work. It will become clear below that the work they do is a vital component of our self-containment. Like the plasma membrane of individual eukaryotic cells, however, the skin of an animal is not involved in the task of harnessing chemical energy in the form of ATP.

The role of the prokaryotic cell membrane in the production of ATP might be taken to endow it with a special status on account of its near-ubiquity and its significance. Despite its status as perhaps the original bio-container, however, the diversity of forms that self-containment can assume argues against privileging it as some sort of archetype. Particularly marked is the difference with respect to the tough peptidoglycan cell wall. The plasma membrane has been described as a 'fluid mosaic', a delicate structure resembling 'a sea of mobile lipid molecules full of floating protein molecules'.[748] The fluidity of the membrane is crucial; its normal condition is a liquid crystalline state, and this liquidity must be maintained if the membrane is not subsequently to spring leaks.[749] Variations between bacterial and archaeal phospholipid membranes confer greater stability upon the archaea in dealing with extreme conditions,[750] and in general the membranes of thermophilic micro-organisms tend to have a higher proportion of saturated fatty acids (endowed with stronger bonds between their molecules), while those of *psychrophilic* micro-organisms are richer in unsaturated fatty acids. In all cases, however, the fluidity of the membrane remains essential. By contrast, the peptidoglycan cell wall – a 'single, huge, sack-shaped molecule' comprising a reticulation of sugars and amino acids – has been described as a 'strong, stiff but open-meshed fabric, not unlike nylon'.[751] The strength of the wall is pivotal in giving the cell mechanical and morphological stability, maintaining the cell's integrity and resisting the osmotic pressure generated by the high concentration of solutes (metabolites and ions) in the cellular cytoplasm and the resulting tendency for water to flow into the cell from the surrounding medium. The peptidoglycan wall stretches with the pressure but curbs the inflow of water, giving rise to the phenomenon known as turgor.[752]

The characteristics of the cell wall provide the basis for the fundamental division of bacteria into two categories: Gram-negative and Gram-positive.[753] The former (which include *proteobacteria* such as *E. coli* and *Salmonella*, as well as cyanobacteria and spirochaetes) have a relatively thin peptidoglycan wall (3 to 7 nm), but are endowed with a second, outer membrane containing lipopolysaccharide (LPS), a sugary armour that is thought to have evolved to provide a defence against viruses, foreign digestive enzymes and antibiotics[754] – and is also responsible for inducing inflammation and a potent innate immune response in metazoans. Gram-positive bacteria lack an outer membrane but are enclosed within a much thicker layer of peptidoglycan (33 nm) that can form as much 90 percent of their total dry weight. Unlike the membrane, however, the cell wall is not universal: one class of Gram-positive bacteria known as Mollicutes (meaning 'soft-skinned', by contrast with Firmicutes such as *Streptococcus* and *Bacillus*) has dispensed with the cell wall, instead using sterols such as cholesterol to bolster the membrane and proteinaceous cytoskeleton-like elements for additional morphological support.[755] The Mollicutes tend to be parasites, and some have an intracellular lifestyle; to this extent they possibly exploit their hosts for 'containment'. Their parasitic lifestyle is exemplified by one of their best-known representatives, the tiny pathogen *Mycoplasma genitalium*, which sets up home on the epithelial cells of the genital and respiratory tracts of primates.

Nor are these the only modes of self-containment available to bacteria. We have already come across the multi-layered defensive armoury that enables dormant bacteria – in the form of endospores and microbial cysts – to resist the most unforgiving of environmental hazards, including desiccation, ultraviolet radiation, extreme heat and toxins.[756] The bacterium *Deinococcus radiodurans*, known as 'Conan the Bacterium',[757] on account of its ability to resist unfeasibly high levels of ionizing radiation, is armed not only with an unusually thick cell wall, but with multiple copies of its genome and a particularly efficient DNA repair system. Communities or colonies of bacteria may also secrete sheaths of slime that function both as a physical barrier preventing the entry of exogenous phage and a boundary that binds the bacteria together to form a single multicellular entity.

Yet peptidoglycan cell walls seem to be of particular significance to bacterial cell biology. Bacteria without them are thought to have had them and mislaid them in the course of evolutionary history, much in the way that capsid-less viruses parted company with their capsids. Cavalier-Smith pinpoints the origin of cell walls as marking the transition from proto-cells to bacteria proper.[758] Essential though they may be to many bacteria, however, their presence is also a constraint, as their absence in eukaryotes makes clear. Maynard Smith and Szathmáry refer to the 'catastrophic loss of the rigid cell wall', which possibly occurred when rival bacteria developed antibiotics that blocked cell wall synthesis in their competitors but at the same time paved the way for one of the major transitions in evolutionary history, namely the transition that gave rise to a eukaryotic cell structure.[759] For it is the absence of the cell wall in eukaryotes such as the famously protean amoeba that permits such organisms to engage not only in vigorous shape-changing, but also in the mode of nutrition known as phagocytosis. While bacteria are thus condemned to ingest their nutrients by secreting digestive enzymes into the surrounding medium and then absorbing the degraded matter back across their membrane, shape-shifting eukaryotes can use their flexible outer membrane to surround and engulf the food particle, enclose it in a food *vacuole* within themselves, and then bring the vacuole to fuse with a lysosome containing the requisite digestive enzymes. The membrane that 'contains' the eukaryotic cell is thereby transformed into a much more flexible vessel, for the interiorized vacuoles – topologically equivalent to non-self – effectively increase the cell's surface area in the manner of an animal's digestive tract.

Through the converse process of exocytosis, moreover, vacuoles can be used to sequester potentially harmful material or waste products in the cell and bring them to the outer membrane, where the membranes fuse and unwanted non-self is expelled. There is a sense, therefore, in which eukaryotes are as 'doughnut'-shaped as most animals, though the 'hole' traversing these doughnuts is in fact a constantly shape-shifting array of water-, food- and waste-filled bubbles.[760] Indeed, the cytoplasm of eukaryotes is thoroughly pervaded by a dynamic network of membranous structures, including not only vacuoles and lysosomes, but also the endoplasmic reticulum, the Golgi complex[761] and the membrane surrounding the nucleus. The eukaryotic cell, writes Harold, is a 'diaphanous maze of membranous surfaces that define compartments of specialized function and composition, all of which lie topologically outside the cytoplasm proper and connect, at least intermittently, with the exterior'.[762]

It has been proposed that the loss of the cell wall and the emergence of *phagocytosis* could have played a major role in the appearance of organelles such as mitochondria, produced by a sort of 'cellular indigestion' that occurred when bacteria were ingested but not digested.[763] Whether or not it was phagocytosis that led to the incorporation of the bacteria that were to become mitochondria, the missing wall would certainly have made it much easier for the potential symbionts to fuse, facilitating the union that would give rise to the first, naked eukaryotes. Indeed, while the cell wall precludes cell fusion in prokaryotes, the facility with which eukaryotes can merge with one another has subsequently resulted not only in the emergence of the giant multinucleate cells (syncytia) characteristic of certain fungi and slime moulds, but also prepared the way for the evolution of sexual reproduction.[764] Yet while many eukaryotes have persisted in a wall-less lifestyle – again, the naked amoebae spring to mind – other lineages have invented a wealth of new protective shells and tests, making use of compounds ranging from non-cellulose polysaccharide, *glycoproteins*, *chitin*, peptidoglycans and chalk to the glass frustules of the *diatoms*.[765] Importantly, most plant cells have also surrounded themselves with a rigid wall made of cellulose.[766]

The myriad forms of unicellular armour are believed to serve a variety of purposes besides mere protection. The calcareous scales, or coccoliths, characteristic of the coccolithophorids – the sedimentation of which accumulated during the Cretaceous to form the White Cliffs of Dover – serve not only as a defensive shield but also as a lens, focusing light upon the cell's chloroplasts and thus contributing to energetic efficiency.[767] The ciliate group, which includes the renowned model organism *Paramecium* (traditionally known as the 'slipper animalcule'), has evolved a cortex rather than a shell: this comprises both a 'pellicle' made of membranous vesicles called alveoli, which helps maintain the shape of the cell, and a tough outer cortex composed of proteinaceous cytoskeletal elements that support the cilia and are thus involved in the cell's locomotion.[768]

The factor of differential porosity remains crucial; it is vital that nutrients should be able to enter the cell. Many ciliates have a specialized oral cavity and gullet, into which bacteria and detritus are swept by their cilia; it is in the gullet that food vacuoles are formed. Diatom frustules contain pores that are thought to allow gas, nutrients and waste to be exchanged with the environment, while the tests of foraminiferans – composed of organic materials that may be reinforced with minerals – contain apertures through which there extend sticky, cytoplasm-filled pseudopodia that function both to propel the cell and to trap and engulf prey such as bacteria, diatoms and occasional nematode worms.[769] The morphological exuberance and diversity of foraminiferans and other protists is unmatched.

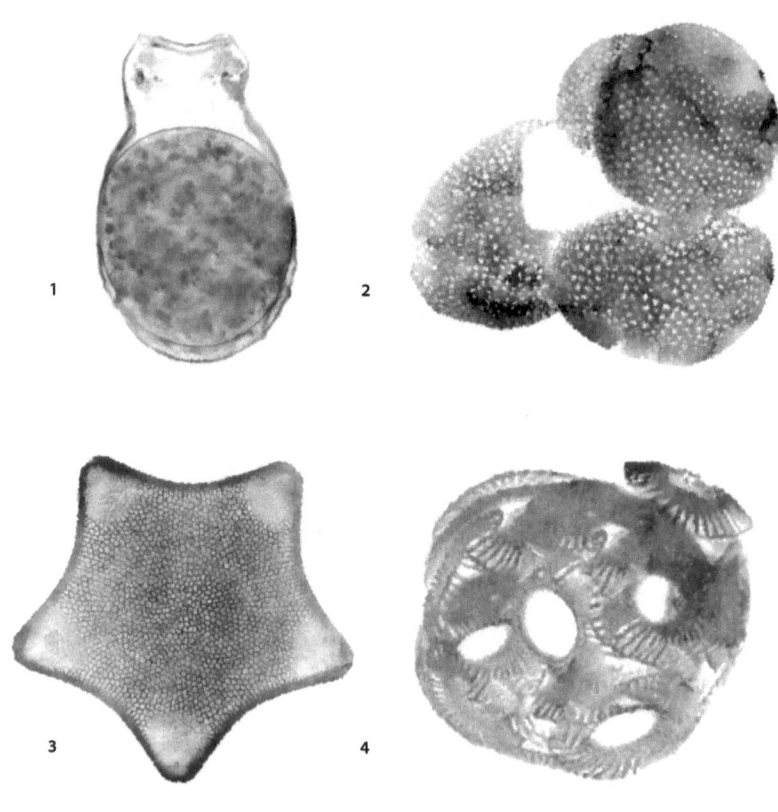

1 Euglyphid   **2** Foraminiferan   **3** Diatom   **4** Coccolithophorid

Figure 5: Diverse Protists

Even some amoebae – known as *testate* amoebae – have turned their back on nudity. One category of such creatures is the euglyphids, described by Nicholas Money:

> The euglyphid shell is produced as a series of plates or scales within the cytoplasm. ... These are secreted by the amoeba and assembled on its surface, leaving an opening at one end. They are shaped like Greek amphorae, without handles. The shell affords protection and the amoeba extends itself through the opening in the form of thin, highly mobile filaments. These operate like pseudopodia, moving the cell and its jar over surfaces in the pond and trapping bacteria. They remind me of hermit crabs.[770]

Again, the variety of the shells worn by testate amoebae is spectacular.[771] While in most cases the test is rigid, some species – such as *Cochliopodium* – wear a flexible sheet of fine scales (the *tectum*) from beneath which the pseudopodia can protrude. Other shells are endowed with spines or horns.

Epithelium, Epidermis

Just as the many physical embodiments of unicellular self-containment can be seen to cover a range of distinct functions, the self-containment characteristic of multicellular selves shows a variety of forms and functions. For a start, there are cases of multicellularity where the individual cell – with its membrane and wall – provides the containment. Fungal *hyphae*, the long filamentous structures whose vegetative growth gives rise to networks called mycelia, are just one cell thick, yielding an enormous surface area through which the fungus can absorb nutrients. In such instances, the filament is 'contained' by the cell wall itself, which in the case of fungi is made of the resilient carbohydrate polymer chitin, also present in the exoskeleton of insects and other arthropods.[772] Plants, by contrast, have a specialized group of cells that form the epidermis, a usually single-layered cellular 'skin' that covers leaves, roots, stems and flowers and provides a clearly demarcated boundary between self and non-self. The tightly bonded epidermal cells, often reinforced with a waxy cuticle, confer mechanical strength upon the plant, present a barrier to fungal and microbial invaders, prevent water loss, and regulate the exchange of gases with the environment. Particularly in the roots, moreover, they absorb water and minerals. In woody plants it is the periderm, or bark, that takes on these protective duties.

In metazoans the relevant term is not so much the epidermis as the epithelium, which along with connective tissue, muscle tissue and nervous tissue represents one of the four basic categories of animal tissue. The epithelium includes not only the epidermis but also the mucous membrane that lines our gastrointestinal tract, in other words the hole in the doughnut that we are. Epithelia are defined by the aligned polarity of their component cells (i.e. the alignment of basal and apical surfaces), the linkage of these cells by tight lateral contacts called 'belt-form junctions', and their basal attachment to a layer of extracellular matrix known as the basal lamina.[773] They are thus constituted by a sheet-like arrangement of cells that can serve as a barrier between different environments, which is what grounds the possibility of compartmentalization and complexity in metazoan bodies. They can also be specified by their ability to regulate the passage of ions and solutes between the interior of the organism – the internal milieu – and the environment, i.e. to generate what is known as a 'transepithelial potential'.[774] This capacity to create an asymmetrical electrochemical potential is another defining characteristic of epithelia, testifying to the presence of sealing junctions.[775] By means of its transepithelial electrical resistance, the epithelium segregates what is inside from what is outside the organism, differentiating self from non-self.

Developmentally, epithelium is the default state of animal cells[776] in all metazoans except basalmost groups such as sponges and placozoans. There has been disagreement on whether sponges have an epithelium[777]; it has widely been thought that environmental waters can circulate freely through the *poriferan* body. Though sponges certainly have an epitheloid or epithelium-*like* layer in the form of the pinacoderm (an outer layer of flattened cells akin to the epidermis), these cells lack a basal lamina and the typical belt-form junctions of true, animal epithelia. Recent work, however, has cast doubt upon the notion that sponges do without a proper distinction between inside and outside and that their tissues are only transiently sealed: the pinacoderm of some freshwater *demosponges* has been found to show transepithelial resistance, impeding the passage of small molecules and controlling the transport of ions to maintain an electric potential.[778] In these terms, sponge epithelia can indeed be considered functionally equivalent to true epithelia.

The other prime candidate for the basalmost metazoan is the *placozoan Trichoplax adhaerens*, the least complex of all animals in terms of morphology and organization. *Trichoplax* is a diminutive, flat but utterly asymmetrical (i.e. blob-shaped) animal that lacks not only organs, muscle cells and nerve cells, but also a basal lamina and extracellular matrix. However, its outer cells are joined in an unbroken layer by regular cell-cell junctions, and the tiny multicellular amoeboid effectively consists of a simple upper and lower epithelium sandwiching a layer of multinucleate fibre cells in between.[779] Indeed, the placozoan self seems to consist predominantly of its container. As with the sponge, the simple organization of its body suggests that the self-containment provided by an epithelium is essential to the most ancestral forms of metazoans.

The physical 'container' that envelops complex animals such as humans is not just a matter of the epithelium. The human skin comprises two main layers: the *epidermis* is constituted in large measure by multiple layers of epithelial cells, whereas the underlying *dermis* is a thick layer of connective tissue made of a combination of collagen and elastin fibres that imparts much of the mechanical strength and toughness to the skin.[780] The very surface of the epidermis, writes Nina Jablonski, is its most remarkable layer, the *stratum corneum*: 'The stratum corneum is sometimes called the epidermal horny layer because it consists of a relatively thin sheet of dead, flattened cells with a smooth, fairly tough and water-resistant surface. ... The skin's effectiveness as a barrier against environmental insult of all kinds, especially oxidative stress such as ultraviolet radiation (UVR), ozone, air pollution, pathological microorganisms, chemical oxidants, and topically applied drugs, depends primarily on the integrity of the stratum corneum'.[781] However, the epidermis as a whole functions as a sort of conveyor belt, with the cells moving through the layers from the *stratum basale* (where they are produced) to the *stratum spinosum* (where they in turn produce keratin), then to the *stratum granulosum* (where they die) and on to the horny outermost stratum, from which the dead cells are constantly being shed as they are replaced from beneath.[782] The epidermis thus consists of a perpetual process of self-renewal; the container is no mere vessel, but rather an ongoing work in progress. Such self-renewal is particularly evident in our stomach, the epithelial lining of which is regenerated every three days to resist the digestive onslaught of the gastric acid it contains.[783] The human gut is likewise endowed with a constantly self-renovating epithelium, casting off 20–50 million cells every minute in the small intestine and two to five million cells per minute in the colon.[784]

The skin's power of self-regeneration also comes to light when we are punctured, slashed or grazed, it being a matter of life and death to reconstruct the boundary between inside and outside, self and non-self. First, platelet cells in the blood clump together, forming a clot that provisionally plugs the leak. The immune system also kicks in; phagocytic cells called neutrophils are rallied to rid the site of debris and unwanted micro-organisms, i.e. potentially deleterious non-self that has infiltrated the organism and must be eliminated. In a communal reconstruction project, millions of specialized cells called fibroblasts arrive to lay down new layers of collagen, new blood vessels are established, and new skin cells are moved to the area.[785] All this activity is accompanied by a sensation of pain, which induces us to recoil initially, to protect the damaged site while it heals, and – in the case of animals capable of learning – to seek to avoid impaling ourselves on sharp or pointed items in the future.

The work performed by the skin is not just a question of its capacity for self-regeneration. The vast majority of the cells in the epidermis belong to the category of keratinocytes, which manufacture the tough fibrous protein called keratin. Such protein complexes not only provide mechanical reinforcement, protection against scuffing and injury, and water resistance, but can also be turned into sturdy keratinized appendages such as the feathers of birds, the hair of mammals, and the claws, nails and hooves exhibited by many tetrapods[786] – an invaluable set of tools for heat regulation, locomotion and generally negotiating the challenges of the environment. The protective shells worn by turtles also include a keratinized layer of epithelial cells as well as modifications of ribs and the spine.[787]

Other forms of protection are furnished by other epidermal cell types. Alongside the keratinocytes in the epidermis are the Langerhans cells, specialized cells belonging to the immune system that are described as the 'sentinels' of the skin, the body's 'first line of defence'[788] against the incursions of microscopic non-self in the form of the bacteria and viruses that might come into contact with the skin. A very different, but equally significant form of protection is provided by the melanocytes, the group of cells responsible for producing the pigment melanin that gives skin cells most of their colour. The prime importance of melanin is that it shields the body from the destructive effects of ultraviolet radiation, which both damages DNA and breaks down vitamins such as folate, itself essential for DNA replication and cell division.[789] It seems likely, indeed, that dark pigmentation evolved because of the beneficial effects of melanin in shielding vital biomolecules and fostering reproductive success. At the same time, however, the skin also *uses* ultraviolet radiation to produce vitamin D, required for the absorption of calcium from one's diet and the construction of a robust skeleton. Given these contradictory tendencies, a balance must be struck between protection from what is harmful and openness to what is beneficial in solar radiation: 'skin pigmentation should be dark enough to prevent or slow the breakdown of important biomolecules in the skin by UVR, but light enough to permit the production of other important biomolecules catalyzed by UVR'. Melanin, suggests Jablonski, is the 'governor'[790] in this process, fine-tuning the complex relationship between self and non-self by controlling the access granted to potentially harmful sources of energy.

Functional Unity as Self-Containment

Organisms as Self-Containing Entities

In the case of unicellular entities and complex metazoans such as humans, the unit of selfhood – as manifest in how the self defines, delimits or contains its self – seems reasonably straightforward. Just as a plasma membrane encloses a single cell, the human skin or epithelium not only protects us, but keeps our constituent parts in close proximity and physically connected to one another, while segregated from everything else outside us. It holds our organs together and fixes the boundaries of cells belonging to different individuals, preventing our bodily cells from migrating to the body of a conspecific (whether friend or foe) or any other living organism. To this extent, the unit defined by our self-generated physical boundary is equivalent to the unit of functional or causal integration. Our spatial and temporal continuity and boundedness coincide with our *unitary selfishness* in the sense elaborated in the Introduction.[791] One might here conceive of two distinct *aspects* of self-containment: the individual and the organism. As an individual self, I 'contain myself' by the ongoing production of a membrane or epithelium that separates me from what is outside me or what is not me; as an organismal self, I 'contain myself' by the functional interdependence of my component parts, i.e. by the fact that in general terms I cannot 'lose' or dispense with my constituent organs without ceasing to perpetuate myself as a whole. Complex metazoans such as human beings seem to be paradigms of self-containment both as individuals and as organisms. Yet these two aspects of self-containment do not necessarily coincide.

The concepts 'individual' and 'organism' have frequently been confused, but are not synonymous.[792] *Individual* refers to a 'particular' that can be localized in space and time. The term has been defined by Thomas Pradeu as 'an entity that can be designated through a demonstrative reference (*this* F), is separable, countable, has acceptably clear-cut spatial boundaries, and exhibits transtemporal identity, that is, the capacity to remain the "same" while changing through time'.[793] As a particular, it is a concrete, specifiable material object as opposed to a class or a universal. In fact, in the context of biological selfhood this is not quite enough: a self is not merely an individual or particular in the sense of an object with boundaries. Rather, it is an individual or particular that – by virtue of its intrinsic reflexivity – constantly *constructs* its own boundaries. In this respect, a self is more accurately termed a *biological* or *physiological* individual. Such a spatially self-containing individual is the self as defined and bounded by its self-made membrane, wall or epithelium.

Organism, by contrast, refers to a self as a composite entity whose constituent parts are causally integrated into a functional unit. The notion can likewise be understood in terms of the intrinsic reflexivity characteristic of selfhood. As Kant recognized, an organism is a self-organizing entity in which each component part exists because of and for the sake of every other component part; the parts are thus produced and sustained by their function within the whole, which in turn exists as a result of the workings of the parts. It is also a self-*containing* entity to the extent that the causal interdependence of the parts and the whole makes them mutually indispensable. As a rule, the parts *must* hold together, for otherwise the whole will cease to perpetuate itself as a self.

However, the physical bounds of selfhood are not necessarily as clear-cut as the membrane of a cell or the epithelium of a mammal might imply. Indeed, a major implication of the *functional* aspect of selfhood and self-containment – where the overall function is the continued self-maintenance of a self-maintaining self – is that particular constituent parts need not inevitably exist in a relationship of immediate physical attachment to the rest of the constituent parts of the self in question. The physical details of the mechanism that carries out a particular function are of only secondary interest, as is the location of that mechanism. It does not matter what or where the mechanism is, so long as it successfully carries out its function: what counts is causal efficacy rather than physical contiguity. As a result, an organism may be inherently ambiguous in the boundaries that define it, making it difficult or impossible – and perhaps irrelevant – to specify in material terms where a given self begins and where it ends.

This applies even to what at first sight may appear to be paradigmatically self-containing selves. Philosopher Mark Rowlands gives an example relating to the biological process of digestion:

> It may seem obvious that what makes a digestive process mine, and not anyone else's, is the fact that it occurs inside of me and not anyone else. This claim, however, should be resisted: spatial containment is only a falli-

> ble guide to the ownership of digestive processes. For a digestive process to be mine, it is neither necessary nor sufficient that it occur inside my body. ... Imagine a case whereby one's digestive processes become externalized. Suppose, for example, one cannot produce enough of the relevant enzymes in one's digestive tract. The solution, drastic and implausible, but nonetheless a solution, is to reroute one's tract into an external device where the relevant enzymes are added, before routing the tract back into one's body where it finishes its work in the usual way. The most natural way of understanding this scenario is, I think, as a case where my digestive processes pass outside my body and receive the required external aid. The processes do not stop being mine just because they are, for a time, located outside my body.[794]

Rowland's example is particularly enlightening given that certain organisms *do* accomplish their digestion outside themselves. The osmotrophic nutrition of bacteria and fungi, which secrete digestive enzymes into the environment and then absorb the degraded nutrients back across their cell wall, is a case in point. A variant is the crown-of-thorns starfish – scourge of corals – which wraps itself around its prey before everting one of its two stomachs through its mouth, spewing enzymes over the polyps and then slurping the resulting chyme back inside itself.[795] Human cooking may also be considered a (partial) externalization of digestion, as may the delegation of much of our more challenging digestive work to a specialized microbial community that has colonized our intestines.[796] Other functions also lend themselves to externalization: as we shall see below, protective structures and tools in general provide endless opportunities for a functionally understood self to 'reach out' beyond its physical boundaries and 'appropriate' non-self in its own interests and for its own benefit.

As an organism, a self is thus constituted by a heterogeneous set of functionally interdependent or causally integrated parts, damage to any of which may lead to the impaired operation of the whole. Wherever my digestive apparatus may be, I depend on its successful activity to maintain myself as a self-maintaining self; the same goes for all my vital organs. Despite the heterogeneity of its parts (its organs and limbs), an organismal self is characterized by a coordinated unity of interest, where the interest in question is that of the self in its entirety. This unitary 'selfishness' normally goes unnoticed and unquestioned. Occasionally, however, it may come to light indirectly when blatantly infringed or undermined. Witness the alien hand syndrome suffered by epilepsy patients who have had the two hemispheres of their brain surgically separated.[797] Such anarchic arms exemplify the importance of coordinating bodily parts that may otherwise have a 'mind of their own' coupled with the potential to do considerable harm.[798]

The parts of an animal are heterogeneous on various levels.[799] It is not only organs and limbs that differ from one another (a liver from a kidney, an arm from a leg), but the cells that compose these very organs: a complex metazoan is thought to be composed of at least 120 different *types* of cell.[800] Indeed, cellular differentiation of this sort – along with cell-cell communication and cell-cell and cell-matrix adhesion – constitutes one of the fundamental prerequisites for the transition from a colony of single cells to a genuinely multicellular organism,[801] i.e. from a multiplicity of first-order selves to a single, new meta-self. A many-celled organism depends upon the functional integration and unity of the differentiated cells of which it is composed, i.e. their capacity to pull together for a common cause, namely the organismal self as a whole. This may involve low-level self-sacrifice, the individual cell overriding its own self-perpetuation as a self in the interests of the meta-organism. Self-sacrifice of this sort manifests itself not just as cell differentiation, but specifically as differentiation into germ line and soma, with the concomitant result that some cells are destined to die without having furthered their lineage.[802] Even more important is the propensity of certain cells to engage in apoptosis[803] for the sake of the organism as a whole, as when they have fulfilled their function and serve no further purpose, or when their demise might benefit the organism as a whole as a result of infection or mutation.

In the case of multicellular organisms such as animals or plants, therefore, the constituent parts of a self (the individual cells) are programmed to subordinate their own selfhood and their own interests (self-perpetuation; self-reproduction) to those of the organismal self in its entirety. This, in essence, is why selfhood is ascribed more appropriately to animals or plants than to the individual cells that compose them. The 'selfless' cells of multicellular bodies in this respect contrast starkly with *free-living* single-celled organisms, which tend *not* to commit suicide but to pursue their own selfish interest in staying alive as long as possible. Especially among animals, one might thus view apoptosis as a mechanism of organismal self-containment, a way of keeping the cellular parts subservient to the multicellular whole. When such self-sacrifice fails to occur (on account, say, of a mutation in the pro-apoptotic gene *TP53*), the result may be the proliferation of a rebellious, non-functional subself, i.e. a cancer.

Outside the realm of complex metazoans, by contrast, it is more often unclear whether selfhood is best ascribed to the part or the whole. Such cases provide further illustration of the potentially blurred nature of self-containment.

A much-discussed example of fuzzy selfhood is the gargantuan clonal mass of the fungus *Armillaria bulbosa*, also known as *A. gallica*. One colony, popularly dubbed 'the Humungous Fungus', aroused particular attention and debate in the early 1990s,[804] covering at least fifteen hectares of a forest in Michigan (most of it underground in the form of networks of hyphae) and weighing more than 100 tons. As the product of vegetative growth from a common ancestor thought to date back some 1500 years, the Humungous Fungus has been described as one of the largest living individuals on Earth, rivalling the blue whale and the giant redwood in biomass. In the case of this venerable clone, the unit of selfhood can perhaps be defined by the geographical area it covers and the considerable genetic homogeneity displayed by its various parts. Yet it has been questioned whether the fungal mass really is *one thing*. For a start, it is unclear whether there are physiological connections between all its genetically near-identical parts or whether fragmentation has occurred. It is perfectly feasible – and would be in keeping with the species *Armillaria bulbosa* – for the clone to have become fragmented into a multitude of independently functioning entities. If so, should we refer to the whole individual, or the now fragmented subunits, as the self? Or perhaps selfhood can exist at both levels. Perhaps the question is as redundant or as unanswerable for a fungus as the question of what happens when one amoeba undergoes fission to become two.[805]

Similar problems are thrown up by clonal plants such as the dandelion and certain types of tree such as the quaking aspen (*Populus tremuloides*), the roots of which sprout runners that spread away from the parent tree – by vegetative growth – to a point from which a new tree shoots forth.[806] Again, one particular clonal protagonist has captured the limelight: in this case, a colony of quaking aspen in central Utah. Commonly known as Pando or the 'Trembling Giant', this clonal colony covers 43 hectares, weighs some 6,000 tons, and is thought to have originated 80,000 years ago.[807] There is a tendency, not surprisingly, to regard the individual tree as the unit of selfhood, or – in more practical term – the unit to be counted by demographers. Each tree is physiologically self-contained (sporting epidermis and bark) and has clear boundaries in space; it is also self-contained in time to the extent that it undergoes a life-cycle involving a path to maturity and subsequent senescence, notions that are scarcely relevant to the clone as a whole, which survives as long as the generations of its constituent trees keep on succeeding one another. Again, however, the matter is not straightforward: it might be countered that the unit of selfhood is the *clone as a whole* provided that the trees remain attached to one another by the subterranean network of propagating runners that gave rise to them, as is believed to occur with the more than 40,000 trees of which Pando consists. It might accordingly be felt that the shared roots and physical attachment as well as the genetic identity of the parts are enough to guarantee the unity of a single self. Yet the duration of these connections is disconcertingly fortuitous, as the runners can be broken by land subsidence or the burrowing activities of animals, an environmental contingency thus turning what had appeared to be a physiologically self-contained individual into a multiplicity of such individuals.[808]

The nature of the connectedness is also relevant. A clone of trees – or even a community of unrelated trees linked by a symbiotic network of *mycorrhizal* roots – may use their reticulum of underground linkages as a means of communication and cooperation, but this does not *in itself* produce the strict functional unity characteristic of an organism. As emerged from the example of complex animals, the functional unity of an organism is generally associated with one or both of two conditions. First, the component parts tend to be mutually interdependent, such that severing any part from the whole will impair the functioning of both the part and the whole. This depends upon a degree of differentiation among the constituent parts, by contrast with the homogeneity (and thus interchangeability) of the members of a clone. Secondly, one part of the whole might be disposed to 'sacrifice' itself *for the sake of* the whole. In the case of the quaking aspen, this would involve a hypothetical tree 'committing suicide' (for example) as a response to a general shortage of nutrients or in order to stop the spread of a microbial pathogen. The first condition is how organs interact with one another within a metazoan organism[809]; the second condition is how individual cells interact with one another within such an organism.

The Strange Case of the Social Amoebae:

Dictyostelium Discoideum

Substantial light is shed on the logic of the transition from unicellular selfhood to the full multicellular selfhood of a complex metazoan by the intermediate case of the 'social' amoebae, exemplified by the cellular slime mould *Dictyostelium discoideum*.[810] These amoebae can exist relatively independently from one another as single cells, albeit exchanging signals amongst one another to monitor the presence and abundance of kindred amoebae and potential prey. In itself, the single-celled *D. discoideum* amoeba represents both aspects of self-containment encountered so far: i.e. as a biological individual ('contained' by its cell membrane) and as an organism (a functionally integrated cellular unit composed of causally interconnected and interdependent parts, including its membrane but also other essential components such as its mitochondria, endoplasmic reticulum, etc.). In this form, it behaves much like any other amoeba, moving through the soil in pursuit of bacteria for consumption and eventually splitting to form two genetically identical offspring.

When food runs short, however, such amoebae emit a chemoattractant known as cyclic AMP which causes the cells in the vicinity to aggregate into a slug-like cylindrical mass or 'grex', a multicellular body that contains up to two million individual amoebae. This elongated slug brings its constituent cells from the feeding area to an area on the surface of the soil that is suitable for spore dispersal. At this point the slug again reorganizes, the anterior fraction of the amoebae (the front 20 percent) differentiating to become stalk cells, and the posterior fraction flowing up the stalk to become a ball of spores that – if all goes to plan – will be picked up and transported to new, bacteria-rich feeding pastures by passing insects.

The question, therefore, is whether selfhood is best attributed to the individual amoeba, a self-contained – i.e. membrane-bound and functionally integrated – organism that eats, grows and reproduces in its own right, or to the multicellular grex. To put it differently, to what extent can self-containment be ascribed to the grex, as it can to its constituent cells? Certainly, the grex shows cohesive behaviour, moving towards light and heat and showing exquisite sensitivity to gas gradients (a strong aversion to the common waste product ammonia, and an attraction towards oxygen). It may appear morphologically simpler than most metazoans, but this is partly because – having engaged in feeding at the single-celled stage – its shape is freed from the constraints of an alimentary canal and a doughnut topology. Its cells not only show the differentiation characteristic of an organism (transmuting either into stalk or spore), but some of them also embody the 'selflessness' or 'altruism' of cells disposed to sacrifice themselves for the good of the collective self, in that the stalk cells die in the process of elevating the spores into the air, whereas the spore cells – akin to germ-line cells – continue the lineage. Such differentiation is induced by a signal molecule called 'differentiation inducing factor' or DIF, which seems to be produced by the better-fed cells, inducing the less robust ones to become stalk and thus suggesting that coercion rather than 'voluntary' selflessness may be at work.[811] Yet one should resist the anthropomorphism implied by 'volition'; a multicellular self is a totalitarian place, where the 'will' of individual cells is simply not an issue.

In terms of physical containment, the slugs are surrounded and supported by a 'thin, transparent slime sheath',[812] though the lack of anything akin to an epithelium – by contrast even with basalmost metazoans such as the blob-shaped *Trichoplax* – is not without consequence. Unlike stably self-contained metazoans from placozoans to primates, the cells of the slime mould can 'escape' from their slug and go and join the body of a nearby conspecific. As evolutionary biologist John Bonner explains, since most of the attractant cyclic AMP is secreted from the *tip* of the slug, the tip can be considered dominant: it 'has all the attendant amoebae in thrall'.[813] As a consequence, if one grex crosses paths with another, its tip can 'steal' amoebae from the posterior part of the other. By the same token, slugs can be split into two and can fuse with one another.[814] What is more, there is unusual flexibility in the cell differentiation shown by *D. discoideum*, so if a slug is cut in two, each of the resulting slugs will still produce a fruiting body. In what was the anterior part of the body (composed of cells previously 'destined' to become stalk), some of the amoebae will revert to being pre-spore cells; in what was the posterior part (composed of cells previously 'destined' to become spores), some will turn into pre-stalk cells.[815] The slugs are not 'indivisible' in the manner of a complex organism, therefore, and are not subject to 'death' in the way that an organism is; like a clonal forest of quaking aspens, they live and die with the cells of which they are composed.[816]

Further factors are involved in the (defective) self-containment of the *D. discoideum* grex. By contrast with the cells of a complex metazoan, whose cells are more or less the same genetically, the cells of the slime mould may aggregate even though not all of them are genetically identical, resulting in what is known as a chimera. In a chimera, it is possible for one genetic type – a so-called 'cheater' – to gain an evolutionary advantage by not 'playing fair'. In this case, such a clone can leave more descendants by inducing the cells of other clones to sacrifice themselves as stalk cells while it makes more than its fair share of spores. One of the practical consequences of genetic conflict and cheating is that such slugs tend to move more slowly because the cheating strains compete to stay at the rear, which is where the future spore cells are aggregated.[817] Rather like a cancer, a part of the self is working against the interests of the unitary whole. As noted in Chapter 3, however, *D. discoideum* has evolved a way of defending itself against cells that fail to cooperate with one another. This takes the form of what is believed to be a 'greenbeard gene' (called *csA*), which encodes a homophilic cell-adhesion protein anchored in the cellular membrane. This cell-adhesion molecule enables the cells that possess it to 'recognize' and then bind to one another, collectively dragging one another into the aggregation (indeed sorting preferentially – selflessly – into the stalk), while leaving the cells that lack it straggling.[818] The cells with the gene are thus better at engaging in 'social' behaviour than those without. This ostensibly selfish gene – 'selfish' to the extent that it only fosters cooperation among cells that possess it – ensures that it is in the (collective) interests of those cells to be selfless.

To the extent that the gene distinguishes self from non-self (i.e. from genetically *similar* but non-identical competitors), *csA* functions as a sort of immune mechanism, separating and excluding what might be termed 'near-self'. Through this capacity for self/non-self discrimination, *D. discoideum* is endowed with a variety of *active* self-containment. Yet parasitic 'cheater' cells are not the only type of non-self that can threaten the interests of the slime mould grex. Nor is 'greenbeard' self-recognition the only kind of immune system with which it is provided. Social amoebae can also be infected by bacteria – phylogenetically a much more distant form of non-self – such as the pathogen *Legionella pneumophila*. A subset of the cells in the grex consists of specialized phagocytic cells akin to neutrophils in the human innate immune system. These so-called sentinel cells[819] patrol within the slug as single cells and have the capacity to recognize, attach to and then engulf or sequester harmful bacteria. There is an element of self-sacrifice too, for the sentinel cells – having ingested their fill of harmful non-self – subsequently clump together into immobile groups of five to ten cells that are left behind in the discarded slime sheath deposited by the migrating slug, surrendering themselves to the wellbeing of the whole.[820] Notably, the interaction between the amoebae and the invasive bacterial cells involves a protein that is also characteristic of animal and plant immune systems,[821] suggesting a pathogen-recognition mechanism that may predate the diversification of eukaryotes into various multicellular lineages.

Genetic Individuals

Social behaviour in many respects akin to that of *D. discoideum* is also in evidence among certain bacteria, specifically a species of slime bacteria by the name of *Myxococcus xanthus*.[822] The cells of *M. xanthus* move through their feeding area in the form of a group-coordinated predatory swarm, secreting high concentrations of digestive enzymes that kill and degrade their prey (including other bacteria such as *E. coli*). Held together by intercellular signals, these multicellular groups can fuse and be split up with impunity, yet they approach organismal status – multicellular selfhood – through a social act that occurs when they are starving. In such circumstances, some of the cells commit suicide by lysis, releasing their contents possibly for general consumption, while others aggregate to become a raised fruiting body, a robust spherical spore entrusted with the business of surviving until conditions improve. Again, it is proposed, mutant cheaters can gain an advantage by lysing less and forming more spores.[823] Providing they are rare enough, such cheaters have been shown to increase in frequency in relation to their wild-type companions in the group, whereas if they become too common, they disrupt sporulation and their excessive presence is detrimental to the group as a whole. The amount of cheating – and thus of 'intraorganismal' disunity – is likely to depend upon the degree of genetic homogeneity in the group. The greater the genetic unity, the less is the potential for conflict within the group.[924]

Whether we interpret the individual bacterium or the whole swarm as the unit of selfhood may thus depend not only on the relative degree of functional integration at the cellular and the multicellular level and on other forms of self-containment (physical cohesiveness or immune-like defence systems), but also on the degree of genetic homogeneity. Indeed, the genetic identity of an organism's constituent cells has often been regarded as an essential feature of a biological individual. Genetically homogeneous components are thought to have a greater tendency to cooperate than genetically heterogeneous components because of the fate they have in common. It makes sense for a kidney cell to continue to fulfil its cooperative function in excretion rather than selfishly de-differentiating and heading for the gonads in the hope of sneaking a ride to the next generation, because its abnegation of duty would impair the functioning of the kidney and thus the survival and fertility of the individual, making the genes in the kidney cell – as well as all the other cells in the body – less likely to reach the next generation anyway.[825]

Biological 'individuality' has thus been understood to encompass not only physiological autonomy but also genetic homogeneity and genetic uniqueness.[826] Individuals failing to show all these attributes have generally been regarded as exceptions. In these terms, the 'genetic individual' might be included alongside the physiological individual and the functional individual (or organism) as representing distinct *aspects* of self-containment that need not always coincide. The philosopher Jack Wilson has defined a genetic individual as a biological entity whose parts 'share a common genotype because of descent without interruption from a common ancestor with that genotype'.[827] Such a conception is taken to incorporate clones of amoebae (an original singularity plus its genetically more or less identical offspring), colonies of bacteria, multicellular bodies such as those of human beings or other complex metazoans, as well as clones comprising multiple multicellular units such as quaking aspens, dandelions or aphids.[828]

The appeal of the notion perhaps lies in its evident applicability to complex metazoans like us, although in other cases this applicability seems less straightforward. For bacteria, amoebae and aphids, the genetic individual – defined in terms of genetic homogeneity and uniqueness – may well be a *plurality* in organismal and physiological terms, composed of a multiplicity of spatially separate functional units. For complex metazoans, by contrast, our genetic individuality provides us with a relatively clear-cut identity that distinguishes us from our conspecifics as reliably as our fingerprints. Yet even here there are problems: identical twins represent a single genetic individual, but two physiological or functional individuals. Indeed, the genomic information simply seems insufficient to capture what it is about an individual that makes it an individual *self*, instead implying an immutability or genetic essentialism which ignores the ongoing interaction of self with non-self, the resulting capacity for self-transformation, and the unique, individualized life-history that this helps engender. More concretely, it leaves out of account the whole dimension of so-called 'epigenetic' factors that determine *which* genes are switched on and *which* switched off. So how are we to understand the idea that selves may be genetic individuals just as they are physiological individuals or functional organisms? Or rather: how far, if at all, can we apply the concept of self-containment to genetic individuals? In what sense can genetic selves be said to be self-contained?

One possible answer, perhaps, is that genetic self-containment comes to expression in the form of its *phenotypic* effects. In this case, it is *indirect* or *secondary* in relation to the physiological and functional forms of self-containment through which it phenotypically manifests itself. Any further attempt to pinpoint genetic self-containment is superfluous.

An alternative answer focuses on the ways in which one genetic individual differentiates itself – creates its identity and maintains its difference – in relation to other genetic individuals.[829] In general, a new genetic individual comes into being when a cell, or group of cells, acquires a genotype distinct from that of its progenitor.[830] However, there are grades of distinctness: mere *point mutation* within the offspring of a clone may not be considered sufficient distinctness for a new genetic individual to have arisen. By contrast, when two gametes fuse in the sexual reproduction of eukaryotes, the resulting zygote – together with all the cells with the same genotype that descend from it – constitutes a new genetic individual distinct from either gamete. The self-containment of a genetic individual may be interpreted as the 'fixing' of any such difference by *increasing* variance with respect to other genetic individuals and *decreasing* the amount of variance within the genetic individual, in this way defining or delimiting its position within the *gene pool*.

Sexual reproduction is one of various means by which this may be achieved. Whereas clonal reproduction merely results in more of the same (without sharp differentiation either between parents and offspring or between siblings), sexual reproduction results in a zygote that is different from other genetic individuals, creating a new genotype by recombination. In this sense it functions as a mechanism of differentiation. Many flowering plants are further characterized by barriers to self-fertilization to ensure outbreeding rather than 'selfing'; these so-called 'self-incompatibility' systems involve an apparatus of self/non-self discrimination such that the recognition of self-pollen leads to the subsequent prevention of egg-sperm interaction.[831] Sexual outcrossing represents a mechanism that fosters genetic variation in offspring, producing a population of differentiated individuals.

While such measures increase the difference *between* genetic individuals, others decrease the difference *within* individuals. The immune systems of fungi and animals capable of fusing with one another – less complex metazoans such as jellyfish-like hydrozoans and other marine invertebrates – deploy 'incompatibility' barriers, in this case to restrict their capacity to merge with closely related individuals. Mechanisms of self/non-self discrimination such as histocompatibility systems in animals and heterokaryon incompatibility systems in fungi serve to maintain the boundaries between self and closely related self, thus *defining* the individual as a genetic self. Genetic homogeneity is further maintained by the single-celled developmental 'bottleneck', which serves as a mutation 'sieve' by only allowing the genome of one cell to pass to the next generation (irrespective of the number of distinct genomes in the parent).[832] The same goes for the 'sequestration' of the germ line, i.e. the separation of germ cells and somatic cells. Even though mutations may occur in somatic cells, such mutations – according to the traditional view at least – cannot cross over into the germ line, making the cells in which they occur an evolutionary dead end. There is a sense in which the genetic identity of an animal is 'contained' within its germ line, or – to expand on the bottleneck metaphor – perhaps the 'container' in question is the bottle through whose neck the genetic individual must squeeze in order to reach a new generation.

Chimeras and Symbionts

The self has been seen to contain itself in the mode of a physiological individual, a functional individual (or organism) and, more contentiously, a genetic individual. The latter is epitomized in the genetic homogeneity and uniqueness that is (broadly speaking) characteristic of complex metazoans, yet these attributes are recognized to be anything but universal among living organisms. For a start, they are undermined by the relative prevalence in nature of somatic embryogenesis over early germ-line sequestration.[833] Genetic heterogeneity may take the form of *mosaicism* and *chimerism*, the former commonly arising from genetic changes caused by somatic mutations, the latter produced by the fusion of genetically distinct organisms.[834] Genetic uniformity seems to be a relatively contingent or non-essential character, subordinate to the functional and physiological unity which it fosters but for which it is neither necessary nor sufficient.

The phenomenon of chimerism in particular demonstrates that genetic identity is not necessarily what *matters*. The fusion of two genetically distinct individuals would normally be thought to generate internal conflicts or intraorganismal disunity that might disrupt the functional integrity of the resulting organism. Such fusion is generally prevented by immune or histocompatibility systems consisting of mechanisms of self/non-self discrimination, but the exceptions are legion. Not only do many red algae (for example) create chimeras through the coalescence of genetically divergent spores, but this has been shown to result in enhanced survival and fertility.[835] Likewise, fungi frequently form chimeric organisms, and the grafting of trees – for example, apple and pear trees[836] – can lead to the creation of tightly integrated functional individuals. It is among metazoans that chimerism proves more problematic. Attempts at xenotransplantation – the transfer of cells or organs from one animal species to another – have as yet generally failed to overcome the violent defensive reaction of the recipient's immune system.

If chimeras raise the question of whether there is one self or two – and if there are two, where the one begins and the other ends – this fuzziness is embodied even more graphically in the phenomenon of symbiosis, which involves a relationship of mutual interaction and interdependence, usually between the members of two (or more) different species. The phenomenon may range from the relatively casual mutualism of the cleaning services offered by certain species of fish, which benefit both parties but are ultimately optional or facultative,[837] to the seamlessly integrated obligate interdependence of lichens, which comprise a cooperative association between a fungus and one or more photosynthetic partners (green algae or cyanobacteria, or both).[838] In this case, the fungus provides the structural framework and protective 'containment' (in the form of a 'cortex' comprising layers of hyphae) but benefits from a constant supply of on-tap sugars produced by the photosynthetic work of its partners. Of course, this invites the question of whether the fungus has 'enslaved' its workers and whether the relationship might not be better regarded as parasitic rather than mutualistic.[839] To human eyes, fungal containment might seem tantamount to the forced confinement of a prisoner or slave labourer. As with the endosymbionts encountered in Chapter 4, however, containment cannot be equated with incarceration in the absence of aspirations to escape, and there is no more reason to ascribe any such aspirations to a cyanobacterium in its fungal confinement than to *Buchnera aphidicola* tucked away in the bacteriocyte cells of an aphid. The bottom line is ultimately the self-maintaining functional unity that in many, though not all,[840] cases makes the two partners mutually indispensable as a single self.

Even more spectacular, perhaps, is the symbiosis formed by humans with roughly 100 trillion (10^{14}) bacteria, as well as rather lower numbers of archaea, yeast cells and protists.[841] Without realizing it (until recently at least), we vertebrates each constitute a moving forest of microbial 'non-self' – the densest bacterial ecosystem found in nature[842] – in which our own bodily cells are heavily outnumbered by the micro-organisms we host. A key feature of this portable ecosystem is the genetic diversity it endows us with; whereas one person's 'own' genome differs from another's by just 0.1 percent, our gut genomes may diverge from each other by as much as 50 percent. The entire cohort generally comprises over a thousand species in each individual human, these species providing us with what researchers have termed a 'minimal gut metagenome' – a core of bacterial genes we all share – capable of performing more than six thousand biochemical functions.[843]

Studies have shown that the identity of our *microbiota* is determined more by what we eat than by evolutionary kinship. Two main phyla, Firmicutes and Bacteroidetes, dominate the community; species belonging to *Lactobacillus*, a member of the Firmicutes, are prevalent in infant guts, but yield to genera such as *Prevotella* and *Bacteroides* when plant carbohydrates and animal proteins are introduced into the diet. The ratio of these two genera in turn reflects whether the diet is based more on cereals and vegetables or on animal proteins and saturated fats.[844] One of the most remarkable gut-inhabiting bacteria in its digestive versatility is a species called *Bacteroides thetaiotaomicron*, whose genome encodes some 260 carbohydrate-degrading enzymes, almost three times as many as the 500-times-larger human genome.[845] Yet the digestion of otherwise indigestible foodstuffs such as plant polysaccharides is just one of a number of favours our microbes do us; indeed, they provide a whole range of services that are essential to the metabolic processes on which our survival and wellbeing depend. These include the synthesis of vitamins such as B12, the regulation of levels of stomach acids and the hormone ghrelin (which in turn regulates appetite), and a major role in fine-tuning the immune system so as to prevent autoimmunity.[846] Crucially, they also endow us with flexibility: because our resident microbes do not constitute a tightly defined or fixed association but a fluid community that varies in its composition in accordance with functional expediency, we are able to adapt to changing environmental circumstances by altering our microbiota.

And what do we do for them? We supply them with regular meals (under the delusion that we are feeding *ourselves*), which they pass on to us in a form we can digest; we also furnish them with the 'containment' of a predictable and sheltered environment. By regularly expelling some of them in faeces, moreover, we provide the dispersal mechanism that is crucial for their ability to propagate themselves in the long run. The question of who is in charge of whom is as unanswerable as it is in the case of the lichen; servant and master – whoever is which – are locked in a Hegelian embrace of mutual interdependency.[847] To the extent that we constitute a single functional individual, we are multiple selves that unite to form a single self. Confounding the law of identity, self coincides with non-self.

Of course, we may bridle at the idea that the community of 'lowly' bacteria that happen to inhabit our intestines partakes of our selfhood: 'I am my brain', we may insist, 'or my body insofar as it consists of cells I can genuinely call my own'.[848] Such a self-conception receives support from the notion of genetic individuality, to the extent that each of us is a clearly differentiated genetic individual with respect to our microbiota. Yet the other aspects of self-containment show the phenomenon in a more nuanced light.

As a physiological individual, my relationship to my bacterial symbionts is intrinsically ambiguous, for my in-house microbial community inhabits my epithelium (not only the gut, but also the mouth and skin), to this extent residing at the very margins where self meets non-self. This ambivalence is compounded by their prevalence in my intestines, where notions of outside and inside are even fuzzier. Yet to the extent that I 'contain' my microbiota (providing them with accommodation and shelter), there is certainly a sense in which my self-containment is theirs. The image of 'containment' has been used, moreover, to designate how our mutualist microbes are as a rule kept in the 'right' compartment; a failure to 'contain' our microbes in this way – allowing them access to forbidden or inappropriate tissues or cells – can transform the most beneficial of mutualists into harmful pathogens. Gut microbes, suggests Gérard Eberl, are not inherently mutualistic or pathogenic, but 'navigate between shades of mutualism and parasitism'[849] according to whether or not they are appropriately 'contained' by the host immune system.[850]

More than genetic and physiological individuality, it is perhaps the third aspect of self-containment that is decisive in defining my relationship to my indwelling microbiota: the functional unity that characterizes this relationship, the shared interests that result from our collaborative interaction, the fact that my metabolic well-being depends on my gut bacteria, just as their collective well-being depends on me. The degree of unity, and thus unitary selfhood, may vary according to whether our symbiotic interdependence is facultative or obligate (humans are born largely germ-free, suggesting that a life without intestinal associates is at least feasible). It may also vary with the level of cohesion and specialization among the symbionts and with the time-scales involved,[851] i.e. the question of whether the association is momentary, life-long or transgenerational, as with the intracellular inhabitants of aphids and other sap-sucking insects. Unlike endosymbionts such as *Buchnera*, our gut microbiota is not bequeathed to our children, but must be individually reacquired each generation.[852] To this extent, therefore, the selfish union of an animal with its microbiota covers only two of the three forms of intrinsic reflexivity that are held to constitute full selfhood: (metabolic) self-maintenance and self-containment, but not self-reproduction.

Yet even this may be an oversimplification, such is the pervasive influence of our resident microbes on what we are and what we do. It is becoming increasingly apparent that our gut bacteria may affect not only our health and welfare but also our moods, stress levels and our general behaviour in ways that have yet to be elucidated.[853] This is most palpably the case with our eating habits. It is in the interests of gut bacteria to induce us to feed on what causes *them* to flourish, and those that succeed in doing so will fare better than competing species that fail to do so.[854] There is accumulating evidence that intestinal microbes communicate with the central nervous system through neural, endocrine and immune pathways,[855] exerting both direct and indirect effects on brain function and behaviour. Indeed, the concept of a 'microbiota-gut-brain axis' has been coined to denote the influence of our microbes on gut-brain communication.[856] A graphic illustration of the influence of gut bacteria on animal feeding behaviour is the giant panda, whose eating habits are dictated by the preference of its intestinal microbes for high-cellulose bamboo – even though the panda genome does not encode the requisite digestive enzymes and pandas themselves are metabolically much better equipped for a carnivorous diet.[857] However, the sway exerted by gut microbiota on the animals they colonize is not limited to eating preferences. Experiments on the fruit fly have shown that this influence may extend to the choice of mating partner.[858] Variations in the presence of one bacterium in particular, *Lactobacillus plantarum*, have been found to be responsible for the fly's mating preferences, suggesting that symbiosis might even contribute to speciation – and that symbiotic associations may in a sense thus foster their own 'reproduction' after all. This has led to the idea of the 'holobiont' (the host *plus* its symbionts) as the 'unit of selection' in evolutionary change.[859]

It is evidently over-hasty to exclude our microbiota from our *selves* – from what we *are* as selves – on any level except purely genetic individuality. Yet if we are magnanimous enough to share our selfhood with a thousand species of prokaryotes, what about the mitochondria we host *within* most of our bodily cells, formerly free-living alpha-proteobacteria which, many hundreds of millions of years ago, are thought to have merged with host archaea and are now regarded as 'mere' organelles? Despite the vast expanse of time that has passed, is this still an instance of two (or more) selves in one? The question, perhaps, is whether it makes sense to attribute any residual selfhood to our mitochondria. Certainly, aerobic metazoans such as humans are still as dependent on our mitochondria as our mitochondria are on us; we rely on the power they generate in the way that the lichen's fungus relies on its algae or cyanobacteria. The association continues to be based on mutual interdependence.

It can be countered, of course, that the relationship is asymmetrical in that mitochondria *are a part of* human cells, whereas human cells are *not part of* a mitochondrion. But this is the nature of endosymbiosis, where one of the symbionts is contained within the other (i.e. where unilateral 'protection' is part of the deal).[860] It might also be argued that mitochondria have 'forfeited' their genetic individuality by ceding most of their genes to the host nucleus; indeed, they may end up losing them altogether, as many hydrogenosomes and all mitosomes have. But perhaps the most relevant question, once again, is whether our dependence on mitochondria ever results, or could result, in functional disunity, with vestigial selfishness on the part of the organelle working against the interests of the organism as a whole.[861] Either way, from the ever more evanescent mitochondrial perspective, there remains a sense in which human beings – like the rest of the animal kingdom – represent not so much an autonomous self as a vehicle by which selfish mitochondria have succeeded in perpetuating themselves through the eons.[862]

Farming, Love and Other Shared Selfhood

Symbiotic relationships are sometimes described in terms of farming. Adopting the point of view of our microbiota, Nicholas Money has referred to the 'symbiosis between bacteria and their farm animals (*us*)'.[863] The metaphor is appropriate: the human farming of non-human animals is also a form of symbiosis, albeit facultative rather than obligate, with the species in question contributing different functions to a relationship of mutual cooperation: in general humans provide protection in return for regular food, mobility, strength or some other attribute or resource in which we are relatively deficient. Complementarity of this sort creates the possibility of a new functional unity.[664]

By the same token, the agricultural cultivation of plants is a mode of collective symbiosis whereby humans compensate for their anatomical limitations by *outsourcing* the process of photosynthesis, in return domesticating or 'containing' what was originally wild, unconstrained vegetation. Here too, the question of who is farming whom, or who has domesticated whom, eschews a straightforward answer. Upending the humans-in-charge perspective naturally favoured by humans, historian Yuval Noah Harari depicts an almost comic *mundus inversus* in which it is the wheat, rice and potatoes that have domesticated *Homo sapiens* rather than the reverse. As a result of the agricultural revolution some ten millennia ago, what had previously been a species of relatively easy-living hunter-gatherers was brought to put more and more effort into tending to every last whim of the plants on which it was becoming increasingly dependent. A crop such as wheat proved to be an unforgiving task-master, writes Harari: 'wheat didn't like rocks and pebbles, so [humans] broke their backs clearing fields. Wheat didn't like sharing its space, water and nutrients with other plants, so men and women laboured long days weeding under the scorching sun. ... Wheat was attacked by rabbits and locust swarms, so the farmers built fences and stood guard over the fields. Wheat was thirsty, so humans dug irrigation canals or lugged heavy buckets from the well to water it. Its hunger even impelled [them] to collect animal faeces to nourish the ground in which wheat grew'.[865] As a consequence, wheat now covers vast swathes of the planet, its numerical success paralleling that of the primate it has domesticated.

Humans are far from being the only animals that engage in such strategies of mutual cooperation. The farming of aphids by ants is well documented.[866] Even more surprisingly, the social amoeba *Dictyostelium discoideum* is known to engage in what has been called 'bacterial husbandry'.[867] When food runs short and the amoebae join together to form a grex, some of the amoebae refrain from consuming all the remaining bacteria before decamping, instead taking a number of bacteria with them in their fruiting bodies. The idea is that the accompanying bacteria will 'seed' a fresh colony if there is a shortage at the new site. Roughly a third of the spores contain such bacteria, though there may be costs involved: when spores are transferred to sites where edible bacteria are abundant anyway, farmer amoebae seem to produce rather fewer offspring, presumably because they have relinquished immediate nourishment out of forward-looking 'prudence'.[868]

In a broad sense, the concept of symbiosis covers a whole spectrum of forms of association ranging from slavery to farming through to love (and even sexual reproduction). Between certain species, the relationship of domestication may thus incorporate an emotional component. The mutual domestication of wolf and man,[869] for example, may be described not only in terms of functional integration or unity of interests, but also in terms of emotions such as friendship or love as well as empathetic identification (i.e. emotional union). In this extended sense, symbioses are even more frequent between members of the same species. Both friendship and love – however we define these notoriously slippery terms – provide a context in which *two selves become one*. Aristotle, as we have seen, identified a friend as 'another self',[870] by which he meant that to be in a relationship of friendship to a person is to seek the good of that person for the sake of that person, just as one does for oneself. It is, one might even say, to care intrinsically for another self as one cares intrinsically for one's own self.[871] In practical terms, this emotional symbiosis may manifest itself not only in one person selflessly-selfishly seeking the wellbeing of another, but also in the physiological unity and mutual interdependence suggested by metaphors of two people being 'inseparable from one another' or 'unable to live without one another' or 'one another's other half'. Conventional or biological gender differences may further foster a division of labour by which each partner contributes a different set of skills to long-term affiliations. Such friendship, or love, may bear a disconcerting similarity to the relationship we share with our gut microbiota. Unsurprisingly, the metaphor of love as a form of symbiosis can be off-putting to those who value free-living autonomy and are keen not to end up playing a green alga to someone else's fungus.

It is a cliché indeed that two selves are turned into one by both the emotion and the act of love.[872] Traditionally, the topos coincides with the folly of romantic love, which causes the (usually male) 'lover' to be besides or outside himself – obsessed with, or perhaps possessed by, his other self – and incapable of acting in his own interests. In fact, the emotional symbiosis of love is a reflection of the brute biological fact that, modern technology apart, it takes two persons to reproduce sexually anyway. In the context of copulation, there is a sense in which the couple *is* the unit of selfhood; sexually reproducing species rely upon an (at least transitory) sharing of selfhood.

The resulting infringement of numerical identity is manifest at the most fundamental level of organization when two gametes fuse in sexual reproduction. The two *gametes* cannot be numerically identical with the ensuing zygote because numerical identity presupposes unity (a one-to-one relationship). As was proposed in the Introduction, however, identity is not always what matters when it comes to selfhood. Trans-individual selfhood, as embodied in the self-perpetuation of a lineage, depends not on the *identity* of the self-producing self through time but on its *continuity*. At the same time, the fusion of two gametes engenders a new *individual* that can be understood to be distinct from either of the original individual selves, 'individuality' denoting a unitary entity that is bounded or 'contained' in space and time and thus endowed with a beginning and an end. This explains why – although there is a real sense in which I am a perpetuation of my progenitors – I am not the same biological individual.

Such eukaryotic fusion was doubtless made possible by the loss of the bacterial cell wall.[873] With this obstacle removed, many simple eukaryotes exhibit a marked tendency for their cells to fuse with one another. Many fungi, for example, are able to form giant multinucleate cells both through hyphal self-fusion within the same individual and through hyphal fusion between different individuals.[874] The resulting 'heterokaryon' is a single cell comprising a common cytoplasm occupied by numerous genetically distinct nuclei, again undermining the association between individuality defined in terms of physical self-containment and specifically *genetic* individuality. More generally, a distinction is often drawn between a *syncytium* (which includes fungal heterokaryons), where cellular aggregation precedes the dissolution of the membranes within the mass to form a single multinucleate cell, and a *coenocyte*, where the multinucleate cell is produced by a series of nuclear divisions that take place without subsequent cell division. One of the best known instances of the latter is the creature known as the plasmodial slime mould (formerly Myxomycetes). Unlike the related cellular slime moulds, whose best-known representative is *D. discoideum*, this creature comprises not a multicellular slug but a multinucleate bag of cytoplasm, which starts life as a single fertilized cell, repeatedly dividing its nucleus as it absorbs food, creates new cytoplasm and expands in size.[875] The growing plasmodium, writes Bonner, 'looks like a viscous liquid and, like a giant amoeba, slowly crawls about seeking food. If the conditions are right, especially if there is sufficient nutrition and moisture, the plasmodium may become very large – the size of one's hand or even larger. It is not an uncommon sight to see a beautiful slimy glob of bright orange, glistening on the surface of a rotten log'.[876] When conditions turn less favourable, the bag of liquid will sprout numerous stalks that rise into the air as fruiting bodies, dispersing itself in the form of multiple spores.[877]

Despite appearing to be little more than a shapeless accumulation of goo 'contained' by a slime-reinforced plasma membrane rather than anything akin to an epithelium, slime moulds such as the much-studied *Physarum polycephalum* exhibit the directed, functional, intelligent behaviour of a unitary self.[878]

Immune Containment: Distinguishing Self from Non-Self

Immunity and Selfhood: A Complex Relationship

The previous section has brought to light the fuzziness that may characterize the boundaries separating self from non-self, or one self from another. The 'self' contained by the process of self-containment may merge and multiply, infringing the dictates of numerical identity (the precept that one is one). This may involve short- or rather longer-term discrepancies between *aspects* of self-containment, between the self as a bounded physiological individual, as an organism and as a genetic individual. Such discrepancies are brought to light particularly clearly by the immune system, which is often understood in terms of genetic identity but where the bottom line must ultimately be the functional unity of a self-maintaining and self-containing self. The present section will seek to shed light on the complex relationship between immunity and selfhood and on the extent to which the former can be considered a universal – or even a definitional – feature of the latter.

The underlying idea is that the immune system forms a critical part of an organism's self-containment. It establishes the boundaries of the self to the extent that it determines what is excluded from the self and what is not excluded. Rather like the bouncers at the entrance to a night-club or the border guards at passport control, cells of the immune system buttress the physical frontiers of the organism, working in close coordination with the skin and mucous membrane.[879] The image of 'sentinel cells' is recurrent in immunology. Such sentinels include not only antigen-presenting cells such as the Langerhans cells encountered above, but amoeboid *macrophages* capable of ingesting microbial non-self. These dedicated phagocytes patrol the tissues just under the skin, in the lungs and around the intestines, and can recognize characteristic surface molecules of bacteria such as mannose and LPS, as well as invaders that have been tagged or 'opsonised' by the immune system's antibodies. Along with neutrophils (specialist phagocytes on call from the blood), such cells are part of the first line of defence in the case of wounds and injuries to the skin. The neutrophils are themselves subsequently engulfed and degraded by the macrophages.

Understood thus, the immune system is a mechanism of self/non-self discrimination, and immunology has been referred to as the science of self/non-self discrimination.[880] It is assumed that whereas elements 'foreign' to a body will trigger an immune response, endogenous elements will not generate such a response but are tolerated by the rest of the body. Essential to this discrimination are the twin processes of recognition and systemic communication. While macrophages are indispensable sentinels of the evolutionarily older *innate* immune system, *lymphocytes* known as B cells and T cells are the 'eyes' of the more specific *adaptive* (or acquired) immune system present only in vertebrates. In the case of B cells, for example, the recognition of non-self antigens induces the production of antibodies that in turn opsonise further such antigens so they can be recognized and eliminated by the innate system. This recognition should not be taken to presuppose 'consciousness'; the antibodies comprise a special class of large proteins known as immunoglobulins that bind to – i.e. 'recognize' – their target antigens as a lock interacts with a key.[881]

Another crucial class of such recognition molecules is the major histocompatibility complex (MHC), a set of cell surface molecules encoded by a tightly linked cluster of genes that play a major role in acceptance of self (histocompatibility) and the rejection of non-self (histoincompability). These surface proteins function as *markers* of cellular identity or selfhood. Notably, one of the two primary classes of MHC proteins (MHC-I), which is constitutively expressed on almost all nucleated self cells (though not on blood cells), is commonly downgraded as a consequence of viral infection or cellular stress: the ensuing 'missing self'[882] is recognized as such by a class of immune agents called natural killer (NK) cells, which in turn trigger apoptosis (i.e. cellular suicide) in the affected cell. This capacity and disposition of infected, stressed or transformed cells to engage in apoptosis – i.e. to 'sacrifice' themselves for the good of the organism as a whole – is another more or less ubiquitous characteristic of immune systems.[883]

The notion of the immunological 'self' has recently been called into doubt by philosophers and biologists. Immunologist Polly Matzinger, for example, has focused on questions raised by borderline cases, such as why the organism generally 'accepts' a genetically foreign body such as the foetus or placenta while other transplants are so forcefully rejected.[884] Indeed, the placenta can be seen as akin to a parasitic presence of (paternal) non-self within (maternal) self and to this extent a natural theatre for conflict and self-division.[885] In practice, cells such as NK cells are prevented from attacking this invasive non-self by modulations that take place in the signalling system of the mother's immune system. Matzinger understands this as an indication that 'the immune system is more concerned with damage than with foreignness, and is called into action by alarm signals from injured tissues, rather than by the recognition of non-self'. She accordingly advocates what she terms the 'danger model' for its greater explanatory value.[886]

The traditional, narrowly genetic notion of immune selfhood undoubtedly has considerable limitations, and 'danger' is undoubtedly a relevant notion in explaining what is going on. However, 'danger' is always 'danger *to*' and inevitably raises the question 'danger *to whom or what*?' Perhaps the first and most obvious answer to suggest itself is 'danger *to self*',[887] but how are we to define the 'self' in question? While genetic individuality yields one (apparently inadequate) answer, a more flexible conception of self-containment as referring to an *organism* sheds a different light on the 'self' that has to be contained. In this case, 'danger to self' denotes a threat to a composite yet functionally integrated unity together with all the symbiotic associates with which it exists in a relationship of mutual interdependence – with the foetus assuming pride of place among such symbionts. One may query whether the mother-child relationship really amounts to a case of symbiosis. Surely the mother does not *depend* upon her foetus? Indeed, there is asymmetry in their relation precisely to the extent that the mother is much more likely to survive the loss of her foetus than vice versa. In this context, however, their mutual interdependence resides in the fact that neither of them will pass on their genes to future generations without the help of the other: mothers whose over-zealous NK cells attack their own foetuses will produce fewer offspring than those whose immune systems are successfully held in check.

Understood in this broad sense, the phenomenon of symbiosis makes it clear that a merely genetic notion of self/non-self discrimination fails to yield a full explanation of immune selfhood; again, genetic individuality is not the final word. A more robust explanatory framework is provided by a functional understanding of the self as an organism, i.e. a composite entity consisting of heterogeneous yet causally integrated components whose unitary 'function' is to sustain itself through time and perpetuate itself through the generations. This is corroborated by the association of a host organism with its microbiota. While a narrowly genetic view would suggest that the body's own cells should be in a state of perpetual conflict with the microbial non-self that inhabits our intestines, the mutualistic nature of the relationship between self and benign non-self implies that such an aggressive immune system would effectively be cutting off its nose to spite its face, leaving us with a crippled digestive system and bereft of a whole array of metabolic capabilities that enhance our flexibility and promote our survival.

The implication is that immunity is not so much a matter of attacking as of *managing* the bacterial non-self we harbour. The idea, indeed, goes back at least to the physician and essayist Lewis Thomas, who in the 1970s foresaw the possibility of coming to regard 'immune reactions, genes for the chemical marking of self, and perhaps all reflexive responses of aggression and defense as secondary developments in evolution, necessary for the regulation and modulation of symbiosis, not designed to break into the process, only to keep it from getting out of hand'.[888] In these terms, our immune system is a mechanism required to 'contain' symbiosis, to channel and control it and ensure that our resident bacteria continue to behave *in* our interests rather than *against* them.[889] To the extent that our bacterial associates are essential to our development, protection and overall metabolic welfare, the role of the immune system is to supervise and shape the composition of the microbiota rather than to wage war blindly on whatever is non-self.

It is now becoming apparent, moreover, that our symbiotic gut microbiota is itself an active and crucial participant in our immune system.[890] This participation may take a variety of forms. Benign bacteria may not only 'crowd out' the harmful contingent, but also activate the immune responses that are required to keep pathogens at bay. As Jon Turney describes it, the resident bacteria 'promote coordinated production of plentiful mucus, antibacterial peptides, immunoglobulin and immune cells in a collective that has been called a "mucosal firewall". The microbes secure peaceful co-existence by bringing on the conditions that ensure their own containment'.[891] The model symbiont *B. thetaiotaomicron*, for example, is known to provide protection against invasion by modulating expression of a species-selective antibacterial peptide known as Ang4, not only benefiting its host but also keeping a measure of control over the composition of its bacterial neighbourhood.[892] More generally, the gut microbiota plays a major role in developing, maturing and 'educating' the intestinal immune system, which has been shown to be correspondingly underdeveloped in specially raised germ-free mice.[893] Bacteria such as *Bacteroides fragilis* help to maintain our immune balance by stimulating the production of anti-inflammatory immune players such as regulatory T cells (cells that counter the effects of other, pro-inflammatory T cells). For example, one of the surface molecules by which *B. fragilis* is recognized – the sugar molecule polysaccharide A – contributes to this placatory effect, protecting the bacterium itself and also sparing the host organism the trauma of inflammation. Polysaccharide A functions rather like an identity card or passport, announcing 'look, it's only me!' and thus signalling the presence of a friend, i.e. of symbiotically shared self. Strains of the bacterium without this means of identification do not last long in the mucosal lining of the gut; they are attacked by our immune system like any other pathogen.

The role of benign microbes in our immune 'containment' of course raises the question of whether we can still claim to be *self*-contained. Genetically speaking, the answer is yes and no, to the extent that self *cooperates with* non-self in the process of self-containment. A functional approach to self-containment tells a slightly different story, in which what counts is the *shared selfhood* of the resident microbiota with its host organism, the symbiotic unity ensuring that 'containment' is in the (selfish) interests of both.[894] Similarly knotty questions are raised by the far-from-implausible scenario of a nanotechnological immune system, which might be conceived as consisting of an army of microscopic robots that performed the work of our macrophages.[895]

Part of the reason for the distrust shown towards the concept of immune 'selfhood' is the sheer *complexity* of our immune system (scarcely reflected in the present brief sketch), which makes it seem doubtful that any *single* concept could do justice to the phenomenon. As outlined above, the discrepancy between genetic and functional individuality – the divergent limits they may imply – gives rise to situations in which the distinction between self and non-self is necessarily fuzzy. Tumours, i.e. mutated self, are another of the borderline cases referred to by Matzinger: 'why do we fail to reject tumors', she asks, 'even when many clearly express new or mutated proteins?' According to the danger model she proposes, the answer is that the healthily growing cells of cancers do not send alarm signals.[896] Yet two further points shed additional light on the matter. First, to the extent that the immune system is conceived as including mechanisms of apoptosis and programmed cell death, the immune system *does* seek to avert cancerous growths, albeit at a unicellular rather than a systemic level: whenever the p53 protein encoded by the *TP53* gene, for example, detects mutation or irreparable damage to the individual cell's DNA, its response is to instigate suicide in the cell in question. Mutations to the pro-apoptotic *TP53* gene are thus one of the defining features of cancer.[897] Secondly, the importance of a stout defence against cancer – which rarely strikes until after a reproductive age has been reached – has to be weighed against the importance of *self-tolerance*, and a balance has to be struck. It is vital that B and T cells should not interpret self cells as a threat unless they really are a threat, and a whole range of mechanisms have evolved to prevent inappropriate self-recognition from occurring.[898] Failures of such self-tolerance lead to autoimmune diseases – self waging war on self – such as type 1 diabetes, multiple sclerosis, rheumatoid arthritis and lupus.

The complexity of immunity is also illustrated by the extent to which it goes beyond mere self/non-self discrimination. Macrophages, for example, are not just bacteria-eating sentinels, but 'garbage men' that hoover up cellular debris and ageing self cells (such as neutrophils that have fulfilled their function). There is evidence of special populations of lymphocytes that respond to stressed self molecules rather than to invasive foreign entities.[899] In this sense, the immune system is not merely a form of border-reinforcement, but a mechanism of homeostasis and 'housekeeping'. This has again been interpreted as betraying the inadequacy of the notion of immune 'selfhood'.[900] In fact, the contrary is the case: such self-surveillance provides additional evidence of the inextricability of self-containment and self-maintenance as two intertwined aspects of a single functional unit, both sustaining the order within and upholding the boundaries that separate within from without. This homeostatic self-regulation applies not just to the individual host organism, but to the host-symbiont meta-organism as a whole.[901]

One further cause for confusion is generated by the potentially infinite nature of negation. As seen in the case of *D. discoideum*, 'not self' can refer equally to entities from different domains[902] or to different individuals from the same species, i.e. to the most phylogenetically distant of bacterial microorganisms (*remote non-self*), but also to transplantations or grafts from individuals belonging to the same or closely related species (*near-self*). On the one hand, identifying bacterial non-self involves a coarse-grained recognition system based on an evolutionary memory of typical 'microbe-associated molecular patterns' (MAMPs)[903] such as mannose and LPS. This is done by venerable 'pattern recognition receptors' (PRRs). On the other hand, when humans or other animals reject grafts or transplants that are not from themselves but from conspecifics, this is because 'foreign' MHC molecules are recognized as such by the host organism's army of NK cells and cytotoxic T cells (CTLs). The immune cells respond by attacking the cells that express such molecules, targeting the blood vessels in the donated organ and thus cutting off its supply of blood and oxygen. Of course, transplants are not a 'peril' faced by complex metazoans such as humans in the struggle for survival. However, the same principle of defence against near-self is of critical importance to less complex animals such as certain marine invertebrates (e.g. hydrozoans), which can fuse with conspecifics and – since they do not sequester their germ-line – are vulnerable to parasitism from competing individuals. In the face of this threat, *allorecognition* mediated by multi-gene complexes akin to the human MHC[904] endows an organism with the ability to differentiate between its own tissues and those of other individuals of the same species, thus allowing it both to fuse (and thus avoid wasteful competition) if it encounters clone mates[905] and to reject fusion with unrelated rivals for space and natural resources. In these terms, there are two primary realms of non-self: intra-species non-self, or near-self; and inter-domain microbial non-self. To this we should add the protean non-self of viruses, masters of disguise and imposture, to which the vertebrate adaptive immune system is thought to be a response.

Immunity and Selfhood: A Necessary Relationship?

Despite the diversity of forms it can take, immunity remains intricately intertwined with selfhood. However, while *some* kind of self-containment pertains to full minimal selfhood by definition (as one of the three forms of intrinsic reflexivity: self-maintenance, self-reproduction and self-containment), a key question is whether such self-containment always includes an immune system: is immunity as essential a feature of selfhood as the membrane of a cell or the epithelium of an animal? Immune defences are well known to be ubiquitous in jawed vertebrates. A brief empirical answer will thus involve looking at a variety of organisms *other than* vertebrates in order to ascertain whether they too display an immune system as outlined above, i.e. whether they too show a capacity to discriminate between self and various forms of non-self (near-self; remote non-self) and a potential disposition to engage in apoptosis.

An appropriate starting point in this context is our trusty slime mould *D. discoideum*, i.e. a non-metazoan 'multicellular' lineage. As a slug-like grex, this has little more than a slimy sheath in the way of physical containment and a tendency to 'lose' its constituent amoebae to any passing 'slug' that emits the requisite whiff of cyclic AMP. Yet it is nonetheless endowed both with cell-adhesion molecules that allow its cells to recognize and bind to one another and thus get the better of mutants and cheaters (near-self) and with sentinel cells similar to neutrophils capable of recognizing and engulfing pathogenic bacteria (extremely remote non-self). Though its 'multicellular' status is ambiguous, *D. discoideum* has also been shown to be capable of undergoing programmed cell death not only in the context of stalk cell differentiation, but also in ways that bear a marked resemblance to mammalian cell apoptosis.[906]

Given the example of *D. discoideum*, therefore, it is perhaps hardly surprising that even the most ancestral of metazoans such as sponges show a complex and multi-faceted immune system. Lacking a nervous system, 'true' musculature and a basal lamina, sponges have tended to be regarded as 'almost animals' (*Parazoa*) rather than the real thing like the rest of us (*Metazoa*).[907] As with *D. discoideum*, there is a flexible relationship between the individual self of the constituent cells and the collective self of the organism as a whole: if a living sponge is forced through a fine mesh and its cells separated, the resulting multitude of individual cells will simply hook up with one another to reconstitute a communal entity. And yet the apparent functional independence of the individual sponge cells is emphatically countered by the complexity and coordination of the collective immune system, which contains and unifies the whole organism no less effectively than its epithelium-like outer layer of flattened cells.

As in complex metazoans, the sponge's immune defences have two broad targets, distant non-self and near-self, providing protection against microbes on the one hand and mechanisms of histo(in)compatibility to ward off potentially parasitic conspecifics on the other. In the first place, sponges are equipped with a specialized class of phagocytic amoeboid cells known as archaeocytes. Like the macrophages of mammals, these have specific pattern recognition receptors – in this case called 'scavenger receptors'[908] – that enable them to identify evolutionarily defined non-self, recognizing molecules such as LPS typical of bacteria that need to be engulfed. At the same time, sponges have been found to display a high degree of precision in discriminating between self and near-self, fusing with autografts and rejecting allografts either by forming physical barriers to fend off non-self tissue or deploying toxins to destroy the attempted graft. Noteworthy is that the sponge histoincompatibility reaction involves a signalling molecule, or cytokine, that bears a striking resemblance to one of the cytokines at the heart of the histoincompatibility response in humans and other mammals.[909] Some sponges have even been shown to possess so-called 'sponge adhesion molecules',[910] which exhibit a high sequence similarity to the immunoglobulin proteins characteristic of the mammalian adaptive immune system. There is also evidence that sponges have the machinery required for apoptosis, allowing the elimination of unwanted and possibly infected tissue.[911]

As one of the other major multicellular lineages – a lineage from which metazoans diverged prior to the evolution of multicellularity – plants provide an invaluable point of contrast with animals. Unlike most animals, plants do not have mobile phagocytes capable of ingesting pathogenic invaders; nor are they thought to possess the adaptive immune system with which vertebrates are endowed. However, they *are* equipped with a system-level response – known as 'systemic acquired resistance' (SAR)[912] – that provides long-term protection against harmful forms of phylogenetically remote microbial non-self.[913] As in the mammalian innate response, SAR depends upon the recognition by transmembrane receptors of microbe-associated molecular patterns (MAMPs), such as the flagellin present on nearly all flagellated bacteria.[914] In many cases, moreover, a specific form of programmed cell death, known as the hypersensitive cell death response, is induced at sites of infection. Essential to SAR is the signal molecule salicylic acid, the chemical precursor for aspirin. The salicylic acid that is produced when a plant is attacked by bacteria or viruses potentiates the plant's defence system, prompting the healthy parts of the plant to take various measures – such as erecting a barrier of dead cells around the infected site – to prevent the microbes from spreading.[915] Once more, selfless cells sacrifice themselves for the sake of the collective self, i.e. for the wellbeing of the plant as a whole.

Yet there are also interesting differences with respect to animal defences. Under microbial attack, leaves emit not only endogenous salicylic acid, but also its volatile equivalent, methyl salicylate. Under herbivorous attack they emit a different gas, methyl jasmonate, corresponding to the defence hormone jasmonic acid. In other words, writes Daniel Chamovitz, 'when a leaf is attacked by an insect or by bacteria, it releases odours that warn its brother leaves to protect themselves against imminent attack, similar to guard towers on the Great Wall of China lighting fires to warn of an oncoming assault. In this way, the plant ensures its own survival as leaves that have "smelled" the gases given off by the attacked leaves will be more resistant to the impeding onslaught'.[916] Significantly, *neighbouring* plants are also able to 'eavesdrop' on this internal 'conversation' among the leaves of an infested plant, giving them the chance pre-emptively to ramp up their own defence systems. Immunological communication is not confined to the individual plant.[917] So just as plants have been seen to have rather fuzzy physiological, functional and genetic boundaries, their shared – or at least not jealously guarded – defence systems likewise suggest that the relevant unit of selfhood might reside not at the level of the individual plant, but of the clone, lineage, species (or even kingdom?).[918]

Such interplant communication has also been shown to take place by means of mutualistic associations between the roots of many higher plants[919] and so-called arbuscular mycorrhizal fungi, giving rise to underground mycorrhizal networks. Hyphal connections between plants produce communication systems as extensive as forests that serve not only to distribute nutrients such as nitrogen and phosphorus but also convey information alerting neighbouring plants to the threat of imminent attack. The plants do not even have to be of the same species to participate in a mycorrhizal network and benefit from the information transmitted. Again, plant selfhood – with its associated modes of self-containment – seems to be less focused on the individual organism.

Our brief glance at *slime moulds*, sponges and plants has so far suggested a positive answer to the question of the universality of immune defence as a feature of selfhood. However, this answer can only be as provisional as any other inductive generalization. We might simply have considered the wrong selves. What about the single cell, the cellf, which after all represents the paradigmatic level of selfhood?[920]

Bacteria provide perhaps the best-studied case. Programmed cell death has already been seen to be a common practice among bacteria. As the lysis of certain cells in the formation of *Myxococcus xanthus* fruiting bodies makes clear, however, this in turn implies some sort of collective selfhood. 'It is not immediately apparent, to put it mildly, that a defective unicellular organism will benefit from committing suicide', writes Kim Lewis, yet 'it is becoming increasingly apparent that bacteria live and die in complex communities that in many ways resemble a multicellular organism'.[921] In such a context, apoptosis may prove beneficial at a collective level by containing the spread of a viral infection; the suicide of cells damaged by toxic factors enables these cells to donate vital nutrients and genetic material to neighbouring cells rather than struggling in vain to repair themselves. Yet bacterial colonies exposed to antibiotics and lethal factors such as heat or oxidants must not allow their suicidal tendencies to be *universal*: this would clearly be counterproductive. Instead, bacterial populations are believed to harbour a small fraction (one per million) of 'persistor cells' in which the apoptotic machinery is disabled and full viability is maintained.[922] These persistors – responsible for the survival of a population that would otherwise wipe itself out – are not cheaters or mutants (though they may be vulnerable to cheating). The bacterial 'decision' to survive or not has been shown to be regulated by genes such as *hip* and *sulA*, which function rather like the *TP53* gene that regulates apoptosis in human cells.[923]

Bacterial suicide is also thought to provide protection against the opportunistic mutants (i.e. near-self) that tend to arise when a bacterial population arrives unscathed at the 'stationary' phase of its life cycle, i.e. when nutrients start to run out, growth ceases and toxins accumulate. The drastic reduction in numbers observed to take place in this phase is likely to represent a form of mass suicide designed to prevent proliferating dead-end mutants from turning the colony into an 'unhopeful monster'.[924] As pointed out above,[925] moreover, addiction modules such as toxin/antitoxin (T/A) systems – originally lysogenic phage – may serve to equip their host with an immune system capable not only of triggering suicide if the cell is infected by competing phage, but also eradicating closely related strains of bacteria in which the module is lacking, thus defending the cell both from phylogenetically remote viral non-self and from rival near-self.

To the extent that the immune defence furnished by apoptosis implies a collective rather than a single-celled self, however, it leaves unresolved the issue of unicellular immunity. It is the second fundamental mechanism of immunity – self/non-self discrimination – that sheds light on this question. Two major systems of self/non-self differentiation have been identified in bacteria. The better characterized of these is the restriction-modification (RM) mechanism,[926] which involves the bacteria methylating (adding methyl groups to) their own DNA as an 'identity mark' to label it as 'self'. Lacking such identification, unmodified DNA is recognized as 'foreign' or 'non-self' and is usually 'restricted' by being cleaved into fragments and subsequently degraded. Remarkably, this work is itself commonly carried out by relatively autonomous genetic elements known as restriction-modification systems, some of which are known to be mobile ('moving' by horizontal gene transfer), are themselves considered selfish and have even been designated 'alive' in their own right.[927] The *methylation* that takes place in prokaryotes differs significantly from what occurs in many eukaryotes, where it is transposable elements – i.e. invasive *non-self* – that are methylated as a way of switching them off or silencing them[928] and where methylation has also been recruited for regulatory purposes crucial to the development of multicellular organisms.[929]

The second main mechanism of self/non-self discrimination, found in 90 percent of archaeal genomes and 40 percent of bacterial genomes, is known as the CRISPR-Cas system.[930] Whereas the RM system is relatively indiscriminate in its attacks on non-self, the CRISPR-Cas system is more akin to an adaptive immune system, providing the cell with a 'memory' of previously met genetic invaders that can then be picked out for attack when re-encountered. It does this by incorporating captured fragments of viral DNA – known as spacers – into its characteristic CRISPR loci, and then using the RNA transcripts of these spacers (crRNA) to 'recognize' the corresponding segments of invading viruses.[931] Adjacent *cas* genes encode the requisite enzymatic machinery to cleave and ultimately degrade the viral material that is recognized in this way. A facility for self/non-self discrimination again proves imperative, for the crRNA must avoid targeting the spacer DNA within the encoding CRISPR locus (i.e. 'self'). This is thought to be achieved by means of specific mismatches between the flanking regions of the crRNA and its viral target, which contrast with the more extended pairing between the crRNA and the host's CRISPR DNA. Such differential complementarity *outside* the spacer region of a crRNA thus allows self to be distinguished from non-self.[932]

According to Koonin and Dolja,[933] as much as 10 percent of prokaryotic genomes may be taken up by genes encoding defence systems, and an even greater proportion of the eukaryotic protein-coding gene complement. However, there remain many cases where defence systems have not yet been identified. This is relatively unsurprising, for example, in mutualists with small genomes, where protection – *allo*-containment – might come as part of the symbiotic package. Yet there are also some bacteria with large genomes that still lack identifiable defence systems.[934] The question is whether it is the lifestyle of these organisms that makes immune systems surplus to their needs or whether further mechanisms of self/non-self discrimination are yet to be discovered.

Managing the Interface of Self and Non-Self

Respiration

Immunity can be considered a mechanism for ensuring the *differential porosity* or *permeability* of our boundaries, granting (limited) access to benign cells recognized as 'self' (in the sense of symbiotically shared selfhood) and refusing access to pathogenic 'non-self'. Yet it is far from being the only such mechanism, for access must also be granted to the appropriate nutrients and fuels; waste must be expelled; and water levels must be maintained constant. In short, the cell's inner environment – the acidity, ionic composition and osmotic pressure – must be kept within the narrow limits that permit continued metabolic activity. In multicellular organisms, it is a question of upholding the chemical stability of what has been called the *milieu interieur*, the blood plasma and tissue fluid that bathes and surrounds the individual cells of the body, providing them with nutrients, carrying away waste and creating a chemical environment – inherited from the ancient oceans 500 million years ago – in which they can flourish.[935] Such *homeostasis*, classically defined as 'the coordinated physiological reactions which maintain most of the steady states of the body,'[936] is a prerequisite for selfhood, denoting the self-sustained stability of what is inside, irrespective of what is outside. The term 'homeostasis' implies 'sameness' (in the Greek *homos*), though again it should be borne in mind that this sameness is founded on continuity rather than identity.[937] The selfsame self is not a static self, but is engaged in an ongoing dynamic conversation with the environmental non-self. The border or interface between self and non-self is the organ of controlled exchange that provides the raw materials (and removes the waste) enabling a self to sustain itself as the 'same' self. The present section will look at how self-containment can be modified to facilitate such self-sustaining selfhood.

As the medium of access for the fuel and nutrition that keeps us going, our boundary is anything but marginal in its importance. In his essay 'On Being the Right Size', J. B. S. Haldane famously explains how matters become critical as organisms increase in dimension:

> A typical small animal, say a microscopic worm or rotifer, has a smooth skin through which all the oxygen it requires can soak in, a straight gut with sufficient surface to absorb its food, and a simple kidney. Increase its dimensions tenfold in every direction, and its weight is increased a thousand times, so that if it is to use its muscles as efficiently as its miniature counterpart, it will need a thousand times as much food and oxygen per day and will excrete a thousand times as much of waste products.
>
> Now if its shape is unaltered its surface will be increased only a hundredfold, and ten times as much oxygen must enter per minute through each square millimetre of skin, ten times as much food through each square millimetre of intestine. When a limit is reached to their absorptive powers their surface has to be increased by some special device.[938]

Comparative anatomy, writes Haldane, is 'largely the story of the struggle to increase surface in proportion to volume'.[939] When it comes to fuelling organisms larger than prokaryotes, the greater the boundary is between self and non-self, the better.

Bacteria breathe across their skin and are therefore generally condemned to remain small. If they were to grow any bigger than they are, they would pay the price in the form of energetic inefficiency caused by the corresponding decline in their surface-area-to-volume ratio. Unlike the much larger eukaryotes, moreover, they depend largely on diffusion – the random thermal motion of molecules in the cytoplasmic slurry – to ensure that nutrients and key metabolites reach their targets. Cases of bacterial gigantism thus pose a particular challenge to the rapid diffusive transport of metabolites and nutrients within the cell, making it vital that no part of the cytoplasm should be far from the boundary. Larger-than-normal bacteria are instructive in how they meet these challenges, for example adopting a long and slender shape that restricts the cytoplasm to a thin tube.

Some of the gargantuans in the bacterial world belong to the genus *Epulopiscium*,[940] cigar-shaped cells that exist in a symbiotic relationship with surgeonfish and are known to attain volumes more than 100,000 times (i.e. five orders of magnitude) greater than *E. coli* bacteria,[941] exempting them from predation by almost all the ciliates that otherwise feast on bacteria. These bacteria display the condition of polyploidy, harbouring tens of thousands of copies of their genome around the periphery of the cell; this arrangement, it is thought, enables them to transcribe the necessary genes at disparate points within the cell and thus minimize the time taken for metabolites to travel to wherever they are required. This allows the bacterium to function 'like a microcolony, with different regions of the cell independently responding to local stimuli'.[942] An even more extreme case of bacterial gigantism is *Thiomargarita namibiensis*, the spherical cells of which can reach 800 mm in diameter and are likewise characterized by a peripheral arrangement of their multiple chromosomes. Much of their volume (98%) is taken up by a fluid-filled vacuole that confines the cytoplasm to a thin layer just beneath the cell membrane.[943]

Part of the eukaryotic solution to the problem of surface area has been to internalize their bioenergetic membranes in the form of (usually multiple) mitochondria, each serviced by a specialized genome that ensures flexible and locally fine-tuned power provision. The mitochondria are in turn characterized by highly convoluted inner membranes, whose numerous invaginations serve to maximize the efficiency of ATP synthesis by increasing the surface area across which the proton gradient can be established; it is for the same reason that the membranes of chloroplasts, known as thylakoids, are also so tightly folded.[944] The energetic riches provided by these internalized 'bacteria' are believed to have made possible the development of increasingly sophisticated subcellular structures such as the cytoskeleton, reducing the reliance on cellular diffusion for metabolite transport.

Even so, oxygen and carbonaceous fuel – or carbon dioxide in the case of plants – still need to be imported. As regards oxygen provision, various options present themselves. Just as single-celled eukaryotes such as amoebae breathe across their outer boundary (the cell membrane), relatively simple metazoans such as flatworms and the blade-shaped chordate amphioxus are small enough to breathe across their epithelium.[945] Amphioxus possesses gill slits, but these are used as filters for capturing food particles. In fish, by contrast, the gill slits are transformed into a complex system of slender filaments across which water is pumped, providing a densely folded, specialized surface for extracting the oxygen from water. By means of such gills, therefore, a specific portion of the self/non-self interface undergoes twin processes of *expansion* and *specialization*. The incorporation of a pumping mechanism – the fact that it is not just a matter of free diffusion – further highlights that self-containment is an ongoing process involving *work*.

Much less work is required to extract oxygen from air than from water, as a consequence of which the energetic costs of breathing are generally lower for insects than for fish.[946] Insects breathe through their cuticle, which contains small breathing pores called spiracles. These open up into a network of air-filled tubes called tracheae that ramify through the whole organism, ending in tracheoles that bring oxygen directly to individual cells. Such a system results, again, in a huge increase in the area of the interface between self and non-self. As Haldane pointed out, however, this system relies on diffusion alone, placing severe restrictions on how rapidly oxygen can penetrate to the finer branches of the tracheal network. Parts of the organism more than a few millimetres – a quarter of an inch – away from the air at the surface will always tend to be short of oxygen, which is why few insects ever grow to be more than 'half an inch thick'.[947]

Unlike insects and spiders, the descendants of the earliest reptiles (including mammals) evolved gas exchange systems known as lungs that rely on the pumping of blood rather than the diffusion of air for the distribution of oxygen; the resulting mechanism is known as a 'coupled convection-diffusion exchange'.[948] Lungs work by bringing together two convective flows – air and blood – at a thin, extremely convoluted gas exchange surface, where there is only a micrometre between the air in the alveoli and the blood that will subsequently transport the oxygen round the body. Again, the principles of work (the pumping of the heart), specialization and a drastic expansion of the self/non-self interface are involved, the alveoli of mammalian lungs providing an epithelial surface area at least 40 times greater than the skin in its entirety (roughly 80 as opposed to two square metres in humans) and hugely amplifying our capacity for oxygen uptake.[949] The drawbacks of using a water- or blood-based rather than an air-based system of gas distribution (as insects do) are compensated by the additional control it confers; the heart can modulate the convective flow of blood and thus regulate the gas exchange rate. This double act performed by the heart and lungs has allowed animals endowed with lungs to attain much greater sizes than insects. Though commonly considered 'inner' organs (i.e. contained within us), therefore, the heart and lungs are in fact essential aspects of our self-containment, greatly increasing its range and flexibility. While our skin tends to grab the headlines owing to its role in getting us identified, our lungs make up a much greater proportion of the boundary between self and non-self than our skin does.

The twin processes of specialization and enlargement of the boundary surface area are also in evidence in the absorption of nutrients. In humans, this takes place primarily in the small intestine, the walls of which exhibit a whole array of different-sized folds: tiny microvilli, millimetre-long villi and relatively large flaps called Kerckring's folds. These serve to augment the area available for the extraction of nutrients from the mass of chyme delivered by the stomach and to slow this mass down as it passes on its way towards the large intestine. Ninety percent of nutrients are absorbed in the small intestine, for the colon and rectum are incapable of extracting much more than water, salt and a few vitamins and minerals. Indeed, the small intestine tends to run out of time and surface area before passing on its load to the colon, and as a result of the limitations of the colon as an organ of absorption, valuable nutrition is often discarded with the waste.[950] Accordingly, further measures may be taken with a view to increasing the effective self/non-self interface. One frequently adopted such measure is the autocoprophagia keenly practised by certain mammals, which has been likened to rumination as a way of getting the most out of one's meal: by eating their own faeces, rabbits, rats and even dogs are providing themselves with otherwise missing nutrients, giving their intestinal boundary a second chance to do its job.[951]

The phagocytosis of amoebae can likewise be interpreted in terms of the flexibility it bestows upon the bounds between self and non-self. While bacteria remain obliged to ingest their nutrients across their outer membrane, amoebae – freed from the constraints of the cell wall – are able to engulf their prey whole, internalizing their own boundary (and the prey) in the form of a vacuole called a phagosome. Other classes of *protozoa* such as the heliozoans, traditionally known as the sun-animalcules, also illustrate the value of a flexible and extended surface area, comprising an amoeboid central body from which there project stiff, needle-like, cytoplasmic arms, known as axopods.[952] These delicate projections, supported from within by a bundle of cytoskeletal microtubules, again confer the benefit of a greatly increased interface with the environment, serving not only as mechanisms of buoyancy but also as a means of capturing small animals and other motile protozoa, which adhere to the axopods before being engulfed by cytoplasm and transported towards the centre of the cell for digestion. To the extent that they impart a shape that amplifies the surface area, the axopods of these single-celled eukaryotic predators bear a functional resemblance to the myriad folds of the human small intestine.

Osmoregulation

As a consequence of their relatively high surface-area-to-volume ratio, small organisms have few problems with oxygen uptake, but the other side of the coin is a heightened vulnerability to desiccation, i.e. a tendency to lose water through the greater relative surface area of the skin. A balancing act is required. As David Wharton puts it, small organisms cannot prevent desiccation simply by developing an impermeable outer layer, for 'if the organism was impermeable to water, it would also not be able to breathe. There are no biological structures that are impermeable to water but permeable to oxygen. If water loss from the body is reduced by an impermeable skin or cuticle, there need to be openings, such as our noses or the pores in an insect's cuticle (spiracles) or in the surface of a plant (stomata), which let the organism breathe'.[853] Accordingly, insects and other arthropods generally restrict water loss by means of a waxy cuticle that is punctuated with pores.[954] Nematode worms are also provided with a waxy, pore-studded cuticle that slows the rate of water loss by its relative impermeability. Behavioural options are also available. Tiny microorganisms such as nematodes, *rotifers* and *tardigrades* may survive severe desiccation by entering into the 'suspended selfhood' of dormancy or anhydrobiosis. Nematodes reduce their exposed surface area by coiling up, while tardigrades turn themselves into a mini-barrel or 'tun' by withdrawing their legs into their body.[955] An even more remarkable evolutionary response to the constant water loss to which terrestrial animals are subject was the invention of thirst, a sensation triggered by an increase in the salt concentration of the blood – tantamount to an inadequate replacement of water that has been lost – which is monitored by specific cells in the hypothalamus at the base of the brain.[956] This sensation expresses itself as a motivation to seek and ingest water from the environment, resulting in the intentional behaviour that in turn leads to the re-establishment of homeostatic balance.

Like terrestrial animals, marine animals are also vulnerable to desiccation. While the major force extracting water from an animal on land tends to be evaporation, in a marine environment it is the force of osmosis that draws water from an organism. Osmosis is a result of the differences in solute composition between the water inside an animal and the water in the external environment. The Second Law of Thermodynamics dictates that these differences in ionic concentration[957] will drive fluxes of salts and water through the semipermeable membrane separating the inner and outer environment until the two solutions – self and non-self – are of the same concentration.[958] By one form of self-containment or another, a self must resist this tendency for inside to become indistinguishable from outside. Animals living in seawater tend to be characterized by a lower osmotic pressure than the waters surrounding them; in other words, they face an environment that is saltier than they are, resulting in an influx of salts and an osmotic outflow of water (desiccation). To counter this thermodynamic propensity, the bony fish of the oceans drink the seawater around them, but must perform *work* in order to rid themselves of the excess of salts. This time it is the kidney that constitutes the self/non-self interface responsible for maintaining the appropriate balance of water and solutes in the body. With the help of the heart, its job is to perform the physiological work of counteracting the thermodynamically favoured fluxes of water and salt.[959] As a result of this work, marine animals produce small quantities of relatively concentrated urine.

In fact, the greater osmotic challenge is faced by freshwater organisms.[960] The fluid contents of such organisms are markedly saltier than the water around them, the thermodynamic tendency thus being for solutes to diffuse from the organism to the surrounding water and for water to flood into the organism by osmosis. Without self-containment either in the form of a physical barrier or physiological work, no organism would survive the influx of water and efflux of solutes. Evolution has invented various mechanisms for coping with the osmotic challenge. In bacteria the peptidoglycan wall confers upon the cell the mechanical and morphological stability to resist the inflow of water. The wall distends with the pressure, but curbs the potentially destructive influx, in the process becoming rigid or *turgid* and adopting a stress-bearing spherical or cylindrical shape.[961] An amoeba, by contrast, lacks a cell wall to protect it from the onslaught of water inflow, but cheats death by means of contractile vacuoles that fill with water and then empty themselves at the cell surface every few seconds.[962] This is made possible by the amoeba's flexible boundary, the very feature that permits phagocytosis with all its attendant benefits. Yet the ongoing expulsion of surplus water of course exacts a price in the form of work.

In the case of animals such as fish it is the kidney that performs the physiological work required to offset the thermodynamically advantaged flows of ions and water. However, the task varies greatly depending on whether the fish inhabits a salt- or a freshwater setting. While animals living in a marine environment produce small quantities of relatively concentrated urine, freshwater fish must generate large amounts of very dilute urine to counter the osmotic influx of water and the efflux of salts. The urine excreted by freshwater fish is thus basically water which – like the contents of the amoeba's vacuole – must be returned to the environment to balance the inflow. These environmental differences are reflected in the structures of the kidneys of the animals in question. In both cases the kidney is composed of tiny tubules called nephrons that form the specialized interface between the blood (self) and the urine (shortly-to-be-non-self), functioning as a mechanism of selective filtration and reabsorption. In both cases it is the heart that does the work of pumping the blood and generating the elevated pressure to power the filtration and reabsorption. But whereas the nephrons of marine fish tend to have relatively small filtration structures that produce little filtrate (the resulting liquid) and short tubules with a low capacity for salt reabsorption, those of freshwater fish foster the production of large quantities of filtrate and are characterized by long tubules, with a high capacity for salt reabsorption and low permeability to water.[963] Once more, an expanded and specialized surface area is required to ensure that a self can maintain its inner homeostatic balance as a self distinct from the surrounding non-self.

The complexity of such adaptations makes it difficult for organisms to cross over from one medium to another. Transferred to a river, a marine microbe would burst apart under the influx of water; relocated to the sea, a freshwater amoeba would have all the water sucked out of it. There are exceptions. Some diatoms seem to be able to adapt to both a marine and a freshwater environment, though it is uncertain what adaptive mechanisms have enabled marine species to avoid bursting at the seams in lakes, and freshwater species to avoid shrivelling to death in the sea.[964] Migratory fish such as salmon and eel pull off the feat through physiological flexibility. In a marine context they ingest water constantly, excrete salt from their gills and reduce urine-production to a minimum, whereas in a river environment they do not drink but excrete copious quantities of urine. Amphibians, which also alternate between the challenges of osmosis and desiccation, produce great quantities of urine when in water but virtually none when on land. Their skin helps out, providing a layer of mucous to prevent desiccation, as well as specialized cells known as flask cells that help maintain the proper internal concentrations of ions and water.[965] By contrast with other classes of tetrapod, amphibians appear to lack the faculty of thirst that would trigger water-seeking behaviour in response to dehydration.[966] They thus remain rather fish-like to the extent that fish too, unsurprisingly enough, are without water-seeking behaviour within their behavioural repertoire.

Thermoregulation

As Haldane noted, one advantage of having a low relative surface area is that one loses less heat to the environment. In other words, the good thing about being big is that the accompanying reduction in the surface-area-to-volume ratio keeps one warm:

> *All warm-blooded animals at rest lose the same amount of heat from a unit area of skin, for which purpose they need a food-supply proportional to their surface and not to their weight. Five thousand mice weigh as much as a man. Their combined surface and food or oxygen consumption are about seventeen times a man's. In fact a mouse eats about one-quarter its own weight of food every day, which is mainly used in keeping it warm.*[967]

In truth, many animals have relatively little control over the temperature of their body, which tends to be the same as that of their immediate surroundings.

Birds and mammals are a minority in being able to keep a steady internal temperature in the face of fluctuations in the environmental temperature.[968] Their respective temperatures of 41 °C and 37 °C are generally rather higher than those of their surroundings, which means that metabolic work has to be done to maintain them – yet overheating is also possible in a hot environment.[969] Mechanisms of thermoregulation include sweating and panting, where the evaporation of water absorbs heat from an external surface,[970] although such measures have the accompanying drawback of water loss and dehydration.[971] Other adaptations also involve evolutionary modifications of the boundary between self and non-self, for example in the form of fur, feathers or the specifically mammalian invention of hair. The built-in insulation provided by feathers and fur was one of the key innovations that allowed the forebears of mammals and birds to evolve towards warm-bloodedness, keeping the energy costs of constantly warm bodies to a minimum.[972] This would have been particularly useful given the nocturnal niche to which the small mammals of the Mesozoic were confined while dinosaurs called the shots.

Behavioural options may also play a part in heat regulation (i.e. keeping warm), again involving modification of the self/non-self interface. We saw in Chapter 2 how groups of male Emperor penguins huddle together in conditions of extreme cold over a nine-week incubation period, dramatically reducing the surface area exposed to the Antarctic winter.[973] East African wild dogs have been seen to huddle together in a similar style when a cold wind blows, with the individual dogs occasionally swapping a windward for a leeward spot such that – over the course of a few hours – the 'huddle' ends up shifting to a completely new location.[974] Eusocial groups of mammals such as naked mole rats, as well as hymenopteran insects such as bees, also engage in forms of 'huddling', collectively reducing their surface area and in this sense approaching a form of communal selfhood by creating a shared boundary. Such communal selfhood is highlighted by the specialization characteristic of the bee 'huddling' that may often take place on a cool morning, with a core of protected bees surrounded by a circular shell of shivering (i.e. heat-generating) bees, in turn surrounded by an outer layer of bees that insulate the cluster by interweaving the chitinous hairs on their body to form a 'downy coat'.[975] This may occur in conjunction with, or as an alternative to, the construction of forms of *external* insulation, i.e. of intentionally built, 'artificial' containers such as dens, burrows, mounds and houses. For diminutive mammals who would not survive the dehydration associated with panting or sweating and whose size limits their capacity to wear a thick coat of fur (which would restrict their movement), the building of burrows and other forms of shelter is an indispensable way of keeping themselves at the proper temperature. Hares, lemmings, shrews and voles are able to survive the Arctic winter by burrowing into the snow.[976]

Extending One's Self

Houses and Other Shells

William James famously defined 'a man's self' as 'the sum total of all that he CAN call his, not only his body and his psychic powers, but his clothes and his house, his wife and children, his ancestors and friends, his reputation and works, his lands and horses, and yacht and bank-account'.[977] The ideological confusion created by ambiguous notions of 'ownership' and 'property' need not concern us here: in the functional terms introduced above, a husband 'belongs' to his wife and children as much as vice versa; the family may 'belong' to the house as much as the house to the family. The point in this context is that just as human selfhood may be considered to include the building owned or rented or squatted or otherwise lastingly occupied by the self in question, the self of a lugworm, an earthworm, a naked mole rat or a prairie dog may be seen to encompass its burrow, which constitutes a form of *reinforced self-containment*. The focus in this section will initially be on animals, including humans, which display particular behavioural flexibility in this respect. However, the principle is a basic one to the extent that it pertains to one of the three forms of intrinsic reflexivity, and single-celled variations on the theme will subsequently emerge too.

The degree to which we are prepared to include an artificially fabricated structure as a *part* of a living self will depend on the degree of functional interdependence between the living entity and that structure: in particular, the role of the animal in its construction and maintenance, and the reliance of the animal on the protection or the energetic benefits it provides (i.e. how far it is willing or able to exchange it for another such construction or for a homeless existence).[978] A dwelling is part of the self that inhabits it to the extent that house and inhabitant exist in an *intrinsic* rather than a merely contingent relationship.

Further aspects of dwellings *mimic* the living self that inhabits them. At the risk of comic anthropomorphism (or more general zoomorphism),[979] one might highlight the need for points of ingress for nutrition and egress for waste; the dwelling must be able to 'breathe'. In modern human housing, the sewerage system and the concomitant throughflow of water – a piped influx of clean drinking water and an efflux of waste water – reflect the throughflow of water embodied by its human residents. Instead of glucose, other carbonaceous fuels (such as wood, peat, coal, oil or gas) may be imported to provide a form of auxiliary thermoregulation, as well as serving 'digestive' functions in the hearthplace.[980] Inhabitants may furnish their house with additional insulation to reduce the amount of carbonaceous fuel required to maintain the desired temperature, and the amount of work that has to be done to pay for it. As well as providing protection, a house thus constitutes a *physiological* extension of the self inside. It may even be considered a *cognitive* extension of the self, yielding a realm of regularity and predictability that does not, as a rule, require exploration, active attention or conscious decision-making. Psychologists have referred to the 'automaticity of being' that comes to prevail in contexts of repeated and consistent experience.[981] To the extent that a self can be viewed as an entity that is predictable to itself,[982] a house – a home – may likewise form a part of that self. Witness the cognitive disorientation that may result when elderly people are removed from accommodation where they have spent much of their lives. It is as though a portion of their self is excised in the process; suddenly, life is full of cognitive gaps, problems and challenges.

Another form of extended self-containment – human clothing – illustrates some of these issues from a slightly different angle. As with human housing, the degree of integration tends to be less than absolute: our clothes can be removed and exchanged and put back on again. Indeed, this exchangeability generates increased flexibility when it comes to thermoregulation: I can wear a thick coat, or a skimpy T-shirt, or nothing at all, depending on what is called for by the environment. Anatomical self-containment is much less flexible. The difference in integration is highlighted by the fact that I am not connected to my clothes by nociceptors; it does not hurt to take them off. I may get very 'attached' to my favourite baggy jumper; I may be 'inseparable' from my most threadbare jeans. But this attachment and inseparability is metaphorical compared to the literal attachment and inseparability that binds me to my skin. The containment conferred by clothing is subsidiary in relation to the primary containment provided by my epidermis or epithelium.

Though not truly self-integrated, however, clothing *is* self-generated in the broader sense that we have to expend energy either to fabricate garments or to perform the work to be able to acquire them. As with other forms of supplementary self-containment, moreover, the metaphor of ownership can be subverted by the appropriation of clothing belonging to other selves. It is not just a question of the ease with which garments can be stolen, but rather the fact that – ever since the first, prehistoric pelts – coats have traditionally been purloined from other selves in the form of animal hides and fleeces. It has been speculated that the ability of modern humans to sew and thus assemble clothing and tents may have provided them with a decisive advantage that was not available to the Neanderthals when the two species coincided in Europe some 50,000 years ago.[983] Killing animals for their skins, our species has flourished by parasitizing the self-containment of other selves.[984]

Auxiliary forms of self-containment employed by many non-human organisms show similar features to human housing and clothing, combining in varying measure both protective and physiological or thermoregulatory functions, and displaying the same vulnerability to re- or misappropriation. Burrowing, for example, seems likely to have arisen primarily as a protective measure. Palaeontologists have distinguished two major bursts of diversification in the construction of burrows in the pre-Cambrian (Ediacaran) and Early Cambrian periods roughly 650 million and 570 million years ago, probably as a response to the emergence of macropredation and the progressive evolution of ever bigger predators.[985] One of the best ways to avoid being eaten in such a competitive setting was to dig vertical burrows and ensconce oneself safely inside them. At the same time, burrows, dens and lairs produce reliable forms of insulation and a relatively constant temperature, thus providing protection not only from predators but from inclement or variable environmental conditions.

Yet this is not all. As Scott Turner has argued in *The Extended Organism*,[986] the physiological work performed (for example) by earthworms in constructing their tunnels modifies the environment in such a way as to increase the hydraulic capacity of the soil, optimize the water balance and thus *reduce* the work that has to be done by their internal organs, in particular the osmoregulatory organ akin to the mammalian kidney. These originally freshwater animals – with bodies designed to prioritize the expulsion of large quantities of water – are naturally ill-equipped to face the constant threat of dehydration in dry soils. Having ventured onto land, however, their strategy has not been to 'retool' their internal physiology to cope with terrestrial desiccation (which would involve an evolutionary reorganization of their 'kidney'), but rather to undertake the burrowing work that effectively allows them to 'co-opt the soil as an accessory organ of water balance'.[987] As Turner puts it, an animal's physiology really consists of two physiologies: 'the conventionally defined "internal physiology," governed by structures and devices inside the integumentary boundary of the organism, and an "external physiology", which results from adaptive modification of the environment'.⁹⁸⁸ When annelids construct their burrows, they turn the soil into an 'accessory kidney' that helps them overcome the threat of desiccation associated with life on land.

Among the most celebrated animal constructions are the houses assembled on riverbeds by caddis fly larvae, described by Dawkins as 'among the most remarkable creatures on earth':

> *Using cement of their own manufacture, they skilfully build tubular houses for themselves out of materials that they pick up from the bed of the stream. The house is a mobile home, carried about as the caddis walks, like the shell of a snail or hermit crab except that the animal builds it instead of growing it or finding it. Some species of caddis use sticks as building materials, others fragments of dead leaves, others small snail shells. But perhaps the most impressive caddis houses are the ones built in local stone. The caddis chooses its stones carefully, rejecting those that are too large or too small for the current gap in the wall, even rotating each stone until it achieves the snuggest fit.*⁹⁸⁹

Impressive indeed. Equally impressive, however, is the ruthless skill displayed by parasitic ichneumonid wasps of the genus *Agriotypus*. These 'nasty little wasps'⁹⁹⁰ lay their eggs on a caddis larva; the hatchling wasp larvae devour their host, take possession of the now ownerless caddis house, and then make a number of adaptations to its structures – sealing off the ends, extracting the water from the enclosed space, and adding a piece of silk ribbon – to turn it into an accessory gill that extracts oxygen from the flowing water and allows them to pursue an aquatic existence. The caddis larva's self-containment has been *appropriated* by the parasitic wasp, i.e. made its own property, made proper to its own needs.

Dawkins likens the caddis house to the shell of a snail or hermit crab, while highlighting the apparently intentional behaviour behind its construction. Like burrows, shells are assumed to have arisen as a defensive response to the emergence of macropredation in the pre-Cambrian arms race, with organisms secreting a form of external armour made of silica or calcite and predators in turn developing the hard mouth parts capable of breaking through them.⁹⁹¹ The extent to which intentionality, planning or choice are involved in building such structures seems to vary from case to case and is not essential to the nature of the protective self-containment afforded. However, the repeatedly observed phenomenon of veined octopuses (*Amphioctopus marginatus*) using a pair of coconut halves as a makeshift 'shell' shows the existence of intentional and improvised tool use in invertebrate species to which such attributes have not traditionally been applied.[992] The octopuses are frequently encountered lugging their coconuts around with them in a rather ungainly form of 'stilt-walking', during which time the prospective shells grant no protection to their head or body and represent a considerable energetic cost – lower efficiency – in relation to unencumbered locomotion. The only benefit is the future use of the coconut halves as a shelter or lair.[993]

The deployment of coconut husks as shells is presumed to have evolved from the use of large, empty bivalve shells before coastal human communities started producing an abundant source of discarded husks. The use of bivalve shells again shows how the 'container' associated with one self can be appropriated by another. This occurs even among single-celled eukaryotes. The diversity of the shells and tests sported by these organisms has already been broached: the siliceous frustules of the diatoms, the calcareous scales of the coccolithophorids, the pore-studded tests of the *foraminiferans* and the variety of shells with which the testate amoebae are endowed. The provenance of the building materials may vary. One of the most commonly found of the testate amoebae, *Euglypha*, for example, secretes a test that consists of an orderly disposition of flat, overlapping siliceous scales; such self-produced components are known as 'idiosomes'.[994] By contrast, another of the most widespread genera, *Difflugia*, constructs a test comprising a layer of organic matter beneath a coating of irregularly-shaped pieces of 'grit' that are often foreign in origin; these extraneous bodies, which may include diatom shells and detritus, are known as 'xenosomes'.[995] A third alternative, used by predators such as *Nebela* and *Heleopera*, is to eat other testate amoebae and appropriate *their* idiosomes for one's own self-containment.[996] In fact, it is not the 'individual' amoeba that provides the building materials. The constituents – whether autogenous or xenogenous – are prepared by the mother amoeba prior to fission, with the offspring cell thus receiving what the mother cell has either produced or ingested beforehand. In some cases, if the ingestion of xenosomes is prevented, fission does not even take place.[997] Again, the shells produced by testate amoebae may in turn be appropriated by other micro-organisms. Equipped with a highly extensible and mobile neck, the predatory *ciliate Lacrymaria* shows a particular predisposition for life in empty *Difflugia* shells, which provide a fine receptacle from which its neck can protrude in search of passing prey.[998] Nematodes too are known to make themselves at home in *Difflugia* shells.

Perhaps the most remarkable unicellular 'house' of all belongs to a species of giant multinucleate amoeba, *Xenophyophorea*, which inhabits the hadal depths of the world's ocean trenches.[999] These plate-sized coenocytes – whose name is Greek for 'bearer of foreign particles' – form a test consisting not only of an accumulation of particles from other (ex)-selves such as sponge spicules, *radiolarian* skeletons and foraminiferan tests held together by a cement-like organic glue, but also dark strings of faecal pellets called 'stercomes'. Despite the fragility of their structures, the xenophyophores – which tend to be mistaken for fragments of damaged sponges – are extremophiles that have been encountered at depths of 10.6 kilometres in the Mariana Trench, where they are subject to pressures a thousand times greater than those at sea level.

Tools as Extensions of Self

Containers such as coconut husks are a form of tool, though most shelters are not usually regarded as tools because their function is ongoing rather than specific to a particular task.[1000] One of the archetypal human tools is the hammer, or percussive tools in general.[1001] A functional definition of selfhood might be understood to permit an appliance such as a hammer to be included as a constituent part of a unitary self. In this sense, the notion of an extended self would refer to the intentional incorporation of 'non-self' within the functional unity of a self-caring self (pursuing the goals and interests of that self). When successfully using a hammer, the hammer effectively becomes an extension of our intentionality and is 'transparent' to us; there is no awareness of myself as a distinct entity from the hammer. It is only if something *goes wrong* that my attention is brought to the hammer as an obstacle in the path of my intentions.[1002]

It will be countered that no hammer is deeply enough *integrated* within our network of needs for it to be incorporated into our selfhood in this way. We are too easily, or too frequently, *de-coupled* from our hammer. Any relationship between human and hammer is likely to be episodic or transient: tools can be put away, swapped and lost, and few people, if any, take their hammer to the shower with them, or to bed. Only for the brief period that we use the hammer, and in ideal circumstances of mutual human-hammer harmony, might we speak of a person as forming – or ourselves have the feeling of forming – a unity with the hammer.[1003]

However, there are other sorts of tools, such as sensory and cognitive tools, where the boundary between self and non-self may be fuzzier. A much-discussed example, which dates back to Maurice Merleau-Ponty's analysis in *The Phenomenology of Perception*, is the cane of a blind person. As Mark Rowlands explains, 'the cane can be both an *object* of awareness and a *vehicle* of awareness. But when the blind person uses the cane, it functions as a vehicle, not an object, of awareness. The cane is not something of which the blind person is aware; it is something *with* which he is aware. Phenomenologically, the consciousness of the blind person passes all the way through the cane to the world'.[1004] The cane is metaphorically transparent not only in the way that a pair of glasses is literally transparent (unless the lens cracks or steams up) but also in the way that my eyes are 'transparent': i.e. to the extent that we are not normally aware of the role of our retina and optic nerve in processing the information that reaches them from the environment, and are not normally aware of our eyes at all unless they malfunction. Sensory tools of this sort mediate the relationship between self and non-self in the same way that the rest of our sensory apparatus tacitly mediates this relationship. It tends only to be when something goes wrong – when there is some sort of breakdown – that they return to our explicit attention as objects that are 'external' to our selves.

Such tools may also be cognitive in nature rather than merely sensory.[1005] The philosophers Andy Clark and David Chalmers have coined the notion of the 'extended mind'[1006] to refer to the hypothetical case of a man, Otto, who suffers from Alzheimer's disease and resorts to a notebook in order to access the information he requires in order to organize his life. Provided certain conditions are fulfilled relating to the reliability of the coupling between man and notebook, it seems arbitrary to restrict mental states or processes such as believing or remembering to states or processes that occur only within the cranium, or even within the whole body.[1007] In helping him achieve specific aims, the information in Otto's notebook plays the same role for him as the information available within the brain of any healthy person without Alzheimer's.

Digital technology has led to the 'outsourcing'[1008] of our brain in a wealth of previously unimagined ways. As David Brooks has (only half-ironically) noted, the magic of the information age – embodied in his case in an almost mystical union with his GPS – is not that it allows us to know more, but that it allows us to know less: 'it provides us with external cognitive servants – silicon memory systems, collaborative online filters, consumer preference algorithms and networked knowledge. We can burden these servants and liberate ourselves'.[1009] Freeing us from the need to 'think' or solve problems, these cognitive tools come to form part of ourselves precisely to the extent that they in turn become 'transparent' to us (i.e. we cease to notice their presence) and we become dependent on them (i.e. we cease to be able to get from A to B *without* a GPS).

A natural objection to such considerations invokes what has been termed 'cognitive bloat'[1010]: if we grant that notebooks, GPSs and mobile phones are a part of ourselves (or our selves, or our minds), it is countered, then where do we stop? Over-extending our mind takes us on a 'slippery slope' to union with all the other informational aids at our disposal: telephone directories, libraries and the whole of the Internet. It has been well argued[1011] that the answer lies in the notion of 'ownership', though a more relevant concept is possibly 'belonging' in the sense of functional unity.[1012] A process – and the tool I use to carry it out – is 'mine' to the extent that it 'belongs' to the system of causally integrated processes by which I seek to achieve my goals as a self-caring self. Such 'mineness' might be considered to encompass the dog-eared dictionary by my desk or the whole of my personal library, or even a particular section of my local library. Yet the Internet lacks this 'mineness': it is an amorphous network of relatively independent functions, most of which I am unconnected to. It makes no sense to expand my selfhood into a realm of purely hypothetical possibility, embracing all those books and web pages that I *could* consult if only I had heard of them. Nonetheless, it is perhaps not too far-fetched to regard the sum of all informational tools created by humankind, including the Internet, as forming part of – belonging to – a *collective* human self, a higher-level human superorganism that technological connectivity has now allowed to extend itself globally.[1013]

Transcending One's Self

Concepts of extended organisms, minds and selves underscore that selfhood may reach *beyond* its biological boundaries and that the boundaries between self and non-self are often blurred. Self-containment may coincide with self-transcendence in other ways too. The notion of self-adaptability – first touched upon in the Introduction – denotes an aspect of intrinsic reflexivity that may go further than merely passive self-maintenance, including the flexibility of a self that is able to move itself or manipulate non-self to its own advantage, as when *E. coli* cells perform the work of manoeuvring themselves in the direction of aspartate or away from toxic metals.[1014] This involves a *normative* interaction between self and non-self,[1015] in that the self in question inhabits a world imbued with value, where non-self may be good (for self) or bad (for self) and the rational course is always to head for the good and shun the bad.

    A remarkable feature of the self-moving self is that the cause of its behaviour can be located within its self; its behaviour can be self-caused. When an animal goes in pursuit of prey, for example, its hunting activity can be attributed to an internal, homeostatic imbalance that triggers its behaviour in the form of a sensation of 'hunger' and an appetite for food; if the same animal, in the same circumstances, does not chase a potential quarry, this is likely to be because it has just eaten and is not hungry. However, the activity of a hungry organism is not *merely* self-caused; an active self must also be *open* to its environmental non-self so as to be able to scent or see its prey.[1016] At the cellular level represented by *E. coli*, this openness takes the form of transmembrane receptor proteins – akin to gateways or windows spanning the boundary between self and non-self – that 'recognize' certain molecules (amino acids or toxins) on the outside and activate the biochemical circuitry on the inside of the cell.[1017] In turn, a protein-based signal pathway involving the addition or removal of phosphates from a small protein called CheY regulates the rotary motor activity of the bacterium's four to six flagella, causing the cell either to 'tumble' (i.e. change direction in search of food) or to continue to swim smoothly in the same direction. Thanks to some ten thousand such transmembrane protein receptors (clustered mainly at one end of the organism), a bacterium inhabits a chemical universe comprising over fifty attractants and repellents. As a result of its legendary sensitivity, even the 'slightest whiff'[1018] of aspartate – a concentration of less than one part in ten million – will elicit a change in its swimming activity.

It is this 'openness' to its environment that permits a hungry organism not just to grope around at random, but to engage in intentional, directed behaviour, i.e. to go after what is good (for itself). By sensing environmental non-self, the organism can be said to reach *beyond* its boundaries. A self-contained self thus also *transcends itself* and opens out onto the universe, enabling it to behave (move itself) in a manner that is appropriate to its (self-generated) needs.[1019] This openness manifests itself immediately in our sense of touch. Our skin is not just a container that holds us in, but one of the 'main sensory portals'[1020] by which we open onto the world. Even the single-celled *Paramecium* reacts to a bump from behind by speeding up its swimming and to a bump at the front by swimming off in a new direction; these responses are mediated by movements of charged ions through ion channels in the cellular membrane that cause changes in the beating of the organism's cilia.[1021] The doughty human dermis, by contrast, contains a variety of specialized receptor cells that communicate with the central nervous system about the external world and the state of the skin. These include mechanical pressure receptors, temperature receptors and diverse pain sensors that alert us to the presence of potentially harmful physical stimuli and to inflammation and injury. The sensation of pain, nociception, is a homeostatic mechanism that prompts us to recoil from what might threaten our bodily integrity and to protect areas where damage already has occurred.

Much greater, even astronomical distances are opened up by light-sensitivity, but once again the principle at work is the mediation or coupling of 'outside' and 'inside'. One venerable molecule, or family of molecules, here plays a central role. Though the eye – in the sense of 'image-forming optics'[1022] – is thought to have evolved independently as many as forty times in various parts of the animal kingdom, it is the same transmembrane protein, *rhodopsin*, that is responsible for the absorption of photons across the whole range, from the single photosensitive cells of some cnidarians to the camera-like lenses of vertebrates, where an image is projected onto a whole sheet of photoreceptors. Rhodopsin consists of the protein opsin linked to a form of vitamin A called retinal, the light-induced *isomerisation* of which results in a change of molecular shape both in the retinal itself and the protein surrounding it. This conformational switch in the membrane-spanning protein is what transmits the signal from outside to inside, initiating the biochemical cascade of events in our neural circuitry that in turn gives rise to a behaviour appropriate to changes in the environment around us.

Such changes are exemplified by the shadow reflex of the barnacle, whose simple eyes – each comprising a few photoreceptor cells, but with no lens – do not form an 'image', but are acutely sensitive to a sudden decrease in illumination. This measured drop in light intensity, which can be taken as a reliable indicator of the shadow cast by a potential predator, promptly causes the animal to withdraw into its protective shell.[1023] Rhodopsins are also present, though not ubiquitous,[1024] in unicellular light-sensitive organisms, where some varieties govern the phototactic locomotion of cells towards sources of light (and thus energy) while others function as proton pumps.[1025] Perhaps the most intriguing case among unicellular organisms is that of the warnowiids. These remarkable dinoflagellates, which nourish themselves by eating other dinoflagellates rather than feeding on the energy of the sun, are equipped with a photoreceptor system called an 'ocelloid' that is no less complex than a metazoan eye in its organization, incorporating cornea, iris, lens and retina.[1026] It is not currently known how this organism transmits signals from its eye to its *flagellum* and thus guides its locomotion, but its lack of a brain (or perhaps we should consider *the whole cell* to be the 'brain') does not prevent it from being an extremely successful predator. The warnowiid eye, which likewise seems to use rhodopsin,[1027] is believed not only to have a cornea made of mitochondria, but also a retinal body composed of highly modified *chloroplasts*, derived ultimately from cyanobacteria that were engulfed by eukaryotic organisms in an ancient endo-symbiotic embrace.[1028] It has been conjectured that the rhodopsin dates back to the ancestral cyanobacteria from which these chloroplasts – and warnowiid eyes – descend,[1029] serving to guide the phototactic movement that would take them to where the sun was shining.

Admiring the rich behavioural repertoire of *Paramecium* in the early 20th century, the pioneering protozoologist Herbert S. Jennings wondered whether the busily moving slipper animalcules might be conscious.[1030] In the present work I have more or less avoided the issue. Yet the idea of self-transcendence suggests a self-caring self that is able and inclined to move itself through the world in a way that is directional and intentional. For this self-movement to be appropriate to the interests of the self in question, it makes sense to suppose that that self may, at least sometimes, be *conscious* of the world through which it is moving and the goal towards which it is moving. The question of rudimentary consciousness will be taken up in a separate study.

Glossary

Actin: microfilament-forming protein, abundant in eukaryotic cells and essential to functions such as locomotion and cell division

Aerobic: describes an organism that requires oxygen; the opposite is anaerobic, which refers to an organism that does not require oxygen, or that requires the absence of oxygen

Allele: one version of a gene among others in a population

Allo-: preface signalling the opposite of auto-, i.e. by 'non-self' or 'other': e.g. if autopoiesis denotes self-creation, allopoiesis is creation by non-self or other; in the present context allo-containment is used to denote containment by non-self or other, as opposed to self-containment

Aminoacyl-tRNA synthetase: an enzyme that plays a crucial role in DNA translation and protein synthesis

Apoptosis: a highly controlled process of programmed cell death, or cell 'suicide'

Archaea: microorganisms that are similar in size to bacteria and likewise lack a nucleus, but are very different in their biochemistry; along with Bacteria and Eukarya, they constitute one of the three domains of living organisms

Arthropod: member of the phylum Arthropoda ('animals with jointed legs'), which includes insects, spiders, scorpions, crabs and the extinct trilobites; they have an exoskeleton, or external skeleton

ATP: adenosine triphosphate: a molecule that stores and transports the energy required for living processes; release of a phosphate group successively yields adenosine diphosphate (ADP), then adenosine monophosphate (AMP)

ATP synthase: the enzyme that catalyzes the synthesis of adenosine triphosphate (ATP) from adenosine diphosphate (ADP) and phosphate, using energy derived from a proton gradient

Autotroph: an organism that can produce complex organic compounds from simple inorganic compounds, for example by using the energy from sunlight (photosynthesis)

Bacteriophage / phage: a virus that infects bacteria

Base pair: two chemical bases linked to one another by hydrogen bonds to constitute a single 'rung' of the nucleic acid 'ladder'

Bilateria: the clade of animals characterized by bilateral symmetry at some stage in their life cycle, i.e. possessing a front and a back, a top and a bottom, and a right and a left; it includes the protostomes and the deuterostomes (q.v.), but not the sponges or cnidarians such as corals or jellyfish

Binding site: a region of a protein or nucleic acid to which a specific molecule or ion (a 'ligand') may bind

Capsid: the protein shell that envelops viral genetic material

Carbaquism: an understanding of life as necessarily based on carbon compounds in liquid water

Carboxylic acid: any of a diverse class of organic acids that contains a carboxyl (-COOH) group; examples include formic acid, acetic acid, citric acid, fatty acids and amino acids

Cell-adhesion molecule (CAM): proteins on the surface of a cell that associate or bind with other cells or with molecules of the extracellular matrix

Cell membrane: see cytoplasmic membrane

Cell wall: a tough layer surrounding certain types of cell, including plants, fungi and many prokaryotic cells

Chemiosmotic coupling: the use of energy from respiration to pump protons across a membrane and thus create a proton gradient, the flow of protons back across the membrane in turn driving the synthesis of ATP

Chitin: a tough polysaccharide found in the exoskeletons of arthropods and the cell walls of fungi

Chloroplast: organelle within which photosynthesis is carried out

Ciliate: group of protists whose cell surface features hair-like extensions called cilia; like flagella (q.v.), cilia serve as organelles of motility but they are generally shorter and more numerous than eukaryotic flagella

Coenocyte: a multinucleate cell resulting from repeated nuclear division without corresponding cell division

Cofactor: a chemical compound required by some enzymes for their catalytic activity to take place; cofactors may either take the form of inorganic ions or complex organic molecules called coenzymes

Conjugation: transfer of genetic material between bacterial cells

Cryptobiotic: capable of surviving a state of ametabolism, i.e. a cessation of metabolism

Cyanobacteria: a division of bacteria that derive their energy from photosynthesis in a similar way to chloroplasts

Cytoplasm: the contents of a cell that are outside the nucleus (if there is one) but within the cell membrane

Cytoplasmic membrane, plasma membrane, cell membrane: membrane separating the inside of a cell from the external environment; it consists of a double layer of phospholipid molecules

Cytoskeleton: dynamic protein structure in the cytoplasm of cells, fulfilling a wide range of functions including the maintenance of cell shape, locomotion, intracellular transport and cell division

Cytosol: the fluid part of the cytoplasm (q.v.); it does not include the organelles

Demosponge: the major class of sponges

Deuterostomes: a superphylum of bilaterian animals that includes the chordates (which in turn include the vertebrates), echinoderms and hemichordates; they are opposed to the protostomes (q.v.)

Diatoms: group of mainly unicellular photosynthetic algae endowed with glass tests or shells known as frustules; they rank among the world's most abundant aquatic organisms

Dinoflagellates: major category of flagellate, i.e. flagellum-bearing, protist

Diploid: provided with chromosomes in pairs (one from each parent in the case of sexual reproduction); a haploid cell, such as a gamete (q.v.), only has a single set of chromosomes

DNA polymerase: a type of enzyme that catalyses the synthesis of DNA from its constituent nucleotides (q.v.), generally using a DNA template; essential to the replication of DNA

dsDNA, dsRNA: double-stranded DNA or RNA molecules

Endergonic: of a biochemical reaction, requiring energy in order to take place, by contrast with exergonic reactions, which release energy and can thus power work

Endonuclease: an enzyme able to cleave DNA or RNA

Endoplasmic reticulum: an organelle consisting of a complex network of membranes, with various functions including the regulation of the synthesis, folding and transport of cellular proteins

Endosymbiont: an organism that lives inside the body or cells or another organism in a mutually beneficial relationship of *endosymbiosis*

Epithelium: type of animal tissue, taking the form of one or more layers of cells that cover a body's outer surface and line its cavities

Euglena: a genus of flagellate protist, traditionally known as the 'eye animalcule', most species of which have chloroplasts and can photosynthesize but are also able to feed by phagocytosis (q.v.)

Euglyphida: a prominent category of testate, or shell-bearing, amoeba; it belongs to the supergroup Rhizaria, which also includes Foraminifera and Radiolaria (q.v.)

Eukaryote: an organism whose cells contain their genetic material within a membrane-bound nucleus

Flagellum (plural: *flagella*): whip-like appendage in certain prokaryotic and eukaryotic cells, used primarily for locomotion in a fluid medium

Foraminifera: class of mainly marine protists with pore-studded tests or shells from which microtubule-reinforced projections emerge

Gamete: a typically haploid (q.v.) cell that fuses with another cell in sexual reproduction, i.e. sperms and eggs in animals

Gene pool: the set of all genes in a population or species

Genotype: the set of genes of organisms

Germ line: the lineage of specialized cells in animals that give rise to the sex cells or gametes

Glycolysis: the breakdown of glucose, releasing energy to form ATP (q.v.)

Glycoprotein: a protein covalently bonded to a carbohydrate moiety

Golgi apparatus: membrane-bound organelle found in most eukaryotic cells that plays a major role in the processing, packaging and transport of cellular proteins

Gram-negative bacterium / Gram-positive bacterium: two main classes of bacteria, differentiated by their response to a certain staining procedure

Halobacterium: a group of halophilic ('salt-loving') archaea, i.e. archaea that tolerate highly saline conditions

Heterotroph: an organism that requires complex organic molecules as its principal source of food; it contrasts with an autotroph (q.v.)

Heterozygous: of a diploid organism, having non-identical paired alleles at a gene locus

HGT, horizontal gene transfer (also: *lateral gene transfer*): transfer of genes between organisms other than by parent-offspring transmission; it contrasts with vertical *gene transfer*, which is by sexual or asexual reproduction

Homophilic binding: binding between cell-adhesion molecules (q.v.) of the same kind

Hydrolysis: the cleavage of chemical bonds in a molecule by the action of water

Hyphae: threadlike tubular filaments of fungi

Isomerisation: process by which one molecule can change into another with the same atoms but arranged in a different configuration

Kilobase, kb: unit of length of chains of nucleic acids such as DNA or RNA, equalling one thousand base pairs (q.v.)

Kinase: an enzyme that catalyses the addition of phosphate groups to proteins, thus activating protein function; the enzymes that catalyse the removal of phosphate groups and thus the de-activation of protein function are called phosphatases.

Kinetoplastid: a group of flagellated protozoa, members of which include *Leishmania* and *Trypanosoma brucei* (the cause of leishmaniasis and 'sleeping sickness', respectively, in humans)

Lipid: any of a large and diverse group of organic compounds that are insoluble in water but soluble in organic solvents such as alcohol, ether and chloroform; examples include fats, oils, waxes and steroids; they are among the main constituents of plant and animal cells

Lipopolysaccharide, LPS: a complex molecule consisting of both lipid and carbohydrate parts, and making up the outer membrane of Gram-negative bacteria (q.v.)

Lymphocyte: a type of white blood cell that belongs to the vertebrate immune system and includes B cells and T cells

Lysogenic, temperate: describes a virus able to integrate its genetic material into the host chromosome

Lysosome: membrane-bound vesicle (q.v.) that contains enzymes capable of digesting food particles and breaking down alien viruses or bacteria

Lytic, virulent: describes a virus that does not integrate its genetic material into the host chromosome, but replicates separately; the process usually results in the lysis, or destruction, of the host cell

Macrophage: a type of white blood cell whose functions include the phagocytosis (q.v.) of pathogens as part of the immune system

Megabase, Mb: unit of length of chains of nucleic acids such as DNA or RNA, amounting to one million base pairs (q.v.)

Metazoa: (also known as *Animalia*) the kingdom of multicellular eukaryotic animals

Methylation: the addition of a methyl group ($-CH_3$), for example to DNA or a protein

Micelle: a single-layered, spherical arrangement of lipid molecules

Microbiota: the collective of microorganisms that inhabit a particular space, such as the gut or skin of an animal; the *microbiome* denotes the total genetic material of the microorganisms in question

Mitochondrion: organelle in eukaryotic cells that uses energy from aerobic respiration to synthesize ATP (q.v.), commonly termed the 'powerhouse' of the cell

Mutagenesis: the production and development of mutations in a genome

Mutualism: a symbiotic relationship from which both partners benefit

Mycorrhiza: a symbiotic association between a fungus and the roots of many plants

Myosin: a type of motor protein, i.e. a molecule that turns the chemical energy of ATP (q.v.) into mechanical energy

Myxobacteria: also known as 'slime bacteria': a group of bacteria that includes the model organism *Myxococcus xanthus*; noted for travelling as 'swarms' and aggregating as 'fruiting bodies' when nutrients are scarce

NCLDV, nucleocytoplasmic large DNA viruses: various families of large DNA viruses that infect eukaryotes; they include genera such as *Mimivirus, Megavirus, Pandoravirus, Mamavirus, Pithovirus* and *Poxvirus*

Neurogenesis: the generation of neurons

Nucleotide: the biochemical molecule that constitutes the basic building block of nucleic acids such as DNA and RNA; each nucleotide comprises a nitrogenous base, a sugar and one or more phosphate groups; a nucleoside is a nucleotide minus the phosphate groups

Oligonucleotide: a relatively short chain of nucleotides (q.v.)

Oncovirus: a virus that can cause cancer

Organelle: a specialized structure within a eukaryotic cell, examples being mitochondria and chloroplasts

Paramecium: one of the best-known genera of ciliates (q.v.), also known traditionally as 'slipper animalcules' on account of their shape

Peptide: organic compound consisting of short chains of amino acids

Peptidoglycan: characteristic polymer that forms the cell wall of most bacteria, consisting of a mesh of amino acids and sugars

Phage: see bacteriophage

Phagocytosis: process by which a cell engulfs a solid food particle

Phagosome: a vesicle (q.v.) formed during phagocytosis (q.v.) when a food particle or prey item is engulfed and internalized by the cell membrane; the phagosome subsequently fuses with a lysosome (q.v.) for digestion to take place

Phenotype: the bodily characteristics of an organism

Phospholipid: one of a class of lipids (q.v.) that includes both a phosphate group and one or more fatty acids

Placozoa: one of the most basal groups of Metazoa

Plasma membrane: see cytoplasmic membrane

Plasmid: a circular, self-replicating molecule of double-stranded DNA that is found in cells but is independent of the chromosomal DNA

Polymer: a molecule that consists of many repeated elements (monomers): e.g. proteins are polymers of amino acids; DNA and RNA are polymers of nucleotides

Porifera: the phylum of sponges

Positive-stranded RNA viruses, negative-stranded RNA viruses: the major division among the viruses that have a single strand of RNA as their genetic material; RNA viruses may also be double-stranded

Prokaryotes: cells that have no membrane-bounded nucleus or membrane-bounded organelles such as mitochondria; they include the bacteria and archaea and are contrasted with the eukaryotes (q.v.)

Promoter: a stretch of DNA that initiates the transcription of a gene

Prophage: the latent form of a bacteriophage (q.v.), in which its genetic material is integrated within the bacterial chromosome or exists as a plasmid outside the chromosome

Protease: an enzyme that cleaves proteins into smaller pieces

Proteobacteria: a major group of Gram-negative bacteria that includes the genera *Rickettsia*, *Escherichia*, *Salmonella* and *Buchnera* as well as myxobacteria such as *Myxococcus*

Protist: informal term referring to a diverse group of mainly unicellular eukaryotes

Protostome: a superphylum of bilaterian animals that include the arthropods (q.v.), molluscs, annelid worms and nematode worms

Protozoa: informal term referring to a diverse group of non-photosynthetic (i.e. 'animal'-like rather than 'plant'-like) unicellular protists such as amoebae and ciliates

Provirus: a virus genome that is integrated into the genetic material of the host cell; referred to as a prophage (q.v.) in the case of bacterial viruses

Pseudopod, pseudopodium: a temporary protrusion of the cytoplasm (q.v.) of amoeboid cells that is used for locomotion and the capture of prey

Psychrophilic: describes organisms that thrive at low temperatures; *psychrotolerant* describes organisms that tolerate low temperatures

Radiolarians: major class of protozoa characterized by a delicate silica skeleton and long thin projecting pseudopods known as axopods

Replicase, RNA replicase, (also known *as RNA-dependent RNA polymerase):* an enzyme that catalyses the replication of RNA

Retroelement, retrotransposon: a genetic element that can multiply its presence within a genome by using the enzyme reverse transcriptase (q.v.) to turn RNA copies of itself back into DNA, which may then be inserted into the genome

Reverse transcriptase: an enzyme that generates DNA from an RNA template

Rhodopsin: a light-sensitive receptor protein

Ribonucleoprotein complex: a structural association between a protein and RNA, e.g. a ribosome

Ribosome: intracellular organelles made of RNA and various proteins, present in all cells and responsible for protein synthesis

Ribozyme: a catalyst composed of RNA, as opposed to an enzyme (which is a protein that acts as a catalyst)

Rotifer: a phylum of mainly microscopic invertebrates

Slime moulds: a group of amoeboid protists that include the cellular slime moulds or social amoebae such as *Dictyostelium discoideum* and the plasmodial or acellular slime moulds such as *Physarum polycephalum*

Somatic, soma: refers to the cells of an organism that do not belong to the germ line (q.v.)

Squamate: a member of the order Squamata, or scaled reptiles, comprising lizards and snakes

ssDNA, ssRNA: single-stranded DNA or RNA molecules

T4 phage: virulent phage that infects *E. coli*

TP53: a gene with a major role in tumour suppression, one of whose functions is to initiate apoptosis (q.v.)

Tardigrades / water bears: phylum of microscopic invertebrates capable of surviving in extreme conditions

Testate: of amoebae, possessing a shell or test

Transcription: the process by which a stretch of DNA is used as a template to produce a complementary messenger RNA molecule

Translation: the process by which ribosomes synthesize proteins, using messenger RNA as a template to specify the order of the amino acids that make up the protein

Vacuole: a type of vesicle (q.v.), a membrane-bound space within the cytoplasm of a cell, often used for storing food, water or waste

Vesicle: a membrane-bound compartment within the cytoplasm of a cell

Virion: a complete virus particle comprising both the genetic material and the protective capsid (q.v.)

Viroid: a short, circular, infectious, single-stranded RNA molecule that does not code for any proteins and does not have a capsid (q.v.)

Wild type: genotype most frequently found in a natural population (by contrast with a knockout, where one of the organism's genes has been rendered inoperative or 'knocked out')

X chromosome, Y chromosome: the two sex-determining chromosomes in mammals; the presence or absence of the Y chromosome dictates whether offspring are male or female, for female individuals generally have two X chromosomes, whereas male individuals generally have an X and a Y

Zygote: cell produced by sexual fusion between two gametes

List of Figures

Figure 1: Self across cultures and scripts 21
Figure 2: Me, myself and a typographical gap 23
Figure 3: Nicolas-Joseph Cugnot's automotive contraption 89
Figure 4: T4 phage... 149
Figure 5: Diverse Protists 234

All graphics/illustrations by Christina Nath, 2017

Endnotes

1 There may seem to be a contradiction in simultaneously applying the epithets 'full' and 'minimal' to selfhood. It will become clear that there is not. Such selfhood is considered *minimal* in that it provides the foundation for the more complex aspects of selfhood characteristic of animals such as humans, most notably the moral and autobiographical dimensions of selfhood. It is considered *full* in that it displays all three forms of intrinsic reflexivity, by contrast with the merely self-like or selfish entities that do not display all three.

2 In what follows, I shall thus frequently refer to 'biological selfhood' and 'living selfhood' as synonyms for full minimal selfhood.

3 Intrinsic reflexivity, in its various forms, might well be such a property, but then it would be *primarily* a self (or something self-like) that was being recognized. By contrast with life and living entities, the possibility of *radical* difference within the class of minimal selves – and thus the problem of recognizing what is radically unrecognizable – is ruled out by the intrinsic reflexivity that provides a defining characteristic common to all selfhood. However different it may be from the selfhood found on our planet, any entity that exhibits intrinsic reflexivity is at least self-like.

4 I use the term 'self-like' to refer to entities that only comply with one or two of the three underlying categories of intrinsic reflexivity. Here too there is considerable, though not complete, overlap with the attribute 'life-like'. In other cases, the entities in question tend rather to be described as 'selfish'.

5 Kenny (1989), 87.

6 In *Sein und Zeit* (*Being and Time*) Heidegger refers to *das Selbst* as the answer to the question of the 'who' of *Dasein* (*die Frage nach dem Wer des Daseins*); see Heidegger (1926; 1986), 114ff., 267. He makes particularly extensive reference to *das Selbst*, as well as employing coinages such as *Selbstwelt* (selfworld), in his 1919-20 lectures entitled *Grundprobleme der Phänomenologie* (*Fundamental Problems of Phenomenology*); see Heidegger (1919/20; 1993), for example 62-64. We shall return below (pages 33-34) to his better-known *Grundbegriffe der Metaphysik: Welt - Endlichkeit - Einsamkeit* (*The Fundamental Concepts of Metaphysics*).

7 This emphatic use can be further subdivided into adnominal emphasis ('the president himself opened the meeting') and adverbial emphasis ('he built his house himself'). Of 72 languages included in a survey carried out by Volker Gast and Peter Siemund (2006), 30 use the same expression for all three functions: these include English, Mandarin, Arabic, Bengali, Cantonese, Irish, Hebrew, Hungarian, Persian, Quechua, Turkish and Ndyuka (a South American Creole language); 25, including German, distinguish the two forms of adnominal and adverbial intensifiers from the reflexive; others have different lexical items for all three.
8 Ibid., 347.
9 'Da ist ze wissenne, daz ein ieklicher mensch hat fúnfley Sich. Daz eine Sich ist im gemein mit dem steine, und daz ist wesen. Ein anders mit dem krute, und daz ist wahsen. Daz dritte mit den tieren, und daz ist enphinden. Daz vierde mit allen menschen, daz ist, daz er ein gemeine menschlich nature an im hat, in dem dú andern ellú eins sint. Daz fúnfte, daz im eigenlich zu gehert, daz ist sin persenlicher mensch beidú nah deme adel und och nach dem zuval' (Seuse, ca. 1330; 1993, 18–20, trans. R. G.).
10 Another fascinating case of the substantive use of the *Sich* is found in the early 20th-century work of the philosophical anthropologist Helmuth Plessner. Contrasting the *Selbst* with the *Sich*, Plessner notably downplays the element of reflexivity in the former. According to Plessner, it is with the *Sich* – a characteristic of animals – that genuine reflexivity enters the organic realm. The *Sich*, he says, is *ein rückbezügliches Selbst*, a reflexive self. See Plessner (1928; 1975), 238.
11 See Gast and Siemund (2006), 347–48.
12 It should be stressed that I am referring here (and below) to the subject and object in a grammatical sense and not in the epistemological sense of a subject and object of knowledge. As we shall see in the case of self-consciousness and self-awareness, these two senses of 'subject' and 'object' need not necessarily coincide.
13 Hume (1739; 1962), 301–2.
14 Taylor (1989), 113.
15 See Aristotle (trans. J. A. K. Thomson; 1953), 267, 277, 280: Thomson's translation gives 'second self' twice and 'alter ego' once. The translation by W. D. Ross uses 'another self' on all three occasions (*Works*, vol. IX, trans. W. D. Ross; 1915), 66a31, 69b6, 70b6. On the reaction to Aristotle's formulation, see Stern-Gillet (1995), 12–13.
16 Bowker, ed. (1997), 106–7.
17 This tendency is reflected in such locutions as: 'self should be measured against self' and 'self is protector of self'; see Harvey (1995), 19–20; Pérez-Remón (1980), 9–10.
18 For a discussion of the Arabic word *nafs*, see Anghelescu (2011).
19 My use of the word 'reflexivity' will be based throughout on the grammatical use of the word 'reflexive', suggesting something 'turned back' on itself, in other words a relationship of something to itself. The term 'reflexivity' is not to be confused with the notion of a reflex in the sense of an automatic bodily response to a stimulus. The adjective I use in the latter case is 'reflex-like' or simply 'reflex', as in a 'reflex reaction'. It is also to be distinguished from 'reflective', which refers to the process of reflection or thinking and occurs in the present context in the form of 'pre-reflective', denoting a form of awareness taken to be independent of, or prior to, thought processes.

20 As I have been politely reminded on a couple of occasions by non-native English speakers, it is more normal in English to drop the 'myself' (as redundant) and simply wash and shave, or have a wash and a shave. However, in both cases the explicit reflexive remains optional. In other languages, such as German and Spanish, it is the norm: *ich wasche mich, ich rasiere mich; me lavo, me afeito*, etc.

21 Human selfhood and human identity are such complex phenomena that it is often impossible to disentangle what I am from what I am seen to be, and this in turn from what I want to be seen to be (beardless and clean, perhaps) and from what I see myself as being seen to be (stubbly and in need of a wash).

22 In fact, it would certainly be possible to produce interpretations of self-depilation and auto-grooming in terms of the three categories of intrinsic reflexivity I propose here. Other, apparently more *ex*trinsic cases of reflexivity are scratching oneself or tickling oneself. To the extent that such activities constitute forms of adaptive self-movement, however, these may likewise be considered to partake of intrinsic reflexivity (by contrast with accidental or non-adaptive reflexive movements such as shooting oneself in the foot). Importantly, viewing – and recognizing – oneself in a mirror is also an act of extrinsic rather than intrinsic reflexivity. The very notion of representation suggests the non-identity of what represents with what is represented, precisely insofar as the former only *represents* the latter. This has profound implications for any representational theory of self-consciousness or self-awareness: such self-knowledge is not a form of intrinsic reflexivity, yet it *presupposes* intrinsic reflexivity (see note 30).

23 A further possible objection to this grammatically grounded conception of intrinsic reflexivity is that it suffers from a certain fuzziness. It will be noted that some of the cases of intrinsic reflexivity *could* take the form of merely intransitive verbs: this is so, for example, with 'to adapt' and 'to replicate'. In such contexts, the additional reflexive pronoun may seem pedantic or superfluous. In all the cases in question, however, the reflexive pronoun is a possibility and makes logical sense. Sometimes other languages provide a clue, as with *adaptarse* in Spanish and *sich adaptieren* in German. Two points of contrast further clarify the matter. Firstly, in the case of a verb such as 'adapt' there is an evident distinction with respect to its transitive use, as when I adapt *something else* to my needs as opposed to adapting (myself) to my new circumstances. Secondly, the intransitive 'adapt' can be compared with other intransitive verbs that are *neutral* regarding causal agency. The English verb 'grow', for example, is completely indifferent to whether the cause is endogenous or exogenous: an animal can grow, but so can a record collection; the verb simply means 'to get bigger', irrespective of what causes the increase in size. The verb 'adapt', used intransitively or reflexively (as when an animal adapts, or adapts itself, to its surroundings'), implies some degree or form of *endogenous* causality, by contrast with when a car or machine is adapted for some purpose by a human agent.

24 See pages 63 ff.

25 Hood (2012), 80.

26 In a recent anthology called *This Idea Must Die: Scientific Theories That Are Blocking Progress*, edited by John Brockman (2015), Hood pinpoints 'the self' as his personal bête noire, a concept that should be put out of its misery even though 'like a conceptual zombie [it] refuses to die' (147). The 'self' Hood is sentencing to death seems to be the 'self' as a unitary decision-making entity,

a 'free-willing' self. Certainly, any concept that has never been satisfactorily defined – as is the case with the 'self' – is best viewed with suspicion. My aim here is to provide it with an appropriate definition and a new lease of life.
27 Hood (2012), 160: of course, the fact that something *might as well be* non-existent does not provide good grounds for inferring its actual non-existence.
28 Metzinger (2009), 1.
29 Ibid., 8.
30 In fact, part of the problem is Metzinger's reliance upon a purely representational notion of self-awareness. Self-representation is not a form of intrinsic reflexivity: a self does not constitute itself by representing itself; one can be a self without having an explicit self-model. In self-representation, a logical breach is opened up between self (as the subject of representation) and self (as the object of representation), the very term 'representation' implying their non-identity. In other words, the self has no criteria for recognizing itself *as itself* unless it has some form of pre-representational self-awareness that *does* involve intrinsic reflexivity.
31 Bennett and Hacker (2003), 325–26, 331–32.
32 *Acaranga Sutra*, I.1.3, quoted in Chapple (1993), 11.
33 On Hobbes's conception of 'endeavour', see Hobbes (1651; 1968), 118–22 (i.e. chapter 6); on Spinoza, see for example Spinoza (1667; 1955), 202–3 (i.e. part IV, propositions 20, 22).
34 Jonas (1966; 2001), 80, 126.
35 In the case of offspring, one might say that it is 'life' rather than the 'living individual' that is perpetuating itself.
36 Glasgow (1997), 16.
37 Schopenhauer (1986), 3.28; see also Glasgow (1999), 260.
38 On the godlike attributes of 'nothing' and 'nobody', see Glasgow (1999), 117–18.
39 Maynard Smith and Szathmáry (1999), 11.
40 Characterized by what Kant calls an 'intrinsic purposiveness', a natural organism is 'one in which every part is reciprocally both end and means': again, an organism is both the cause and effect of itself. See Kant, *Kritik der Urteilskraft*, § 64–66, pp. 340, 343.
41 Even more recently, the term 'adaptive self-organization' has been used by Jamie A. Davies (2014) to describe the development of the human embryo. Davies resorts to imagery of 'self-creation' and 'bootstrapping', yet it remains clear that this conception of self-organization as a process by which complex structures emerge from the application of simple rules to simple components always presupposes a throughflow of energy. Embryos are not mini-Münchhausens.
42 Morowitz (1992), 77. This raises the question of what is meant by 'complexity'. One definition suggested by the above is a thermodynamic one, which identifies complexity as 'a measure of the rate of energy flowing through a system of given mass'; see Chaisson (2001), 13. However, the nature of complexity is an ongoing bone of contention, and many other definitions have been proposed. An algorithmic approach to the complexity of a system is more static, measuring it in terms of the shortest list of instructions required to generate it, or the information needed to describe its structure and function. On complexity, see Morowitz, 74–84; Maynard Smith and Szathmáry (1999), 15–16.

43 For a clear account of the background to the BZ reaction, see Coveney and Highfield (1990), 188–201.
44 Prigogine and Stengers (1984), 14.
45 Gell-Mann, for one, denies that the eddies that form in turbulent flow can be considered adaptive; see Lewin (1992), 15.
46 On this view, the spatial structure of living organisms is the product not merely of a genetic program dictated by historical contingency, but of the internal dynamics of a complex system and the naturally resulting 'morphogenetic field'. As Franklin M. Harold puts it (2001), 'biological forms are not fragile and contrived; quite the contrary, they are the "generic forms" most likely to be found by self-organizing dynamic systems, and therefore both probable and robust'. They are no longer 'artifices cobbled together by a capricious history, but the outward expressions of their own dynamics', 198.
47 Bray (2009), 190.
48 Shapiro and Feinberg (1982; 1995), 168.
49 Ibid., 169.
50 The logical relationship between self-organization and natural selection is complex. They are commonly seen as complementary processes. For a helpful discussion see Hoelzer, Smith and Pepper (2006), who themselves see natural selection within a more general context of self-organizing systems and thermodynamic evolution.
51 The notion of complexification is in fact rendered superfluous by that of self-adaptation: the 'self' in question is not necessarily becoming more 'organized' (with connotations of increased complexity) but simply *adapting itself* to changing environmental circumstances.
52 As will become clear below, there are three fundamental categories of intrinsic reflexivity that are required for 'full' selfhood. A deficiency of *self-containment* results in dissipative systems, where no (construction) work is possible; a lack of *self-reproduction* or *self-replication* rules out heredity and thus puts a severe restriction on the possibility of variation and selection; a lack of *self-maintenance* limits selfhood to viruses or virus-like entities.
53 Thompson (2007), 75. Elsewhere, Thompson reassures the reader that there is no homunculus 'self' inside a self-organizing system. 'Such spontaneous pattern formation is exactly what we mean by self-organization,' writes J. A. S. Kelso, quoted by Thompson; 'the system organizes itself, but there is no "self", no agent inside the system doing the organizing' (61). According to the definition I am proffering here, the self *is* the self-organizing or self-producing system by virtue of its intrinsic reflexivity; there need be no talk of agents or homunculi within.
54 Joyce (1982; 1995), 140.
55 'Metabolism' is thus meant in the sense of the German term *Stoffwechsel*, i.e. 'stuff-change'. There is no hidden implication that the chemical processes in question must be directed by the genetic apparatus of nucleic acids. On the uses of the term 'metabolism' see Dyson (1985; rev. ed. 1999), 6–7.
56 See Maynard Smith and Szathmáry (1999), 3–5.
57 Ibid., 3.

58 What is common to these two concepts is the element of self-multiplication. The distinction between them is largely contextual and has been summarized by Dyson (1985; rev. ed. 1999), 6: 'For a cell, to reproduce means simply to divide into two cells with the daughter cells inheriting approximately equal shares of the cellular constituents. For a molecule, to replicate means to construct a precise copy of itself by a specific chemical process. Cells can reproduce, but only molecules can replicate. In modern times, reproduction of cells is always accompanied by replication of molecules, but this need not always have been so in the past'.
59 Joyce (1982; 1995), 140.
60 Heidegger (1929/30; 1983), 325: 'Selbstherstellung überhaupt, Selbstleitung und Selbsterneuerung sind offenbar Momente, die den Organismus gegenüber der Maschine kennzeichnen'. Heidegger also uses *Selbsterzeugung* instead of *Selbstherstellung* (326); in English one might refer to self-manufacture or self-generation; the point is the same.
61 Ibid., 332.
62 Ibid. It was his pupil Hans Jonas who – with his concept of 'self-concern' – subsequently extended this intrinsic reflexivity to the organic world at large.
63 Ibid., 340: 'Wir behalten uns den Ausdruck des "selbst" und der Selbstheit zur Kennzeichnung der *spezifisch menschlichen Eigentümlichkeit*, seines Sich-zu-eigen-seins vor. .... Die Art und Weise, wie das Tier sich zu eigen ist, ist nicht Personalität, nicht Reflexion und Bewusstsein, sondern einfach nur *Eigentum*'. The distinction is almost impossible to reproduce in English, based as it is on idiosyncratic wordplay relating to property and propriety (a thematic link between selfhood and ownership that we shall re-encounter in other contexts). When Heidegger describes animals as *Eigentum*, the implication is on the one hand that – as selves – they are proper to themselves; on the other that they are mere property. This contrasts with the *Eigentümlichkeit*, the characteristic uniqueness, of human selfhood.
64 Ibid., 376. This corresponds to the self-formalism I have referred to above.
65 The word *heteropoiesis* may also be used to denote the specific subcategory of *allopoiesis* involving humans as designers and producers (as in the case of cars or cookers). See Thompson (2007), 98.
66 Ibid., 44.
67 Autonomy implies self-rule or having a law of one's own; here we might take it to mean primarily self-regulating.
68 Maturana and Varela (1987; 1998), 46–47.
69 See Thompson (2007), 448 (footnote 4).
70 Ruiz-Moreno and Moreno (2004), 237.
71 Ibid., 240.
72 See Ruiz-Mirazo et al. (2004), 332: such regulatory flexibility is 'only possible if the system is chemical, because the variety of constraining mechanisms required to achieve that capacity simply is not at reach for bare physical systems'.
73 Ruiz-Mirazo and Moreno (2004), 240.
74 Schrödinger (1944; 1992), 77.
75 Aristotle, *De Anima*, (Book II.1) 412a; Aristotle (1986), 156.

76 Grammatically speaking, the term 'self-regulation' likewise implies intrinsic reflexivity, but caution is due. In practice, the concept refers not only to the biological phenomenon of homeostasis, where the self-adjustment serves the self-perpetuation of a living self, but may also incorporate other negative-feedback-based automatic control systems such as thermostats. Indeed, Daniel Dennett is prompted by the self-regulating capabilities of thermostats to suggest that these – along with self-replicating macromolecules, unicellular organisms, plants, animals and chess-playing computers – are what he calls 'intentional systems'. Sensitive to environmental conditions, such systems are seen by Dennett as behaving *as though* they had goals or intentions (in this case maintaining a constant temperature in a particular context) and as being correspondingly 'mindlike'; see Dennett (1996), 26, 34. In fact, a thermostat does not in itself exhibit intrinsic reflexivity, or selfhood, because the *function* of its activity is ultimately to regulate not itself, or its self, but a more broadly defined system. Even so, some sort of thermostat may well *form part of* a self-maintaining, self-adapting self, i.e. an intrinsically reflexive system. Our bodies thus contain internalized thermostats – which keep our inner environment at a constant temperature – as one of various aspects of their overall homeostasis.

77 Thompson (2007), 147–48, refers to a distinction drawn by Ezequiel Di Paolo between the 'intrinsic teleology' of self-production and the 'projective teleology' of adaptivity and cognition.

78 In this respect there is an asymmetry between self-adaptation and the deeper or more radical change suggested by self-transformation. A self-maintaining system must necessarily adapt itself to changes in its environment (for otherwise it will fail to maintain itself), yet this need not entail permanent or irreversible self-transformation. A self-maintaining system may or may not transform itself as it maintains itself.

79 Maturana and Varela (1987; 1992), 57–58.

80 Wharton (2002), 268.

81 See Morono et al. (2011).

82 Thompson (2007), 122.

83 Joyce (1995), 140.

84 See Harold (2001), 101.

85 In *Reasons and Persons* (1984) Derek Parfit argues that there may indeed be cases in which there is no answer to questions about 'identity', using the analogy of a club that disbands and subsequently reforms with the same name, the same members and the same rules. Is this the same club as before? If not arbitrarily specified, the question has no answer. And what if the members subsequently split into two groups and form two clubs, albeit with the same name and the same rules? Which of the two clubs is the old one? Again, Parfit argues, identity is not what matters, for it can be indeterminate. Parfit gives the example of the French Socialist Party, which in 1881 split into two new parties, raising the issue of whether it had ceased to exist or whether it continued its existence as one or the other, or both, of these new parties. If we know what there is to be known about spatio-temporal continuity, says Parfit, we know all that needs to be known (see pp. 213, 260).

86 More or less: direct conscious memories are unlikely to stretch back to our life *in utero* or in infancy, yet most of us know when we were born. My autobiographical selfhood incorporates what others tell me about myself.

87 Locke (1689: 1975), 340–41, provided a much-cited definition of selfhood in terms of what we can remember of ourselves: 'It is plain, consciousness, as far as ever it can be extended, should it be to ages past, unites existences and actions, very remote in time, into the same person, as well as it does the existence and actions of the immediately preceding moment: so that whatever has the consciousness of present and past actions is the same person to whom they both belong. Had I the same consciousness that I saw the ark and Noah's flood, as that I saw an overflowing of the Thames last winter, or as that I write now, I could no more doubt that I who write this now, that saw the Thames overflowed last winter, and that viewed the flood at the general deluge, was the same self, place that self in what substance you please, than that I who write this am the same myself now whilst I write … that I was yesterday.'
88 Turney (2015), 41.
89 Ruiz-Mirazo and Moreno (2004), 253, 254–55.
90 Ruiz-Mirazo et al. (2004).
91 Moreira and López-García (2009), 306.
92 Dawkins (1976; 1989).
93 In practice, this takes the form of what is known as 'semi-conservative replication', such that each of the resulting two copies of the double-stranded DNA contains one of the original strands and one new strand.
94 On the distinction between numerical and qualitative identity see Parfit (1984). If a perfect replica is made of me, my replica and I are qualitatively identical or exactly alike. However, we may not be numerically identical, i.e. one and the same person. The point is sometimes known as the identity of indiscernibles, which holds that if two or more things share all their properties (including their spatiotemporal location), they are identical in the sense of being really only one thing.
95 This is perhaps just a variation on the theme of the enigmatic *ur*-self.
96 Dawkins (1982; 1999), 83. This ambiguity is pointed out in McMullin (1995).
97 This is, of course, logically equivalent to the slightly disquieting notion derived from the concept of self-reproduction, namely that the self that reproduces itself is in some sense the same as – or at least continuous with – the self that is reproduced.
98 Harold (2001), 72–73: 'the cellular context impinges upon the transfer of information, for the chain [of amino acids] will only fold "correctly" in a medium of "appropriate" ionic composition and pH. Indeed, the very translation of the messenger RNA depends upon the cellular context, for ribosomes only work properly in the presence of high concentrations of potassium ions – a special milieu that the cell must do work to provide'.
99 Researchers from the European Bioinformatics Institute have used a small amount of DNA to archive digital data including all 154 of Shakespeare's sonnets, a spoken excerpt from Martin Luther King's 1963 'I have a dream' speech, the 1953 paper by Crick and Watson describing the structure of DNA, a colour photograph of the researchers' workplace, and a file about the encoding system itself. The five files in question were represented by 153,335 strings of DNA, each comprising 117 nucleotides. See Goldman et al. (2013).
100 Again, this distinction is not absolute. Single-stranded DNA can also behave as an enzyme;

see Breaker and Joyce (1994), Santoro and Joyce (1997); also Cavalier-Smith (2001), 556. Despite this potential for catalytic activity, however, DNA enzymes, or deoxyribozymes, are not known to occur in nature or have any biological function. Though there are single-stranded DNA viruses, most biological DNA occurs in a double-stranded form, precluding the complex secondary and tertiary structures associated with catalysis. Whatever the case, the logical point remains the same.

101 Banzhaf et al. (1999), 85–86; see also Bray (2009), 145–51.

102 The hypothesis of the RNA world is itself not without its critics; see Holmes (2015), discussing work by Loren Williams and Nick Hud. Given the relative inefficiency of RNA as an enzyme, it has been suggested that RNA cooperated and coevolved with proteins from the outset. Yet the principle remains the same: the possibility of selfhood rests on reflexivity, whether embodied in one or two different kinds of macromolecules.

103 On the logic of the limit or *Grenze*, see Hegel (1986), 5.136–39.

104 See, for example, Cavalier-Smith (2001), 557.

105 Ibid., 569–70.

106 Thompson (2007), 46.

107 Ruiz-Mirazo et al. (2004) lay particular weight on the 'active' role of the membrane.

108 See Ackerman (2012), 26–27; Turney (2015), 149–69.

109 Woese (2002), 8746. See also Koonin et al. (2006).

110 See Glasgow (1997), 13, 105–6.

111 See for example Schopenhauer (1986), 1.217–18.

112 In fact, any such 'reduction' would be a merely collateral effect of the present argument, which is first and foremost an analysis of the implications of a certain conception of 'selfhood' and only secondarily concerned with whatever it is that life is.

113 Marder (2013), 131.

114 See Prigogine and Stengers (1984), 14: consciously adopting 'somewhat anthropomorphic language', they suggest that 'in equilibrium matter is "blind", but in far-from-equilibrium conditions it begins to be able to perceive, to "take into account," in its way of functioning, differences in the external world'.

115 Maturana and Varela (1987; 1998), 102–3.

116 An autonomous system is structurally coupled to its environment to the extent that 'the conduct of each is a function of the conduct of the other'. Structural coupling thus denotes 'the history of recurrent interactions between two or more systems that leads to a structural congruence between them'. By contrast with self-adaptation, therefore, the stress is on the reciprocity of influence. See Thompson (2007), 45.

117 The concept of 'entelechy' has on occasion been linked with immaterial or vitalistic principles, but these bear no logical connection to the idea of being 'an end in oneself'.

118 Dennett (1991), 174.

119 Dennett (1996), 32.

120 See Thompson (2007), 162.

121 Locke (1689; 1975), 341 (my italics).

122 Heidegger himself seems to have recognized the reflexivity in this deeper sense of 'care' (in his terms: *Sorge*), pointing out that the notion of 'self-care' (*Selbstsorge*) is a tautology or pleonasm; see Heidegger (1926; 1986), 193. In what follows, I shall nonetheless continue to use the rather awkward terms 'self-care' and 'self-concern' because in normal usage the English concepts of 'care' and 'concern' are not themselves taken to be reflexive.

123 Nozick (1981), 108–9.

124 See Zahavi (2005), 11–13, for an account of the phenomenological understanding that self-consciousness is presupposed by consciousness itself, as expressed in the writings of Husserl, Heidegger and Sartre.

125 Here we see how the grammatical and the epistemological senses of the subject-object distinction may fail to coincide. See above page 20, note 12.

126 Strawson (2011), 282.

127 Strawson (1997), 424–25: 'I will call my view the Pearl view, because it suggests that many mental selves exist, one at a time and one after another, like pearls on a string, in the case of something like a human being. According to the Pearl view, each is a distinct existence, an individual physical thing or object, though they may exist for considerably different lengths of time. The Pearl view is not the view that mental selves are necessarily of relatively short duration – there may be beings whose conscious experience is uninterrupted for hours at a time, or even for the whole of their existence (if I believed in God, this is how I'd expect God to be). But we are not like this: the basic form of our consciousness is that of a gappy series of eruptions of consciousness from a substrate of apparent non-consciousness. … I don't suppose the Pearl view will be much liked. … The proposal, in any case, is that the mental self – *a* mental self – exists at any given moment of consciousness or during any uninterrupted or hiatus-free period of consciousness. But it exists only for some short period of time'.

128 Nozick (1981), 110.

129 See Parfit (1984), 204–6.

130 Part of the problem is that – as a form of self-representation – explicit autobiographical memory does not *in itself* provide a satisfactory yardstick for distinguishing true from false memories. Indeed, to the extent that a memory of self is a form of self-representation, it does not strictly speaking constitute a case of intrinsic reflexivity. A representation is necessarily non-identical with what is represented, which raises the question of how a self can recognize a representation of itself *as itself* unless it in some sense already knows itself.

131 Parfit (1984), 205.

132 An interesting case is the episodic memory of corvids such as Western scrub jays, which have been shown to remember 'what', 'where' and 'when' they hide their food caches; see Emery and Clayton (2001). The question of whether this implies the use of concepts need not concern us here; it certainly implies highly complex social cognition.

133 Wedekind and Füri (1997).

134 See Bonner (1993), 3–5.

135 It may seem as though the global self – life on Earth as a whole – *may* have something like an unchanging core: the ribosome, for example, which carries out protein synthesis. The notion of 'selfhood' as laid out here does not in itself *rule out* an unchanging nucleus. Selective constraints may make it difficult to change certain elements of the biological apparatus. Yet the virosphere provides a counterpoint, for there is no single gene common to all viruses. Either way, the point is that such an unchanging core is not *necessary* for 'selfhood'; continuity is what matters.

136 See Rose (1992), 137–42.

137 See Shapiro (1998), 96–97, also Jolivet-Gougeon et al. (2011).

138 Wharton (2002), 257. The question is whether increased mutation is merely a symptom of stress – in that cells in extreme or nutrient-scarce conditions are less able to produce accurate copies of their DNA and to generate the proteins required for DNA maintenance and repair – or a case of evolutionary legerdemain allowing a proliferation of 'trial and error' solutions to a particular environmental challenge. The idea that hypermutation may be an evolved adaptation is corroborated by cases where it is *localized* within the genome, e.g. the somatic hypermutation that occurs in limited chromosomal regions of the B cells of the adaptive immune system, fine-tuning the ability of the collective of antibody molecules to recognize non-self antigens.

139 See Dawkins (2004), 622–27. Dawkins himself speculates that such considerations might imply the existence of 'a kind of high-level, between-lineage selection in favour of evolvability' – an example of what has been called clade selection (622).

140 Ibid., 623.

141 Plant modularity is rather different in character but brings up similar issues. Indeed, the modules of plants are endowed with an even greater degree of autonomy and – provided they have the requisite nutrients – can survive and sexually reproduce independently of the rest of the plant. On plant modularity see Clarke (2012), 324–25, who applies the term 'structural modularity' to plant modules, by contrast with the less autonomous forms of 'evolutionary' or 'developmental' modularity. To call a plant modular, she suggests, 'is to say that it grows by the accumulation of smaller constructional building blocks called modules', each of which 'has its own life cycle; its own program of growth and senescence'. Clarke describes such modules as 'semi-autonomous' where the 'semi' refers to the fact that they do not usually live alone but interact and share resources with other modules.

142 Pepper and Herron (2008), 622–23.

143 Ibid., 625, citing a definition given in *Webster's Ninth New Collegiate Dictionary* (1983).

144 Once more, we encounter the (grammatical) duality of subject and object, the subject of interest coinciding with the object of interest.

145 Ibid., 626.

146 A notable exception is provided by the germ-free laboratory animals (e.g. mice) used in microbiota research. Such animals are kept in a sterile environment from birth, ruling out the postnatal colonization process that otherwise occurs in the gastrointestinal tract.

147 See Glover (1988), 33–35. One of the most memorable images of this self-conflict is Peter Seller's Dr Strangelove being throttled by his own anarchic hand in Stanley Kubrick's 1964 film *Dr Strangelove, or How I Learned to Stop Worrying and Love the Bomb*.

148 Quoted in Miller (1985), 355–56.

149 On inner disunity see Glasgow (1997), 31–36.

150 The ordered structure may arise without any input of energy or it may require energy in the form of stirring, but once it is formed, it is stable or metastable. On self-assembly see in particular Whitesides and Grzybowski (2002) and Whitesides and Boncheva (2002). There is still a certain amount of terminological inconsistency. These authors distinguish between dynamic self-assembly and static self-assembly, and use the former to refer to what is more commonly referred to as self-organization.
151 Whitesides and Grzybowski (2002), 2419.
152 See Benner et al. (2004).
153 The Victorian writer and critic John Ruskin was particularly sensitive to the 'life-like' attributes of crystals. In *The Ethics of the Dust* (1865; 1877), 203, the elderly lecturer admits that crystals 'look as if they were alive' and make him 'speak as if they were'. The process of crystallization leads back, he suggests, to the question, 'what is it to be alive?' The conclusion he draws is that things are neither wholly alive nor wholly dead; being alive is a matter of degree.
154 Whereas the stability of covalent bonds allows configurations of up to 1000 atoms to synthesize, the molecular self-assembly of larger structures relies on non-covalent or weak covalent interactions such as van der Waals, electrostatic or hydrophobic interactions (Whitesides and Grzybowski (2002)). In non-biological contexts self-assembly may also take place at larger scales, involving micrometre to millimetre-sized components. Mesoscale self-assembly of this sort may employ magnetic or capillary interactions; see Boncheva and Whitesides (2005), 737.
155 On protein folding see Dobson (2003).
156 See Harold (2001), 50–51. The enzyme ribonuclease catalyzes the breakdown of RNA.
157 There are some molecular chaperones that not only oversee the correct folding of proteins, but 'rescue' proteins that have misfolded, giving them a second chance to fold properly. Such active intervention in the folding process does require energy in the form of ATP; see Dobson (2003), 886.
158 See Li et al. (2010), 871–72: 'prions show the hallmarks of Darwinian evolution: they are subject to mutation, as evidenced by heritable changes of their phenotypic properties, and to selective amplification, as documented by the emergence of distinct populations in different environments'.
159 Harold (2001), 80. Here too qualification is required. As Harold points out, ribosome self-assembly requires the initial RNA transcripts to be processed by cellular proteins that remain outside the ribosome. The process is completed 'only if the mixture is gently warmed at a particular stage'. It is believed that 'in the living cell constituents external to the ribosome intervene in its assembly'. Like the self-replication of DNA, in other words, ribosome synthesis is ultimately dependent upon a highly specific context provided by the self-maintaining and self-reproducing cell.
160 Deamer et al. (2002), 371, 374.
161 See Cavalier-Smith (2000), 176. See also Harold (2001), 105.
162 Harold (2001), 105.
163 Ibid., 56.
164 Ibid., 244.
165 See Chapter 5. On the properties of water that have proved crucial to the development of life on

Earth, see Glasgow (2009), 45–55; see in general Ball (1999). Noteworthy is water's double role as both matrix and nutrient, fuelling the photosynthesis that produces high-energy carbohydrates for cyanobacteria and plants; combustion of these carbohydrates in turn powers the animal kingdom.
166 Morowitz (1992), 53.
167 Ruiz-Mirazo and Moreno (2004), 255.
168 Clegg (2001), 613, quoting David Keilin.
169 The largest animal known to survive anhydrobiosis is the larva of the midge *Polypedilium vanderplanki*, which can lose 99 percent of its body water. See Wharton (2002), 49.
170 On anhydrobiosis in general see Wharton (2002), 27–49, 92–128; see also Clegg (2001).
171 Wharton (2002), 101–2, reporting on research into the metabolism of an anhydrobiotic nematode, measured in terms of oxygen uptake, heat output and carbon dioxide production. See also Clegg (2001), 619, reporting on research into the encysted embryo of the brine shrimp during anoxybiosis, where metabolism – if present – would have to be 50,000 times slower than the aerobic rate.
172 Wharton (2002), 76.
173 Ibid., 77.
174 Cano and Borucki (1995).
175 Clegg (2001), 619.
176 Johnson et al. (2007).
177 Clegg (2001), 616.
178 See Lennon and Jones (2011), 123, on the diversity of phenotypes shown by cryptobiotic microbes.
179 See this description by Wharton (2002), 47–48, of the cocoon constructed by the African lungfish when its river habitat dries out: 'as the water level falls, it burrows into the mud of the river and secretes a cocoon of mucus.... The cocoon is waterproofed by a layer of lipid, and the fish lies folded on itself with its head next to a small opening at the top of the cocoon. The fish's oxygen uptake reduces to 10% of normal, its heartbeat slows, its tissues partly dehydrate, urine production ceases ... The lungfish can survive in this dormant state for up to six months'.
180 Blackiston et al. (2008).
181 Lennon and Jones (2011), 124–25.
182 Morowitz (1992), 52.
183 In fact, desiccation is one of the best strategies for surviving extreme cold, since the main threat posed by cold is a result of freezing, which cannot happen in the absence of water. In practice, animals have two broad options in facing low temperatures: either avoiding freezing, or tolerating freezing. Freeze-avoidance may be by means of desiccation, or it may involve freezing-point depression (where water is kept in its liquid state at temperatures below zero), for example by using antifreeze sugars or antifreeze proteins. Freeze-tolerance seems a more drastic measure, for ice is by common consensus the very antithesis of life, flow and process. It is generally assumed that metazoans will only survive freezing providing that ice is confined to extracellular spaces: such is the case with the frog *Rana sylvatica*, which can withstand temperatures down to -6 °C for four weeks, with 65–70 percent of its body water frozen. Yet the nematode worm *Panagrolaimus davidi* confounds even this assumption, surviving freezing in water to temperatures as low as -80°C. This Antarctic nematode can withstand

82 percent of its water turning to ice, including extensive intracellular freezing (though apparently restricted to the cytoplasm, and thus not including the organelles). Impressive though this is, it is still a far cry from the cold tolerance of the waterless tardigrade. On cold tolerance see Wharton (2002), 150–197, esp. 177–80 on the freeze-tolerant nematode.

184 Clegg (2001), 615.

185 Of course, 'life-like' is not meant in the common sense of 'tetrapod-like', i.e. endowed with four limbs and a physiognomy. The likeness is with life as a whole or in its deepest manifestations.

186 See Introduction, page 29. The reaction itself involves an appropriately proportioned mixture of an organic acid (malonic acid) with potassium bromate in the presence of a catalyst such as cerium ions and sulphuric acid. It was first conceived in the early 1950s by the Soviet biophysicist Boris Belouzov in an attempt to throw light on the workings of the Krebs cycle, a series of metabolic reactions by which aerobic organisms break down organic foodstuffs into energy and carbon dioxide. Given a constant supply of the requisite ingredients, Belouzov's solution was found to switch regularly back and forth between two distinct colours, confounding the scientific community of the time by defying the tendency to degenerate into disorder and thus seeming to challenge the Second Law. See Coveney and Highfield (1990), 197ff.

187 Quoted in ibid., 200.

188 Ruiz-Mirazo et al. (2004), 332. Clearly, such adaptability is not an all-or-nothing attribute. It may vary in degree and in form, ranging from internal homeostasis to active intervention in the environment. If the external perturbations exceed a certain limit in strength or duration, any self-maintaining system will fail to cope.

189 The hydrosphere can be considered the very heart of the biosphere. Indeed, it is only by internalizing the ocean's waters within ourselves as sap or blood that certain plants and animals have succeeded in escaping onto dry land.

190 Leonardo da Vinci provides one of the best-known formulations of the timeless analogy between the blood of a living body and the waters of the planet in his *Notebooks* (1952), 45–46: 'while man has within him a pool of blood wherein the lungs as he breathes expand and contract, so the body of the earth has its ocean, which also rises and falls every six hours with the breathing of the world; as from the said pool of blood proceed the veins which spread their branches through the human body, so the ocean fills the body of the earth with an infinite number of veins of water'.

191 Winchester (2010), 21.

192 Zimmer (2011), 42; Suttle (2007), 801.

193 Quoted in Ball (2009), 76; on self-organizing sand flows in general, see 75–123.

194 See the work of Hans Herrmann and colleagues at Stuttgart University; e.g. Durán et al. (2005). In this paper, computer simulations of interacting Barchan (i.e. crescent-shaped) dunes show a small and thus fast-moving dune approach and collide with a larger, slower one from behind. Four basic outcomes emerge, depending on the relative size of the two dunes: coalescence (simple absorption of one dune by the other), breeding (where 'baby' dunes emerge from the horns of the big dune), soliton behaviour (where the small fast-moving dune passes right through the big one), and budding (where the small dune passes through the big one, but then splits into two).

195 Quoted in Ball (2009), 48–49.
196 On the various sorts of atmospheric and hydrospheric convective cells see Ball (2009), 59–64.
197 Leaving surface tension out of account (by considering fluids that are contained between two parallel plates so there is no free surface), this number specifies a ratio between convection-driving forces such as the temperature difference and the resistance to such forces in the form of viscosity as well as the fluid's thermal conductivity. When surface tension is included (as in an open saucepan), a rather different form of convection is produced, known as Marangoni convection and resulting in Marangoni cells.
198 In the Earth's interior, the mantle is a layer almost 3,000 km thick located between the planet's core and its crust. Though made of rock, it is hot enough to behave like a viscous fluid, undergoing sluggish convective flow in geological time.
199 On the Kármán vortex street, see Ball (2009), 25–32.
200 Shear instability is often known as Kelvin-Helmholtz instability, after two of the pioneering 19th-century researchers into fluid dynamics.
201 This feedback is a product of Bernoulli's principle of fluid dynamics, according to which the pressure exerted by a fluid perpendicular to the direction of flow decreases as the flow velocity increases. When a bulge appears at the interface of the two flows, the widening produced by the bulge causes the bulging flow to slow down, while the adjacent, squeezed flow is simultaneously made to speed up. As a result of Bernoulli's principle, this difference in speed produces a difference in pressure that further accentuates the bulge. While positive feedback thus dictates that bulges forming at the interface of two flows will tend to reinforce their own growth, in practice viscosity holds this self-amplification in check until a critical threshold is crossed in terms of the relative velocity of the two flows. See Ball (2009), 32–36.
202 Turner (2000), 3–6.
203 Ibid., 4.
204 Ibid., 5.
205 It was for a long time thought that all animals need oxygen. However, certain species belonging to a phylum of tiny marine bottom-dwelling organisms called loriciferans have now been found to spend their entire life cycle in a completely anoxic environment; they do not need free oxygen to be metabolically active or able to reproduce. They manage this by dispensing with mitochondria as power-generating organelles, instead seeming to use hydrogenosome-like organelles in association with prokaryotic endosymbionts. Of course, loriciferans are equally limited in their powers of adaptation. See Danovaro et al. (2010); on mitochondria and getting by without them, see also Chapter 4.
206 Turner (2000), 5.
207 This is reported on the webpage of the Jet Propulsion Laboratory of the California Institute of Technology (9 Nov 2006): http://saturn.jpl.nasa.gov/news/newsreleases/newsrelease20061109/.
208 Ball (2009), 39.
209 Turner (2000), 4.
210 Ball (2009), 43.

211 Kauffman (1995), 20–21: 'the lifetime of the Great Red Spot is far longer than the average time any single gas molecule has lingered within it. ... The similarity to a human organism, whose molecular constituents change many times during a lifetime, is intriguing'. This point, of course, applies to any long-lasting self-organizing system – whether The Whirlpool beneath the Niagara Falls, Saturn's polar hurricanes or the Hadley convection cell – and not only the Great Red Spot.
212 Ibid., 21.
213 Ball (2009), 40–42.
214 One could provide it with a mouth and an anus to make it more animal-like. But prokaryotes such as bacteria and archaea manage perfectly well with the differential permeability of their membrane.
215 Ruiz-Mirazo and Moreno (2004), 239.
216 Dawkins (2004), 575–76.
217 Ibid., 576.
218 Maynard Smith and Szathmáry (1999), 5.
219 Again, 'containment' need not always take the form of a physical boundary. A candle flame provides an intermediate case, where the flame maintains its own stability by a self-sustaining sequence of events. For the flame to persist in time, it must be provided with new energy as fast as it emits heat and light. This comes from the heat of the flame itself, which melts the wax, which is in turn drawn up the wick by capillary action. The melted wax then vaporizes and burns within the heart of the flame, thus perpetuating the process.
220 Oxygen is the usual oxidant, although in anaerobic respiration sulphate, sulphur or nitrate may take its place. The other major mechanisms of energy provision are fermentation, which is also anaerobic, and photosynthesis, which feeds directly on the energy of the Sun.
221 Quoted in Bray (2009), 138.
222 Harold (2001), 40.
223 To illustrate the extent of this ongoing resynthesis, human beings typically *contain* 250g of ATP but *use up* their own body weight of it every day.
224 See Turner (2000), 29–30.
225 Ibid., 32. Of course, heat generation is anything but 'useless' to a warm-blooded creature. Yet warm blood is certainly an energetic extravagance, not only in terms of the organism's high fuel requirements but also because in hot conditions the organism will have to cool itself back down again, whether by panting, sweating or turning on the air conditioning. The advantages it confers are niche expansion, nocturnal activity and possibly – controversially – larger brains. Nick Lane provides a succinct assessment: 'hot blood exacts a cruel toll. It spells a short life, spent eating dangerously. It depresses the population size and the number of offspring. ... In recompense we have the boon of staying up at night and hanging out in the cold'. On warm blood see Lane (2009a), 205–31; 210.
226 Wharton (2002), 62–63.
227 Turner (2000), 7: whereas the 'internal physiology' refers to 'structures and devices inside the integumentary boundary of the organism', the 'external physiology' is a product of 'adaptive modifications of the environment'.
228 As Wrangham (2009; 57) explains, 'cooking gelatinizes starch, denatures protein, and softens

everything'. Such processes make it substantially easier to obtain energy from food.

229 See especially Wrangham (2009) and Aiello and Wheeler (1995), who agree that an increase in relative brain size was made possible by a reduction in relative gut size, while diverging somewhat on the precise chronological relationship between brain-size increase among the various species of hominins since australopithecines and the emergence of meat-eating, cooking and a more digestible diet. The point in the present context is that the use of *externalized* combustion (cooking) to make food more digestible meant that less *metabolic* combustion was required to power one's gastrointestinal tract and more was available to power one's brain.

230 'The use of inanimate sources of power', writes historian Paul Kennedy (1989; 188), 'allowed industrial man to transcend the limitations of biology and create spectacular increases in production and wealth without succumbing to the weight of a fast-growing population'.

231 Kauffman, *Investigations* (2000), quoted in Ruiz-Mirazo and Moreno (2004), 241.

232 A nuclear explosion is self-propagating or autocatalytic in the sense that the decay of a uranium nucleus creates a shower of neutrons, each of which may then collide with another uranium nucleus to produce a further shower of neutrons. The chain reaction feeds on itself, mushrooming exponentially (for a while). In a nuclear reactor control rods absorb the excess neutrons, and the energy stays below a threshold value.

233 Steam engines are technically known as 'external' combustion engines (by contrast with the 'internal' combustion engines of modern-day cars), in that the fuel is burnt *outside* the engine, in an exterior boiler. However, this distinction is not relevant in the present context: the combustion of an external combustion engine is external in relation to the engine, but internal in relation to the 'system' as a whole. The difference is one of efficiency.

234 Aristotle, *De Anima*, (Book I.2) 404a; Aristotle (1986), 133.

235 *Phaedrus*, 245e; in the *Laws*, Plato says that 'soul' is the name that language gives to 'the motion that can move itself' (894c-895b). Plato sees this self-movement as evidence of the immortality of the soul insofar as that which moves itself – that which is the sole source and initiator of its own actions – can move without cease. The reason for Plato's leap from self-motion to immortality is that he (perhaps understandably) neglects thermodynamics and the need for *fuel*. The self-caused movement that he envisages is the logical equivalent of Baron von Münchhausen dragging himself from the morass by his own hair – the sort of sleight-of-hand of which only gods and nobodies are capable (see Introduction, page 28).

236 This too was mocked by Aristotle in *On the Soul* (Book I.2; 404b) and has usually been given short shrift by commentators. If the concept of 'number' is taken to denote something akin to a ratio, harmony or attunement, however, the notion seems less silly. In such terms, soul becomes a form of self-moving harmony or self-attunement.

237 This is hardly surprising given that the original French 'automobile' had gauchely yoked together a Greek prefix with a Latin root word.

238 Let's say wood rather than coal for the sake of the argument; it is too much to ask Cugnot's lumbering contraption to engage in sophisticated mining operations at this stage of the thought experiment. Even as it is, the reader will be requested to engage in a fairly generous suspension of disbelief.

239 Ieropoulos et al. (2003), 792; David McFarland refers to 'energy autonomy' (2008; 15). One of the earliest examples of an energetically autonomous 'robot' was the work of W. Grey Walter in 1950, who gave his tortoise-like 'species' the mock-biological name of *Machina speculatrix* and referred to the individuals as Elmer and Elsie. See W. Grey Walter (1950).
240 Kelly et al. (2000), 470.
241 Ibid., 471. See Chapter 6, page 240–41, for further examples of externalized digestion.
242 Ibid. As Kelly and colleagues put it, even with unlimited supplies of slugs SlugBot is at best 'on the borderline of survivability'. This is because its mode of energy recovery is 'likely to be at least an order of magnitude worse than any biological system' (474).
243 By contrast, the small, solar-powered drones that are currently being developed will doubtless attract unlimited military and commercial funding. Work is also in progress on drones that can 'scavenge' energy by perching like birds on power lines. The 'selfhood' of drones requires a study in its own right. On new technologies for extending the limited flight times of small drones, see Hambling (2015), 126–37.
244 See Brodbeck et al. (2015).
245 McFarland (2008), 14.
246 McFarland draws parallels with the selective breeding of turkeys and other domesticated animals by humans. Here too the evolution of species is closely tied up with the satisfaction of market demand (ibid., 28–30).
247 Such marketplace selection is strikingly evident in the case of small drones, whose 'reproductive' success depends upon their ability to satisfy their human users. On the evolution of drones see Hambling (2015).
248 Many thanks go to Adam Stokes of Edinburgh University for drawing my attention to EcoMow.
249 One way round this quandary is the use of batteries. These circumvent – or at least postpone – the need for self-fuelling, but also represent a restriction on autonomy. Deeper levels of autonomy involve the robot being able to locate, harvest or hunt, and assimilate its own fuel, as illustrated by the small drones that are capable of feeding on solar energy or recharging themselves by perching on power lines to scavenge from the electricity grid (or doing both).
250 McFarland (2008), 15: Kelly and colleagues, the designers of SlugBot, refer to 'computational' autonomy, an ability to carry out actions independently.
251 Ibid., 31.
252 Ibid., 34.
253 Ibid., 43.
254 On self-assembly, see Introduction. Self-assembly is difficult to conceive on this macroscopic scale, but not impossible on principle. A car with a self-repairing or self-healing body would certainly seem closer to biological selfhood, albeit only on a rather superficial level. On self-healing materials, see for example Hager et al. (2010) and Hansen et al. (2009).
255 Ruiz-Mirazo et al. (2004), 332–33: biological systems, they continue, 'are component production systems (chemical networks) that manage their material and energetic resources in such a way that they continuously accomplish a global self-construction dynamics in a plastic way'.

256 For an image of cellular self-production, see the online animation by the excellent *Kurzgesagt* (now known as 'In a Nutshell'), at https://www.youtube.com/watch?v=QOCaacO8wus, who suggest that we 'imagine driving a car at 100 km an hour while constantly rebuilding every single part of it with stuff [we] collect from the street'.

257 By contrast, modern-day transplantation even makes a machine-like replacement of parts possible, although the immune system – one of our primeval forms of self-containment – does what it can to resist this disruption of selfhood.

258 Aboobaker (2011), 304–11.

259 Dennett (1996), 70.

260 Ibid., 71; 74–80.

261 On proteins as computational elements and the cell 'wiring' they form, see Bray (2009), 71–108. Bray writes: 'the term *biochemical circuits* is flawed in several respects, a product, no doubt, of our propensity to attach spatial metaphors to processes of all kinds. In reality, a signal traveling through a cell is a change in the numbers of specific molecules at particular locations. Signals move from one place to another by diffusion and the influence of enzyme catalysis. ... Try mapping all the protein-protein interactions in even a small region of the cell, and you will create a mass of densely interwoven lines impossible to unpack' (87, 89).

262 In fact, the Introduction made two references to tautology, i.e. to propositions considered logically necessary and whose negation is self-contradictory. The first was the tautological understanding of selfhood in terms of the proposition 'I = I'; i.e. your 'self' is what you are. This was dismissed as an unhelpful or vacuous account of selfhood.

The second reference to tautology was to the claim that selves are inherently and reflexively 'selfish' (in a sense related to their intrinsic reflexivity). This claim would be regarded by many as incorrect rather than as tautological. In fact, the claim is that a proper understanding of the concept 'self ' shows it to be associated by definition – tautologically or analytically – with a certain understanding of the concept of 'selfishness'. This tautology is not useless, because it involves a reconsideration and re-examination of the concepts of 'selfhood' and 'selfishness'; we do not normally face up to this definitional connection between selfhood and selfishness. On the contrary, we resist it vehemently as an attack on our moral dignity.

263 It is not to be understood as a hypothesis providing a 'deeper' (possibly even unconscious) reason underlying all particular actions, whether apparently altruistic or otherwise. It is not a psychological theory of action, although to the extent that the concept of 'action' is logically linked to that of 'selfhood' it may be considered an analysis of what 'action' means.

264 Cynicism of this sort finds famous expression in the 17th-century maxims of La Rochefoucauld (1665; 1976), for whom our virtues are but concealed vices and our honour and nobility are rooted in amour-propre. It is also essential to the type of satirical comedy that understands itself in terms of an unmasking of hypocrisy.

265 Actor and spectator thus commonly hold conflicting views on what a person's interests actually *are*, as when people smoke 80 cigarettes a day or sacrifice their life for a base or noble cause. Yet even in cases where a person's behaviour may seem (to an onlooker) to be in patent contradiction with

his or her own interests, the tautological bottom line is that – in the absence of outer constraints – that person still does what he or she is in some sense *motivated to do*.
266 See Parfit (1986), 3–4, on the self-interest theory of rationality.
267 This is a tautology to the extent that it is part of what the concept of rationality means.
268 Aristotle (1953), 274; (1915), 68b. The concept at issue here is the venerable Greek notion of *philautia* or self-love rather than the English 'selfishness', which only dates back to the 17th century. Traditional Christian thought generally dismissed *philautia* as akin to excessive pride, running counter to the principle of *agape*, the selfless concern for others.
269 Ibid. (1953), 275; (1915), 68b–69a.
270 G. E. Moore (1948), 96. Moore himself dismissed the doctrine of ethical egoism as contradictory. The contradiction, as Moore understood it, was between the absolute or universal goodness he demanded of an ethical principle (the 'good in itself') and the relative nature of what is good 'for me'.
271 Another formulation is provided by Jesse Kalin in 'In Defense of Egoism', in Gauthier, ed. (1970), 64–87.
272 On this level, the selfless bomb disposal expert should be understood as behaving in his or her own interests as well as for the collective good. The moral satisfaction derived from the job – say, the feeling of serving the community – in some sense 'outweighs' the risk to life and limb. This is precisely what makes such people admirable (by contrast with someone who performs such a task *under coercion*). Admirable people are people who *want* to help others.
273 Here we may draw a distinction between *extrinsic* self-reward (social or divine approval, reputation or material gain) and *intrinsic* self-reward (the pleasure of helping, altruism as an end in itself). Only the latter provides a genuine foundation for morality.
274 See Hobbes (1651; 1968), 183–88.
275 Dawkins (1976; 1989), 28.
276 Ibid., 33.
277 Ibid., 36. See also ibid., 86: '"Good" genes are blindly selected as those that survive in the gene pool. This is not a theory; it is not even an observed fact: it is a tautology'.
278 Ibid., 33–34: 'a gene is not indivisible, but it is seldom divided', he writes. 'It is either definitely present or definitely absent in the body of any given individual'.
279 Ibid., 36.
280 Ibid., 2.
281 Dawkins (2004), 194.
282 Midgley (1979), 439.
283 Ibid., 451.
284 See also Daston and Mitman (2005), 3: 'Although a metaphor like the "selfish gene" might be tolerated in popularizations, to use the term literally is to be accused of making a category mistake. Genes (or radios or planets) are not the kind of things that can think or feel; to believe otherwise is considered a mark of childishness or feeblemindedness'. In these terms, what Dawkins is saying is not merely empirically wrong but logically or philosophically 'absurd' in the sense of being self-contradictory, unverifiable, nonsensical, infinitely regressive, or simply so self-evidently and

flagrantly aberrant that no one in their right mind could possibly assent to it. But how are we to distinguish between an absurd statement and one that may indeed be true or false? What is absurd to one generation of scientists may be self-evident to the next. On the problematic notion of 'category mistakes' (as opposed to mere misclassifications) see Passmore (1961), 119–47.

285 Ibid., 448.

286 Dawkins (1976; 1989), 45: 'at times, gene language gets a bit tedious, and for brevity and vividness we shall lapse into metaphor. But we shall always keep a sceptical eye on our metaphors, to make sure they can be translated back into gene language if necessary'.

287 Dawkins (1981), 557.

288 Whatever the case, Dawkins is being consistent to the extent that his above-cited definition of genetic selfishness incorporates the idea of genes 'behaving' in such a way as to increase their own chances of survival within the gene pool. The concept of 'behaviour' will be taken up again below and in greater depth in a forthcoming work.

289 Dawkins (1976; 1989), 24: 'Genes have no foresight. They do not plan ahead. Genes just are, some genes more so than others, and that is all there is to it'. Subsequently, with precautionary inverted commas, he writes: 'the true "purpose" of DNA is to survive, no more and no less' (45).

290 Any conception of selfishness or its opposite presupposes an axiological framework, an implicit theory of what is good and bad in the world, to the extent that egoism is taken to focus on what is good for oneself, and altruism on what is good for other selves. 'Pleasure' and 'pain' have been frequent candidates for the 'good' and the 'bad', respectively. It is not clear that mere persistence or replication or proliferation are 'good' except insofar as these *ground the possibility* for some sort of pleasure. Many humans have traditionally aspired to immortality, but what is the point of immortality devoid of either pleasure or pain, well-being or suffering? In what sense can this be said to be 'better' than non-existence?

291 Midgley (1979), 446.

292 The relationship between selfhood and the brain is anything but straightforward. Bereft of pain receptors and incapable of movement, the brain seems strangely un-self-like. Hidden away in an exoskeletal box, it lacks any form of pre-reflective self-awareness. Without the benefit of post-mortem examinations of *other* selves, we would be more or less oblivious to its presence. It is more akin to a *blind spot* of the self. If anything, however, this perhaps makes the analogy with DNA all the more robust.

293 Benner (1999), 126.

294 Ruiz-Mirazo and Moreno (2004), 255: the qualification ('in large measure') reflects the fact that chromosomal structures are proteinaceous in nature and subject to ongoing processes of epigenetic modification. In this respect it would be misleading to imply that the genetic material is wholly 'off-line'.

295 Santoro and Joyce (1997), 4262.

296 Benner (1999), 129.

297 Ibid.

298 Ibid., 130: 'A biopolymer specialized for catalysis must be able to change its physical properties rapidly with few changes in its sequence, enabling it to explore "function space" during divergent evolution. A biopolymer specialized for genetics must have physical properties largely unchanged even after substantial change in sequence'.

299 Lincoln and Joyce (2009), 1229–32. In fact, the system in question is a cross-catalytic system in which two RNA enzymes catalyse each other's synthesis from a total of four component substrates. In other words, a first ribozyme catalyzes the joining together of two oligonucleotides to form a complementary ribozyme, which in turn catalyzes the joining together of two other oligonucleotides to create more of the first ribozyme. More recently, Sczepanski and Joyce (2014) have discovered a single type of ribozyme that is capable of catalyzing the production of copies of *itself*, albeit in the form of its mirror image. The mirror-image ribozyme is in turn able to catalyze the synthesis of the original. This solves a particular problem associated with the earlier work on systems of self-replicating ribozymes, namely the tendency of RNA to form base pairs with the RNA it is supposed to be copying, drastically curbing its enzymatic efficiency. This does not occur when the ribozyme works cross-chirally, i.e. on opposite-handed RNA. On the chirality or 'handedness' of biological molecules, see for example Rutherford (2013), 38–42.
300 Lincoln and Joyce (2009), 1232.
301 Thompson (2007), 123–24.
302 Ibid., 185–86. Thompson concludes: 'this notion of information as something that preexists its own expression in the cell, and that is not affected by the developmental matrix of the organism and environment, is a reification that has no explanatory value' (187).
303 The incoherencies associated with dualism carry less weight when the focus is on RNA, which – as we have seen – unites its function as a template ('information') with its biological activity as a catalyst. Yet this does not invalidate Thompson's objections to the misuse of the term 'information'.
304 See Jonas (1966; 2001), 52, who describes Weismann's theory as 'a strange parody of the Cartesian model of two noncommunicating substances': For the Weismann doctrine and a critique of its validity, see also Thompson (2007), 174–79.
305 Thompson (2007), 175.
306 See Fletcher and Mullins (2010), 490–91.
307 See Cavalier-Smith (2000), 176: 'Two universal constituents of cells never form de novo: chromosomes and membranes. ... Genetic membranes are as much a part of an organism's germ line as DNA genomes; they could not be replaced if accidentally lost, even if all the genes remained'.
308 Goldenfeld and Woese (2007), 369.
309 Ibid.
310 Moreira and López-García (2009), 310: given such genomic plasticity, 'trying to reconstruct the evolutionary history of each individual gene of a viral lineage and inferring HGT events is possible, but such histories will not reflect the evolution of the viral lineage as a whole, as lineages cannot have genomic persistence in the presence of high HGT rates'.
311 See Breitbart and Rohwer (2005), 281: such gene clusters are autonomous enough to move around 'while retaining their functionality': distinct phage genomes can then assemble themselves by a process of 'mixing and matching' their component modules.
312 Or perhaps selfhood is again better viewed as a function of continuity rather than identity.
313 Whereas most of the roughly 20,000 protein-coding genes in the human genome have a counterpart in all other vertebrates (from sharks to chimpanzees) and over a third (37%) are even

shared with bacteria, an analysis of viruses from four oceanic regions has revealed some 1.8 million viral genes, the great majority of which show no recognizable homology to genes from microbes, animals, plants or any other virus known to science. See Suttle (2007), 806. Koonin and Dolja (2013) refer to this vast realm of previously undetected sequences as the 'dark matter' of the viral world. In recent years 'dark matter' has become a rather commonplace scientific metaphor for stuff about which disquietingly little is known.

314 Goldenfeld and Woese (2007), 369.
315 See review by Boto (2009), 820; Dagan et al. (2008).
316 Lawrence and Ochman (1998); see review by McInerney et al. (2008), 277.
317 Ibid., 278.
318 Harold (2001), 205–6.
319 Medini et al. (2005), 589.
320 See Turney (2015), 38.
321 See Medini et al. (2005), 589. Species such as *E. coli* and *Streptococcus agalactiae* are accordingly said to have an 'open' pan-genome.
322 Ibid., 591–92.
323 Jain et al. (1999).
324 Ibid., 3805.
325 However, see Sorek et al. (2007), 1451–52: although transfer-resistant genes were identified from a wide range of prokaryotes, 'no single gene was untransferable among all genomes examined'.
326 This is corroborated by a noteworthy exception to the link between genes encoding translation apparatus and resistance to HGT, *viz.* the aminoacyl-tRNA synthetases (aaRS), which have a marked propensity to engage in HGT. Woese et al. (2000; 206) explain why the synthetases show such unusual behaviour: 'The aaRSs are in essence modular components of the cell; they function in isolation from the rest of the translation apparatus and from the rest of the cell, except for their individual contacts in each case with a small subset of the tRNAs. Because of this and because of their universality, the aaRSs can function in a wide spectrum of cellular environments, often without disadvantage to the host'. Remarkable in this context is that genes for as many as seven of the 20 aminoacyl-tRNA synthetases are even found in a family of large viruses, the nucleocytoplasmic large DNA viruses (which include mimivirus and mamavirus and which we shall encounter again below).
327 Medini et al. (2005), 593.
328 See Itoh et al. (2002).
329 Tamas et al. (2002), 2376–79.
330 Silva et al. (2003).
331 See Wernegreen (2002), 857.
332 See, for example, Boto (2009), 823; McInerney (2008), 277; Medini et al. (2005), 593.
333 The concept of the species as a self-contained self will be the subject of a forthcoming work.
334 Sonea and Mathieu (2001), 68, 70.
335 Goldfenfeld and Woese (2007), 369.

336 See Gould (1983), 174. A similar scale of selfhood informs the realm of eukaryotes. With or without scare quotes (depending, presumably, on whether or not we are willing to ascribe full selfhood to the entity in question), selfishness can be found among genes, cells, multicellular organisms and species.
337 Orgel and Crick (1980), 604.
338 Clark et al. (2012).
339 See for example Carey (2015), 40–42.
340 Dawkins (1982; 1999), 159: 'It is becoming increasingly evident that, in addition to the large, orderly chromosomes with their well-regimented gavotte, cells are home to a motley riff-raff of DNA and RNA fragments, cashing in on the perfect environment provided by the cellular apparatus'. Orgel and Crick (1980) introduced the term 'junk' (604) but this lacks the dimension of (humorous or poetic) anthropomorphism present in imagery of hangers-on and parasites, knaves and rascals.
341 Gould (1984), 173: Gould chose the term 'self-centered' in an attempt to avoid the anthropomorphism and the 'opprobrious overtones' associated with 'selfish'. In common usage, however, 'self-centred' and 'selfish' are near-synonyms with equally powerful anthropomorphic associations and equally negative psychological connotations.
342 Ibid., 174–75. Gould's conception of self-centred DNA illustrated his deep understanding of the hierarchical nature of evolutionary processes, and how hierarchical levels of selfhood are not walled off and separate from one another, but leak and interact through complex ties of feedback.
343 Orgel and Crick (1980), 606: Orgel and Crick believed that this was unlikely to be the norm: most selfish DNA would not have a specific function. However, there is now an increasing awareness that the epithet 'junk' was a misnomer.
344 Dawkins (1982; 1999) makes the distinction between allelic and laterally spreading outlaws. I have added non-genomic DNAs as these elements have been considered 'selfish' as well. Nonetheless, the following classification of selfish DNA makes no claims to exhaustiveness.
345 Ibid., 133. For a detailed account of allelic outlaws see 133–55.
346 In fact, a common form of meiotic drive requires two closely associated genes, one producing a toxin that kills gametes *without* the gene complex, and the other protecting gametes *with* the gene complex against the toxin. See Maynard Smith and Szathmáry (1999), 96. A rather similar toxin-antidote mechanism underlies another selfish element, called the *Medea* gene, which is found in the flour beetle, *Tribolium castaneum*. See Beeman et al. (1992), 89–92.
347 Quoted in Dawkins (1982; 1999), 138; see also Maynard Smith and Szathmáry (1999), 23–24, 96.
348 As Dawkins himself explicitly points out (ibid., 139), the proponents of the 'parliament of genes' hypothesis are well aware that they are using a metaphor.
349 Ridley (1999), 110.
350 This is for the simple reason that while female mammals have two X chromosomes, males have an X and a Y, so three quarters of all sex chromosomes are X chromosomes (ibid., 111).
351 Ibid., 108, quoting a paper by Amos and Harwood (1998), 'Factors affecting levels of genetic diversity in natural populations', published in the *Philosophical Transactions of the Royal Society of London, Series B*.

352 Dawkins (1982; 1999), 145.
353 Ibid., 144; see also Dawkins (1976; 1989), 89.
354 Queller et al. (2003), 105–6. As the authors put it, 'when wild-type cells are mixed with *csA*-knockout cells, the wild type is more altruistic, but is also able preferentially to direct the benefits to other wild-type cells. Both properties derive directly from homophilic cell adhesion of the protein encoded by *csA*'.
355 It has been suggested that the green-beard gene is not in fact an outlaw, since other genes within the genome's 'parliament of genes' will actually benefit by sharing a body with a green-beard gene. For a discussion, see Dawkins (1982; 1999), 148–50.
356 Harold (2001), 71.
357 There are other theories of the origins of mitochondria, for example that they were formed in early eukaryotes by a compartmentalization of plasmid-like entities within internalized host membrane. In the present work, however, I shall follow the consensus in assuming them to be bacterial in origin. This is supported in particular by the fact that they encode their own ribosomes, which bear a closer resemblance to bacterial ones than to eukaryotic ones. In addition to being broadly accepted in contemporary thought, endosymbiotic theory is conceptually feasible at the very least, and has fascinating implications for any theory of minimal selfhood. See Archibald (2014), 66–87, for a summary of the arguments.
358 See Clark et al. (2012); Schnable and Wise (1998). Cytoplasmic male sterility has also been found to occur in crop species such as beet, carrot, maize, onion, rice, rye, sorghum, sunflower and wheat. See also Maynard Smith and Szathmáry (1999), 23–24.
359 See Schnable and Wise (1998), 178.
360 Clark et al. (2012): this deletion-bearing mtDNA is a selfish element in that it benefits from a marked transmission bias relative to variants without the deletion, yet it produces chemically reactive molecules that are damaging to the organisms themselves.
361 On endogenous retroviruses see for example Belshaw et al. (2004); Magiorkinis et al. (2012).
362 Belshaw et al. (2004), 4894; Dewannieux et al. (2006), 1548; Kazazian (2004) gives a figure of 8.5 percent for the presence of LTR retrotransposons in the human genome.
363 See Magiorkinis et al. (2012), 7385.
364 Ibid., 7388: mammalian ERVs are believed to have 'evolved independently into retrotransposons multiple times, and this process underlies their relative abundance in mammal genomes. Integrating this information into the known biology of ERVs suggests that genome invasion by XRVs generates ERV lineages that typically expand through reinfection in the initial stages but often adapt to become intracellular retrotransposons. This adaptation leads to the degradation of the now-redundant *env* gene and confers increased intracellular but diminished interhost mobility'. Among invertebrates, however, there have been various instances of LTR-retrotransposons being converted back to retrovirus-like elements through the *acquisition* of an *env*-like gene.
365 The impression of living mobility is exemplified by the efforts of Thierry Heidmann and colleagues in France to bring an apparently degenerate HERV 'back to life'. To this end, they focused on the most recently active family of endogenous retroviruses, the HERV-K(HML2) family, which

first integrated into the genome of the common ancestor of humans and Old World monkeys over 30 million years ago, but is thought to have amplified considerably in the last five million years. By comparing mutated sequences of a particular retrovirus-like segment in different people – mutations that had presumably occurred *since* the 'endogenization' of the retrovirus in the genomes of ancestral humans – Heidmann and colleagues were able to infer the DNA sequence that must have originally infected those genomes. When this DNA sequence was synthesized and inserted into human cells in culture, the resulting provirus sequence was shown to contain the *gag, pol, env* and other genes expected of a bona-fide retrovirus, to produce viral particles exhibiting all the structural and functional properties of such a retrovirus, and thus to be able to infect human cells. Even though the resuscitated retrovirus – appropriately named *Phoenix* for having risen from the 'dead' – in fact shows a relatively low level of infectivity, the amplification of the HERV-K family subsequent to infection by *Phoenix* is thought to have involved reinfection and an extracellular pathway rather than retrotransposition. See Dewannieux et al. (2006).

366 Goodier and Kazazian (2008), 23.

367 Both LTR and non-LTR retrotransposons duplicate via RNA intermediates that are reverse transcribed and inserted at new loci on the genome. Whereas the reverse transcription of the former takes place in viral or virus-like particles in the cytoplasm, the retrotransposition of the latter involves a different mechanism whereby RNA copies of the element are shuttled back into the nucleus, with the reverse transcription taking place on the DNA itself. See Kazazian (2004), 1626–27; Goodier and Kazazian (2008), 23–24.

368 On LINE-1, see especially Cordaux and Batzer (2009), 692; also Goodier and Kazazian (2008), 23–25; Belgnaoui et al. (2006). The second most abundant of the four clades of autonomous mammalian non-LTR retrotransposons is LINE-2, now fossilized and inactive, which accounts for over two percent of the human genome. It takes up a greater proportion of the genome in the non-placental mammals, i.e. marsupials and monotremes; see Goodier and Kazazian (2008), 24.

369 Kazazian (2004), 1628; see also Carey (2015), 39–40.

370 Schulz (2006) gives a germ-line retrotransposition rate of one event per 100 births; Cordaux and Batzer (2009) give a rate of one event per 20 births; Kazazian (2004) suggests that one in 50 human infants has a new genomic L1 insertion, while Stenglein and Harris (2006) suggest one in 10–250.

371 Kazazian (2004), 1627.

372 Ibid., 1628.

373 Cordaux and Batzer (2009), 692. Perhaps unsurprisingly, L1 elements mobilize themselves preferentially, their proteins tending to act on the RNA that encodes them; they are said to have a 'cis preference'. Even so, *Alu* elements continue to benefit from the 'trans-mobilization' provided by L1.The profusion of *Alu* sequences in the human genome is thought to be the result of an expansion some 40 million years ago, when the *Alu* elements of the era apparently had special access to the enzymatic machinery provided by three now inactive L1 families. During this period, there would have been approximately one *Alu* retrotransposition event per birth. See Kazazian (2004).

374 On DNA transposons see Kazazian (2004), 1626.

375 See Engels (1997), 14.

376 Cordaux and Batzer (2009), 691.
377 On the P element in general see Engels (1997), 11–15.
378 Maynard Smith and Szathmáry (1999), 98–99.
379 Ibid.
380 As Bertram Gerber has pointed out to me, modified P elements are used in experimental manipulations of the *Drosophila* genome and may thus be said to contribute to *Drosophila*'s success as a laboratory animal. In this respect, it might be argued that the P elements *do* benefit the fruit fly.
381 The other two families are retrons and diversity-generating retroelements (DGRs). On retrons see Lampson et al. (2005); on DGRs see Medhekar and Miller (2007).
382 On group II introns see Lambowitz and Zimmerly (2004); Toro et al. (2007).
383 The mobility of group II introns is primarily site-specific. Group II introns typically move to alleles that lack them, a process called 'retrohoming'. In this, they are rather like the 'allelic outlaws' encountered above, which replace rival alleles with copies of themselves. In addition to retrohoming, however, there is evidence of low-frequency retrotransposition to non-allelic sites that merely *resemble* the normal homing site, thus allowing for the element to become more widely dispersed in the genome. This is known as 'ectopic' transposition; see Lambowitz and Zimmerly (2004), 16.
384 Ibid., 23. This is only a tendency; some group II introns are also found in essential genes; see Toro et al. (2007), 354.
385 See Lambowitz and Zimmerly (2004), 24, for alternative hypotheses.
386 Ibid., 3.
387 See Kazazian (2004), 1630. Although non-LTR retrotransposons account for roughly a third of the human genome, and LTR retrotransposons for 8.5 percent, the figure does vary from species to species and is substantially lower (for example) in the fruit fly *Drosophila*, where LTR and non-LTR retrotransposons account for only 2.7 and 0.9 percent of the genome, respectively.
388 Goodier and Kazazian (2008), 26.
389 Ibid.
390 Orgel and Crick (1980), 605.
391 See Money (2014), 12. The genome of another amoebozoan, *Polychaos dubium*, is reported to be over twice as big again, although McGrath and Katz (2004; 33) point out that it has yet to be measured with current molecular techniques. Even if these figures are an order of magnitude out, the point stands.
392 For an exhaustive account of the possible effects of retrotransposition on genome evolution, see Cordaux and Batzer (2009), 694–700; On insertion mutagenesis see ibid., 695.
393 See Schulz (2006), 4.
394 See Di-Poï et al. (2009), 605–6.
395 See ibid., 602. However, the exclusion of transposable elements from *Hox* clusters is neither absolute nor universal. Though a general feature of vertebrates, it does not extend to the single *Hox* cluster in protostomes such as arthropods and molluscs. Among vertebrates, the exclusion seems not to apply to squamates such as the green anole lizard, where the *Hox* clusters show a 'massive accumulation' of non-LTR retrotransposons. The presence of such elements, it is conjectured, may

have laid the foundation for the evolution of the abundant morphological novelties characteristic of squamates and the ensuing diversity among squamate body plans. Even mouse and human *Hox* gene clusters contain *a few* selfish elements, mainly non-LTR retrotransposons, albeit in positions of 'minimal functional and regulatory impact' (ibid., 607–8).

396 Yoder et al. (1997); Carey (2015), 121.
397 Schulz (2006), 6.
398 Ibid., 9.
399 See Hanahan and Weinberg (2000), 61–62, on the evasion of apoptosis as one of the defining features of cancer.
400 See Goodier and Kazazian (2008), 29; Carey (2015), 255–58.
401 A recent study has suggested that the human genome may contain at least 800 microRNAs, each of which may recognize many mRNAs. See Bentwich et al. (2005); also Carey (2015), 257–58.
402 Piriyapongsa et al. (2007) found 55 miRNAs to be derived from mobile elements and predict the presence of many more. Those in question come from all the major classes of transposable element. The ancient and now fossilized LINE-2 (L2) family of non-LTR retrotransposons is one of the major sources, as are DNA transposons, but elements derived from L1 and *Alu* are also represented.
403 A fourth mode of genomic self-protection involves a family of enzymes called the APOBEC proteins, which – by induced hypermutation and other mechanisms still to be fully determined – are able to block the replication of a wide range of retroelements; see for example Bogerd et al. (2006); Esnault et al. (2008); Stenglein and Harris (2006).
404 The significance of the notion of 'containment' in the context of a host's relationship to a parasite or symbiont will become clearer in Chapter 6.
405 I have put 'symbiotic' in quotation marks because symbiosis generally denotes an association of two living things; here its meaning is being extended to include an association of merely life-like or self-like things.
406 Goodier and Kazazian (2008), 23.
407 See Jordan et al. (2003), who found roughly 24 percent of the promoters analysed (475 out of 2004) to contain sequences derived from transposable elements.
408 See Goodier and Kazazian (2008), 27.
409 One of the most prominent examples is a protein called syncytin, which evolved from a HERV *env*-encoded protein that enables retroviruses to target, attach to and penetrate specified cell types by means of membrane fusion. This protein has now been appropriated for the formation of the syncytial cells (multinucleated cells produced by multiple cell fusions) required in the outer part of the mammalian placenta during pregnancy. It has been joked that without this protein – i.e. without the genetic invader from which we acquired it – humans would still be laying eggs.
410 See Nakamura and Cech (1998) for an analysis of the various possible relationships.
411 Ibid., 589.
412 Interestingly, telomerase is not the only solution to the problem of telomere maintenance. The fruit fly *Drosophila* lacks functional telomerase and uses a variety of other non-LTR

retrotransposons to replicate its telomeres. If telomerase was indeed already present in ancestral eukaryotic cells, it may well be that *Drosophila* lost its telomerase in the course of its evolution but subsequently recruited a different retroelement for the same purpose. See ibid.

413 See Muotri et al. (2009); Muotri et al. (2010). On L1 retrotransposition in the human brain, see also Baillie et al. (2011); Singer et al. (2010).

414 See Baillie et al. (2011). The other side of the coin is the possibility of L1-induced neurological pathologies.

415 See Agrawal et al. (1998). In fact, evidence for the transposon has also been found in non-vertebrate deuterostomes such as the lancelet or amphioxus (a chordate) and the purple sea urchin (an echinoderm); see Holland et al. (2008). It can thus not be ruled out that the transposon made its 'hop' before vertebrates had appeared on the scene and was *subsequently* co-opted by the adaptive immune system.

416 It is by means of this diversity-generating mechanism that a genome such as ours with considerably fewer than 25,000 genes is able to produce tens of millions of distinct antibodies.

417 Plasterk (1998), 718–19.

418 A different type of self-defence mechanism may also involve the most recently acquired human ERV family, HERV-K, which appears to serve an immunoprotective function by inhibiting viral infection in early embryonic cells; see Grow et al. (2015).

419 See Rogozin et al. (2012).

420 See Carey (2015), 238.

421 For an overview of alternative hypotheses on the evolutionary origins of introns, see Rogozin et al. (2012).

422 Lane (2009a), 116.

423 Carey (2015), 238.

424 Goodier and Kazazian (2008), 28.

425 Kazazian (2004), 1631.

426 Again, this is to say that the attribution of 'interests' implies an ability to pursue them.

427 It would be less imprecise, though a lot more clumsy, to speak not of selves-within-selves, but of self-like-or-selfish-entities-within-selves, given that we have not yet established the extent to which viruses comply with the criteria for full selfhood. There are times, however, when pretensions to conceptual rigour are best sacrificed for the sake of a slightly snappier title, or relegated to a footnote.

428 This claim is based on an understanding of viruses as entities that replicate themselves but do not maintain themselves by means of metabolism. In these very provisional terms, a virus is a self-replicating and self-containing but not a self-maintaining entity. All these points will come under scrutiny below.

429 The apparent synonymy of 'being a self' and 'having a self' normally goes unnoticed. In the case of humans, a similar logic comes to light in how we talk about character and personality. I may be said both to have and to be a certain sort of personality; my identity too is something I both have and am. What is implied is an association of selfhood with self-possession or self-ownership that will be called into question below.

430 On the distinction between self-organization and self-assembly see Introduction, esp. pages 63ff.
431 Fraenkel-Conrat and Williams (1955); on viral self-assembly in general see also Kushner (1969).
432 Budin and Devaraj (2011).
433 Kushner (1969), 315-19; on the structure and morphogenesis of T4 phage see Leiman et al. (2003).
434 See Introduction, page 32.
435 Thompson (2007), 123.
436 A prominent case is the relatively huge mimivirus, which has a 1.2 Mb genome (larger than many bacterial genomes) and includes various genes involved in transcription and translation. See Moreira and López-García (2009), 309.
437 For a discussion of the debate between cytoplasmic and genocentric views, see ibid., esp. 306-7.
438 Ibid., 307.
439 Ibid., quoting Alexander and Bridges.
440 See ibid.
441 On movement proteins see Kehr and Buhtz (2008), esp. 86-87; also Lough and Lucas (2006), esp. 210-12.
442 On coat proteins, see ibid.
443 See Chapter 3, pages 119-20.
444 See Moreira and López-García (2009), 310.
445 See Breitbart and Rohwer (2005), 281. Many virologists prefer to limit the concept of 'species' to a context of sexually reproducing organisms, yet viruses still need to be classified and the word 'species' is often used. Since 1991, the International Committee on Taxonomy of Viruses (ICTV) has accepted a definition that combines the idea of a lineage with that of an ecological niche ('a virus species is a polythetic class of viruses that constitutes a replicating lineage and occupies a particular niche'). Such a 'polythetic' approach means that members of the group share many but not all properties, and that no single property is necessary or sufficient to define group membership. This has not met with universal approval, and virus taxonomy remains a controversial issue. See Van Regenmortel et al. (2013); O'Malley (2014), 78.
446 The term 'virosphere' is used, for example, by Suttle (2007), 801, who defines it as 'the portion of the Earth in which viruses occur or which is affected by viruses'; the term 'virus world' is also in currency.
447 In the context of micro-organisms in general, O'Malley (2014; 164) cites the well-known words of the microbiologist Baas Becking: 'everything is everywhere, but the environment selects'. She also provides a nuanced discussion and review of this assumption (ibid.).
448 See Koonin et al. (2006) for a fuller discussion.
449 Hendrix et al. (1999) describe how a global gene pool might work for dsDNA (double-stranded) bacteriophages (though their description is not couched in terms of a virosphere, let alone a 'selfish' virosphere). They describe a model 'in which all of the dsDNA phage and prophage genomes are mosaics with access by horizontal exchange to a large common gene pool. However, access is clearly not uniform.' The frequency and ease of access 'depends strongly on the number of barriers (e.g., host

ranges) between any particular sequence and that phage and, therefore, how many individual steps of genetic exchange are required to bring them together' (2196).
450 Koonin et al. (2006).
451 Ibid.
452 Many scientists, for example, espouse 'cell-first' hypotheses for the origins of viruses, according to which viruses derive from a cellular context from which they either 'broke free' as infectious systems in their own right or evolved reductively through a gradual process of functional streamlining that dispensed with all genes superfluous to their parasitism. See ibid.
453 Koonin and Dolja (2013), 549.
454 Whether this global self is given the appellation 'biosphere' or the more unwieldy 'biosphere + virosphere' depends on whether or not viruses are themselves considered *part* of the biosphere.
455 Suttle (2007), 802–3; in other words, viruses represent roughly 94 percent of all RNA or DNA-containing particles.
456 The statistics are bewildering: if tailed phages were lined up end to end they would span the distance between the Earth and the Sun more than 10^{13} times, reaching out beyond the nearest 60 galaxies. See Hendrix (2002), 471; Hendrix (2003), 506; see also Zimmer (2011), 42.
457 Suttle (2007), 802–3. However, this still represents a weight equivalent to 75 million blue whales. See Zimmer (2011), 42.
458 See Suttle (2007), 803, who cites tentative estimates to the effect that 20–40 percent of the oceans' prokaryotes are wiped out by viral lysis each day, approximately the same percentage as succumb to grazing by protozoa.
459 Less frequently, it may form an extra-chromosomal plasmid in the cytoplasm.
460 Our theoretical imagination serves precisely this purpose of taking us out of ourselves and our selves.
461 Or it may be that the accident-essence dichotomy itself misses the point. However fleetingly or enduringly it lasts, it might be argued, an intrinsically reflexive system – say, a self-regulating or self-organizing system fed by the requisite energy – simply *is* its own end. To be an end in oneself, and an end to oneself, is part of the nature of intrinsic reflexivity. What this does *not* imply is that the *components* of the system – in this case the virosphere or the biosphere or any parts thereof – themselves seek or strive to perpetuate the system. The purposiveness, if such there is, exists at the systemic level.
462 On the history of its discovery see Mukherjee (2011), esp. 349–72.
463 See ibid., 358–59; also Schwartz et al. (1983).
464 Mukherjee (2011), 359.
465 On HPV see Zimmer (2011), 23–29. Unlike RSV, HPV is not a retrovirus but a DNA virus that gets itself incorporated into the host genome as part of a lysogenic cycle.
466 Mankertz (2008), 360. The precise mechanism by which the virus enters the host cell is not clear, but it is thought to occur by endocytosis, a form of cellular engulfment. The steps leading to the release of the virus from the host cell have not yet been clarified either.
467 Zimmer (2011), 10: on rhinovirus, see 9–13; on the equally diminutive influenza virus, see also 15–20.

468 Mills et al. (1967).
469 In other words, a sample of freshly synthesized RNA was extracted from one test tube and added to a second test tube to continue its replicating activity, and a sample from this second test tube was decanted into a third test tube, and so on. In effect, this 'serial transfer' technique simulated a process of Darwinian selection, as for each test-tube 'generation' it was the RNA that multiplied fastest that was passed on to the next test tube in the series; see ibid., 217.
470 Ibid.
471 Ibid., 224.
472 See Dawkins (2004), 591–93.
473 Mills et al. (1967), 224.
474 In the real-life conditions provided by its host *E. coli*, the phage provides just one of the four proteins needed to produce Qβ replicase; the rest are supplied by the bacterium, which produces them anyway for its own purposes.
475 In this they contrast with another class of virus-like elements, designated virusoids or satellite RNAs; these are circular ssRNAs of similar length, but they have a capsid and rely on the presence of a helper virus both for encapsidation and replication.
476 For a general account of viroids, see Daròs et al. (2006); see also Diener (1989).
477 Unlike the *Avsunviroidae*, the *Pospiviroidae* require a host factor for this cleavage to occur.
478 Diener (1989), 9370.
479 Ibid. Another candidate is the self-splicing group II intron we met in the last chapter, but Diener argues that the much greater simplicity of the viroid ribozyme makes it the more likely precursor.
480 On viroid trafficking see especially Ding et al. (2005) and Gómez and Pallás (2004); more generally Kehr and Buhtz (2008) and Lough and Lucas (2006).
481 See below, page 169.
482 Ding et al. (2005), 606.
483 On the capsid-less RNA viruses, see Dolja and Koonin (2012); on the narnaviruses in particular see also Hillman and Cai (2013).
484 Having forfeited their infectivity, the viruses propagate via non-infectious intracellular pathways such as cell division; see Dolja and Koonin (2012). The 'confinement' of the virus to its host leads to peaceful coexistence rather than destructive lysis; no obvious ill effects have been found to be exerted by such viruses. Dolja and Koonin suggest that the origin of the mitoviruses dates back to a bacteriophage that had infected the 'proto-mitochondrial endosymbiont' in the early eukaryotic cell; this subsequently 'resigned' itself to replicating within the evolving mitochondria.
485 For the example of the R64 plasmid see Villarreal (2009), 53–54.
486 Double-stranded RNA viruses such as reovirus and rotavirus – a major cause of gastroenteritis in young children – are particularly susceptible to detection (as non-self) by the host cell, which may often resort to apoptosis as a form of defence. It is presumed to be for this reason that dsRNA virions consist of multiple protein layers and maintain considerable structural integrity within the host. On the structure of dsRNA virions see Bamford et al. (2002), 466–67.
487 Daròs et al. (2006), 593. In other words, viruses are not viroids that happen to wear a coat.

488 Kushner (1969), 307.
489 On mimivirus see Suzan-Monti et al. (2007).
490 See Zauberman et al. (2008), 1110.
491 See Moreira and López-García (2009), 308-9. Such membranes are referred to as 'genetic membranes'.
492 Raoult and Forterre (2008).
493 Ibid., 315. The term 'nucleocapsid' denotes the capsid together with the genetic material it encloses.
494 Ibid., 317.
495 Ibid., 318: it has been found, for example, in viruses that infect the bacterium *E. coli*, the archaeon *Sulfolobus solfataricus* and the eukaryote *Paramecium bursaria*, a single-celled ciliate.
496 Bamford et al. (2002), 468.
497 Raoult and Forterre (2008), 319. A replicon is a genetic unit of replication.
498 Ibid.
499 In an influential essay entitled 'The Concept of Virus' (1957), microbial geneticist André Lwoff pinpointed infectiousness as an essential feature of viruses, yet recoiled at the implication that the concept would therefore exclude proviruses, i.e. non-infectious phases of the life-cycle. A more recent definition characterizes viruses as 'biological entities that infect cells and replicate themselves'; see Breitbart and Rohwer (2005), 278.
500 See Dolja and Koonin (2012).
501 Bamford et al. (2002), 462.
502 Ibid., 462-66.
503 Ibid., 468; see also Moreira and López-García (2009), 308.
504 Bamford et al. (2002), 467-68.
505 Ibid., 468.
506 In these terms, the selfhood of the individual viral particle is completely subsumed by, and subordinate to, the unchanging selfhood of the lineage.
507 Human narrative selfhood in particular tends to depend heavily upon such identity, which grounds my sense of having a fixed personality or character, of being recognizable and identifiable to others and myself, whether through predictable behavioural patterns, style preferences, or the birth mark or tattoo in a public or private place. However, though the fixity implied by personality and identity may be reassuring to us as humans, it is not essential to us as selves; it is the *continuity of a process* that is essential to selfhood, with the possibility of self-change that this always logically harbours.
508 A capsid must be able to interact with the host, although it is precisely the rapidly evolving host-specific diversity of viruses that Bamford and colleagues seek to exclude from selfhood as mere 'noise'. It is significant that the authors also pinpoint the viral envelope as a possible embodiment of viral self 'despite' its role in host interactions (ibid.).
509 Raoult and Forterre (2008), 316. On mimivirus see also Zimmer (2011), 89-94; Zakaib (2011); Suzan-Monti et al. (2007); Zauberman et al. (2008).

510 Quoted in Pearson (2008), 677. In English a link between health and selfhood is manifest in the everyday idiom 'I'm not myself (today)'. Infected by its virophage, poor mamavirus is also 'not itself'. This anthropomorphism amounts in practice to a reduced efficiency in replication.
511 See Philippe et al. (2013); Yutin and Koonin (2013). Even bigger is a genus of giant virus known as *Pithovirus*, first described in 2014. At 1.5 micrometres in length and 0.5 micrometres in diameter, it is half as big again as pandoravirus, though its genome is not as large and it contains only a fifth the number of genes (fewer than 500). It was discovered in a sample of permafrost dating back to the Late Pleistocene (30,000 years ago), bouncing back to 'life' to infect amoebae after all this time. See Legendre et al. (2014); Coghlan (2014).
512 The class of NCLDVs or nucleocytoplasmic large DNA viruses includes not only *Mimiviridae* and *Megaviridae*, but other eukaryotic viruses such as *Poxviridae*, *Iridoviridae*, *Asfarviridae* and *Phycodnaviridae*. Pandoraviruses are thought to be highly derived forms belonging to *Phycodnaviridae*, with which they have certain signature genes in common, rather than to the *Mimiviridae* family. This suggests that giant viruses such as mimivirus and pandoravirus have evolved from smaller viruses at least twice independently. See Yutin and Koonin (2013).
513 Zimmer (2011), 92. It is notable that such virus factories have so far only been found in viruses that infect the relatively large eukaryotes; in the case of bacterial or archaeal viruses it perhaps makes sense to consider the factory to be the cell *as a whole*, which is recruited-hijacked in its entirety in pursuit of viral interests.
514 See Castro et al. (2013), 30: 'it is proposed that viruses kidnap the aggresome pathway to concentrate the numerous factors needed for replication and morphogenesis, and to avoid being recognized by cell defences'.
515 On the VV factory see Novoa et al. (2005), 149–53.
516 For example, a class of ssRNA viruses called the togaviruses, which include the human pathogen rubella, modify membranous structures such as lysosomes and endosomes to turn them into special protective vesicles known as cytopathic vacuoles. See ibid., 158–61.
517 For examples see Castro et al. (2013), 24; Novoa et al. (2005), 147.
518 It should be added that the verb 'recruit' – unlike 'hijack' – can also be used when the mitochondria are 'properly' deployed by the host cell for its own metabolic purposes; i.e. the host cell is said to 'recruit' even its own organelles.
519 Such misappropriation of selfhood is exemplified on a slightly larger scale by the single-celled parasite *Toxoplasma gondii*, which can set up home indefinitely in most mammals, including mice (as well as humans), but can only complete its life-cycle by sexual reproduction inside cats. Its strategy is to 'recruit' certain parts of the brain (possibly including the amygdala) of an infected mouse to make it lose its normal self-preserving fear of cat urine, with predictable consequences: the mouse is eaten, and the parasite can complete its life-cycle inside a cat. Failing to shun its arch-enemy, the cat-friendly mouse *is no longer itself* to the extent that it is not in control of its own behaviour and so neglects to act in its own interests; it is 'possessed' (by toxoplasmic non-self) rather than 'self-possessed'. On *Toxoplasma gondii* see Koch (2011).
520 Claverie (2006), 110.4.

521 While virulent viruses (as understood by Claverie) thus provide a graphic illustration of the concept of 'disposable soma' in that the viral factories – like the somatic cells of an organism – are utterly secondary to the replicative interests of the germ line (and are destroyed once they have served their purpose), the life cycle of temperate viruses need not involve this destructive antagonism of soma and germ line, host and parasite.
522 Villarreal (2009), 35–37.
523 See ibid., 62–64.
524 Yarmolinsky (1995), 836.
525 Hendrix (2003), 506.
526 This distinction also applies to the human immune system, which on the one hand protects us from phylogenetically remote antagonists such as bacteria and viruses, but on the other also hampers attempts to transplant limbs from one human to another. See below, Chapter 6.
527 Villarreal (2009), 43–44.
528 Ibid., 57–58.
529 Ibid., 58.
530 On *R. prowazekii* see Andersson et al. (1998); Renesto et al. (2005).
531 Renesto et al. (2005), 105–6; see also Winkler (1976).
532 Winkler (1976), 390.
533 Moulder (1985), 299. The mechanism of host infection is thought to involve *Rickettsia* inducing phagocytosis in its prospective host, i.e. causing the cell to 'eat' it. Once phagocytosed, the parasite escapes directly into the cytoplasm from the host vacuole enclosing it (the phagosome) before this merges with the lysosome that digests its contents.
534 Andersson et al. (1998), 135.
535 Moreira and López-García (2009), 307.
536 Admittedly, the binary fission required for multiplication itself involves a limited form of internalized movement, and intracellular movement may be required to exit the host cell. Some forms of *Rickettsia* (members of the spotted fever group) escape from the host cell by recruiting host-derived actin, which is assembled into a tail and used for locomotion; *R. prowazekii*, by contrast, simply multiplies until the cell bursts.
537 For a comparison of various intracellular parasites in their relationship to their host, see Moulder (1985).
538 Andersson et al. (1998), 133. Future analyses might well revise this phylogenetic interpretation, which remains provisional. It has been argued that a facultatively anaerobic bacterium might represent a more plausible origin for mitochondria than an obligately aerobic bacterium resembling *Rickettsia*; see Tielens et al. (2002). However, the precise degree of kinship is secondary in comparing mitochondrial selfhood with that of *Rickettsia*.
539 Andersson et al. (1998), 133. Another feature that these distant cousins have in common is the possession of ATP-ADP translocases, the transmembrane proteins that allow ATP and ADP to pass from one side of the membrane to the other. What is curious is that this movement is in a different direction in the case of *Rickettsia* from mitochondria: while the parasite uses the translocases to

assimilate ATP from the host cytoplasm, the organelle utilizes them in order to *export* ATP to its host. In fact, differences between the translocase molecules suggest that they may have originated independently, possibly entering *Rickettsia* by HGT from *Chlamydiae*, the only class of bacterial intracellular parasites also known to possess them. No free-living bacteria are believed to have homologues of ATP-ADP translocases. On the ATP-ADP translocases in mitochondria and *Rickettsia*, see Andersson et al. (1998), 139–40; Renesto et al. (2005), 100, 106.

540 I follow Eberl (2010) in using 'symbiosis' as an umbrella term referring to persisting biological interactions, usually between organisms belonging to different species: such interactions may be mutualistic (in which both parties benefit), commensalistic (in which one party benefits while the other remains unaffected) or parasitic (in which one party benefits at the expense of the other).

541 Chan (2006), 1241.

542 In the case of *Amborella* (considered the basalmost extant flowering plant and thus of outstanding interest in its own right), the outsize mitochondrial genome is believed to be the product of otherwise unheard-of levels of HGT. The mitochondrial DNA includes a number of foreign genomes 'swallowed' more or less in their entirety from mosses and green algae. Most of the foreign DNA engulfed by the mitochondria of *Amborella* is thought to be 'junk'. On *Amborella* and its unfeasibly large mitochondrial genome, see Rice et al. (2013).

543 Burger et al. (2003), 711; see also Burger et al. (2013). The DNA of the jakobid mitochondrion bears a greater resemblance to that of a free-living bacterium than does that of any other mitochondrion.

544 Burger et al. (2003), 711.

545 Harold (2001), 178.

546 See Koonin et al. (2006): the mitochondria 'donated numerous genes that integrated into the host genome, including genes coding for components of the essential organelles of the eukaryotic cells, such as ... the bacterial-type plasma membrane that displaced the original archaeal membrane'.

547 In fact, the number of mitochondria per cell varies greatly according to the organism. Whereas the cells of animals have several hundred, unicellular eukaryotes such as kinetoplastids and jakobids have just a single, relatively large mitochondrion per cell. Some anaerobic eukaryotes have lost their mitochondria; human red blood cells also do without. See Ameisen (2002), 382.

548 Chan (2006), 1243.

549 Lane (2009a), 109.

550 See ibid., 109–10, citing the work of biochemist John Allen. Archibald (2014; 138–42) assesses this and various alternative hypotheses. The fact that some protists, such as the jakobids, have just a single, gene-rich mitochondrion, implies that this is not the only reason organelles retain their genomes. Another possible explanation is that the proteins encoded by some genes are simply too difficult to import back from the host cytosol into the mitochondrion. See also Daley and Whelan (2005).

551 See van der Giezen et al. (2005), 175: the authors propose that mitosomes, like mitochondria, are involved in the maturation of vital iron-sulphur proteins required for fundamental catalytic processes. On hydrogenosomes see also Palmer (1997); on mitosomes see also Tovar et al. (1999).

552 One possible comparison would be with peroxisomes (formerly known as 'microbodies'), which are organelles enclosed by a single membrane that are present in most groups of eukaryotes; see Gabaldón (2010). Like most hydrogenosomes and mitosomes but unlike mitochondria, peroxisomes do not have an organellar genome, so all peroxisomal proteins have to be encoded in the nuclear genome and imported into the organelle. The enzymatic functions associated with peroxisomes vary greatly according to the eukaryotic taxon in which they happen to be found, although common functions include fatty acid metabolism, lipid biosynthesis and the detoxification of reactive oxygen species (ibid., 768). There are two main theories on the origin of peroxisomes. The fact that – like bacteria-derived organelles such as mitochondria – new peroxisomes are formed by the division of existing ones led to the idea that they too were acquired by endosymbiosis (ibid., 771). The present consensus is rather that they are derived from the cell's own internal membrane system (specifically the endoplasmic reticulum). Does this make them any less self-like than hydrogenosomes?

553 See for example Cavalier-Smith (2000), 177.

554 See Gavelis et al. (2015); on the warnowiid eye, see also Chapter 6, page 289.

555 Lane (2009a), 299, cf. 186.

556 Thomas (1974), 71. Thomas is only half-joking when he claims that it is the mitochondria who are the lucky ones: 'Each of them, by all accounts, makes only enough of its own materials to get along on, and the rest must come from me. And I am the one who has to do the worrying' (72). So who is the real master?

557 As we have seen, one of the most plausible scenarios for the provenance of eukaryotic cells is the merger between a host archaeon and the bacterium that subsequently evolved into a mitochondrion. See Chapter 3, page 126, note 357. For a discussion, see Maynard Smith and Szathmáry (1999), 59–78; Archibald (2014), 88–119.

558 Ameisen (2002), 383.

559 The issue is complicated by the fact that mitochondria may shrivel to tiny mitosomes that perform a single function unrelated to ATP generation, such as the synthesis of iron-sulphur clusters (cofactors that are crucial to many cellular pathways). Such 'mitochondrion-related organelles' may be extremely difficult to find. Archibald (2014; 113), for example, hazards that 'all eukaryotes possess mitochondria or organelles derived from them'. Findings by Karnkowska et al. (2016), by contrast, point to the existence of protists that have managed to dispense with their mitochondria *entirely*, lacking even hydrogenosomes and mitosomes. The species in question appears to have acquired alternative mechanisms both for energy production and iron-sulphur cluster synthesis.

560 Raoult and Forterre (2008), 317: the authors regard both mitochondria and chloroplasts as REOs rather than mere organelles 'because they contain their own translation apparatus'. Perhaps impressed by the distinguished heritage of mitochondria as free-living bacteria, Raoult and Forterre are being charitable. All the mitochondrial ribosomal proteins of mammals, for example, are now encoded in nuclear genes and subsequently imported into the mitochondria. The 16 kb mitochondrial genome of humans contains 37 genes, only two of which encode ribosomal RNAs. Yet one might ask whether it genuinely matters in which of the two genomes the 'mitochondrial' genes happen to be located. Does it really reduce mitochondrial selfhood if some of its genes have been 'handed over' to the nuclear genome for safe-keeping? On the human mitochondrial genome see Chan (2006), 1241.

561 See Chapter 3, page 126.
562 On mitophagy as crucial to cellular well-being, see Kim et al. (2007).
563 See Rugarli and Langer (2012), 1340, and Vives-Bauza et al. (2010).
564 It is currently unclear whether elongation and hyperfusion rescue mitochondria from mitophagy because their increased size makes them impossible to 'swallow' or because the mitophagy machinery fails to recognize them in a hyperfused form. See Rambold et al. (2011), 10194.
565 See ibid.
566 Lane (2009a), 265, 267. On programmed cell death in general see Raff (1998); see also Koonin and Aravind (2002); Huettenbrenner et al. (2003); Ameisen (2002).
567 In fact, apoptosis is said to be either caspase-dependent or caspase-independent. The caspase-independent cell death pathway might well have different evolutionary roots; an archaeal origin has been proposed. This would imply that both parties brought their own death-producing equipment to the marriage of convenience that became eukaryotes. Both mechanisms of apoptosis are now entrusted to the mitochondrion.
568 It is also found, for example, in the slime mould *Dictyostelium discoideum*, single-celled social amoebae that also build multicellular bodies and are best viewed as an intermediate form between a unicellular and a multicellular organism. See Ameisen (2002), 374; Arnoult et al. (2001).
569 See Huettenbrenner et al. (2003), 242–43, on cell death programmes as a 'prerequisite of organized life': 'during embryonic development of the nervous system, the finger digits or the ovary, but also in adult organisms, minutely regulated daily death processes maintain health and integrity. Every second, millions of cells of the human body undergo apoptosis, i.e. in conditions of homeostasis each mitosis is compensated by one event of apoptosis'.
570 Lane (2009a), 268.
571 Koonin and Aravind (2002), 402.
572 In this section I have focused on the route from alpha-proteobacteria to mitochondria (and relatives) as a paradigm of intracellular selfhood, but a similar analysis could apply to the relationship between the chloroplasts and the cyanobacteria from which they are believed to descend. This is possibly a more complex scenario. Not only has the primary endosymbiotic uptake of cyanobacteria occurred more than once, but there are also cases of secondary endosymbiosis – which involves the uptake of a primary chloroplast-bearing alga by an unrelated eukaryotic host – and even tertiary endosymbiosis, as well as the fascinating phenomenon of kleptoplastidy (the 'stealing' of plastids). For a full account of these phenomena see Archibald (2014), 120–72.
573 McCutcheon and Moran (2011), 23.
574 See Chapter 3, pages 119ff.
575 See Gil et al. (2002); Tamas et al. (2002).
576 Wernegreen (2002), 855–56; see also Pérez-Brocal et al. (2006).
577 Wernegreen (2002), 858, referring to the strain of *B. aphidicola* associated with the pea aphid *Acyrthosiphon pisum*.
578 Pérez-Brocal et al. (2006), 312–13: *Cinara cedri* is a species belonging to the genus of conifer aphids.

579 Genes required for transcription and translation are the best preserved, and the DNA replication machinery is likewise complete. See ibid.

580 The term 'Candidatus' (subsequently abbreviated to Ca.) is used to designate provisional taxonomic status in the case of organisms that cannot be isolated and cultured as required for the establishment of a new taxon.

581 On the phylogenetic links between these various endosymbionts see Thao and Baumann (2004).

582 In both cases we are considering an obligate as opposed to a facultative (i.e. optional) association. The exact degree of dependence is variable. See Wernegreen (2002).

583 Theissen and Martin (2016), R1016; see also Cavalier-Smith (2000), 177.

584 One conjecture is that the host insect may produce sugar transport proteins that enable it to cater to the fuel requirements of its bacteria. Another hypothesis is a direct supply of ATP from host to endosymbiont. See Archibald (2014), 169.

585 See Bhattacharya and Archibald (2006).

586 See McCutcheon and Moran (2011), 23–24.

587 Cavalier-Smith (2000), 177.

588 Limited locomotion may take place when the endosymbiont is transmitted from host mother to offspring. In the case of *Buchnera*, for example, the symbionts leave the specialized cells that host them via a small opening and then travel through the host body fluids until they reach and enter the fertilized egg. As the aphid embryo develops, the *Buchnera* cells then migrate to the cells specially earmarked for them. In other cases the specialized host cells themselves migrate to the ovaries. See Wernegreen (2002), 853.

589 The idea that the possibility of self-movement grounds the possibility of it 'being like' anything to be oneself and thus of consciousness will be explored in greater depth in the forthcoming work on rudimentary consciousness.

590 See von Dohlen et al. (2001).

591 See McCutcheon and Moran (2011).

592 Ibid., 17: it 'has no functional tRNA synthetase genes' and 'lacks several other genes found even in the smallest symbiont genomes'.

593 Gil et al. (2002), 4454. As Wernegreen puts it (2002), '*Rickettsia* and other intracellular pathogens invest a considerable portion of their small genomes in synthesizing elaborate cell structures and can rapidly change the cell surface to avoid detection by the host' (859).

594 Wernegreen (2002), 853.

595 McCutcheon and Moran (2011), 19; Wernegreen (2002), 859.

596 See Gil et al. (2004), 531.

597 Wernegreen (2002), 858: *Wigglesworthia* might need the flagellum at some point in its life cycle, or the flagellar proteins might be required to provide the apparatus for the invasion of a new host.

598 Pérez-Brocal et al. (2006), 312; see also Gil et al. (2004), 528.

599 On the effects of genome reduction in '*Ca*. Tremblaya princeps' and '*Ca*. Carsonella ruddii' see in particular McCutcheon and Moran (2011; 19). Of the five smallest endosymbiotic genomes cited, none is able to synthesize a complete cell envelope (ibid., 24).

600 At the time of writing (or, more truthfully, revising) this chapter, 'Ca. Tremblaya princeps' no longer boasts the smallest genome. The size of the smallest bacterial genome sequenced has now shrunk to 112 kb; this belongs to the endosymbiont 'Ca. Nasuia deltocephalinicola', which lives in association with a species of leaf hopper, co-residing with another symbiont with a somewhat larger genome. It has retained genes involved in DNA replication, transcription and translation, as well as the synthesis of two amino acids for its host. See Bennett and Moran (2013).
601 McCutcheon and Moran (2011), 20: it is believed that the relatively high expression of so-called 'heat shock proteins' in symbiotic bacteria may counter the deleterious effects of their high mutation rates.
602 Ibid., 21.
603 Ibid.
604 Ibid., 24.
605 'Ca. Carsonella ruddii' is somewhat bigger than 'Ca. Tremblaya princeps', with 182 predicted coding sequences in a 159-kb genome.
606 Tamames et al. (2007).
607 Maniloff (1996), 10004.
608 Mushegian and Koonin (1996), 10272.
609 Itaya (1995).
610 Quoted in Gil (2004), 518.
611 See McCutcheon and Moran (2011), 14.
612 Ibid.
613 Giovannoni et al. (2005), 1242: the reduction of its genome is described as being a consequence of 'streamlining'; it encodes nearly all the most basic functions of alpha-proteobacterial cells but dispenses almost entirely with apparently redundant or non-functional genetic elements such as introns or transposons. It codes for just short of 1400 genes, fewer than any other known free-living microorganism.
614 This division between heterotrophic and autotrophic ways of life has been described as the 'most fundamental' in biology; see Wächtershäuser (1994), 4283. 'Ca. P. ubique' is a heterotroph, feeding on the ocean's reservoir of dissolved organic carbon.
615 We could perhaps call this mutualism to the extent that we heterotrophs do at least provide carbon dioxide for those autotrophs that use it.
616 On the cyanobacteria see Morowitz (1992), 66–68. As Morowitz puts it, 'mycoplasma and cyanobacter demonstrate two very different kinds of simplicity'.
617 On the self-organizing universe, see for example Smolin (1997) and Chaisson (2001). The notion of self-organization at the level of a universal 'self' is not unproblematic. The conceptual difficulties associated with the idea of the universe as a self relate in particular to the question of self-containment and the seeming incoherence of the concept of 'non-self' in such a context – though some sort of non-self is ostensibly required by any self-organizing self for the provision of energetic sustenance. Such puzzles are tied up with the problematic nature of concepts such as 'everything' and 'nothing', which are prone to entangle us in our own cognitive limitations. On 'nothing', see Glasgow (1999), 107–28.

618 Of course, the problem of bootstrapping remains, but now elevated (or relegated) to the overarching (or underlying) level of the cosmos.

619 The metaphor is intentionally dissonant in that roots imply 'below' and über implies 'above', subverting spatial connotations of height or ascent. The evolutionary notion of 'descent' hits the nail on the bottom: upside-down, we are descended from our roots.

620 For the distinction between, and application of, bottom-up and top-down approaches see Morowitz (1992).

621 'Downwards' has the advantage of being consistent with the spatial imagery of a 'top-down' approach. Again, however, the metaphor of verticality or height should not be swallowed whole.

622 Ibid., 88 (I have modified the capitalization).

623 Ibid., 89.

624 See for example Cavalier-Smith (2001), 588; Harold (2001), 244–45.

625 Morowitz (1992), 44. See also Harold (2001), 56: 'from the chemical viewpoint, rabbits and grass are very much alike, and their molecular constituents comprise but a tiny fraction of the structures known to chemistry. All cells contain virtually the same set of small molecules – amino acids, sugars, sugar phosphates, nucleotides, dicarboxylic acids, perhaps a hundred in all, dissolved in water, which makes up as much as nine tenths of the total mass'.

626 Morowitz (1992), 47.

627 See Harold (2001), 58: 'The molecules of life make up a minute fraction of the organic substances known to chemists: why just these and not others? ... What adenosine triphosphate does, guanosine triphosphate could do just as well; the fact that ATP serves as the universal energy currency while GTP performs specialized tasks (in protein synthesis and cell signaling) is not explained by the difference in chemical structure'.

628 On XNAs, see Rutherford (2013), 97–99 (*The Future of Life*). It is not only the backbones of our genetic macromolecules that have been shown to be modifiable; two new bases (P and Z) have also been added to the 'natural' genetic alphabet of A, T, C and G (see ibid., 96–97).

629 On PNAs, see Nielsen (2008). Peptide nucleic acids resemble RNA and DNA in their capacity to store information, but the greater stability of double-stranded PNA impairs its ability to separate into two daughter strands, i.e. to replicate. PNA-based selves can indeed be (and are) imagined, but such imaginings remain largely speculative.

630 One cannot rule out the existence of what has been termed a 'shadow' biosphere, an alternative form of terrestrial life that has so far gone undetected. The most likely candidate is thought to be some kind of 'RNA organism', a direct descendent from the primordial 'RNA world' that would have survived more than two billion years of competition with protein-based organisms by retreating to a niche suitable for micro-organisms smaller than the most diminutive known cells (since an 'RNA organism' would not need the bulky translation machinery required for protein synthesis). See Benner et al. (2004), 686, for a more detailed discussion. Such a proposal is not absurd, but it is flagrantly speculative. It is also hard to envisage it having any practical implications, though this might change if all DNA- and protein-based life went extinct – in which case its possible practical implications would still not be of great relevance *to us*.

631 Morowitz (1992), 39.

632 Ibid., 42. Sodium, magnesium, chlorine, potassium and calcium have been identified as a secondary set of atomic constituents; micro-constituents include iron, silicon, manganese, zinc and molybdenum.

633 Ibid., 134: 'If one looks at the core of metabolism: glycolysis, the citric acid cycle, and the pentose phosphate pathway, all of the compounds contain only C, H, O, P, and the phosphorus is always in the form of phosphates. None of those compounds contains nitrogen. Likewise, there are major portions of lipid pathways that involve C, H, O, S, and phosphate. This suggests a possible prenitrogen chemistry'. This implies a form of biochemistry prior to amino acids (and thus proteins) and to nucleotides (and thus RNA and DNA).

634 Benner et al. (2004), 675.

635 Although silicon is the element most frequently proposed as a substitute for carbon in an alternative biochemistry, the two elements show major differences in their capacity for forming stable long-chain molecules. While silicon-silicon bonds are so weak that they are incapable of forming a lasting polymer backbone of more than 30–40 atoms at room temperature (whereas carbon chains can contain millions of atoms, as in DNA), silicon reacts so strongly with oxygen that the resultant polymers – which exist in the Earth's crust in the form of silicates – are too stable to participate in a biochemistry akin to our own. See Fry (1999), 246–49. See also Benner et al. (2004), 675–76, who are rather more open to the possibility of silicon-based scaffolding.

636 See Introduction.

637 The cases of extreme desiccation examined in the Introduction all involved forms of cryptobiosis or ametabolism, in other words the cessation of function. See Introduction, pages 67–71.

638 Even the necessity of a *liquid* solvent can be questioned. While recognizing the advantages of a solvent in the liquid phase, Benner et al. (2004; 676) do not rule out the possibility of biochemical reactions taking place in the gas phase: in such conditions 'chemistry is limited to molecules that are sufficiently volatile to deliver adequate amounts of material to the gas phase at moderate temperatures, and/or to molecules sufficiently stable to survive higher temperatures where vapor pressures are higher. Obviously, if volume is abundant, pressures are low, and time scales are long, even low concentrations of biomolecules might support a biosystem'. Solid-phase diffusion is so slow that 'cosmic lengths of time' and an energy input from extremely high-energy particles would be required for a biochemical system capable of Darwinian evolution to be conceivable.

639 The chemical instability of RNA in water represents a serious drawback for aqueous 'RNA world' scenarios. One alternative hypothesis is that RNA was in fact preceded by a more stable molecule resistant to the corrosiveness of water. The peptide nucleic acids we encountered above (page 198) have been postulated as candidates for such a pre-RNA scenario, yet – despite their virtues as repositories of information – no PNA molecules have yet been shown to possess catalytic qualities. In other words, they (at present) appear to lack the duality of information-storage and biological function that is such a significant feature of RNA. See, for example, Nielsen (2008) and Nelson (2000) on PNA as a possible pre-RNA genetic molecule.

640 For a perspicacious discussion and critique of non-carbaquist approaches to the origin and nature of life, see Fry (1999), esp. 235–54. Fry's work as a whole provides a fine account and assessment of origin-of-life theories. For an account of some of the alternatives to the carbaquist approach, see Benner et al. (2004). On the role of water in the emergence of life and in particular the properties that are conducive to nurturing and sustaining a biosphere, see also Glasgow (2009), 49–55.

641 Benner et al. (2004) suggest supercritical dihydrogen. On gas planets such as Saturn, they suggest, a habitable zone would be where the temperature and pressure are high enough for dihydrogen to become supercritical, yet not too high for stable carbon-carbon covalent bonding and thus organic molecules to exist.

642 Catling (2013), 82.

643 For a discussion of the possibility of life on Titan see ibid., 102–6.

644 Saladino et al. (2012) write: 'the most abundant organic (HCN) and inorganic (H_2O) combinations of the four most frequent atoms of the Universe H, C, O, N … react to yield formamide' (98).

645 See ibid. and also Benner et al. (2004), 678–79.

646 Fry (1999), 248.

647 *New York Times*, 11 August 1996; quoted in Fry (1999), 217.

648 Quoted in Fry (1999), 56. Charles's grandfather Erasmus Darwin had written a poem, 'The Temple of Nature' (1804), in which he had described how 'the first specks of animated earth' came into being 'beneath the waves' of the primordial seas (quoted in ibid., 35).

649 See ibid., 54–57.

650 Ibid., 1–8.

651 Troland's speculations foreshadowed much of what was subsequently established about genetic material in the course of the century; see ibid., 74–76.

652 Ibid., 65–78.

653 On the Miller-Urey experiments see ibid., 79–83.

654 On pyrimidines see for example Powner et al. (2009); on purines see Becker et al. (2016).

655 See Fry (1999), 245.

656 Lane et al. (2010), 271–72.

657 For an overview of recent findings in space chemistry see Mueck (2013).

658 Fry (1999), 113–17. The 19th century theory known as panspermia – whose advocates included Lord Kelvin and Hermann von Helmholtz – likewise held that life originated elsewhere in the universe. By contrast with the modern-day study of complex chemistry in interstellar space, panspermia was born from a conviction that life was too complex to have its origins in inanimate or 'dead' matter; life and matter were two distinct categories, both of them eternal. The 'seeds' of life – and selfhood – can thus only have come to Earth ready-made. Both Kelvin and Helmholtz conjectured that meteorites were the vehicle responsible (ibid., 59–62).

659 In itself, the 'soup' metaphor is not objectionable. Soups can be chunky broths or thin consommés; they can be heated and maintained in a state far from thermodynamic equilibrium; they can undergo convective self-organization produced by thermal gradients. They can also be held in 'containers' (of whatever size or provenance), thus creating an interface between the liquid and the vessel that contains it.

660 On Oparin and Haldane see ibid., 65–74.
661 Ibid., 86.
662 Ibid., 184.
663 Kauffman (1995), 73.
664 See Dyson (1985; rev. ed. 1999), 16: Dyson's idea is that the first living creatures were 'cells with a metabolic apparatus directed by enzymes ... but with no genetic apparatus' (15). This protein-based life form would have been 'infected' by RNA, which may have originated as an indigestible by-product of ATP metabolism (caused by a build-up of the nucleotide AMP). With time, the RNA parasite would have come to be not only tolerated but also *harnessed* on account of the capacity for exact replication associated with its chemical structure. The parasite would have turned into an obligate symbiont, proteins and nucleic acids thus merging to form a harmonious unity. Dyson himself describes this scenario as a 'poetic fancy' (16).
665 Ruiz-Mirazo and Moreno (2004), 250.
666 Ibid.
667 Maynard Smith and Szathmáry (1999; 33–39) describe the primordial dilemma as a catch-22 situation inhering in the origin of life: without specific enzymes, genome size is limited to just a few dozen bases (if it were any greater, the inaccuracy of replication would rise above an 'error threshold' and result in an unfeasible accumulation of mutations); but with just a few dozen bases the genome is too small to code for the enzymes that would allow for an increased genome size.
668 Benner (1999; 130) summarizes the contradictory demands placed on RNA by its double nature as catalytic and genetic material.
669 Ibid.
670 Ruiz-Mirazo et al. (2004), 235–36.
671 See Introduction, note 100. On catalytic DNA, see Breaker and Joyce (1994), Santoro and Joyce (1997); also Cavalier-Smith (2001), 556.
672 Breaker and Joyce (1994), 227–28: the most likely scenario, they contend, is that 'DNA was invented subsequent to RNA as a more stable repository of genetic information. Once DNA became trapped in the form of a complete duplex structure, which was selectively advantageous because it provided a means for mutational repair, the catalytic potential of DNA would have been stifled'.
673 See Joyce (1982; 1995), 142–43, for a more detailed exposition of the fundamental role of RNA in our present-day biology and other arguments in support of the view that RNA-based life preceded DNA and protein-based life.
674 Benner (1999; 131) makes the point that the RNA components in modern metabolism perform functions to which they are *not* ideally suited: 'this suggests that these fragments originated during a time in natural history where RNA was the only available biopolymer rather than by convergent evolution or recruitment in an environment where chemically better-suited biomolecules could be encoded'.
675 Richard Dawkins (1976; 1989) is often cited as a major proponent of the 'naked gene' hypothesis. Such scenarios have tended to invoke 'chance' or 'random' events that require extremely long stretches of time to become slightly less improbable. However, even Dawkins implies the need for some sort of clustering or aggregation, conjecturing that the 'organic substances became locally concentrated,

perhaps in drying scum round the shores, or in tiny suspended droplets' (15). This would reduce the factor of 'chance'.

676 Harold (2001), 246.
677 Quoted in Fry (1999), 173. In his subsequent work Eigen revised this view, developing the notion of 'compartmented hypercycles' of cooperating RNA strands. See ibid., 107–111.
678 Cavalier-Smith (2001), 557; see Introduction, page 47.
679 Koga et al. (2011), 720–724.
680 See ibid., 724; on self-assembly see Introduction.
681 See Fry (1999), 172–78, on lipid vesicles.
682 This goes for autopoietic theory.
683 Fry (1999), 173.
684 Morowitz (1992), 174–75.
685 A similar principle governs the extant halophilic archaeon *Halobacterium salinarum*, which employs a light-sensitive pigment akin to rhodopsin to harvest sunlight. This is used to pump protons out of the cell, and the resulting transmembrane protein gradient drives the synthesis of ATP. See ibid., 145–46.
686 See Lane et al. (2010), 275–78.
687 Materials extracted from the Murchison meteorite – which landed in Australia in 1969 and also contained amino acids such as glycine – have been shown to contain amphiphiles that spontaneously form membranous vesicles in aqueous solutions: see Deamer (2002), 374.
688 Ibid., 373, 375.
689 Ibid., 377.
690 Ibid., 376–77: 'if the chain lengths of phospholipids composing a lipid bilayer are reduced from the 18 carbons of modern biological membranes to 14 carbons, thereby thinning the membrane, the permeability to ionic solutes increases by three orders of magnitude. … Such membranes could capture and concentrate macromolecules, yet still provide access to ionic nutrient solutes in the external aqueous phase'.
691 See Budin and Szostak (2011).
692 Cavalier-Smith (2001), 575.
693 On fermentation and its explanatory limitations see Lane (2010), 272.
694 Ibid., 275–78.
695 See Fry (1999), 176–77.
696 Wächtershäuser (1998), 206.
697 Ibid., 206-7: the cell envelope and the genetic machinery, he writes, 'are both derivatives of, and ancillary for, the metabolism, with the first having the main function of keeping all the constituents of the metabolism together, and the second having the main function of controlling all the metabolic reactions. Therefore, we may hold that the metabolism is logically and phylogenetically prior to cellular organization and genetic control; and we may conjecture that a rudimentary metabolism was the primordial life process and that the corresponding primordial organism ("metabolist") later came to "invent" cellular organization and genetic control'.

698 What is meant by 'semi' in this context will be illustrated by the three examples below and by the implicit contrast with the 'full' self-containment of modern cells. In a nutshell, there is less enclosure and less 'control' exerted by the entity in question over its boundaries.
699 Fry (1999), 129–30.
700 On Cairns-Smith see ibid., 126–29.
701 Morowitz (1992), 90.
702 On Wächtershäuser see Fry (1999), 162–72.
703 See Wächtershäuser (1998), 208: 'it is a necessary condition of a surface metabolism that the surface bonding of the metabolites is strong enough ... to assure a sufficiently long residence time, but weak enough to allow a two-dimensional surface diffusion'.
704 Wächtershäuser (1994), 4284: it is also telling that he resorts to precautionary inverted commas. In fact, the notion of two-dimensionality is a geometrical abstraction. The surface morphology of most solid materials is fractal, characterized by non-integral dimensionality ranging between two and three depending on the degree of roughness and convolution. One can thus conceive of 'interiority' (and thus 'containment') in the context of a strongly fractal 2+ dimensional surface.
705 Ibid.
706 Morowitz (1992), 91.
707 Harold (2001), 249.
708 Lane (2010), 276.
709 Cavalier-Smith (2001), 577.
710 Ibid., 578.
711 Ibid., 555–56: Cavalier-Smith prefers this term to the more commonly used 'RNA world' to allow for the possibility that catalytic single-stranded DNA might have also been present. He likewise refers to a nucleozyme rather than a ribozyme.
712 Ibid., 563.
713 Ibid., 562.
714 Ibid., 558–59 (my emphasis).
715 Ibid., 576. Hemicells denote flattened obcells attached to phosphate surfaces forming curved membranous elevations.
716 Ibid., 572–74.
717 Ibid., 559.
718 Ibid., 581: 'The concepts of the cenancestor and the proto-organism have been repeatedly confused in evolutionary discussions. The tremendous difference in complexity between them ... can be conceptually filled by contrasting ideas of the obcell and the protocell and their distinctive contributions to the growth in biological complexity'. The obcell, writes Cavalier-Smith, 'was not the first true cell, but a precursor of it. All cells are organisms, but not all organisms are cells'.
719 I do not know whether Cavalier-Smith himself would approve of my use of the word 'self' in this context.
720 For a more detailed account of hydrothermal vents as possible 'hatcheries' for emergent life, see Lane et al. (2010) and Lane (2009b).

721 See Lane (2009b), 41; Lane et al. (2010), 273–75.
722 Quoted in Lane (2009b), 41.
723 See Lane et al. (2010), 275–79.
724 On LUCA see Lane et al. (2010).
725 Notable among such differences are the mechanisms of DNA replication, which show a deep disparity between the two domains (intimating that LUCA lacked a large DNA genome), and of fermentation, which involve markedly divergent gene sequences and enzymes (intimating that fermentation was not the ancestral power source).
726 The chemistry of their cell walls has even less in common.
727 Koonin and Martin (2005), 647. One alternative hypothesis is that LUCA was capable of synthesizing both types of lipid and cell wall, but afterwards lost one of these pathways in the archaeal lineage and the other in the bacterial lineage. However, this is a much less parsimonious sort of explanation, for it would lumber LUCA with 'functionally redundant parallel pathways for a plethora of essential functions' (ibid., 652). The other alternative hypothesis is that the cells of one of the lineages – despite inheriting from LUCA the ability to synthesize their membrane and cell wall perfectly well – subsequently invented a *new* type of membrane and cell wall that replaced what they had before. This explanation seems equally far-fetched.
728 Lane et al. (2010), 276–77. 'So LUCA was chemiosmotic', they write, 'requiring a membrane, but apparently did not have a membrane comparable to that in either modern archaea or bacteria. While this might look like a paradox, it is not. The bubbly mineral cells that riddle alkaline vents have their own inorganic walls, which we envisage were lined in some regions by hydrothermally synthesised hydrophobic substances – lipids – that were eventually replaced by enzymatically derived lipid membranes, independently, in the archaeal and eubacterial stem lineages. ... It is worth noting here that we do not envisage the ancestral ATPase as embedded in the inorganic walls, but rather in organic lipids lining the walls'.
729 Koonin and Martin (2005), 650.
730 As will become clear in Chapter 6, self-containment need not necessarily manifest itself as a material enclosure or vessel, but may take the form of the functional integration of a set of mutually interdependent components. The conception of a precellular 'pool of genes' – a single, collective entity with a distributed communal genome – thus raises the question of the unit of selfhood, i.e. the level at which 'selfhood' is best ascribed. Carl Woese, for example, contemplates the existence of a 'communal ancestral gene pool' in the earliest stages of evolution up to (and including) LUCA. Woese holds that the notion of LUCA as an individual organism is misguided, for LUCA would have instead existed as a *population* of primitive protocells: 'the universal ancestor', he writes, 'is not a discrete entity. It is, rather, a diverse community of cells that survives and evolves as a biological unit'. Understood thus, the urself might not have been a membrane-bound cell, but a community of mutually interacting and interdependent protocells. See Woese (1998), 6854; see also Woese (2002).
731 See Lane et al. (2010), 278: 'chemiosmosis in modern free-living cells requires more than simply tapping a ready-made gradient. Cells must have learnt at some point to generate their own proton gradient'.
732 ab

733 On cell theory see Harold (2001), 18–20; Rutherford (2013), 16–21; Morowitz (1992), 39–41.
734 See Bianconi et al. (2013). 'Trillion' is here being used in the sense of 'million million' (10^{12}), corresponding to 'billion' in former British English as well as to the German word *Billion*. The figure given is $3.72 \pm 0.81 \times 10^{13}$.
735 Cavalier-Smith (2001), 570.
736 Harold (2001), 113.
737 Ibid.
738 Ibid.
739 Rutherford (2013), 105.
740 On the question of how selfhood can be both 'minimal' and 'full', see also Introduction, page 18, note 1.
741 The selfhood of super-organisms and species will only be touched upon in the present chapter, requiring a more exhaustive study in its own right.
742 See Hegel (1986), 5.136–39.
743 Rozin and Fallon (1987), 26.
744 Feuerbach (1970), 9.151 ('Einige Bemerkungen über den "Anfang der Philosophie" von Dr. J. F. Reiff' (1841)). For an account of the blurred boundaries of the human self, see Glasgow (1997), 27–31.
745 On the remarkable job done by our skin, see Jablonski (2006), 10.
746 Morowitz (1992), 8.
747 The mitochondrion has two membranes, the inner one of which provides the transmembrane proton gradient and energetically separates the organelle from the cell that surrounds it. As a result of channels in the outer membrane, the region between the inner and the outer membranes – the intermembrane space – is similar in chemical composition to the cytoplasm of the host cell.
748 Singer and Nicolson (1972), quoted in Bray (2009), 228.
749 If its water is removed, the molecules move more closely together to form a gel; when water is added again, the molecules revert to the liquid crystalline state, but with the risk of leakiness. As we saw in the Introduction, many xerotolerant creatures use the sugar trehalose to keep the membrane liquid. See Wharton (2002), 111–16.
750 Bacterial and archaeal membranes both consist of phospholipids, but whereas bacterial (and eukaryotic) membranes are made of so-called glycerol-ester lipids, archaeal membranes use glycerol-ether lipids. Some archaea have a lipid monolayer rather than a bilayer, which is also thought to endow them with increased stability at high temperatures. See Harold (2001), 166; Wharton (2002), 146–48.
751 Harold (2001), 104.
752 Ibid.
753 The archaea too have a cell wall, in some cases made from a polymer similar to that in bacteria (pseudopeptidoglycan), in other cases consisting of a rigid protective layer of proteins known as an S-layer, which may also be present in both Gram-positive and Gram-negative bacteria.
754 See Cavalier-Smith (2001), 587.
755 See Norris et al. (1996), 199, on the case of *Mycoplasma pneumoniae*.

756 See Introduction, page 69.
757 See Money (2014), 165–67: Conan the Bacterium can cope with exposure to 5,000 grays (Gy) of radiation, whereas a single dose of 5 Gy can prove fatal to human beings.
758 Cavalier-Smith (2001), 586–87.
759 Maynard Smith and Szathmáry (1999), 59–66.
760 Bacteria too may have lipid-enclosed vesicles, such as the protein-bound gas vesicles that are used to regulate cellular buoyancy, but these exist in a much less dynamic relationship to the cell membrane.
761 Both the endoplasmic reticulum and the Golgi apparatus are involved in the packaging and transport of proteins.
762 Harold (2001), 122.
763 Maynard Smith and Szathmáry (1999), 61; see Lane (2009a; 111) for a discussion of the problems associated with such a hypothesis.
764 See Lane (2009a), 141.
765 On diatoms see Barnes (ed.) (1998), 70–73. See also Money (2014), 64–67: diatom frustules, notes Money, have the advantage that constructing them 'consumes less than one tenth of the energy of a sugar-based wrap'.
766 As a consequence, cellulose is the prevalent organic molecule on the planet, accounting for over half its total biomass. See Hallé (2002), 130.
767 On the coccolithophorids see Money (2014), 67–72.
768 On the ciliates, see Barnes (ed.) (1998), 51–53.
769 On foraminiferans see ibid., 42–44; also Black (1970; 1988), 256–65.
770 Money (2014), 24–25.
771 On the testate amoebae, see also Patterson and Hedley (1992; 1996), 87–96; also Schönborn (1966).
772 Again, the chitinous insect cuticle provides support and protection, but it must also be porous; i.e. the barrier it forms has to be selective or differential to the extent that insects also breathe through it. This takes place through openings known as spiracles that lead to the internal respiratory system.
773 Tyler (2003), 55.
774 Adams et al. (2010), e15040.
775 Ibid.
776 Tyler (2003), 56.
777 Ibid., 55–56; see also Nickel et al. (2011), 1693.
778 Adams et al. (2010), e15040.
779 For an engaging description of *Trichoplax*, see Schierwater (2005); see also Srivastava et al. (2008).
780 On the human skin see Jablonski (2006); on the composition of skin see in particular 9–20. Notably, collagen is the most abundant protein in mammals, present not only in skin but also in tendons and ligaments, as well as bones and cartilage.
781 Ibid., 11–12.
782 Ibid., 13.

783 See Roach (2013), 143–45: this is why it is not unknown for the stomach of a cadaver to burn a hole in itself; the self-regenerating mucous membrane shuts down upon death, while the digestive juices may continue to do their work.
784 Xu and Gordon (2003), 10452.
785 For a fuller account of wounds, scabs and scars, see Jablonski (2006), 123–26.
786 See ibid., 28–32.
787 Many reptiles (including crocodylians and lizards) and a few mammals (including xenathrans such as armadillos) have bony osteoderms that also incorporate keratin and can function both as armour and mechanisms of thermoregulation. This is not to mention the heavily armoured thyreophoran dinosaurs such as stegosaurs and ankylosaurs.
788 Ibid., 177. By contrast with the 'foot soldier' neutrophils that phagocytose micro-organisms in an emergency, Langerhans cells are antigen-presenting cells, which transport foreign proteins to lymph nodes to spur the immune system into action. On the neutrophils see Sompayrac (1999; 2008), 17–20.
789 Jablonski (2006), 65–75.
790 Ibid., 80: see 76–96 on how melanin – in an evolutionary context – has resolved the dilemma.
791 In the Introduction we noted the intrinsic reflexivity in my self-care: I care about myself because that is who I am. This extends to the parts of my body. I care about the organs of my body – insofar as I am aware of them – because they are mine. I do not care for my liver because it happens to be a particularly fine specimen of a liver (I suspect it does not), but because it is inseparable from me. If it goes, I go with it. If it malfunctions, the pain and inconvenience is mine.
792 For an interesting but slightly different analysis of the meaning of 'individual' and 'organism' see Wilson (1999), esp. 60: Wilson argues that the claim that a living being is an individual may refer to one or more of six attributes of that entity: that it is (1) a particular; (2) a historical entity; (3) a functional individual; (4) a genetic individual; (5) a developmental individual; (6) a unit of evolution.
793 Pradeu (2013), 78–79.
794 Rowlands (2010), 141. Notably, Rowlands uses the metaphor of 'ownership' to describe the relationship of a particular process to the functional whole. A digestive process is *mine*, he says, if it fulfils its proper function with respect to me, i.e. breaking down the food that I have ingested and releasing the energy that allows my respiratory processes to continue. In fact, the metaphor is slightly ambiguous, connoting both property (possession) and appropriateness or propriety. The former sense has rather misleading socioeconomic implications; the latter sense is ultimately another way of describing functional integration: the parts and the whole self *belong together*.
795 Henderson (2012), 41.
796 This in turn begs a question to which we shall return below: is our microbiota part of our self, or not? Is it 'inside' or 'outside'?
797 Almost equally blatant is the case of smoking in people who want to give up.
798 The common octopus (*Octopus vulgaris*) provides an alternative illustration of 'anarchic arms'; see Nesher et al. (2014). Controlling the movements of its arms is a constant challenge for the octopus due to the animal's apparent lack of proprioceptive 'awareness' of them, their tendency to stick to

virtually any object they touch, and the almost infinite number of degrees of freedom they display. It is vital for the organism to minimize this risk of mutual interference and entanglement in order to be able to behave in its own interests. It does this in part by using predefined, stereotypical motor programmes to reduce the number of degrees of freedom to a manageable number (three), but this is supported by a chemical self-recognition system that prevents octopus suckers from activating their attachment mechanism when faced with other octopus skin. As a result of this self-recognition system, self avoids entanglement with self.

799 See Wilson (1999), 51–52.
800 Ibid.
801 See King (2004), 321–22.
802 Plants, fungi and even some animal phyla do not sequester the germ line in this way, but may propagate through a process of 'somatic embryogenesis', which dispenses with a distinct germ line. In this case, somatic cells are capable of giving rise to embryos at any stage in the organism's development. However, the fact remains that not all cells *do* become embryos and so not all of them *do* further their lineage.
803 Programmed cell death is a considerably more widespread phenomenon than germ-line sequestration, present as it is in animals, plants and fungi.
804 For an account of the dispute over the status of *Armillaria bulbosa*, see Wilson (1999), 23–25.
805 Such entities represent a marked contrast with animals such as humans, which have relatively determinate boundaries and whose unitary selfhood does not support being 'fragmented' in this way. The act of splitting us in two infringes both our physical self-containment (our internal milieu ceases to be held in place; our innards spill out) and our functional integration (our body fails to function if parts of it are removed; by the same token, those parts fail to function if removed from our body).
806 For a discussion of plant individuality with reference to the quaking aspen (amongst other organisms), see Clarke (2012), 321–61.
807 On Pando, see for example Grant (1993).
808 Clarke (2012), 338.
809 Though a clone (and thus genetically more or less identical), the cells of a metazoan body also undergo differentiation. This is as a consequence of epigenetic factors.
810 On *D. discoideum* see Bonner's wonderful monograph (2009); see also Strassmann and Queller (2007). Similar questions regarding transitions between 'levels' of selfhood are raised by the case of super-organisms such as bee, ant and wasp colonies. The degree of physiological and functional self-containment, as well as the genetic and immune factors we shall encounter below, determine the extent to which selfhood can be ascribed to the super-organism, as well as – or instead of – the individual organisms. These vary considerably with the species.
811 Bonner (2009), 119; Strassmann and Queller (2007), 29.
812 Bonner (2009), 12.
813 Ibid., 53.
814 Ibid., 56.
815 Ibid., 103–5.

816 The nearest they come to a collective death is perhaps when they are attacked by a rare, aggressively carnivorous species of slime mould called *Dictyostelium caveatum*: 'since slime molds feed as separate amoebae', explains Bonner, 'this species attacks by entering the aggregate of another species, and the *caveatum* amoebae systematically eat – by engulfing – the amoebae of the victim species. It is a carnivore from within. Its effectiveness is quite remarkable. If the slug of *D. discoideum* has as few as one *caveatum* amoeba in ten thousand *discoideum* amoebae, after a period of what looks like normal migration it will suddenly stop, looking a bit piqued, and small fruiting bodies will sprout out all over its surface. These are all the fruiting bodies of *caveatum*; not one *discoideum* spore can be found' (ibid., 34).
817 Strassmann and Queller (2007), 27–28.
818 In itself, 'straggling' could be an advantage for those without the gene; in practice, however, they tend to 'straggle' so much that they fail even to enter the aggregate. See Queller et al. (2003), 105–6.
819 Chen et al. (2007), 678–81.
820 Ibid.
821 Ibid.: the protein is TirA, a Toll/interleukin-1 receptor (TIR) domain protein.
822 On *Myxococcus xanthus* see Strassmann (2000), 555–56. On bacterial populations considered as multicellular organisms see also J. A. Shapiro (1998).
823 Strassmann's account remains speculative. It is not certain, she says, that lysed cells are genuine altruists and that their contents are actually eaten by the sporulating cells. Nor is it clear that cheating clones cheat specifically by avoiding lysis.
824 Strassmann (2000), 556.
825 See Maynard Smith and Szathmáry (1999), 21–22.
826 See Santelices (1999), 152.
827 Wilson (1999), 86–87: Wilson, as noted above, proposes genetic individuality as one of six possible conceptions of individuality.
828 See ibid., 86–89. It is striking that the focus is on pluralities of cells and on multicellular organisms. Single eukaryotic cells partake of 'genetic individuality' only insofar as they belong to a clone or body.
829 It is significant that genetic individuality defines itself with respect to other genetic individuals, whereas physiological individuality is usually defined with respect to its environment. This perhaps reflects the fact that genetic identity is informational rather than physiological in nature; different *sorts* of entities are being defined. It may be felt that the notion of 'containment' in such a context is uncomfortably metaphorical.
830 Wilson (1999), 87.
831 On plant self-incompatibility, see for example Nasrallah (2005).
832 See Clarke (2013), 341. Dawkins (1982; 1999) defined the 'organism' as the 'unit which is initiated by a new act of reproduction via a single-celled developmental bottleneck' (258) (italics and inverted commas omitted).
833 See Wilson (1999), 54; as an illustration of somatic embryogenesis in animals, Wilson (94) describes the case of a hydra, a small freshwater cnidarian endowed with a population of so-called *I*-cells that can 'give rise to any kind of somatic cell, undergo reductive division to produce gametes, or remain totipotent (able to generate a complete new organism)'. Other organisms do sequester the

germ line, but not until relatively late in development.

834 See Santelices (1999), 152–55; also Pineda-Krch and Lehtilä (2004), 1169.

835 Santelices (1999), 153; also Pineda-Krch and Lehtilä (2004), 1172.

836 Wilson (1999), 97–98.

837 See Balcombe (2006), 138–39: 'cleaner fish of a variety of species nibble loose skin, fungal growths and fish lice from other fish. Cleaners also pluck at wounds, which appears to relieve infection and speed healing. It's a definitive mutualism: cleaners get food (delivered buffet-style by clients who line up patiently to await their turn) and clients get a body-spruce-up service'.

838 On the dog lichen as an example of a tripartite symbiosis, see Money (2014), 98–100.

839 Both mutualism and parasitism are modes of symbiosis. Whereas mutualism implies a shared self in the sense of a complete coincidence of interests, parasitism suggests that the overlap of interests is only partial and there is residual or persisting selfishness in one of the symbionts at the expense of the other. See page 175, note 540.

840 *Nostoc* is the most common cyanobacterium in lichen symbioses, but can also support itself without fungal protection.

841 On the gut microbiome see Qin et al. (2010), 59–65.

842 Money (2014), 150: metagenomic work on the gut microbiome of invertebrates has unearthed a simpler ecology with communities comparable to various free-living habitats. Termites are a notable exception, housing complex communities that aid them in fermenting cellulose.

843 Qin et al. (2010), 62.

844 Money (2014), 132–35.

845 On *B. thetaiotaomicron*, see Turney (2015), 101–2; Xu and Gordon (2003), 10453–55.

846 See Ackerman (2012); also Money (2014), 138.

847 It rather depends on whether the focus is on the microbiota as a whole or the individual species, some of which keep *one another* in check. The new field of 'faecal transplants' perhaps suggests a way in which humans might be starting to gain a certain mastery over some of our more unruly associates, in particular the potentially destructive gut inhabitant *Clostridium difficile*. See Roach (2013), 301–17.

848 This of course begs the question of what is meant by 'my own'.

849 Eberl (2010), 455.

850 It is noteworthy that some bacterial communities have indeed been found to penetrate *beneath* the epithelia, reaching both the dermis and the fatty tissue underneath. See Turney (2015), 69.

851 Philosopher Maureen O'Malley (2014, 153) thus asks: 'how cohesive a community is the one in the human gut? Does it really work as something with a division of labour, an entity that has functional specialization and is reproduced over generations and across environments, with community-level properties selected *for*?'

852 However, symbiotic microorganisms may be 'indirectly' transmitted from one generation to the next. Direct parental contact (for example through the birth canal) is one such mode of transmission; newly hatched termites are fed on parental faeces by colony workers; bovine offspring acquire the microbiota by grazing on pastures rich in the faeces and sputum of their parents. On these and other forms of transmission see Zilber-Rosenberg and Rosenberg (2008).

853 Foster and Neufeld (2013), 305–12.
854 Turney (2015), 205.
855 See Cryan and Dinan (2012) for a fuller account of how the gut microbiota modulates mood, cognition and pain. For example, bacteria are known to be capable of generating a whole range of neurotransmitters and neuromodulators, including noradrenalin, serotonin, dopamine and GABA. It is certainly conceivable that secretions of such substances might 'induce epithelial cells to release molecules that in turn modulate neural signalling within the enteric nervous system, or act directly on primary afferent axons' (ibid., 704).
856 Ibid. The authors themselves acknowledge that it is not yet resolved 'whether the role of the microbiota is sufficiently predominant to warrant its nomenclature being included in an axis independent from the well-described gut-brain axis or whether it should simply be recognized as an important node within the gut-brain axis' (ibid., 702).
857 O'Malley (2014), 151.
858 Sharon et al. (2010) found fruit flies to show a strong mating preference for individuals reared on the same diet as they were. Antibiotic treatment abolished this preference, implying that the microbes rather than the diet were responsible for the choice of mate. Inoculation of treated flies with microbes from the corresponding microbiota restored the preference.
859 See ibid., 20054. This idea is known as the 'hologenome theory of evolution', where 'hologenome' denotes the sum of the genetic material of host and microbiota. Hologenome theory presupposes that the partnerships making up the holobiont are reliably maintained from generation to generation. This requires the faithful transmission of the symbiotic microorganisms down the generations. In practice, such transmission is often 'indirect', involving interaction with the environment. On the hologenome theory of evolution see Zilber-Rosenberg and Rosenberg (2008).
860 In fact, ectosymbiosis can also result in such 'containment'. Consider the case of the large protozoan *Mixotricha paradoxa*, which is propelled through its environment by the coordinated undulation of what appear to be thousands of 'cilia' or hair-like appendages; these appendages have been shown to be hundreds of thousands of tiny spirochaete bacteria, which – like 'galley slaves' – are held in place at the cell surface by yet other bacteria. On *Mixotricha*, see Dawkins (2004), 544–48.
861 See Chapter 4.
862 Nor should we forget the 'symbiotic' relationship in which we exist with the profusion of mobile genetic elements that have established themselves within our genome, elements such as the originally exogenous retroviruses that have been 'endogenized' and retrotransposons such as the prolific LINE-1. Occupying much more of our genome than our protein-coding genes, these elements also perform functions that are crucial to our continued existence. In genetic terms, we are half-mammal, half-virus. See Chapter 3.
863 Money (2014), 134 (emphasis in original).
864 This is not to say that the individual farmer is 'one' with his cows. Given the division of labour on which modern society is based, the interdependence of humans and cows operates at a collective level or species level. The benefits of such a symbiosis are also above all collective in nature. The agricultural revolution – the collective transformation of humans from free-living hunter-gatherers into sedentary

farmers – did not result in increased prosperity or security for individual peasants and their families. What was fostered was the 'well-being' of the species in terms of sheer numbers. More people could be kept alive, albeit under worse conditions. See Harari (2011), 87–94.

865 Ibid., 90–91. Of course, it will be countered that the question of 'agency' is what distinguishes wheat from human beings. A plant does not *do* anything to manipulate us; it manipulates us simply by being what it is. Individual humans, by contrast, take decisions and act on those decisions. While this is true at the individual level, collectively the shift from hunter-gathering to agriculture seems to have followed its own irresistible, irreversible and self-reinforcing logic (see ibid., 94–100).

866 See, for example, Dawkins (1976; 1989), 180–81, on the farming practices of ants. The sap-feeding aphids provide the ants with a nutrient-rich 'honey-dew' which passes from their back end; the ants 'milk' the aphids by stroking their backsides with their feelers and legs. In return for this nectar, the ants give the aphids protection from their enemies and all in all a sheltered life. Aphid species that are farmed in this way tend to lose their normal defence mechanisms.

867 On the farming activity of *D. discoideum* see Brock et al. (2011).

868 Such behaviour also suggests a collective self rather than individual selfishness. As with human and ant farming practices, the benefits are communal and trans-generational. As Brock et al. put it (2011; 393), 'the striking convergent evolution between bacterial husbandry in social amoebas and fungus farming in social insects makes sense because multigenerational benefits of farming go to already established kin groups'.

869 See Grandin (2005), 303–7, on how humans have co-evolved with wolves, the two species mutually modifying one another to create a more efficient association in which humans specialize in the planning and organizational tasks, and dogs in the sensory tasks. Domestication is not a matter of subjugation, but of an overcoming of fear, and thus an overcoming of *distance*.

870 See Introduction, page 22.

871 Aristotle (trans. J. A. K. Thomson; 1953), 266.

872 See Shakespeare's poem 'The Phoenix and the Turtle': 'So they lov'd, as love in twain / Had the essence but in one; / Two distincts, division none: / Number there in love was slain' (lines 25–28); 'Property was thus appall'd, / That the self was not the same; / Single nature's double name / Neither two nor one was call'd' (lines 37–40). Comic and bawdy vernacular captures the image in the metaphor of the sexual act as the 'two-backed beast' or *la beste à deux doz*; see Rabelais (1973), 47.

873 In bacterial conjugation, by contrast, genetic material is swapped between cells by establishing a sort of bridge – a sex pilus – between one bacterium and another from the same or a different species. In this case it is the mating bridge that (temporarily) allows separateness to be overcome. Despite the brief 'union', the two cells involved maintain their integrity.

874 See Wu and Glass (2001), 1045.

875 On the plasmodial slime mould see Ashworth and Dee (1975).

876 Bonner (1993), 55–56.

877 Ashworth and Dee (1975), 16. Sporulation in fact depends on exposure to light. In the absence of light, the starving plasmodium will form a sclerotium, a resistant mass surrounded by a leathery crust that remains dormant until conditions improve.

878 A comparable phenomenon in bacteria is exhibited by just a few species, as large size in general does not pay for bacteria. Some of the largest of all bacteria belong to the genus *Epulopiscium*. This is known to attain lengths of up to 600 μm (larger than many paramecia) and is characterized by the presence of tens of thousands of copies of its genome arranged around the cell periphery.

879 This cooperation is especially close in the intestines, where the tight junctions characteristic of the epithelium are reinforced by layers of mucus secreted by specialized cells. The gut – considered the body's largest immune organ – also houses roughly 70 percent of all the body's immune cells in and just beneath the epithelium in a complex called the gut-associated lymphoid tissue. See Turney (2015), 163–64.

880 See Tauber (2009).

881 There is no more reason to posit consciousness in the activities of immune cells than there is to suggest that an eye might be conscious when a photon is absorbed by a photoreceptor protein such as rhodopsin in the cells of a vertebrate retina.

882 On 'missing self' see Medzhitov and Janeway Jr. (2002), 298–300. The strategy of recognizing 'missing self' is an efficient way of identifying abnormal selfhood and possible viral infection, yet it is in turn vulnerable to 'fraud' and 'imposture': many examples of 'stolen identity' are known in which viruses have acquired the genes for self markers by horizontal gene transfer and thus been able to protect themselves from detection by the host.

883 Medzhitov and Janeway (2002) raise the question of why stressed cells seek the assistance of NK cells to commit suicide when they can do so perfectly well autonomously. They suggest that this may be a way of simultaneously activating the NK cells to produce intercellular signalling molecules – cytokines – such as interferon-gamma, which in turn galvanize other nearby defence cells into action. Alternatively, it may be a way of counteracting viral strategies that block the intrinsic apoptotic pathway.

884 Matzinger (2002), 301–5.

885 According to the notion of genomic imprinting, the question of which allele is expressed in offspring is determined for certain genes by the parent of origin; specifically, paternal genes (inherited from the father) are thought to be responsible for producing the placenta. On this view, propounded by David Haig, the placenta represents a parasitic takeover of the maternal body by the paternal genes in the foetus. The placenta strives, against the mother's resistance, to parasitize the maternal blood supply, producing hormones to raise her blood pressure and blood-sugar levels for the benefit of the foetus. See Ridley (1999), 206–18.

886 Matzinger (2002), 301.

887 Matzinger herself does not reject the concept of 'selfhood' outright; her own analysis aspires to provide us with a 'renewed sense of self' (2002; 304).

888 Thomas (1974), 29.

889 We have already encountered this conception of 'containing' one's microbiota in Eberl (2010), 455: it implies physiological containment but also containment in the sense of functional integration and unity.

890 See Ackerman (2012), 26–27.

891 Turney (2015), 165.

892 Xu and Gordon (2003), 10454: Ang4 is bactericidal for Gram-positive gut pathogens such as *Listeria monocytogenes*, which may cause bacterial meningitis.
893 Eberl (2010), 451.
894 In a nutshell, my immune system helps 'contain' my symbiotic partners; my symbiotic partners themselves participate in this process of self-containment.
895 In such a situation, the 'containment' would not be produced by the individual self, but might be understood as the work of a collective self or species self (humankind as a whole).
896 Matzinger (2002), 301, 304.
897 Hanahan and Weinberg (2000), 62.
898 On self-tolerance see Sompayrac (1999; 2008), 81–90. For example, B and T cells are 'educated' in the bone marrow and thymus, respectively; any cells that 'recognize' self antigens are eliminated. Virgin B and T cells are restricted in their traffic patterns, preventing them from venturing out into tissue. Recognition depends on co-stimulation from other cells. The very safeguards that reduce the risk of a cytotoxic T cell – a killer T cell – misguidedly recognizing 'self' in the bodily tissues of a lung also make it less likely that it will recognize the mutated 'self' of a metastatic tumour cell.
899 Matzinger (2002), 304.
900 See also Tauber (2009).
901 See Eberl (2010).
902 In other words: bacteria or archaea (or prokaryotes in general) as distinct from eukaryotes.
903 A slightly older term is 'pathogen-associated molecular pattern' (PAMP), yet this overlooks that benign microbes as well as pathogens express molecules such as LPS. This in turn raises the problem of how a host organism knows *which* forms of LPS to recognize: major symbionts such as *Bacteroides* express variants of LPS that evade recognition by PRRs, but so do some pathogens. See Eberl (2010).
904 On allorecognition in the hydrozoan *Hydractinia* see Cadavid (2004) and Rosa et al. (2010), who have shown the gene complexes to encode transmembrane receptor proteins with highly variable extracellular regions similar to immunoglobulin proteins.
905 Such a re-encounter might follow fragmentation caused by environmental factors.
906 Arnoult et al. (2001).
907 See Müller and Müller (2003), 281, who provide a detailed description of the sponge immune system and the many features shared with the immune systems of other, more complex metazoans. The authors likewise stress that sponges *are* in fact endowed with precursor elements of nervous systems, as well as with dynamic contractile systems and elementary structures of the basal lamina.
908 Ibid., 282.
909 Ibid., 285: the cytokine in question is allograft inflammatory factor 1 (AIF-1). The sponge AIF-1 shows a greater similarity to its mammalian counterpart than to corresponding molecules in the nematode and fruit fly.
910 Ibid., 287–88. Müller and Müller cite a range of other features suggesting that the sponge immune system is more closely related to that of the class of animals known as the deuterostomes (which include vertebrates and thus mammals) than to the protostomes (which include the arthropods, nematodes and molluscs).

911 Müller (2003), 6–8.
912 See Durrant and Dong (2004), 185–209. SAR is not the only defence mechanism available to plants. Another defence pathway is 'induced systemic resistance', which uses a different set of signalling molecules to protect the plant against a range of pathogens.
913 Hallé (2002; 204), by contrast, argues that plants do not have an immune system. He is right to the extent that plants lack mechanisms of defence against *near-self* and are thus more tolerant of genetic diversity within the 'individual'. However, plants do defend themselves against *remote non-self* (e.g. bacteria), albeit not by means of phagocytes. Moreover, plant roots have also been shown to have powers of self/non-self discrimination, thereby enabling self to avoid competing with self for scarce resources. In some cases this self-recognition relates to other roots of the same individual, in other cases to the roots of other individuals of the same species. This suggests that the 'self' is defined in different ways in the two scenarios. On plant self/non-self discrimination see Gruntman and Novoplansky (2004).
914 Jones and Dangl (2006), 323.
915 Chamovitz (2012), 54–55.
916 Ibid., 52–53.
917 See ibid., 48–54, on the work of Martin Heil on plant olfactory signals. Such signals need not be read as stemming from an 'intention' to help other plants. The point, perhaps, is that no evolutionary measures have been taken to *prevent* the signal reaching other plants.
918 The idea here would be that the kingdom of plants pulls together in the face of a common prokaryotic enemy.
919 Roughly 80 percent of terrestrial plants establish symbiotic mycorrhizal networks with such fungi. On mycorrhizal networks as media of interplant communication, see Song et al. (2010).
920 Or: what about apparently more abstract selves such as species? Mechanisms of reproductive isolation have an analogous defining role, but are not obviously 'defensive'. This topic will require further consideration in future work.
921 Lewis (2000), 503.
922 Ibid., 505.
923 Ibid., 507.
924 Ibid., 508–9.
925 On T/A systems, see Chapter 4, page 172.
926 See Makarova et al. (2013), 4364, for an account of other, similar mechanisms, such as the 'DND' system, which uses a different chemical marker to label self DNA.
927 Kobayashi (2001), 3742: Kobayashi notes that 'RM systems sometimes behave as discrete units of life' and suggests that they may represent 'one of the simplest forms of life, similar to viruses, transposons and homing endonucleases'. They use three distinct strategies to increase their relative frequency within a cell population, defending their host bacteria from invasive 'non-self' DNAs, killing cells that get rid of them and moving between genomes.
928 See Chapter 3, page 136.
929 Methylation is far from universal, however, having been lost in lineages leading to the fruit fly and

the nematode and remaining uncommon in fungi. See Zemach and Zilberman (2010).

930 CRISPR stands for 'clustered regularly interspaced short palindromic repeats'; Cas stands for 'CRISPR-associated genes'. On the CRISPR-Cas system, see for example Makarova et al. (2013), Horvath and Barrangou (2010), and Marraffini and Sontheimer (2010a, 2010b).

931 Analogies have accordingly been drawn with the eukaryotic RNA-induced gene silencing encountered in Chapter 3 (page 137). See Marraffini and Sontheimer (2010b), 187.

932 Recognition of non-self thus involves two factors: a) recognition of identity (i.e. the identity of the spacer region of the crRNA and the viral material: this is a way of 'drawing attention to' or 'focusing on' the element); b) recognition of difference (i.e. the mismatch at specific positions *outside* the spacer region of the crRNA). See Marraffini and Sontheimer (2010a), 570.

933 Koonin and Dolja (2013), 551.

934 Makarova et al. (2013), 4361, cite *Paenibacillus* sp., which has a genome of more than seven megabases.

935 See Denton (2005), 81–82.

936 See Damasio (2000), 138, citing the physiologist W. B. Cannon, writing in the early 20th century. Damasio himself defines homeostasis as 'the coordinated and largely automated physiological reactions required to maintain steady internal states in a living organism. Homeostasis describes the automatic regulation of temperature, oxygen concentration, or pH in your body' (ibid., 39–40).

937 Other terms such as homeorhesis and homeodynamics have been proposed and are certainly more accurate. The important point is that even such suggestions maintain the 'sameness' (*homeo*), albeit within a context of flow or dynamics rather than stasis.

938 Haldane (1927), in Dawkins (ed.) (2008), 55–56.

939 Ibid., 56.

940 Mendell et al. (2008).

941 Bresler et al. (1998), 5601.

942 Mendell et al. (2008), 6732.

943 Ibid.

944 See Archibald (2014), 106, on mitochondria; 127–28, on chloroplasts.

945 Unlike other bilaterians, flatworms lack a coelom or internal body cavity in which circulatory or respiratory organs can be housed, reducing them to flat shapes that allow oxygen to diffuse through the whole body. Oxygen diffusion is likewise used by amphioxus, also known as the lancelet. Amphioxus is closely related to the vertebrates and does have a coelom, yet it lacks a vertebral column, as well as a true brain or eyes.

946 Oxygen is more plentiful *in* air, and also easier to extract *from* it. See Turner (2000), 106–7. Turner suggests that the cheaper 'costs' of physiological respiration for air-breathing animals were a major factor explaining why animals first moved from the sea onto the land.

947 Haldane (1927), in Dawkins (ed.) (2008), 56.

948 Turner (2000), 122.

949 Ibid.

950 See Roach (2013), 259–75.

951 The colon of rodents and rabbits houses bacteria that produce vitamins B and K, yet there is no opportunity for these to be absorbed prior to being expelled. The 'self-manufactured pellet' thus serves as a daily vitamin supplement. Roach cites the work of Richard H. Barnes, who found that rats eat between 45 and 100 percent of what they had excreted each day. Prevented from doing so, they rapidly became deficient in certain key vitamins and essential fatty acids (ibid., 265).

952 On the heliozoans see Barnes (ed.) (1998), 97–98, who includes them as a class of radiolarians; see also Patterson and Hedley (1992; 1996), 168–75, who regard the group as polyphyletic, i.e. containing taxa that do not share a recent common ancestor but are defined on the basis of convergent characteristics.

953 Wharton (2002), 25.

954 See ibid., 40–41.

955 Ibid., 108–11.

956 See Denton (2005), 84, 119–20. Surgical removal of the relevant part of the hypothalamus causes a loss of the faculty of thirst. However high the salt concentrations in the blood may be, the animal no longer shows an appetite to imbibe water.

957 Ions in fact have both concentration differentials and charge differentials across a membrane. The membrane potential denotes the difference in electric charge between the cell's interior and the fluid surrounding the cell.

958 For a more detailed account see Turner (2000), 17–19.

959 See Turner (2000), 19: this work takes the form of the *mechanical deformation* of heart muscle proteins (for pumping blood) or transmembrane transport proteins (for actively moving solutes across the membrane against a gradient). In both cases, it is powered by the chemical energy in ATP.

960 The saltiness of cellular cytoplasm is relatively close to the salinity of the sea. By contrast with terrestrial animals too, the water requirements of marine animals remain fairly steady, for they are exempt from water losses either as a result of thermoregulation (sweating) or respiration. See Denton (2005), 120, citing the work of James Fitzsimons.

961 Prokaryotic cells living in hypersaline media such as soda lakes, by contrast, are able to dispense with turgor and have greater freedom in the range of shapes available to them. This explains the existence of certain halophiles – 'salt-loving' archaea – that can take the form of thin flat squares. In a freshwater context, sheet morphology of this sort would rapidly tear open under the hydrostatic pressure. Freed from the constraints of turgor, square sheets provide a larger area for nutrient uptake and light absorption. See Walsby (2005), 194.

962 Money (2014), 109.

963 See Turner (2000), 102; see also 17–19.

964 Money (2014), 110–11.

965 Jablonski (2006), 27–28, on amphibian skin.

966 See Denton (2005), 122: a dehydrated frog placed near water in a laboratory does not approach the water, but may die of dehydration though just a few centimetres away from it. However, if it stumbles across water through its movements, it will stay there. Some lizards show a similar deficiency.

967 Haldane (1927), in Dawkins (ed.) (2008), 58.

968 Insects are a special case. Though traditionally regarded as having a body temperature dependent on ambient temperature, many classes are now known to have considerable thermoregulatory capacities. See Heinrich (1993).
969 Wharton (2002), 129–33.
970 Sweating leads to evaporative cooling when water is secreted onto the surface of the skin. Panting works by increasing the airflow through the respiratory system and mouth, resulting in the evaporative cooling of these surfaces. See ibid., 135–36.
971 By contrast with most mammals, camels thus set a premium on avoiding water loss. Instead of sweating or panting to regulate their inner temperature, they allow this to vary by as much as 6°C each day. They are believed to save up to five litres of water a day by doing so. See ibid., 34.
972 Jablonski (2006), 18. While most mammals sport fine coats for insulation (as well as decoration), however, certain species of mammal have waylaid their hair over the course of evolutionary time. Examples include naked mole rats, which live in warm, underground colonies; certain aquatic mammals, whose naked skin reduces drag when swimming and diving and who compensate for the lack of an external coat with subcutaneous blubber; and terrestrial giants such as elephants, hippopotamuses and rhinoceroses, whose size puts them at risk of overheating. Human beings too are much less hirsute than their primate cousins. It has been forcefully argued by Nina Jablonski that our hairlessness derives from the benefits of naked skin when it comes to efficient sweating and the thermoregulatory advantages this confers. See ibid., 42–55.
973 See page 87.
974 Balcombe (2006), 141.
975 See Turner (2000), 187, and 186–194 on the social thermoregulation of honeybee colonies.
976 Wharton (2002), 68, 75–76. Many mammals engage in dormancy, torpor or hibernation. Migration is another option available to larger mammals and birds, circumventing the need for physiological thermoregulation.
977 James (1890; 2007), 291 (italics omitted).
978 In the case of modern-day urban buildings, this interdependence is less than in many animals. Most humans are uninvolved in the building of their house; it is a *collective* human self – characterized by specialization and the division of labour – that constructs the aggregation of brick or concrete containers that shelter us collectively from the environment. These containers may be inhabited for only a few hours a day, and swapped at regular intervals throughout a lifetime or when something better turns up. The burrows of naked mole rats, the hives of bees and the mounds of termites are likewise associated with collective selfhood, though in these cases the degree of dependence, continuity and 'belonging' may be much greater.
979 Juxtapositions of the animate and the inanimate – as when objects such as houses or cars are treated as though they were alive, had a face or personality, etc. – are a timeless source of comedy, drawing laughter from the interplay of similarity and incongruous difference. Equally, it would usually be considered 'absurd' (and perhaps also a disconcerting infringement of autonomy) to extend the domain of selfhood, especially *our* selfhood, to incorporate inanimate objects. For an account of the relationship between laughter, anxiety and the boundary between self and non-self, see Glasgow (1997).

980 See Chapter 2, page 88.

981 See Bargh and Chartrand (1999).

982 This is not the place to explore the relationship between selfhood and self-predictability, which is embodied most graphically in the phenomenon of corollary discharge and the fact that we cannot tickle ourselves. Rodolfo Llinás has defined the 'self' as the 'centralization of prediction', but such a definition lacks the necessary element of reflexivity. One might instead describe a self as a unit of 'self-predictability' in the sense not of active prognosis but the fact that a self *tends not to surprise itself*; it is what comes from outside – non-self – that runs the risk of catching us unawares. On corollary discharge see Blakemore et al. (1998) and Crapse and Sommer (2008). See Llinás (2002), 33–35, on the self as the centralization of prediction.

983 See Wong (2013), 80.

984 More benign – and more recent – alternatives include merely shearing the animals, or using plants for garments made of linen or cotton.

985 See Turner (2000), 81–84.

986 See ibid., 99–119.

987 Ibid., 119.

988 Ibid., 6–7.

989 Dawkins (1976; 1989), 238.

990 Turner (2000), 135–6: see 120–41 in general on how diving spiders and aquatic beetles adapt their environment to create accessory gills and lungs, organs of external physiology that complement their internal physiology.

991 Turner (2000), 82.

992 Finn et al. (2009), R1069–70.

993 Ibid.

994 On *Euglypha* see Patterson and Hedley (1992; 1996), 93.

995 On *Difflugia* see ibid., 95–96.

996 Schönborn (1966), 18, 33–37.

997 Ibid., 36: this is observed in the difflugiid *Pontigulasia*.

998 Ibid., 68; Patterson and Hedley (1992; 1996), 138.

999 On xenophyophorea see Barnes (ed.) (1998), 44–45; also Money (2014), 172–73.

1000 See Finn et al. (2009), R1069.

1001 The archetypal *modern* tool, perhaps, is the car; the same sort of argument applies in considering cars as extensions of self.

1002 See Heidegger's account of 'stuff' (*Zeug*) in *Sein und Zeit* (1926;1986), 66–76.

1003 By contrast, many people frequently seem to enter into such a union with their car.

1004 Rowlands (2010), 197.

1005 Language itself may be viewed as such a cognitive tool, at least metaphorically. Just as the physical tools that we use (our car, our glasses) may come to form a part of what we are, so we are partially *constituted* by the language we use. On such a view, this constitutive relationship is likewise characterized by its 'transparency': it is only when something 'goes wrong' (as in poetry, humour or some philosophy) that we focus on the tool *in itself* as an object rather than on the inner or outer world that it is its function to disclose.

1006 Clark and Chalmers (1998), 7–19.

1007 The philosophers engaged in this debate have tended to focus on 'mind' and its extendedness or otherwise, yet analogous arguments apply to the extensibility of selfhood. The idea is that the mind is not localizable merely in the brain or the body, but may extend to incorporate informational structures or processes in the environment. In fact, the concept of 'mind' has always been notoriously resistant to attempts at definition or localization anyway.

1008 See Brooks (2007).

1009 Ibid.

1010 Rowlands (2010), 93–95.

1011 See ibid., 135–62.

1012 This is not to deny the undoubted role of material property and possessions in our human sense of self and the importance of the objects we possess in defining who we are. Psychologists use the concept of the 'extended self' to denote how people incorporate 'self-owned' objects into their sense of self. On this sense of the extended self, see Kim and Johnson (2013). Diverse affective and cognitive effects are triggered by the ownership of objects, a well-documented example being the 'endowment effect', which induces us to ascribe greater value to objects that *are ours*. Recent research has shown that specific neural substrates – notably the medial prefrontal cortex – underlie these associations between selfhood and ownership. Given the huge cultural variations in attitudes to the possession of material goods, however, the relatively contingent relationship between selfhood and 'property' cannot be straightforwardly equated with that between selfhood and 'belonging' in the functional sense.

1013 The implications and limitations of this notion of a collective human self will be explored in a future study.

1014 See Introduction, page 37.

1015 See Thompson (2007), 79.

1016 Of course, random or non-directional movement – known as chemokinesis – may also be a perfectly plausible predatory strategy. However, this has a very different set of implications for the relationship between self and non-self.

1017 See Bray (2009), 89–93.

1018 Ibid., 6.

1019 Self-transcendence can also be conceived in terms of indexicality: while the concept of 'containment' entails that I am always here now (this is tautologically true of the first-person perspective associated with selfhood: here is where I always am; now is the time it always is), my self-transcendence allows for me to be there and then (e.g. intentionally directed towards where my food will be in the near future).

1020 Jablonski (2006), 17.

1021 On *Paramecium*, see Greenspan (2007), 5–21. As Greenspan points out, the ion channels would have originally served to allow cells to adapt to osmotic variability in the environment, but have subsequently been co-opted for the regulation of swimming behaviour.

1022 Dawkins (2004), 398.

1023 On the shadow reflex of barnacles and the molecular basis of photoreception in general see Greenspan (2007), 23–40; on the evolution of sight see Lane (2009a), 172–204.

1024 The single-celled 'eye-animalcule' *Euglena*, for example, seems to employ different photoreceptors, called flavoproteins, to guide its phototactic movements.

1025 In the case of *Halobacterium*, the absorption of light by bacteriorhodopsin serves to provide the chemical energy that pumps protons out of the cell and thus generates a proton gradient across the cell membrane. It is this proton gradient that drives the synthesis of ATP and powers cellular activity. See Morowitz (1992), 145–46.

1026 On warnowiids such as *Erythropsidinium*, see F. Gómez et al. (2009).

1027 Hayakawa et al. (2015) have identified a gene fragment in the warnowiid genus *Erythropsidinium* that appears more closely related to bacterial than to eukaryotic rhodopsin. This may well have been acquired by horizontal gene transfer.

1028 It is in fact thought to be a case of tertiary endosymbiosis: the cyanobacteria were originally engulfed by a red alga that was in turn engulfed by a dinoflagellate. However, the history of plastids in dinoflagellates is more complex than this: several dinoflagellates have lost the original plastid and subsequently reacquired one from other secondary endosymbionts such as diatoms, which themselves harbour chloroplasts derived from the same source. See Gavelis et al. (2015), 204.

1029 See Gehring (2014); Hayakawa et al. (2015).

1030 Jennings (1906), 335–37; see also Greenspan (2007), 6.

Bibliography

ABOOBAKER, A. A. (2011) 'Planarian stem cells: a simple paradigm for regeneration'. *Trends in Cell Biology* 21(5), 304–311

ACKERMAN, J. (2012) 'The ultimate social network'. *Scientific American* 306(6), 22–27

ADAMS, E. D. M., GOSS, G. G., LEYS, S. P. & LAUNIKONIS, B. S. (2010) 'Freshwater sponges have functional, sealing epithelia with high transepithelial resistance and negative transepithelial potential'. *PLoS One* 5(11), e15040

AGRAWAL, A., EASTMAN, Q. M. & SCHATZ, D. G. (1998) 'Transposition mediated by RAG1 and RAG2 and its implications for the evolution of the immune system'. *Nature* 394(6695), 744–751

AIELLO, L. C. AND WHEELER, P. (1995) 'The expensive-tissue hypothesis: the brain and the digestive system in human and primate evolution'. *Current Anthropology* 36(2), 199–221

AMEISEN, J. C. (2002) 'On the origin, evolution and nature of programmed cell death: a timeline of four billion years'. *Cell Death and Differentiation* 9(4), 367–393

ANDERSSON, S. G. E., ZOMORODIPOUR, A., ANDERSSON, J. O. ET AL. (1998) 'The genome sequence of *Rickettsia prowazekii* and the origin of mitochondria'. *Nature* 396(6707), 133–140

ANGHELESCU, N. (2011) 'From Lexical to Grammatical: *Nafs* and Other Identifiers', in B. Orfali (ed.) *In the Shadow of Arabic: The Centrality of Language to Arabic Culture: Studies Presented to Ramzi Baalbaki on the Occasion of His Sixtieth Birthday*, Leiden: Brill

ARCHIBALD, J. (2014) *One Plus One Equals One: Symbiosis and the Evolution of Complex Life*. Oxford: Oxford University Press

ARISTOTLE (1915) *The Works vol. IX: Ethica Nicomachea*, trans. W. D. Ross. Oxford: Oxford University Press

ARISTOTLE (1931) *The Works vol. III: De Anima*, trans. J. A. Smith. Oxford: Clarendon Press

ARISTOTLE (1953) *The Ethics*, trans. J. A. K. Thomson. Harmondsworth: Penguin

ARISTOTLE (1986) *De Anima (On the Soul)*, trans. H. Lawson-Tancred. London: Penguin

ARNOULT, D., TATISCHEFF, I., ESTAQUIER, J. ET AL. (2001) 'On the evolutionary conservation of the cell death pathway: Mitochondrial release of an apoptosis-inducing factor during *Dictyostelium discoideum* cell death'. *Molecular Biology of the Cell* 12(10), 3016–3030

ASHWORTH, J. M. AND DEE, J. (1975) *The Biology of Slime Moulds*. London: Edward Arnold

BAILLIE, J. K., BARNETT, M. W., UPTON, K. R. ET AL. (2011) 'Somatic retrotransposition alters the genetic landscape of the human brain'. *Nature* 479(7374), 534–537

BALCOMBE, J. (2006) *Pleasurable Kingdom: Animals and the Nature of Feeling Good*. London: Macmillan

BALL, P. (1999) *H2O: A Biography of Water*. London: Weidenfeld and Nicolson

BALL, P. (2009) *Flow: Nature's Patterns: A Tapestry in Three Parts*. Oxford: Oxford University Press

BAMFORD, D. H., BURNETT, R. M. & STUART, D. I. (2002) 'Evolution of viral structure'. *Theoretical Population Biology* 61(4), 461–470

BANZHAF, W., DITTRICH, P. & ELLER, B. (1999) 'Self-organization in a system of binary strings with spatial interactions'. *Physica D: Nonlinear Phenomena* 125(1), 85–104

BARGH, J. A. AND CHARTRAND, T. L. (1999) 'The unbearable automaticity of being'. *American Psychologist* 54(7), 462–479

BARNES, R. S. K. (ed.) (1998) *The Diversity of Living Organisms*. Oxford: Blackwell Publishing

BECKER, S., THOMA, I., DEUTSCH, A., GEHRKE, T., MAYER, P., ZIPSE, H. & CARELL, T. (2016) 'A high-yielding, strictly regioselective prebiotic purine nucleoside formation pathway'. *Science* 352(6287), 833–836

BEEMAN, R. W., FRIESEN, K. S. & DENELL, R. E. (1992) 'Maternal-effect selfish genes in flour beetles'. *Science* 256(5053), 89–92

BELGNAOUI, S. M., GOSDEN, R. G., SEMMES, O. J. & HAOUDI, A. (2006) 'Human LINE-1 retrotransposon induces DNA damage and apoptosis in cancer cells', *Cancer Cell International* 6(1), 13

BELSHAW, R., PEREIRA, V., KATZOURAKIS, A. ET AL. (2004) 'Long-term reinfection of the human genome by endogenous retroviruses'. *Proceedings of the National Academy of Sciences* 101(14), 4894–4899

BENNER, S. A. (1999) 'How small can a micro-organism be?', in *Size Limits of Very Small Microorganisms: Proceedings of a Workshop*. Washington, D. C.: National Academy Press

BENNER, S. A., RICARDO, A. & CARRIGAN, M. A. (2004) 'Is there a common chemical model for life in the universe?' *Current Opinion in Chemical Biology* 8(6), 672–689

BENNETT, G. M. AND MORAN, N. A. (2013) 'Small, smaller, smallest: the origins and evolution of ancient dual symbioses in a phloem-feeding insect'. *Genome Biology and Evolution* 5(9), 1675–1688

BENNETT, M. R. AND HACKER, P. M. S. (2003) *Philosophical Foundations of Neuroscience*. Oxford: Blackwell Publishing

BENTWICH, I., AVNIEL, A., KAROV, Y. ET AL. (2005) 'Identification of hundreds of conserved and nonconserved human microRNAs'. *Nature Genetics* 37(7), 766–770

BHATTACHARYA, D. AND ARCHIBALD, J. M. (2006) 'Response to Theissen and Martin'. *Current Biology* 16(24), R1017-R1018

BIANCONI, E., PIOVESAN, A., FACCHIN, F. ET AL. (2013) 'An estimation of the number of cells in the human body'. *Annals of Human Biology* 40(6), 463–471

BITBOL, M. AND LUISI, P. L. (2004) 'Autopoiesis with or without cognition: defining life at its edge'. *Journal of the Royal Society Interface* 1(1), 99–107

BLACK, R. M. (1970; rev. ed. 1988) *The Elements of Palaeontology*. Cambridge: Cambridge University Press

BLACKISTON, D. J., CASEY, E. S. & WEISS, M. R. (2008) 'Retention of memory through metamorphosis: can a moth remember what it learned as a caterpillar?' *PLoS One* 3(3), e1736

BLAKEMORE, S.-J., WOLPERT, D. M. & FRITH, C. D. (1998) 'Central cancellation of self-produced tickle sensation'. *Nature Neuroscience* 1(7), 635–640

BOGERD, H. P., WIEGAND, H. L., DOEHLE, B. P., LUEDERS, K. K. & CULLEN, B. R. (2006) 'APOBEC3A and APOBEC3B are potent inhibitors of LTR-retrotransposon function in human cells'. *Nucleic Acids Research* 34(1), 89–95

BONCHEVA, M. AND WHITESIDES, G. M. (2005) 'Making things by self-assembly'. *MRS Bulletin – Materials Research Society* 30(10), 736–742

BONNER, J. T. (1993) *Life Cycles: Reflections of an Evolutionary Biologist*. Princeton, N. J.: Princeton University Press

BONNER, J. T. (2009) *The Social Amoebae: The Biology of Cellular Slime Molds*. Princeton, N. J.: Princeton University Press

BOTO, L. (2010) 'Horizontal gene transfer in evolution: facts and challenges'. *Proceedings of the Royal Society B: Biological Sciences* 277(1683), 819–827

BOUCHARD, F. AND HUNEMAN, P. (ed.) (2013) *From Groups to Individuals: Evolution and Emerging Individuality*. Cambridge, Mass.: MIT Press

BOWKER, J. (ed.) (1997) *The Oxford Dictionary of World Religions*. Oxford and New York: Oxford University Press

BRAY, D. (2009) *Wetware: A Computer in Every Living Cell*. New Haven and London: Yale University Press

BREAKER, R. R. AND JOYCE, G. F. (1994) 'A DNA enzyme that cleaves RNA'. *Chemistry & Biology* 1(4), 223–229

BREITBART, M. AND ROHWER, F. (2005) 'Here a virus, there a virus, everywhere the same virus?' *Trends in Microbiology* 13(6), 278–284

BRESLER, V., MONTGOMERY, W. L., FISHELSON, L. & POLLAK, P. E. (1998) 'Gigantism in a bacterium, *Epulopiscium fishelsoni*, correlates with complex patterns in arrangement, quantity and segregation of DNA'. *Journal of Bacteriology* 180(21), 5601–5611

BROCK, D. A., DOUGLAS, T. E., QUELLER, D. C. & STRASSMANN, J. E. (2011) 'Primitive agriculture in a social amoeba'. *Nature* 469(7330), 393–396

BRODBECK, L., HAUSER, S. & IIDA, F. (2015) 'Morphological evolution of physical robots through model-free phenotype development'. *PLoS One* 10(6), e0128444

BROOKS, D. (2007) 'The outsourced brain'. *The New York Times*, 26 October

BUDIN, I. AND DEVARAJ, N. K. (2011) 'Membrane assembly driven by a biomimetic coupling reaction'. *Journal of the American Chemical Society* 134(2), 751–753

BUDIN, I. AND SZOSTAK, J. W. (2011) 'Physical effects underlying the transition from primitive to modern cell membranes'. *Proceedings of the National Academy of Sciences* 108(13), 5249–5254

BURGER, G., GRAY, M. W. & LANG, B. F. (2003) 'Mitochondrial genomes: anything goes'. *Trends in Genetics* 19(12), 709–716

BURGER, G., GRAY, M. W., FORGET, L. & LANG, B. F. (2013) 'Strikingly bacteria-like and gene-rich mitochondrial genomes throughout jakobid protists'. *Genome Biology and Evolution* 5(2), 418–438

CADAVID, L. F. (2004) 'Self-discrimination in colonial invertebrates: genetic control of allorecognition in the hydroid *Hydractinia*'. *Developmental and Comparative Immunology* 28(9), 871–879

CANO, R. J. AND BORUCKI, M. K. (1995) 'Revival and identification of bacterial spores in 25-to-40-million-year-old Dominican amber'. *Science* 268(5213), 1060–1064

CAREY, N. (2015) *Junk DNA: A Journey through the Dark Matter of the Genome*. London: Icon Books

CASTRO, I. F., VOLONTÉ, L. & RISCO, C. (2013) 'Virus factories: biogenesis and structural design'. *Cellular Microbiology* 15(1), 24–34

CATLING, D. C. (2013) *Astrobiology: A Very Short Introduction*. Oxford: Oxford University Press

CAVALIER-SMITH, T. (2000) 'Membrane heredity and early chloroplast evolution'. *Trends in Plant Science* 5(4), 174–182

CAVALIER-SMITH, T. (2001) 'Obcells as proto-organisms: membrane heredity, lithophosphorylation, and the origins of the genetic code, the first cells, and photosynthesis'. *Journal of Molecular Evolution* 53(4–5), 555–595

CHAISSON, E. J. (2001) *Cosmic Evolution: The Rise of Complexity in Nature*. Cambridge, Mass. and London: Harvard University Press

CHAMOVITZ, D. (2012) *What a Plant Knows*. London: Oneworld

CHAN, D. C. (2006) 'Mitochondria: dynamic organelles in disease, aging and development'. *Cell* 125(7), 1241–1252

CHAPPLE, C. K. (1993) *Nonviolence to Animals, Earth, and Self in Asian Traditions*. Albany: State University of New York Press

CHEN, G., ZHUCHENKO, O. & KUSPA, A. (2007) 'Immune-like phagocyte activity in the social amoeba'. *Science* 317(5838), 678–681

CLARK, A. AND CHALMERS, D. (1998) 'The extended mind'. *Analysis* 58(1), 7–19.

CLARK, K. A., HOWE, D. K., GAFNER, K. ET AL. (2012) 'Selfish little circles: transmission bias and evolution of large deletion-bearing mitochondrial DNA in *Caenorhabditis briggsae* nematodes'. *PLoS One* 7(7), e41433

CLARKE, E. (2012) 'Plant individuality: a solution to the demographer's dilemma'. *Biology & Philosophy* 27(3), 321–361

CLAVERIE, J. M. (2006) 'Viruses take center stage in cellular evolution'. *Genome Biology* 7(6), 110

CLEGG, J. S. (2001) 'Cryptobiosis – a peculiar state of biological organization'. *Comparative Biochemistry and Physiology Part B: Biochemistry and Molecular Biology* 128(4), 613–624

COGHLAN, A. (2014) 'Biggest-ever virus revived from Stone Age permafrost'. *New Scientist* 221(2959), 10

CORDAUX, R. AND BATZER, M. (2009) 'The impact of retrotransposons on human genome evolution'. *Nature Reviews Genetics* 10(10), 691–703

COSTANDI, M. (2013) 'Brain invaders: meet our mind's maintenance workers'. *New Scientist* 220(2938), 44–47

COVENEY, P. AND HIGHFIELD, R. (1990) *The Arrow of Time: The Quest to Solve Science's Greatest Mystery*. London: W. H. Allen

CRAPSE, T. B. AND SOMMER, M. A. (2008) 'Corollary discharge across the animal kingdom'. *Nature Reviews Neuroscience* 9(8), 587–600

CRYAN, J. F. AND DINAN, T. G. (2012) 'Mind-altering microorganisms: the impact of the gut microbiota on brain and behaviour'. *Nature Reviews Neuroscience* 13(10), 701–712

DAGAN, T., ARTZY-RANDRUP, Y. & MARTIN, W. (2008) 'Modular networks and cumulative impact of lateral transfer in prokaryote genome evolution'. *Proceedings of the National Academy of Sciences* 105(29), 10039–10044

DALEY, D. O. AND WHELAN, J. (2005) 'Why genes persist in organelle genomes'. *Genome Biology* 6(5)

DAMASIO, A. (2000) *The Feeling of What Happens: Body, Emotion and the Making of Consciousness*. London: Vintage Books

DANOVARO, R., DELL'ANNO, A., PUSCEDDU, A., GAMBI, C., HEINER, I. & KRISTENSEN, R. M. (2010) 'The first metazoa living in permanently anoxic conditions'. *BMC Biology* 8(30)

DARÒS, J. A., ELENA, S. F. & FLORES, R. (2006) 'Viroids: an Ariadne's thread into the RNA labyrinth'. *EMBO Reports* 7(6), 593–598

DASTON, L. AND MITMAN, G. (2005) 'Introduction', in L. Daston and G. Mitman (eds), *Thinking with Animals: New Perspectives on Anthropomorphism*. New York: Columbia University Press

DAVIES, J. A. (2014) *Life Unfolding: How the Human Body Creates Itself*. Oxford: Oxford University Press

DAWKINS, R. (1976; rev. ed. 1989) *The Selfish Gene*. Oxford: Oxford University Press

DAWKINS, R. (1981) 'In Defence of Selfish Genes'. *Philosophy* 56(218), 556–573.

DAWKINS, R. (1982; rev. ed. 1999) *The Extended Phenotype: The Long Reach of the Gene*. Oxford and New York: Oxford University Press

DAWKINS, R. (2004) *The Ancestor's Tale: A Pilgrimage to the Dawn of Life*. London: Weidenfeld and Nicolson

DAWKINS, R. (2008) (ed.) *The Oxford Book of Modern Science Writing*. Oxford: Oxford University Press

DEAMER, D., DWORKIN, J. P., SANDFORD, S. A. ET AL. (2002) 'The first cell membranes'. *Astrobiology* 2(4), 371–381

DENNETT, D. C. (1991) *Consciousness Explained*. Harmondsworth: Penguin

DENNETT, D. C. (1996) *Kinds of Minds: Towards an Understanding of Consciousness*. London: Weidenfeld and Nicolson

DENTON, D. (2005) *The Primordial Emotions: The Dawning of Consciousness*. Oxford: Oxford University Press

DEWANNIEUX, M., HARPER, F., RICHAUD, A. ET AL. (2006) 'Identification of an infectious progenitor for the multiple-copy HERV-K human endogenous retroelements'. *Genome Research* 16(12), 1548–1556

DIENER, T. O. (1989) 'Circular RNAs: Relics of precellular evolution?' *Proceedings of the National Academy of Sciences of the United States of America* 86(23), 9370–9374

DING, B., ITAYA, A. & ZHONG, X. (2005) 'Viroid trafficking: a small RNA makes a big move'. *Current Opinion in Plant Biology* 8(6), 606–612

DI-POÏ, N., MONTOYA-BURGOS, J. I. & DUBOULE, D. (2009) 'Atypical relaxation of structural constraints in *Hox* gene clusters of the green anole lizard'. *Genome Research* 19(4), 602–610

DOBSON, C. M. (2003) 'Protein folding and misfolding'. *Nature* 426(6968), 884–890

DOLJA, V. V. AND KOONIN, E. V. (2012) 'Capsid-less RNA viruses'. *eLS*

DOUGLAS, S., ZAUNER. S., FRAUNHOLZ, M. ET AL. (2001) 'The highly reduced genome of an enslaved algal nucleus'. *Nature* 410(6832), 1091–1096

DURÁN, O., SCHWÄMMLE, V. & HERRMANN, H. (2005) 'Breeding and solitary wave behavior of dunes'. *Physical Review E* 72(2), 021308

DURRANT, W. E. AND DONG, X. (2004) 'Systemic acquired resistance'. *Annual Review of Phytopathology* 42, 185–209

DYSON, F. J. (1985; rev. ed. 1999) *The Origins of Life*. Cambridge: Cambridge University Press

EBERL, G. (2010) 'A new vision of immunity: homeostasis of the superorganism'. *Mucosal Immunology* 3(5), 450–460

EDGELL, D. (2009) 'Selfish DNA: homing endonucleases find a home'. *Current Biology* 19(3), R115–R117

EMERY, N. J. AND CLAYTON, N. S. (2001) 'Effects of experience and social context on prospective caching strategies by scrub jays'. *Nature* 414(6862), 443–446

EMERY, N. J. AND CLAYTON, N. S. (2004) 'The mentality of crows: convergent evolution of intelligence in corvids and apes'. *Science* 306(5703), 1903–1907

ENGELS, W. (1997) 'Invasions of P elements'. *Genetics* 145(1), 11–15

ESNAULT, C., PRIET, S., RIBET, D., HEIDMANN, O. & HEIDMANN, T. (2008) 'Restriction by APOBEC3 proteins of endogenous retroviruses with an extracellular life cycle: ex vivo effects and in vivo "traces" on the murine IAPE and human HERV-K elements'. *Retrovirology* 5(75)

FEUERBACH, L. (1841; 1970) 'Einige Bemerkungen über den "Anfang der Philosophie" von Dr. J. F. Reiff'. In vol. 9 of *Gesammelte Werke*. 18 vols, ed. W. Schuffenhauer. Berlin: Akademie

FLETCHER, D. A. AND MULLINS, R. D. (2010) 'Cell mechanics and the cytoskeleton'. *Nature* 463(7280), 485–492

FOSTER, J. A. AND MCVEY NEUFELD, K. A. (2013) 'Gut-brain axis: how the microbiome influences anxiety and depression'. *Trends in Neurosciences* 36(5), 305–312

FRAENKEL-CONRAT, H. AND WILLIAMS, R. C. (1955) 'Reconstitution of active tobacco mosaic virus from its inactive protein and nucleic acid components'. *Proceedings of the National Academy of Sciences of the United States of America* 41(10), 690–698

FRANK, M. (1986) *Die Unhintergehbarkeit von Individualität*. Frankfurt-am-Main: Suhrkamp Verlag

Fry, I. (1999) *The Emergence of Life on Earth: A Historical and Scientific Overview*. London: Free Association Books

Gabaldón, T. (2010) 'Peroxisome diversity and evolution'. *Philosophical Transactions of the Royal Society B: Biological Sciences* 365(1541), 765–773

Gast, V. and Siemund, P. (2006) 'Rethinking the relationship between SELF-intensifiers and reflexives'. *Linguistics* 44(2), 343–381

Gauthier, D. P. (ed.) (1970) *Morality and Rational Self-Interest*. Englewood Cliffs, N.J.: Prentice-Hall

Gavelis, G. S., Hayakawa, S., White III, R. A. et al. (2015) 'Eye-like ocelloids are built from different endosymbiotically acquired components'. *Nature* 523(7559), 204–207

Gehring, W. J. (2014) 'The evolution of vision'. *Wiley Interdisciplinary Reviews: Developmental Biology* 3(1), 1–40

Gil, R., Sabater-Muñoz, B., Latorre, A., Silva, F. J. & Moya, A. (2002) 'Extreme genome reduction in *Buchnera* spp.: toward the minimal genome needed for symbiotic life'. *Proceedings of the National Academy of Sciences* 99(7), 4454–4458

Gil, R., Silva, F. J., Peretó, J. & Moya, A. (2004) 'Determination of the core of a minimal bacterial gene set'. *Microbiology and Molecular Biology Reviews* 68(3), 518–537

Giovannoni, S. J., Tripp, H. J., Givan, S. et al. (2005) 'Genome streamlining in a cosmopolitan oceanic bacterium'. *Science* 309(5738), 1242–1245

Gitai, Z. (2005) 'The new bacterial cell biology: moving parts and subcellular architecture'. *Cell* 120(5), 577–586

Glasgow, R. D. V. (1997) *Split Down the Sides: On the Subject of Laughter*. Lanham: University Press of America

Glasgow, R. D. V. (1999) *The Comedy of Mind: Philosophers Stoned, or the Pursuit of Wisdom*. Lanham: University Press of America

Glasgow, R. D. V. (2009) *The Concept of Water*. R. Glasgow Books

Glover, J. (1988) *I: The Philosophy and Psychology of Personal Identity*. London: Allen Lane

Goldenfeld, N. and Woese, C. (2007) 'Biology's next revolution'. *Nature* 445(7126), 369

Goldman, N., Bertone, P., Chen, S. et al. (2013) 'Towards practical, high-capacity, low-maintenance information storage in synthesized DNA'. *Nature* 494(7435), 77–80

Gómez, F., López-García, P. & Moreira, D. (2009) 'Molecular phylogeny of the ocelloid-bearing dinoflagellates *Erythropsidinium* and *Warnowia* (Warnowiaceae, Dinophyceae)'. *Journal of Eukaryotic Microbiology* 56(5), 440–445

GÓMEZ, G. AND PALLÁS, V. (2004) 'A long-distance translocatable phloem protein from cucumber forms a ribonucleoprotein complex in vivo with Hop stunt viroid RNA'. *Journal of Virology* 78(18), 10104–10110

GOODIER, J. AND KAZAZIAN, H. (2008) 'Retrotransposons revisited: the restraint and rehabilitation of parasites'. *Cell* 135(1), 23–35

GOULD, S. J. (1984) *Hen's Teeth and Horse's Toes*. Harmondsworth: Penguin

GRANT, M. C. (1993) 'The Trembling Giant'. *Discover* 14(10), 82

GREENSPAN, R. J. (2007) *An Introduction to Nervous Systems*. Cold Spring Harbor, N.Y.: Cold Spring Harbor Laboratory Press

GROW, E. J., FLYNN, R. A., CHAVEZ, S. L. ET AL. (2015) 'Intrinsic retroviral reactivation in human preimplantation embryos and pluripotent cells'. *Nature* 522(7555), 221–225

GRUNTMAN, M. AND NOVOPLANSKY, A. (2004) 'Physiologically mediated self/non-self discrimination in roots'. *Proceedings of the National Academy of Sciences of the United States of America* 101(11), 3863–3867

HAGER, M. D., GREIL, P., LEYENS, C. ET AL. (2010) 'Self-healing materials'. *Advanced Materials* 22(47), 5424–5430

HALLÉ, F. (2002) *In Praise of Plants*, trans. D. Lee. Portland and London: Timber Press

HAMBLING, D. (2015) *Swarm Troopers: How Small Drones Will Conquer the World*. Archangel Ink

HANAHAN, D. AND WEINBERG, R. (2000) 'The hallmarks of cancer'. *Cell* 100(1), 57–70

HANSEN, C. J., WU, W., TOOHEY, K. S. ET AL. (2009) 'Self-healing materials with interpenetrating microvascular networks'. *Advanced Materials* 21(41), 4143–4147

HARARI, Y. N. (2014) *Sapiens: A Brief History of Humankind*. London: Vintage

HAROLD, F. M. (2001) *The Way of the Cell: Molecules, Organisms and the Order of Life*. Oxford: Oxford University Press

HARVEY, B. P. (1995) *The Selfless Mind: Personality, Consciousness and Nirvana in Early Buddhism*. Richmond: Curzon Press

HATTORI, D., CHEN, Y., MATTHEWS, B. J. ET AL. (2009) 'Robust discrimination between self and non-self neurites requires thousands of Dscam1 isoforms'. *Nature* 461(7264), 644–648

HAYAKAWA, S., TAKAKU, Y., HWANG, J. S. ET AL. (2015) 'Function and evolutionary origin of unicellular camera-type eye structure'. *PLoS ONE* 10(3):e0118415

HAZAN, R., SAT, B., RECHES, M. & ENGELBERG-KULKA, H. (2001) 'Postsegregational killing mediated by the P1 phage "addiction module" *phd-doc* requires the *Escherichia coli* programmed cell death system *mazEF*'. *Journal of Bacteriology* 183(6), 2046–2050

HEGEL, G. W. F. (1986) *Werke*. 20 vols, ed. E. Moldenhauer and K. M. Michel. Frankfurt-am-Main: Suhrkamp

HEIDEGGER, M. (1919/20; 1993) *Grundprobleme der Phänomenologie (1919/20)*. Frankfurt-am-Main: Klostermann

HEIDEGGER, M. (1926; 1986) *Sein und Zeit*. Tübingen: Max Niemeyer Verlag

HEIDEGGER, M. (1929/30; 1983) *Die Grundbegriffe der Metaphysik: Welt – Endlichkeit – Einsamkeit*. Frankfurt-am-Main: Klostermann

HEINRICH, B. (1993) *The Hot-Blooded Insects: Strategies and Mechanisms of Thermoregulation*. Cambridge, Mass.: Harvard University Press

HENDERSON, C. (2012) *The Book of Barely Imagined Beings*. Granta: London

HENDRIX, R. W., SMITH, M. C., BURNS, R. N., FORD, M. E. & HATFULL, G. F. (1999) 'Evolutionary relationships among diverse bacteriophages and prophages: All the world's a phage'. *Proceedings of the National Academy of Sciences of the United States of America* 96(5), 2192–2197

HENDRIX, R. W. (2002) 'Bacteriophages: evolution of the majority'. *Theoretical Population Biology* 61(4), 471–480

HENDRIX, R. W. (2003) 'Bacteriophage genomics'. *Current Opinion in Microbiology* 6(5), 506–511

HILLMAN, B. I. AND CAI, G. (2013) 'The family *Narnaviridae*: simplest of RNA viruses'. *Advances in Virus Research* 86, 149–176

HOBBES, T. (1651; 1968) *Leviathan*, ed. C. B. Macpherson. Harmondsworth: Penguin.

HOELZER, G. A., SMITH, E. & PEPPER, J. W. (2006) 'On the logical relationship between natural selection and self-organization'. *Journal of Evolutionary Biology* 19(6), 1785–1794

HOLLAND, L. Z., ALBALAT, R., AZUMI, K., ET AL. (2008) 'The amphioxus genome illuminates vertebrate origins and cephalochordate biology'. *Genome Research* 18(7), 1100–1111

HOLMES, B. (2015) 'RNA world may never have existed'. *New Scientist* 226(3027), 10

HOOD, B. (2012) *The Self Illusion*. London: Constable

HOOD, B. (2015) 'The Self', in J. Brockman (ed.), *This Idea Must Die: Scientific Theories that are Blocking Progress*, New York: Harper Perennial

HORVATH, P. AND BARRANGOU, R. (2010) 'CRISPR/Cas, the immune system of bacteria and archaea'. *Science* 327(5962), 167–170

HUETTENBRENNER, S., MAIER, S., LEISSER, C. ET AL. (2003) 'The evolution of cell death programs as prerequisites of multicellularity'. *Mutation Research/ Reviews in Mutation Research* 543(3), 235–249

HUME, D. (1739; 1962) *A Treatise of Human Nature. Book One*, ed. D. G. C. Macnabb. London: Collins (Fontana Library)

IEROPOULOS, I., MELHUISH, C. & GREENMAN, J. (2003) 'Artificial metabolism: towards true energetic autonomy in artificial life', in W. Banzhaf et al. (eds.) *Advances in Artificial Life: 7th European Conference, ECAL 2003*. Berlin, Heidelberg: Springer Verlag

ISHIZAKI, Y., CHENG, L., MUDGE, A. W. & RAFF, M. C. (1995) 'Programmed cell death by default in embryonic cells, fibroblasts, and cancer cells'. *Molecular Biology of the Cell* 6(11), 1443–1458

ITAYA, M. (1995) 'An estimation of minimal genome size required for life'. *FEBS Letters* 362(3), 257–260

ITOH, T., MARTIN, W. & NEI, M. (2002) 'Acceleration of genomic evolution caused by enhanced mutation rate in endocellular symbionts'. *Proceedings of the National Academy of Sciences* 99(20), 12944–12948

JABLONSKI, N. G. (2006) *Skin: A Natural History*. Berkeley: University of California Press

JAIN, R., RIVERA, M. C. & LAKE, J. A. (1999) 'Horizontal gene transfer among genomes: the complexity hypothesis'. *Proceedings of the National Academy of Sciences* 96(7), 3801–3806

JAMES, W. (1890; 2007) *The Principles of Psychology. Vol. 1*. New York: Cosimo

JENNINGS, H. S. (1906) *Behavior of the Lower Organisms*. New York: Columbia University Press (London: Macmillan)

JOHNSON, S. S., HEBSGAARD, M. B., CHRISTENSEN, T. R. ET AL. (2007) 'Ancient bacteria show evidence of DNA repair'. *Proceedings of the National Academy of Sciences* 104(36), 14401–14405

JOLIVET-GOUGEON, A., KOVACS, B., LE GALL-DAVID, S. ET AL. (2011) 'Bacterial hypermutation: clinical implications'. *Journal of Medical Microbiology* 60(5), 563–573

JONAS, H. (1966; 2001) *The Phenomenon of Life: Toward a Philosophical Biology*. Evanston, Illinois: Northwestern University Press

JONES, J. D. G. AND DANGL, J. L. (2006) 'The plant immune system'. *Nature* 444(7117), 323–329

JORDAN, I. K., ROGOZIN, I. B., GLAZKO, G. V. & KOONIN, E. V. (2003) 'Origin of a substantial fraction of human regulatory sequences from transposable elements'. *Trends in Genetics* 19(2), 68–72

JOYCE, G. F. (1982; new ed. 1995) 'The RNA World: Life before DNA and Protein', in B. Zuckerman and M. H. Hart (eds) *Extraterrestrials: Where are They?* Cambridge: Cambridge University Press

KANT, I. (1790; 1963) *Kritik der Urteilskraft*, ed. Gerhard Lehmann. Stuttgart: Reclam

KARNKOWSKA, A., VACEK, V., ZUBÁČOVÁ, Z. ET AL. (2016) 'A eukaryote without a mitochondrial organelle'. *Current Biology* 26(10), 1274–1284

KATZOURAKIS, A., GIFFORD, R. J., TRISTEM, M., GILBERT, M. T. P & PYBUS, O. G. (2009) 'Macroevolution of complex retroviruses'. *Science* 325(5947), 1512

KAUFFMAN, S. (1995) *At Home in the Universe: The Search for the Laws of Complexity*. Oxford and New York: Oxford University Press

KAZAZIAN, H. (2004) 'Mobile elements: drivers of genome evolution'. *Science* 303(5664), 1626–1632

KEELING, P. J. AND ARCHIBALD, J. M. (2008) 'Organelle evolution: what's in a name?' *Current Biology* 18(8), R345-R347

KEHR, J. AND BUHTZ, A. (2008) 'Long distance transport and movement of RNA through the phloem'. *Journal of Experimental Biology* 59(1), 85–92

KELLY, I., HOLLAND, O. & MELHUISH, C. (2000) 'Slugbot: a robotic predator in the natural world'. *Proceedings of the Fifth International Symposium on Artificial Life and Robotics for Human Welfare and Artificial Life Robotics*. 470–475

KENNEDY, P. (1989) *The Rise and Fall of the Great Powers: Economic Change and Military Conflict from 1500 to 2000*. London: Fontana Press

KENNY, A. (1989) *The Metaphysics of Mind*. Oxford and New York: Oxford University Press

KIM, I., RODRIGUEZ-ENRIQUEZ, S. & LEMASTERS, J. J. (2007) 'Selective degradation of mitochondria by mitophagy'. *Archives of Biochemistry and Biophysics* 462(2), 245–253

KIM, K. AND JOHNSON, M. K. (2013) 'Extended self: spontaneous activation of medial prefrontal cortex by objects that are "mine"'. *Social Cognitive and Affective Neuroscience* 9, 1006–1012

KIMBALL, J. W. (1999) *Kimball's Biology Pages*. John W. Kimball

KING, N. (2004) 'The unicellular ancestry of animal development'. *Developmental Cell* 7(3), 313–325

KOBAYASHI, I. (2001) 'Behavior of restriction-modification systems as selfish mobile elements and their impact on genome evolution'. *Nucleic Acids Research* 29(18), 3742–3756

KOCH, C. (2011) 'Fatal Attraction'. *Scientific American Mind* 22(2), 16–17

KOGA, S., WILLIAMS, D. S., PERRIMAN, A. W. & MANN, S. (2011) 'Peptide-nucleotide microdroplets as a step towards a membrane-free protocell model'. *Nature Chemistry* 3(9), 720–724

KOONIN, E. V. AND ARAVIND, L. (2002) 'Origin and evolution of eukaryotic apoptosis: the bacterial connection'. *Cell Death and Differentiation* 9(4), 394–404

KOONIN, E. V. AND MARTIN, W. (2005) 'On the origin of genomes and cells within inorganic compartments'. *TRENDS in Genetics* 21(12), 647–654

KOONIN, E. V., SENKEVICH, T. G. & DOLJA, V. V. (2006) 'The ancient Virus World and the evolution of cells'. *Biology Direct 1*(1), 29. Available at: http://www.biologydirect.com/content/1/1/29

KOONIN, E. V. AND DOLJA, V. V. (2013) 'A virocentric perspective on the evolution of life'. *Current Opinion in Virology 3*(5), 546–557

KUSHNER, D. J. (1969) 'Self-assembly of biological structures'. *Bacteriological Reviews 33*(2), 302–345

LAMBOWITZ, A. AND ZIMMERLY, S. (2004) 'Mobile group II introns'. *Annual Review of Genetics 38*, 1–35

LAMPSON, B., INOUYE, M. & INOUYE, S. (2005) 'Retrons, msDNA and the bacterial genome'. *Cytogenetic and Genome Research 110*(1–4), 491–499

LANE, N. (2009a) *Life Ascending: The Ten Great Inventions of Evolution*. London: Profile Books

LANE, N. (2009b) 'The Cradle of Life'. *New Scientist 2730*, 38–42

LANE, N., ALLEN, J. F. & MARTIN, W. (2010) 'How did LUCA make a living? Chemiosmosis in the origin of life'. *BioEssays 32*(4), 271–280

LA ROCHEFOUCAULD (1665; 1976) *Réflexions ou Sentences et Maximes morales*. Paris: Gallimard

LAWRENCE, J. G. AND OCHMAN, H. (1998) 'Molecular archaeology of the *Escherichia coli* genome'. *Proceedings of the National Academy of Sciences 95*(16), 9413–9417

LEGENDRE, M., BARTOLI, J., SHMAKOVA, L. ET AL. (2014) 'Thirty-thousand-year-old distant relative of giant icosahedral DNA viruses with a pandoravirus morphology'. *Proceedings of the National Academy of Sciences 111*(11), 4274–4279

LEIMAN, P. G., KANAMARU, S., MESYANZHINOV, V. V., ARISAKA, F. & ROSSMANN, M. G. (2003) 'Structure and morphogenesis of bacteriophage T4'. *Cellular and Molecular Life Sciences CMLS 60*(11), 2356–2370

LENNON, J. T. AND JONES, S. E. (2011) 'Microbial seed banks: the ecological and evolutionary implications of dormancy'. *Nature Reviews Microbiology 9*(2), 119–130

LEONARDO DA VINCI (1952) *The Notebooks of Leonardo da Vinci*, ed. I. A. Richter. Oxford: Oxford University Press

LEWIN, R. (1992) *Complexity: Life at the Edge of Chaos*. New York: Collier Books

LEWIS, K. (2000) 'Programmed death in bacteria'. *Microbiology and Molecular Biology Reviews 64*(3), 503–514

LI, J., BROWNING, S., MAHAL, S. P., OELSCHLEGEL, A. M. & WEISSMANN, C. (2010) 'Darwinian evolution of prions in cell culture'. *Science 327*(5967), 869–872

LINCOLN, T. A. AND JOYCE, G. F. (2009) 'Self-sustained replication of an RNA enzyme'. *Science 323*(5918), 1229–1232

LLINÁS, R. R. (2002) *I of the Vortex: From Neurons to Self*. Cambridge, Mass.: MIT Press
LOCKE, J. (1689; 1975) *An Essay Concerning Human Understanding*, ed. P. H. Nidditch. Oxford: Clarendon Press
LOUGH, T. J. AND LUCAS, W. J. (2006) 'Integrative plant biology: role of phloem long-distance macromolecular trafficking'. *Annual Review of Plant Biology* 57, 203–232
LWOFF, A. (1957) 'The Concept of Virus'. *Journal of General Microbiology* 17(2), 239–253
MCCUTCHEON, J. P. AND MORAN, N. A. (2011) 'Extreme genome reduction in symbiotic bacteria'. *Nature Reviews Microbiology* 10(1), 13–26
MCFARLAND, D. (2008) *Guilty Robots, Happy Dogs: The Question of Alien Minds*. Oxford: Oxford University Press
MCINERNEY, J. O., COTTON, J. A. & PISANI, D. (2008) 'The prokaryotic tree of life: past, present … and future?' *Trends in Ecology and Evolution* 23(5), 276–281
MCMULLIN, B. (1995) 'Replicators don't!' *Advances in Artificial Life*. Berlin and Heidelberg: Springer, 158–169
MAGIORKINIS, G., GIFFORD, R. J., KATZOURAKIS, A., DE RANTER, J. & BELSHAW, R. (2012) '*Env*-less endogenous retroviruses are genomic superspreaders'. *Proceedings of the National Academy of Sciences* 109(19), 7385–7390
MAKAROVA, K. S., WOLF, Y. I. & KOONIN, E. V. (2013) 'Comparative genomics of defense systems in archaea and bacteria'. *Nucleic Acids Research* 41(8), 4360–4377
MANILOFF, J. (1996) 'The minimal cell genome: "On being the right size"'. *Proceedings of the National Academy of Sciences* 93(19), 10004–10006
MANKERTZ, A. (2008) 'Molecular biology of porcine circoviruses'. *Animal Viruses. Molecular Biology*, 355–374
MARDER, M. (2013) *Plant-Thinking: A Philosophy of Vegetal Life*. New York: Columbia University Press
MARRAFFINI, L. A. AND SONTHEIMER, E. J. (2010a) 'Self versus non-self discrimination during CRISPR RNA-directed immunity'. *Nature* 463(7280), 568–571
MARRAFFINI, L. A. AND SONTHEIMER, E. J. (2010b) 'CRISPR interference: RNA-directed adaptive immunity in bacteria and archaea'. *Nature Reviews Genetics* 11(3), 181–190
MARTIN, W. AND KOONIN, E. V. (2006) 'Introns and the origin of nucleus-cytosol compartmentalization'. *Nature* 440(7080), 41–45
MATURANA, H. R. AND VARELA, F. J. (1987; rev. ed. 1998) *The Tree of Knowledge: The Biological Roots of Human Understanding*, trans. R. Paolucci. Boston and London: Shambhala Press

MATZINGER, P. (2002) 'The danger model: A renewed sense of self'. *Science* 296(5566), 301–305

MAYNARD SMITH, J. AND SZATHMÁRY, E. (1999) *The Origins of Life: From the Birth of Life to the Origins of Language*. Oxford: Oxford University Press

MEDHEKAR, B. AND MILLER, J. (2007) 'Diversity-generating retroelements'. *Current Opinion in Microbiology* 10(4), 388–395

MEDINI, D., DONATI, C., TETTELIN, H., MASIGNANI, V. & RAPPUOLI, R. (2005) 'The microbial pan-genome'. *Current Opinion in Genetics and Development* 15(6), 589–594

MEDZHITOV, R. AND JANEWAY, C. A. (2002) 'Decoding the patterns of self and nonself by the innate immune system'. *Science* 296(5566), 298–300

MENDELL, J. E., CLEMENTS, K. D., CHOAT, J. H. & ANGERT, E. R. (2008) 'Extreme polyploidy in a large bacterium'. *Proceedings of the National Academy of Sciences* 105(18), 6730–6734

METZINGER, T. (2009) *The Ego Tunnel: The Science of the Mind and the Myth of the Self*. New York: Basic Books

MIDGLEY, M. (1979) 'Gene-Juggling'. *Philosophy* 54(210), 439–458

MILLER, K. (1985) *Doubles: Studies in Literary History*. Oxford: Oxford University Press

MILLS, D. R., PETERSON, R. L. & SPIEGELMAN, S. (1967) 'An extracellular Darwinian experiment with a self-duplicating nucleic acid molecule'. *Proceedings of the National Academy of Sciences of the United States of America* 58(1), 217–224

MOCKFORD, E. L. (1997) 'A new species of *Dicopomorpha* (Hymenoptera: Mymaridae) with diminutive, apterous males'. *Annals of the Entomological Society of America* 90(2), 115–120

MONEY, N. P. (2014) *The Amoeba in the Room: Lives of the Microbes*. Oxford: Oxford University Press

MOORE, G. E. (1948) *Principia Ethica*. Cambridge: Cambridge University Press

MORAN, N. A. AND WERNEGREEN, J. J. (2000) 'Lifestyle evolution in symbiotic bacteria: insights from genomics'. *Trends in Ecology and Evolution* 15(8), 321–326

MOREIRA, D. AND LÓPEZ-GARCÍA, P. (2009) 'Ten reasons to exclude viruses from the tree of life'. *Nature Reviews Microbiology* 7(4), 306–311

MORONO, Y., TERADA, T., NISHIZAWA, M. ET AL. (2011) 'Carbon and nitrogen assimilation in deep subseafloor microbial cells'. *Proceedings of the National Academy of Sciences* 108(45), 18295–18300

MOROWITZ, H. J. (1992) *Beginnings of Cellular Life: Metabolism Recapitulates Biogenesis*. New Haven and London: Yale University Press

MOROZ, L. L. (2009) 'On the independent origins of complex brains and neurons'. *Brain, Behavior and Evolution* 74(3), 177–190

MOULDER, J. W. (1985) 'Comparative biology of intracellular parasitism'. *Microbiological Reviews* 49(3), 298–337

MUECK, L. (2013) 'Cosmic chemistry: life's molecules are everywhere'. *New Scientist* 220(2939), 42–45

MUKHERJEE, S. (2011) *The Emperor of All Maladies: A Biography of Cancer*. London: Fourth Estate

MÜLLER, W. E. (2003) 'The origin of metazoan complexity: Porifera as integrated animals'. *Integrative and Comparative Biology* 43(1), 3–10

MÜLLER, W. E. AND MÜLLER, I. M. (2003) 'Origin of the metazoan immune system: identification of the molecules and their functions in sponges'. *Integrative and Comparative Biology* 43(2), 281–292

MUOTRI, A. R., ZHAO, C., MARCHETTO, M. C. & GAGE, F. H. (2009) 'Environmental influence on L1 retrotransposons in the adult hippocampus'. *Hippocampus* 19(10), 1002–1007

MUOTRI, A. R., MARCHETTO, M. C., COUFAL, N. G. ET AL. (2010) 'L1 retrotransposition in neurons is modulated by MeCP2'. *Nature* 468(7322), 443–446

MUSHEGIAN, A. R. AND KOONIN, E. V. (1996) 'A minimal gene set for cellular life derived by comparison of complete bacterial genomes'. *Proceedings of the National Academy of Sciences* 93(19), 10268–10273

NAGEL, T. (1974) 'What is it like to be a bat?' *Philosophical Review* 4, 435–450

NAKAMURA, T. AND CECH, T. (1998) 'Reversing time: origin of telomerase'. *Cell* 92(5), 587–590

NASRALLAH, J. B. (2005) 'Recognition and rejection of self in plant self-incompatibility: comparisons to animal histocompatibility'. *Trends in Immunology* 26(8), 412–418

NELSON, K. E., LEVY, M. & MILLER, S. L. (2000) 'Peptide nucleic acids rather than RNA may have been the first genetic molecule', *Proceedings of the National Academy of Sciences* 97(8), 3868–3871

NESHER, N., LEVY, G., GRASSO, F. W. & HOCHNER, B. (2014) 'Self-recognition mechanism between skin and suckers prevents octopus arms from interfering with each other'. *Current Biology* 24(11), 1271–1275

NICKEL, M., SCHEER, C., HAMMEL, J. U., HERZEN, J. & BECKMANN, F. (2011) 'The contractile sponge epithelium *sensu lato* – Body contraction of the demosponge *Tethya wilhelma* is mediated by the pinacoderm'. *The Journal of Experimental Biology* 214(10), 1692–98

NIELSEN, P. E. (2008) 'A new molecule of life?' *Scientific American* 299(6), 64–71

NORRIS, V., TURNOCK, G. & SIGEE, D. (1996) 'The *Escherichia coli* enzoskeleton'. *Molecular Microbiology* 19(2), 197–204

NOVOA, R. R., CALDERITA, G., ARRANZ, R. ET AL. (2005) 'Virus factories: associations of cell organelles for viral replication and morphogenesis'. *Biology of the Cell* 97(2), 147–172

Nozick, R. (1981) *Philosophical Explanations*. Oxford: Clarendon Press
O'Malley, M. A. (2014) *Philosophy of Microbiology*. Cambridge: Cambridge University Press
Orgel, L. and Crick, F. (1980) 'Selfish DNA: the ultimate parasite'. *Nature* 284(5757), 604–607
Palmer, J. D. (1997) 'Organelle genomes: going, going, gone!' *Science* 275(5301), 790–791
Parfit, D. (1984) *Reasons and Persons*. Oxford and New York: Oxford University Press
Passmore, J. (1961) *Philosophical Reasoning*. London: Duckworth
Patterson, D. J. and Hedley, S. (1992; rev. ed. 1996) *Free-living Freshwater Protozoa: A Colour Guide*. London: Manson Publishing
Pearson, H. (2008) '"Virophage" suggests viruses are alive'. *Nature News* 454(7205), 677–677
Pepper, J. W. and Herron, M. D. (2008) 'Does biology need an organism concept?' *Biological Reviews* 83(4), 621–627
Pérez-Brocal, V., Gil, R., Ramos, S. et al. (2006) 'A small microbial genome: the end of a long symbiotic relationship?' *Science* 314(5797), 312–313
Pérez-Rémon, J. (1980) *Self and Non-Self in Early Buddhism*. The Hague: Mouton
Philippe, N., Legendre, M., Doutre, G. et al. (2013) 'Pandoraviruses: amoeba viruses with genomes up to 2.5Mb reaching that of parasitic eukaryotes'. *Science* 341(6143), 281–286
Pineda-Krch, M. and Lehtilä, K. (2004) 'Costs and benefits of genetic heterogeneity within organisms'. *Journal of Evolutionary Biology* 17(6), 1167–1177
Piriyapongsa, J., Mariño-Ramírez, L. & Jordan, I. K. (2007) 'Origin and evolution of human microRNAs from transposable elements'. *Genetics* 176(2), 1323–1337
Plasterk, R. (1998) 'V (D) J recombination: ragtime jumping'. *Nature* 394(6695), 718–719
Plato (1914) *Euthyphro. Apology. Crito. Phaedo. Phaedrus*, with an English translation by H. N. Fowler. London: William Heinemann (Loeb Classical Library)
Plessner, H. (1928; 3rd ed. 1975) *Die Stufen des Organischen und der Mensch: Einleitung in die philosophische Anthropologie*. Berlin: Walter de Gruyter
Polilov, A. A. (2012) 'The smallest insects evolve anucleate neurons'. *Arthropod Structure and Development* 41(1), 29–34
Powner, M. W., Gerland, B. & Sutherland, J. D. (2009) 'Synthesis of activated pyrimidine ribonucleotides in prebiotically plausible conditions'. *Nature* 459(7244), 239–242

Pradeu, T. (2013) 'Immunity and the Emergence of Individuality', in F. Bouchard and P. Huneman (eds) *From Groups to Individuals*. Cambridge, Mass.: MIT Press, 77–96

Prigogine, I. and Stengers, I. (1984) *Order out of Chaos: Man's New Dialogue with Nature*. London: William Heinemann

Qin, J., Li, R., Raes, J. et al. (2010) 'A human gut microbial gene catalogue established by metagenomic sequencing'. *Nature* 464(7285), 59–65

Queller, D. C., Ponte, E., Bozzaro, S. & Strassmann, J. E. (2003) 'Single-gene greenbeard effects in the social amoeba *Dictyostelium discoideum*'. *Science* 299(5603), 105–106

Rabelais, F. (1973) *Oeuvres Complètes*, ed. G. Demerson et al. Paris: Seuil

Raff, M. (1998) 'Cell suicide for beginners'. *Nature* 396(6707), 119–122

Rambold, A. S., Kostelecky, B., Elia, N. & Lippincott-Schwartz, J. (2011) 'Tubular network formation protects mitochondria from autophagosomal degradation during nutrient starvation'. *Proceedings of the National Academy of Sciences* 108(25), 10190–10195

Raoult, D. and Forterre, P. (2008) 'Redefining viruses: lessons from Mimivirus'. *Nature Reviews Microbiology* 6(4), 315–319

Renesto, P., Ogata, H., Audic, S., Claverie, J. M. & Raoult, D. (2005) 'Some lessons from *Rickettsia* genomics'. *FEMS Microbiology Reviews* 29(1), 99–117

Rice, D. W., Alverson, A. J., Richardson, A. O. et al. (2013) 'Horizontal transfer of entire genomes via mitochondrial fusion in the angiosperm *Amborella*'. *Science* 342(6165), 1468–1473

Ridley, M. (1999) *Genome: The autobiography of a species in 23 chapters*. London: Harper Perennial

Roach, M. (2013) *Gulp: Adventures on the Alimentary Canal*. W. W. Norton & Company

Rogozin, I. B., Carmel, L., Csuros, M. & Koonin, E. V. (2012) 'Origin and evolution of spliceosomal introns'. *Biology Direct* 7(11), 6150–6157

Rosa, S. F. P., Powell, A. E., Rosengarten, R. D. et al. (2010) '*Hydractinia* allodeterminant *alr1* resides in an immunoglobulin superfamily-like complex complex'. *Current Biology* 20(12), 1122–1127

Rose, S. (1992) *The Making of Memory*. London: Bantam Press

Rowlands, M. (2010) *The New Science of the Mind: From Extended Mind to Embodied Phenomenology*. Cambridge, Mass.: MIT Press

Rozin, P. and Fallon, A. E. (1987) 'A perspective on disgust'. *Psychological Review* 94(1), 23–41

Rugarli, E. I. and Langer, T. (2012) 'Mitochondrial quality control: a matter of life and death for neurons'. *The EMBO Journal* 31(6), 1336–1349

RUIZ-MIRAZO, K. AND MORENO, A. (2004) 'Basic autonomy as a fundamental step in the synthesis of life'. *Artificial Life 10*(3), 235–259

RUIZ-MIRAZO, K., PERETÓ, J. & MORENO, A. (2004) 'A universal definition of life: autonomy and open-ended evolution'. *Origins of Life and Evolution of the Biosphere 34*(3), 323–346

RUSKIN, J. (1865; 2nd ed. 1877) *The Ethics of the Dust: Ten Lectures to Little Housewives on the Elements of Crystallization.* Sunnyside, Orpington, Kent: George Allen

RUTHERFORD, A. (2013) *Creation: The Origin of Life / The Future of Life.* London: Penguin

SALADINO, R., CRESTINI, C., PINO. S., COSTANZO, G. & DI MAURO, E. (2012) 'Formamide and the origin of life', *Physics of Life Reviews 9*(1), 84–104

SANTELICES, B. (1999) 'How many kinds of individual are there?' *Trends in Ecology and Evolution 14*(4), 152–155

SANTORO, S. W. AND JOYCE, G. F. (1997) 'A general purpose RNA-cleaving DNA enzyme'. *Proceedings of the National Academy of Sciences 94*(9), 4262–4266

SCHIERWATER, B. (2005) 'My favorite animal, *Trichoplax adhaerens*'. *Bioessays 27*(12), 1294–1302

SCHNABLE, P. AND WISE, R. (1998) 'The molecular basis of cytoplasmic male sterility and fertility restoration'. *Trends in Plant Science 3*(5), 175–180

SCHÖNBORN, W. (1966) *Beschalte Amöben (Testaceae).* Wittenberg Lutherstadt: Ziemsen

SCHOPENHAUER, A. (1986) *Sämtliche Werke.* 5 vols, ed. W. F. von Löhneysen. Frankfurt-am-Main: Suhrkamp

SCHRÖDINGER, E. (1944; 1992) *What is Life? The Physical Aspect of the Living Cell.* Cambridge: Cambridge University Press

SCHULZ, W. (2006) 'L1 retrotransposons in human cancers' *Journal of Biomedicine and Biotechnology 2006*, 1–12

SCHWARTZ, D. E., TIZARD, R. & GILBERT, W. (1983) 'Nucleotide sequence of Rous sarcoma virus'. *Cell 32*(3), 853–869

SCZEPANSKI, J. T. AND JOYCE, G. F. (2014) 'A cross-chiral RNA polymerase ribozyme'. *Nature 515*(7527), 440–442

SEED, K. D., LAZINSKI, D. W., CALDERWOOD, S. B. & CAMILLI, A. (2013) 'A bacteriophage encodes its own CRISPR/Cas adaptive response to evade host innate immunity'. *Nature 494*(7438), 489–491

SEUSE, H. (ca. 1330; 1993) *Das Buch der Wahrheit,* ed. L. Sturlese and R. Blumrich. Hamburg: Felix Meiner Verlag

SHAKESPEARE, W. (1960) *The Poems,* ed. F. T. Prince. London: Methuen

SHAPIRO, J. A. (1998) 'Thinking about bacterial populations as multicellular organisms'. *Annual Reviews in Microbiology 52*(1), 81–104

Shapiro, R. and Feinberg, G. (1982; new ed. 1995) 'Possible Forms of Life in Environments Very Different from the Earth', in B. Zuckerman and M. H. Hart (eds) *Extraterrestrials: Where are They?* Cambridge: Cambridge University Press

Sharon, G., Segal, D., Ringo, J. M., Hefetz, A., Zilber-Rosenberg, I. & Rosenberg, E. (2010) 'Commensal bacteria play a role in mating preference of *Drosophila melanogaster*'. *Proceedings of the National Academy of Sciences 107*(46), 20051–20056

Silva, F. J., Latorre, A. & Moya, A. (2003) 'Why are the genomes of endosymbiotic bacteria so stable?' *Trends in Genetics 19*(4), 176–180

Simon, D. and Zimmerly, S. (2008) 'A diversity of uncharacterized reverse transcriptases in bacteria'. *Nucleic Acids Research 36*(22), 7219–7229

Singer, S. J. and Nicolson, G. L. (1972) 'The fluid mosaic model of the structure of cell membranes'. *Science 175*(4023), 720–731

Singer, T., McConnell, M. J., Marchetto, M. C., Coufal, N. G. & Gage, F. H. (2010) 'LINE-1 retrotransposons: mediators of somatic variation in neuronal genomes?' *Trends in Neurosciences 33*(8), 345–54

Smolin, L. (1997) *The Life of the Cosmos*. Oxford: Oxford University Press

Sompayrac, L. (1999; 3rd ed. 2008) *How The Immune System Works*. Oxford: Blackwell Publishing

Sonea, S. and Mathieu, L. G. (2001) 'Evolution of the genomic systems of prokaryotes and its momentous consequences'. *International Microbiology 4*(2), 67–71

Song, Y. Y., Zeng, R. S., Xu, J. F. et al. (2010) 'Interplant communication of tomato plants through underground common mycorrhizal networks'. *PLoS One 5*(10), e13324

Sorek, R., Zhu, Y., Creevey, C. J. et al. (2007) 'Genome-wide experimental determination of barriers to horizontal gene transfer'. *Science 318*(5855), 1449–1452

Srivastava, M., Begovic, E., Chapman, J. et al. (2008) 'The *Trichoplax* genome and the nature of placozoans'. *Nature 454* (7207), 955–960

Stenglein, M. and Harris, R. (2006) 'APOBEC3B and APOBEC3F inhibit L1 retrotransposition by a DNA-deamination-independent mechanism'. *Journal of Biological Chemistry 281*(25), 16837–16841

Stern-Gillet, S. (1995) *Aristotle's Philosophy of Friendship*. Albany: State University of New York Press

Strassmann, J. E. (2000) 'Evolution: bacterial cheaters'. *Nature 404*(6778), 555–556

Strassmann, J. E. and Queller, D. C. (2007) 'Altruism among Amoebas'. *Natural History 116*(7), 24–29

STRAWSON, G. (1997) 'The Self'. *Journal of Consciousness Studies* 4(5/6), 405–428
STRAWSON, G. (2011) 'Radical self-awareness', in M. Siderits, E. Thompson and D. Zahavi (eds) *Self, No Self?: Perspectives from Analytical, Phenomenological and Indian Traditions*. Oxford: Oxford University Press
SUTTLE, C. (2007) 'Marine viruses – major players in the global ecosystem'. *Nature Reviews Microbiology* 5(10), 801–812
SUZAN-MONTI, M., LA SCOLA, B., BARRASSI, L., ESPINOSA, L. & RAOULT, D. (2007) 'Ultrastructural characterization of the giant volcano-like virus factory of *Acanthamoeba polyphaga Mimivirus*'. *PLoS One* 2(3), e328
TAMAMES, J., GIL, R., LATORRE, A. ET AL. (2007) 'The frontier between cell and organelle: genome analysis of Candidatus *Carsonella ruddii*'. *BMC Evolutionary Biology* 7(181)
TAMAS, I., KLASSON, L., CANBÄCK, B. ET AL. (2002) '50 million years of genomic stasis in endosymbiotic bacteria'. *Science* 296(5577), 2376–2379
TAUBER, A. (2002; rev. ed. 2009) 'The biological notion of self and non-self'. *The Stanford Encyclopedia of Philosophy* (*2009 Edition*), URL = http://plato.stanford.edu/archives/sum2009/entries/biology-self/
TAYLOR, C. (1989) *Sources of the Self: The Making of the Modern Identity*. Cambridge: Cambridge University Press
THAO, M. L. AND BAUMANN, P. (2004) 'Evolutionary relationships of primary prokaryotic endosymbionts of whiteflies and their hosts'. *Applied and Environmental Microbiology* 70(6), 3401–3406
THEISSEN, U. AND MARTIN, W. (2006) 'The difference between organelles and endosymbionts'. *Current Biology* 16(24), R1016-R1017
THOMAS, L. (1974) *The Lives of a Cell: Notes of a Biology Watcher*. London: Penguin
THOMPSON, E. (2007) *Mind in Life: Biology, Phenomenology and the Sciences of Mind*. Cambridge, Mass. and London: Harvard University Press
TIELENS, A. G. M., ROTTE, C., VAN HELLEMOND, J. J. & MARTIN, W. (2002) 'Mitochondria as we don't know them'. *Trends in Biochemical Sciences* 27(11), 564–572
TORO, N., JIMÉNEZ-ZURDO, J. I. & GARCÍA-RODRÍGUEZ, F. M. (2007) 'Bacterial group II introns: not just splicing'. *FEMS Microbiology Reviews* 31(3), 342–358
TOVAR, J., FISCHER, A. & CLARK, C. G. (1999) 'The mitosome, a novel organelle related to mitochondria in the amitochondrial parasite *Entamoeba histolytica*'. *Molecular Microbiology* 32(5), 1013–1021
TURNER, J. S. (2000) *The Extended Organism: The Physiology of Animal-Built Structures*. Cambridge, Mass. and London: Harvard University Press
TURNEY, J. (2015) *I, Superorganism: Learning to Love Your Inner Ecosystem*. London: Icon Books

Tyler, S. (2003) 'Epithelium – the primary building block for metazoan complexity'. *Integrative and Comparative Biology* 43(1), 55–63

van der Giezen, M., Tovar, J. & Clark, C. G. (2005) 'Mitochondrion-derived organelles in protists and fungi'. *International Review of Cytology* 244, 175–225

Van Regenmortel, M. H., Ackermann, H. W., Calisher, C. H. et al. (2013) 'Virus species polemics: 14 senior virologists oppose a proposed change to the ICTV definition of virus species'. *Archives of Virology* 158(5), 1115–1119

Villarreal, L. P. (2009) *Origin of Group Identity: Viruses, Addiction and Cooperation*. Springer

Vives-Bauza, C., Zhou, C., Huang, Y. et al. (2010) 'PINK1-dependent recruitment of Parkin to mitochondria in mitophagy'. *Proceedings of the National Academy of Sciences* 107(1), 378–383

Von Dohlen, C. D., Kohler, S., Alsop, S. T. & McManus, W. R. (2001) 'Mealybug b-proteobacterial endosymbionts contain g-proteobacterial symbionts'. *Nature* 412(6845), 433–436

Wächtershäuser, G. (1994) 'Life in a ligand sphere'. *Proceedings of the National Academy of Sciences* 91(10), 4283–4287

Wächtershäuser, G. (1998) 'Origin of life in an iron-sulfur world', in A. Brack (ed.) *The Molecular Origins of Life*, Cambridge: Cambridge University Press

Walsby, A. E. (2005) 'Archaea with square cells'. *Trends in Microbiology* 13(5), 193–195

Walter, W. G. (1950) 'An imitation of life'. *Scientific American* 182(5), 42–45

Wedekind, C. and Füri, S. (1997) 'Body odour preferences in men and women: do they aim for specific MHC combinations or simply heterozygosity?' *Proceedings of the Royal Society of London. Series B. Biological Sciences* 264(1387), 1471–1479

Wellman, C. (1975) *Morals and Ethics*. Glenview, Ill.: Scott, Foresman and Company

Wernegreen, J. (2002) 'Genome evolution in bacterial endosymbionts of insects'. *Nature Reviews Genetics* 3(11), 850–861

Wharton, D. A. (2002) *Life at the Limits: Organisms in Extreme Environments*. Cambridge: Cambridge University Press

Whitesides, G. M. and Boncheva, M. (2002) 'Beyond molecules: Self-assembly of mesoscopic and macroscopic components'. *Proceedings of the National Academy of Sciences* 99(8), 4769–4774

Whitesides, G. M. and Grzybowski, B. (2002) 'Self-assembly at all scales'. *Science* 295(5564), 2418–2421

Wilson, J. (1999) *Biological Individuality: The Identity and Persistence of Living Entities*. Cambridge: Cambridge University Press

WINCHESTER, S. (2011) *Atlantic: A Vast Ocean of a Million Stories: The Biography of an Ocean*. London: HarperCollins Publishers

WINKLER, H. H. (1976) 'Rickettsial permeability. An ADP-ATP transport system'. *Journal of Biological Chemistry* 251(2), 389–396

WOESE, C. R. (1998) 'The universal ancestor'. *Proceedings of the National Academy of Sciences* 95(12), 6854–6859

WOESE, C. R. (2002) 'On the evolution of cells'. *Proceedings of the National Academy of Sciences* 99(13), 8742–8747

WOESE, C. R., OLSEN, G. J., IBBA, M. & SÖLL, D. (2000) 'Aminoacyl-tRNA synthetases, the genetic code, and the evolutionary process'. *Microbiology and Molecular Biology Reviews* 64(1), 202–236

WONG, K. (2013) 'Twilight of the Neanderthals'. *Scientific American* 22(1), 76–81

WRANGHAM, R. (2009) *Catching Fire: How Cooking Made Us Human*. London: Profile Books

WU, J. AND GLASS, N. L. (2001) 'Identification of specificity determinants and generation of alleles with novel specificity at the *het-c* heterokaryon incompatibility locus of *Neurospora crassa*'. *Molecular and Cellular Biology* 21(4), 1045–1057

XU, J. AND GORDON, J. I. (2003) 'Honor thy symbionts'. *Proceedings of the National Academy of Sciences* 100(18), 10452–10459

YARMOLINSKY, M. B. (1995) 'Programmed cell death in bacterial populations'. *Science* 267(5199), 836–837

YODER, J. A., WALSH, C. P. & BESTOR, T. H. (1997) 'Cytosine methylation and the ecology of intragenomic parasites'. *Trends in Genetics* 13(8), 335–340

YUTIN, N. AND KOONIN, E. V. (2013) 'Pandoraviruses are highly derived phycodnaviruses'. *Biology Direct* 8(25)

ZAHAVI, D. (2005) *Subjectivity and Selfhood: Investigating the First-Person Perspective*. Cambridge, Mass. and London: The MIT Press

ZAKAIB, G. D. (2011) 'Out on a limb'. *Nature* 476(7358), 20–21

ZAUBERMAN, N., MUTSAFI, Y., HALEVY, D. B. ET AL. (2008) 'Distinct DNA exit and packaging portals in the virus *Acanthamoeba polyphaga mimivirus*'. *PLoS Biology* 6(5), e114

ZEMACH, A. AND ZILBERMAN, D. (2010) 'Evolution of eukaryotic DNA methylation and the pursuit of safer sex'. *Current Biology* 20(17), R780-R785

ZILBER-ROSENBERG, I. AND ROSENBERG, E. (2008) 'Role of microorganisms in the evolution of animals and plants: the hologenome theory of evolution'. *FEMS Microbiology Reviews* 32(5), 723–735

ZIMMER, C. (2011) *A Planet of Viruses*. Chicago and London: University of Chicago Press

www.ingramcontent.com/pod-product-compliance
Lightning Source LLC
Chambersburg PA
CBHW051204300426
44116CB00006B/439